Investing For Dummies,® 2nd Edition
by Eric Tyson

Eric Tyson's Twenty Immutable Investing Laws

1. **Saving is a prerequisite to investing.** Unless you have wealthy, benevolent relatives, living within your means and saving money are prerequisites to investing and building wealth.

2. **Risk and reward go hand in hand.** The way that people of all economic means make their money grow is to take risk by investing in ownership assets, such as stocks, real estate, and small business, where you share in the success and profitability of the asset.

3. **Be realistic about expected investment returns.** Over the long-term, 10 percent per year is about right for ownership investments (such as stocks and real estate). It is possible with running a small business to earn higher returns and even become a multimillionaire, but years of hard work and insight are required. Those who are piling into today's U.S. stock market expecting the 20+ percent annualized returns of the 1990s to continue will be disappointed.

4. **Think long-term.** Because ownership investments are riskier (more volatile), you must keep your long-term perspective when investing in them. Do not invest money in such investments unless you plan on holding them for a minimum of five years, and preferably a decade or longer.

5. **Match the time frame to the investment.** Selecting good investments for yourself involves matching the time frame you have to the riskiness of the investment. For example, for money that you expect to use soon within the next year, focus on safe investments such as money market funds. Invest your longer-term money mostly in growth investments.

6. **Diversify.** Diversification is a powerful investment concept that helps you to reduce the risk of holding more aggressive investments. Diversifying simply means that you should hold a variety of investments that don't move in tandem in different market environments. For example, if you invest in stocks, invest worldwide, not just in the U.S. market. You can further diversify by investing in real estate.

7. **Ignore the minutiae.** Don't feel mystified by or feel the need to follow the short-term gyrations of the financial markets. Ultimately, the prices of stocks, bonds, and other financial instruments are determined by supply and demand, which are influenced by thousands of external issues and millions of investors' expectations and fears.

8. **Allocate your assets.** Besides your individual investment choices, how you divvy up or allocate your money among major investments greatly determines your returns. The younger you are and the more money you earmark for the long-term, the greater the percentage you should devote to ownership investments.

9. **Look at the big picture first.** Understand your overall financial situation and how wise investments fit within it. Before you invest, examine your debt obligations, tax situation, ability to fund retirement accounts, and insurance coverage.

10. **Do your homework before you buy an investment.** You work hard for your money, and many investments cost you to buy and sell. Investing is not a field where acting first and asking questions later works well. Never buy an investment based on an advertisement or a salesperson's solicitation of you.

...For Dummies®: Bestselling Book Series for Beginners

Investing For Dummies,® 2nd Edition

by Eric Tyson

Cheat Sheet

11. **Keep an eye on taxes when choosing investments.** Take advantage of tax-deductible retirement accounts and understand the impact of your tax bracket when investing outside tax-sheltered retirement accounts.

12. **Consider the value of your time and your investing skills and desires.** Investing in stocks and other securities via the best mutual funds is both time-efficient and profitable. Real estate investing and running a small business are the most time-intensive investments.

13. **Where possible, minimize fees.** The more you pay in commissions and management fees on your investments, the greater the drag on your returns. And don't fall prey to the thinking that "you get what you pay for."

14. **Don't expect to beat the stock market averages.** If you have the right skills and interest, your ability to do better than the investing averages is greater with real estate and small business than with stock market investing. The large number of full-time, experienced stock market professionals makes it next to impossible for you to choose individual stocks that will consistently beat a relevant market average over an extended time period.

15. **Don't bail when things look bleak.** The hardest time, psychologically, to hold onto your investments will be when they are down. Even the best investments go through depressed periods, which is the worst possible time to sell. Don't sell when there's a sale going on; if anything, consider buying more.

16. **Ignore soothsayers and prognosticators.** It's nearly impossible to predict the future. Your long-term investments should be based on selecting and holding good investments, not trying to time when to be in or out of a particular investment.

17. **Minimize your trading.** The more you trade, the more likely you are to make mistakes. You'll also suffer increased transaction costs and higher taxes (for non-retirement account investments).

18. **Hire advisors carefully.** Before you hire investing help, first educate yourself so that you better evaluate the competence of those you may hire. Beware of conflicts of interest when you consider advisors to hire.

19. **You are what you read and listen to.** Don't pollute your mind with bad investing strategies and philosophies. The quality of what you read and listen to is far more important than the quantity. Learn how to evaluate the quality of what you read and hear.

20. **Remember the following highest-return, lowest-risk investments.** Your personal life and health are far more important investments than the size of your financial portfolio.

...For Dummies®: Bestselling Book Series for Beginners

Praise for Eric Tyson

Here's what critics and readers have said about Eric Tyson's previous national best-sellers:

"Eric Tyson For President!!! Thanks for such a wonderful guide. With a clear, no-nonsense approach to . . . investing for the long haul, Tyson's book says it all without being the least bit long-winded. Pick up a copy today. It'll be your wisest investment ever!!!'

> — Jim Beggs, VA

"*Personal Finance For Dummies* is the perfect book for people who feel guilty about inadequately managing their money but are intimidated by all of the publications out there. It's a painless way to learn how to take control. My college-aged daughters even enjoyed reading it!"

> — Karen Tofte, producer, National Public Radio's *Sound Money*

"I own many finance and investment books — this is by far the best!"

> — Mike Dodge, Baltimore, MD

"Among my favorite financial guides are . . . Eric Tyson's *Personal Finance For Dummies.*"

> — Jonathan Clements, *The Wall Street Journal*

"The book was well-written, concise, inspirational, excellent for common-folk, and doesn't send you running for a dictionary."

> — Brian O'Connor, Bogota, NJ

"Smart advice for dummies . . . skip the tomes . . . and buy *Personal Finance For Dummies,* which rewards your candor with advice and comfort."

> — Temma Ehrenfeld, *Newsweek*

"Superb reference! Led to my being offered a job as a mortgage originator. [The] bank said I was the 'most informed buyer' they ever sat with!!!"

> — K.A. Carney, Greensburg, PA

"Eric Tyson is doing something important — namely, helping people at all income levels to take control of their financial futures. This book is a natural outgrowth of Tyson's vision that he has nurtured for years. Like Henry Ford, he wants to make something that was previously accessible only to the wealthy accessible to middle-income Americans."

> — James C. Collins, coauthor of the national bestseller *Built to Last;* Lecturer in Business, Stanford Graduate School of Business

"Eric Tyson took a subject — finances — which has always intimidated me and made it manageable. Thanks!"

> — Margaret Holtje, North Sebago, ME

"You don't have to be a novice to like *Mutual Funds For Dummies.* Despite the book's chatty, informal style, author Eric Tyson clearly has a mastery of his subject. He knows mutual funds, and he knows how to explain them in simple English."

> — Steven T. Goldberg, *Kiplinger's Personal Finance Magazine*

"I work with investments and have used this book to help some of my clients understand finances."

> — Bryan Bailey, Mandan, ND

"*Personal Finance For Dummies* offers a valuable guide for common misconceptions and major pitfalls. It's a no-nonsense, straightforward, easy-to-read personal finance book. . . . With this book, you can easily learn enough about finances to start thinking for yourself."

> — Charles R. Schwab, Chairman and CEO, The Charles Schwab Corporation

"Makes financial planning as easy as spending my paycheck."

> — Tim Campbell, Green River, WY

"It can be overwhelming to keep up with the latest developments, which is why you might turn to the book *Mutual Funds For Dummies* by Eric Tyson. A light touch and the use of plenty of graphics help the pages fly by. This book is a primer for those who flinch when contemplating the 7,000 funds you can now buy."

> — Brian Banmiller, FOX-TV

"A nice, easy-to-use format allowed me to skip useless data and glean only the information relevant to me."

> — Steven A. Baffy, Trenton, MI

"Best new personal finance book."

> — Michael Pellecchia, syndicated columnist

"I thoroughly enjoyed the honest, matter-of-fact, straightforward manner in which the book was written. I am grateful to you for providing me with a valuable resource for one of life's great drudgeries."

> — Sven Hagen, Atlanta, GA

"Eric Tyson . . . seems the perfect writer for a ...*For Dummies* book. He doesn't tell you what to do or consider doing without explaining the why's and how's — and the booby traps to avoid — in plain English. . . . It will lead you through the thickets of your own finances as painlessly as I can imagine."

> — Clarence Peterson, *Chicago Tribune*

"Great book!"

> — Cheryl Eichelkraut, Phoenix, AZ

"The best book I've ever bought!"

> — David Clarke, Chicago, IL

"This book was written for real people."

> — Lisa Timco, Westland, MI

"*Personal Finance For Dummies* is, by far, the best book I have read on financial planning. It is a simplified volume of information that provides tremendous insight and guidance into the world of investing and other money issues."

> — Althea Thompson, producer, "PBS Nightly Business Report"

". . . amazingly you were even able to add humor to such a topic."

> — Steve Stachling, Wausau, WI

"This book provides easy-to-understand personal financial information and advice for those without great wealth or knowledge in this area. Practitioners like Eric Tyson, who care about the well-being of middle-income people, are rare in today's society."

> — Joel Hyatt, founder, Hyatt Legal Services, one of the nation's largest general-practice personal legal service firms

". . . very understandable, informative, and enjoyable. . . . This should be required reading for every senior!"

> — Barbara Greub, River Falls, WI

"*Personal Finance For Dummies* is a sane and useful guide that will be of benefit to anyone seeking a careful and prudent method of managing their financial world."

> — John Robbins, founder of EarthSave, author of *May All Be Fed*

"Very informative, lighthearted. . . . I read it cover to cover."

> — Lou Furry, Northampton, PA

"Worth getting. Scores of all-purpose money-management books reach bookstores every year, but only once every couple of years does a stand-out personal finance primer come along. *Personal Finance For Dummies,* by financial counselor and columnist Eric Tyson, provides detailed, action-oriented advice on everyday financial questions. . . . Tyson's style is readable and unintimidating."

> — Kristin Davis, *Kiplinger's Personal Finance Magazine*

"The organization of this book is superb! I could go right to the topics of immediate interest and find clearly written and informative material. The author answered questions that I didn't even know."

> — Lorraine Verboort, Beaverton, OR

"I was able to locate all items that I was interested in by the index. . . . Great!"

> — Robert Linardo, Nas Lemoore, CA

"For those named in the title, such as myself, *Personal Finance For Dummies* is a godsend. It's bright, funny, and it can save you money, too."

> — Jerome Crowe, reporter, *Los Angeles Times*

"Simple and understandable and enjoyable!"

> — Jeanette Johnson, Soldotna, AK

"Eric Tyson has brought his financial experience, investment knowledge, and down-to-earth writing style to create an *outstanding* book on mutual funds for all investors — and an *essential* book for new investors. . . in short, a classic. . . ."

> — Jack Bogle, former CEO, The Vanguard Group

"Understandable to anyone."

> — Pam Smith, Tehachapi, CA

"Confused by finances and taxes? Eric Tyson has written *Personal Finance For Dummies*, a friendly, easy-to-follow guide to smart money strategies."

> — Deb Lawler, anchor, WBZ radio, Boston, MA

". . . by far the best book I've read about the U.S. tax system and personal financial planning."

> — Seva Baykin, Brisbane, CA

"This is a great book. It's understandable. Other financial books are too technical and this one really is different."

> — Shad Johnson, producer, "Business Radio Network"

"Down-to-earth, straightforward information. It was as if Mr. Tyson was a close friend of mine who really cared about me."

> — Arnold L., Monterey Park, CA

"An invaluable, easy-to-read financial help book that should be in every family's library."

> — Stan Schaffer, reporter, *The Morning Call*, Allentown, PA

"I purchased copies for each of my children."

> — M.G. Sher, Marblehead, MA

"I liked his holistic view. He placed money management in perspective to life's important considerations. Invaluable! I'd like to give a copy to each of my sons just starting their 1st jobs."

— Robin Ketchum, Norfolk, CT

"Fantastic. I wish I had it 20 years ago. I'll make sure my children get one."

— C.H. Day, Richmond, VA

"Presents complicated issues with simplicity, clarity, and a touch of humor."

— *The Times-Picayune,* New Orleans, LA

"This book is the first on finances that I have ever read that makes sense to me."

— Tony Toledo, Salem, MA

"Straightforward, readable. . . Tyson is an authoritative writer. . . ."

— *The Orange County Register*

"*Personal Finance For Dummies* is a great book. It addresses everything and helps me feel secure about my finances."

— Phyllis Haber, Kansas City, MO

". . . among tax advice books is far and away the best. *Taxes For Dummies* is fun to read and teaches about the tax system itself. The book also provides excellent advice about dealing with mistakes — created by you or the Internal Revenue Service. And it talks about fitting taxes into your daily financial planning. In other words, it's a book you can use after April 15, as well as before."

— Kathy M. Kristof, *Los Angeles Times*

"*Taxes For Dummies* helped us save $500 on our tax return."

— Bob and Diane Hayman, Mishawaka, IN

"Smart chapters — not just thumbnail sketches — for filling out forms."

— Susan Tompor, Gannett News Service

"Finally, a book about finance that I can understand!"

— Michael K. Owens, Knoxville, TN

"*Taxes For Dummies* will make tax preparation less traumatic. . . . It is a book that answers — in plain English, and sometimes with humor — many puzzling questions that arise on the most commonly used tax forms."

> — Stanley Angrist, *The Wall Street Journal*

"I should never have brought this book into work — everyone wants to borrow it!"

> — Maria Zografos, San Francisco, CA

". . . a witty, irreverent reference . . . And since laughter is good medicine, it most definitely is what it claims. But its focus on humor does not undermine its merit as a research tool. While the guide could be used just to answer individual questions, its friendly format is such fun that you may end up reading Eric Tyson's book from cover to cover. No kidding."

> — *The Times-Picayune,* New Orleans, LA

"This book answered so many questions. Truly, I was completely illiterate financially — now I am becoming the family guru."

> — Jean M., Holt, MO

"There are plenty of books out there that do the job, but if you're looking for one which explains the tax laws using plain English, with a dash of a sense of humor, *Taxes For Dummies* is highly recommended. . . . *Taxes For Dummies* is the ideal guide for getting you through the Ides of April."

> — Bill Peschel, *The Herald*

"It's great! It moves you to a mindset that allows you to control your finances — instead of them controlling you."

> — Sabrina Karl, Madison, WI

"*Dummies* is a primer for those who are tired of making bad choices — or no choices at all — with their money."

> — Barbara Tierney, *Smart Money by The Wall Street Journal*

"This book should be taught in every high school and college in America. Most people, like me, wait until they're in trouble before they get help."

> — Gary Rzepka, APO AP Japan

More ...For Dummies™ Titles by Eric Tyson

Personal Finance For Dummies™

Mutual Funds For Dummies™

Taxes For Dummies™
(co-authored with David Silverman)

Home Buying/House Selling/Mortgages For Dummies™
(co-authored with Ray Brown)

Small Business For Dummies™
(co-authored with Jim Schell)

INVESTING

FOR

DUMMIES®

2ND EDITION

by Eric Tyson, M.B.A.

Financial Counselor, Syndicated Columnist, and Author of
Five National Best-Sellers, including *Personal Finance For
Dummies®* and *Mutual Funds For Dummies®*

**IDG
BOOKS
WORLDWIDE**

IDG Books Worldwide, Inc.
An International Data Group Company

Foster City, CA ◆ Chicago, IL ◆ Indianapolis, IN ◆ New York, NY

Investing For Dummies®

Published by
IDG Books Worldwide, Inc.
An International Data Group Company
919 E. Hillsdale Blvd.
Suite 400
Foster City, CA 94404
www.idgbooks.com (IDG Books Worldwide Web site)
www.dummies.com (Dummies Press Web site)

Library of Congress Catalog Card No.: 99-64904

ISBN: 0-7645-5162-0

Printed in the United States of America

10 9 8 7 6 5 4 3 2 1

2B/RS/QY/ZZ/IN

Distributed in the United States by IDG Books Worldwide, Inc.

Distributed by CDG Books Canada Inc. for Canada; by Transworld Publishers Limited in the United Kingdom; by IDG Norge Books for Norway; by IDG Sweden Books for Sweden; by IDG Books Australia Publishing Corporation Pty. Ltd. for Australia and New Zealand; by TransQuest Publishers Pte Ltd. for Singapore, Malaysia, Thailand, Indonesia, and Hong Kong; by Gotop Information Inc. for Taiwan; by ICG Muse, Inc. for Japan; by Norma Comunicaciones S.A. for Colombia; by Intersoft for South Africa; by Eyrolles for France; by International Thomson Publishing for Germany, Austria and Switzerland; by Distribuidora Cuspide for Argentina; by LR International for Brazil; by Galileo Libros for Chile; by Ediciones ZETA S.C.R. Ltda. for Peru; by WS Computer Publishing Corporation, Inc., for the Philippines; by Contemporanea de Ediciones for Venezuela; by Express Computer Distributors for the Caribbean and West Indies; by Micronesia Media Distributor, Inc. for Micronesia; by Grupo Editorial Norma S.A. for Guatemala; by Chips Computadoras S.A. de C.V. for Mexico; by Editorial Norma de Panama S.A. for Panama; by American Bookshops for Finland. Authorized Sales Agent: Anthony Rudkin Associates for the Middle East and North Africa.

For general information on IDG Books Worldwide's books in the U.S., please call our Consumer Customer Service department at 800-762-2974. For reseller information, including discounts and premium sales, please call our Reseller Customer Service department at 800-434-3422.

For information on where to purchase IDG Books Worldwide's books outside the U.S., please contact our International Sales department at 317-596-5530 or fax 317-596-5692.

For consumer information on foreign language translations, please contact our Customer Service department at 1-800-434-3422, fax 317-596-5692, or e-mail rights@idgbooks.com.

For information on licensing foreign or domestic rights, please phone +1-650-655-3109.

For sales inquiries and special prices for bulk quantities, please contact our Sales department at 650-655-3200 or write to the address above.

For information on using IDG Books Worldwide's books in the classroom or for ordering examination copies, please contact our Educational Sales department at 800-434-2086 or fax 317-596-5499.

For press review copies, author interviews, or other publicity information, please contact our Public Relations department at 650-655-3000 or fax 650-655-3299.

For authorization to photocopy items for corporate, personal, or educational use, please contact Copyright Clearance Center, 222 Rosewood Drive, Danvers, MA 01923, or fax 978-750-4470.

is a registered trademark or trademark under exclusive license to IDG Books Worldwide, Inc. from International Data Group, Inc. in the United States and/or other countries.

About the Author

Eric Tyson is an internationally acclaimed and best-selling personal finance author, lecturer, and advisor. Through his work, he is dedicated to teaching people to manage their money better and to successfully direct their own investments.

Eric is a former management consultant to businesses for which he helped improve operations and profitability. Before, during, and after this time of working crazy hours and traveling too much, he had the good sense to focus on financial matters.

He has been involved in the investing markets in many capacities for the past 25 years. Eric first invested in mutual funds back in the mid-1970s, when he opened a mutual fund account at Fidelity. With the assistance of Dr. Martin Zweig, a now-famous investment market analyst, Eric won his high school's science fair in 1976 for a project on what influences the stock market. In addition to investing in securities over recent decades, Eric has also successfully invested in real estate and started and managed his own business. He has counseled thousands of clients on a variety of investment quandaries and questions.

He earned a bachelor's degree in economics at Yale and an M.B.A. at the Stanford Graduate School of Business. Despite these impediments to lucid reasoning, he came to his senses and decided that life was too short to spend it working long hours and waiting in airports for the benefit of larger companies.

An accomplished freelance personal finance writer, Eric is the author of numerous best-selling books including ...*For Dummies* books on Personal Finance, Mutual Funds, Taxes (co-author) and Home Buying (co-author) and is a syndicated columnist. His work has been featured and quoted in hundreds of national and local publications, including *Newsweek, Kiplinger's Personal Finance Magazine, Los Angeles Times, Chicago Tribune, The Wall Street Journal,* and *Bottom Line/Personal,* and on NBC's *Today Show,* ABC, CNBC, PBS's *Nightly Business Report,* CNN, CBS national radio, Bloomberg Business Radio, National Public Radio, and Business Radio Network. He's also been a featured speaker at a White House conference on retirement planning.

To stay in tune with what real people care about and struggle with, Eric still maintains a financial counseling practice.

ABOUT IDG BOOKS WORLDWIDE

Welcome to the world of IDG Books Worldwide.

IDG Books Worldwide, Inc., is a subsidiary of International Data Group, the world's largest publisher of computer-related information and the leading global provider of information services on information technology. IDG was founded more than 30 years ago by Patrick J. McGovern and now employs more than 9,000 people worldwide. IDG publishes more than 290 computer publications in over 75 countries. More than 90 million people read one or more IDG publications each month.

Launched in 1990, IDG Books Worldwide is today the #1 publisher of best-selling computer books in the United States. We are proud to have received eight awards from the Computer Press Association in recognition of editorial excellence and three from Computer Currents' First Annual Readers' Choice Awards. Our best-selling ...For Dummies® series has more than 50 million copies in print with translations in 31 languages. IDG Books Worldwide, through a joint venture with IDG's Hi-Tech Beijing, became the first U.S. publisher to publish a computer book in the People's Republic of China. In record time, IDG Books Worldwide has become the first choice for millions of readers around the world who want to learn how to better manage their businesses.

Our mission is simple: Every one of our books is designed to bring extra value and skill-building instructions to the reader. Our books are written by experts who understand and care about our readers. The knowledge base of our editorial staff comes from years of experience in publishing, education, and journalism — experience we use to produce books to carry us into the new millennium. In short, we care about books, so we attract the best people. We devote special attention to details such as audience, interior design, use of icons, and illustrations. And because we use an efficient process of authoring, editing, and desktop publishing our books electronically, we can spend more time ensuring superior content and less time on the technicalities of making books.

You can count on our commitment to deliver high-quality books at competitive prices on topics you want to read about. At IDG Books Worldwide, we continue in the IDG tradition of delivering quality for more than 30 years. You'll find no better book on a subject than one from IDG Books Worldwide.

John Kilcullen
Chairman and CEO
IDG Books Worldwide, Inc.

Steven Berkowitz
President and Publisher
IDG Books Worldwide, Inc.

VIII WINNER

*Eighth Annual
Computer Press
Awards ≥1992*

IX WINNER

*Ninth Annual
Computer Press
Awards ≥1993*

X WINNER

*Tenth Annual
Computer Press
Awards ≥1994*

XI WINNER

*Eleventh Annual
Computer Press
Awards ≥1995*

IDG is the world's leading IT media, research and exposition company. Founded in 1964, IDG had 1997 revenues of $2.05 billion and has more than 9,000 employees worldwide. IDG offers the widest range of media options that reach IT buyers in 75 countries representing 95% of worldwide IT spending. IDG's diverse product and services portfolio spans six key areas including print publishing, online publishing, expositions and conferences, market research, education and training, and global marketing services. More than 90 million people read one or more of IDG's 290 magazines and newspapers, including IDG's leading global brands — Computerworld, PC World, Network World, Macworld and the Channel World family of publications. IDG Books Worldwide is one of the fastest-growing computer book publishers in the world, with more than 700 titles in 36 languages. The "...For Dummies®" series alone has more than 50 million copies in print. IDG offers online users the largest network of technology-specific Web sites around the world through IDG.net (http://www.idg.net), which comprises more than 225 targeted Web sites in 55 countries worldwide. International Data Corporation (IDC) is the world's largest provider of information technology data, analysis and consulting, with research centers in over 41 countries and more than 400 research analysts worldwide. IDG World Expo is a leading producer of more than 168 globally branded conferences and expositions in 35 countries including E3 (Electronic Entertainment Expo), Macworld Expo, ComNet, Windows World Expo, ICE (Internet Commerce Expo), Agenda, DEMO, and Spotlight. IDG's training subsidiary, ExecuTrain, is the world's largest computer training company, with more than 230 locations worldwide and 785 training courses. IDG Marketing Services helps industry-leading IT companies build international brand recognition by developing global integrated marketing programs via IDG's print, online and exposition products worldwide. Further information about the company can be found at www.idg.com. 1/24/99

Dedication

Actually, before I get to the thank yous, please allow me a *really* major thank you and dedication.

This book is hereby and irrevocably dedicated to my family and friends, as well as to my counseling clients and customers, who ultimately have taught me everything that I know about how to explain financial terms and strategies so that all of us may benefit.

Acknowledgments

Thanks to chief IDG Books honcho John Kilcullen for recruiting me into the fold and to Kathy Welton and Mark Butler for keeping me focused on writing needed books. Behind every good book (I trust, dear reader, you think that it is) is a great project editor — thank you, Wendy Hatch, for your enthusiasm, insights, and attention to detail. Thanks also to Billie Williams for all her fine editing and to Andy Lewandowski and Justin Wells for additional editorial and research help, and to Tom Missler and the rest of the fine folks in Production for making this book and all my charts and graphs look great! Thanks also to Mimi Sells, Catherine Schmitz, David Kissinger, and Heather Prince for all their sound work behind the scenes, and to everyone else at IDG Books who contributed to getting this book done and done right.

And last but not least, a tip of my cap to the fine lot of technical reviewers who helped to ensure that I did not write something that wasn't quite right. For the 2nd edition, these good folks included Bob Bingham, a truly professional financial advisor with Bingham, Osborn and Scarborough; and Ray Brown, residential real estate guru, fellow author, sometimes mentor, and always great pal. For the previous edition, this book benefited from the wise input of Ed Wholihan, McKinsey & Co. management consultant extraordinaire; Ken Fisher, investment manager and most informed stock market historian; Al Gobar, real estate investing guru; small-business professor Pam Autrey of the University of Texas; and Dennis Ito, Bob Taylor, Madelyn O'Connell, and Marilyn Wilson from KPMG Peat Marwick LLP. Thank you one and all!

Publisher's Acknowledgments

We're proud of this book; please register your comments through our IDG Books Worldwide Online Registration Form located at http://my2cents.dummies.com.

Some of the people who helped bring this book to market include the following:

Acquisitions, Editorial, and Media Development

Project Editor: Kathy Cox

Associate Project Editor: Wendy Hatch

Acquisitions Editor: Mark Butler

Copy Editor: Billie A. Williams

Technical Editor: Bob Bingham

Editorial Coordinator: Maureen Kelly

Associate Permissions Editor: Carmen Krikorian

Editorial Manager: Jennifer Ehrlich

Editorial Assistants: Jamila Pree, Alison Walthall

Production

Project Coordinator: Tom Missler

Layout and Graphics: Amy M. Adrian, Angela F. Hunckler, Barry Offringa, David Mckelvey, Douglas L. Rollison, Brent Savage, Jacque Schneider, Michael Sullivan, Brian Torwelle, Mary Jo Weis, Dan Whetstine

Proofreaders: Melissa D. Buddendeck, Marianne Santy, Rebecca Senninger

Indexer: Infodex Indexing Services, Inc.

General and Administrative

IDG Books Worldwide, Inc.: John Kilcullen, CEO; Steven Berkowitz, President and Publisher

IDG Books Technology Publishing Group: Richard Swadley, Senior Vice President and Publisher; Walter Bruce III, Vice President and Associate Publisher; Steven Sayre, Associate Publisher; Joseph Wikert, Associate Publisher; Mary Bednarek, Branded Product Development Director; Mary Corder, Editorial Director

IDG Books Consumer Publishing Group: Roland Elgey, Senior Vice President and Publisher; Kathleen A. Welton, Vice President and Publisher; Kevin Thornton, Acquisitions Manager; Kristin A. Cocks, Editorial Director

IDG Books Internet Publishing Group: Brenda McLaughlin, Senior Vice President and Publisher; Diane Graves Steele, Vice President and Associate Publisher; Sofia Marchant, Online Marketing Manager

IDG Books Production for Dummies Press: Michael R. Britton, Vice President of Production; Debbie Stailey, Associate Director of Production; Cindy L. Phipps, Manager of Project Coordination, Production Proofreading, and Indexing; Shelley Lea, Supervisor of Graphics and Design; Debbie J. Gates, Production Systems Specialist; Robert Springer, Supervisor of Proofreading; Laura Carpenter, Production Control Manager; Tony Augsburger, Supervisor of Reprints and Bluelines

◆

The publisher would like to give special thanks to Patrick J. McGovern, without whom this book would not have been possible.

◆

Contents at a Glance

Cartoons at a Glance

By Rich Tennant

Table of Contents

Introduction

Since the first edition of *Investing For Dummies* appeared in 1996, times have changed — and then again, they haven't. During the late 1990s, for example, many foreign stock markets plunged — especially those in Asia and select emerging markets. Meanwhile, the U.S. stock market soared to ever higher and gravity-defying levels. The more the supposed market experts and gurus predict a fall, the faster the market seems to climb.

Although a number of things make me feel older these days, few things make me feel as old as the fact that the widely followed U.S. stock market measure — the Dow Jones Industrial Average — once stood at a mere 600 points back in the early 1970s (when I started following stocks in earnest) and it's now practically at a level 20 times that!

With the stock market booming, the media's coverage of stocks and the overall market continues to mushroom. More magazines and news programs are devoted to investing and the markets than ever before. Unless you live in a log cabin in the wilderness without access to television, radio, the Internet, or printed publications, you can't escape the rising tidal wave of investment coverage.

More and more people are stepping into the investment markets for the first time. There's certainly a good side to that: Unless you've got benevolent, loaded relatives, you should take an interest in securing your financial future. That said, I find increasing numbers of people spending much time (too much in my opinion) researching, tracking, and monitoring their investments.

With all the increased interest in and coverage of the investment world, you may think that investing times have changed. To a large degree, things haven't. Investments that were considered lousy — products with high fees and commission — years ago generally are today.

The best investment vehicles for building wealth — stocks, real estate, small business — haven't changed. And, you still need money to play in the investment world. Like the first edition of *Investing For Dummies,* the second edition of this national best-seller includes complete coverage of these wealth-building investments as well as other commonly used investment strategies, such as bonds. Here are the biggest changes in this edition:

  ✔ **Completely revised and updated.** I've freshened up the data and exam-
    ples in this book to provide you with the latest insights and analysis.
    Wondering about getting in on an Internet or technology stock? Curious
    as to what impact Alan Greenspan's comments will have on the stock
    market? Debating whether to invest in a new Roth IRA? You can find the
    answers to these questions and many more in this edition.

  ✔ **Investing resources section.** With the explosion in Internet sites, soft-
    ware, publications, media outlets, and many other information sources
    offering investing advice, I find that more and more people get over-
    whelmed by too many choices. Equally problematic is knowing who you
    can trust and listen to and who you need to ignore. In this new edition, I
    explain how to evaluate the competence or incompetence of various
    investment resources, and I provide tips for who to listen to and who to
    tune out.

Using Your Common Sense

With few exceptions, investing books that rocket onto best-seller lists purport to unveil how to make a fortune investing in individual stocks. These
investment books are usually written by a money manager or someone who
claims to have developed a system that beats the system. Those who fall into
the latter category often have another agenda, such as selling you a newsletter or convincing you to turn your investment dollars over to them to
manage. As Nancy Reagan so eloquently put it, "Just Say No" — and don't
waste your money on these books, either.

As for reading books about those who have publicly available and audited
track records of success as investors — the Peter Lynches and Warren
Buffetts of the investment world — we could perhaps learn something useful.
Problem is, these folks don't write books that can help the rest of us. They're
too busy engaged in other activities that are more lucrative and that they're
better at. As for learning how to "beat the market" by reading such books,
allow me to politely say, "It ain't gonna happen."

Although we may acknowledge and enjoy watching the extraordinary talent
of Michael Jordan playing basketball, Bill Gates developing new computer
technology, and Barbra Streisand or Bette Midler performing, let's not forget
two important points. First, we could read 100 books about them and not
develop their talents. Second, remember that each of these icons is sup-
ported by dozens and, in some cases, thousands of others for their
successful performances.

There's no doubt that over long periods of time, investing in the stock market is a proven and sensible way to build wealth. However, when investing in the stock market, why waste your valuable time trying to learn second-, third-, or fourth-hand the strategies of the investment gods when you can hire them firsthand, at a low cost, through professionally managed investment funds? And why waste your time trying to select and manage a portfolio of individual stocks when you can replicate the market average returns (and beat the majority of professional money managers) through an exceptionally underrated and underused investment fund called an index fund? Plus, you save yourself the heartache of disappointing returns.

As a financial counselor, I know from working with real live people of modest and immodest economic means that the typical best-selling investment books don't focus on the ways that these people build wealth. Quite simply, they increase their wealth by:

- ✔ Living within their means and systematically saving and investing money, ideally in a tax-favored manner.

- ✔ Buying and holding stocks, ideally through the best mutual funds.

- ✔ Building their own small business or career.

- ✔ Investing in real estate.

That kind of investing is what this book is all about. I don't profess to be a guru, but I do have an eye for spotting, through firsthand experience, what works (and what doesn't) for ordinary, yet in many ways extraordinary, people like you!

Equally, if not more importantly, I help you understand and choose investments compatible with your personal and financial goals. Even if you can learn to beat the street, market, or whatever the heck they're calling the stock market today, what good will it do you if you pay gobs more in taxes or don't realize your dreams?

Getting the Most from This Book

Seriously, this stuff isn't rocket science. You see, I wrote this book hoping that you gather enough information in these subject areas so that you won't need to hire people like me.

By all means, if you're dealing with a complicated, atypical issue, get competent professional help. But educate yourself first. As you'll learn from the mistakes that others have made, it's dangerous to hire someone if you yourself are financially challenged. If you do finally decide to hire someone, you'll be much better prepared by educating yourself, and you'll be more focused in your questions and better able to assess that person's competence.

This book helps you fill gaps in your investment knowledge. It's structured so that you can read it cover to cover or simply dive into particular sections that most currently interest you. Here are the major parts:

Part I: Investing Fundamentals

Before you can confidently and intelligently choose investments, you need to be able to cut through the lingo and jargon and get to the heart of what investments are and are not, and how they differ from one another. You find out what rate of return you can reasonably expect to earn and how much risk you need to take to get it. You also clearly see how investments best fit into your specific financial goals and situation.

Part II: Stocks, Bonds, and Wall Street

I know that you probably don't want to trade in your day job for one where you'd wear a three-piece suit and need to know on which page of the daily *Wall Street Journal* you can find yield curves. But you *do* need to understand what the financial markets are and how you can participate in them without suffering too many abrasions and lacerations. I explain what stocks and bonds are all about and how to best buy them and build your fortune.

Part III: Real Estate

We all need places to live, work, and shop, so it makes sense that real estate can be a profitable part of your investment portfolio. Intelligently buying and managing real estate draws on many skills that you may not have used in recent years. I show you the best ways to invest in real estate and provide a crash course in mortgages, landlording, buying low, selling high, and taxes.

Part IV: Small Business

There's nothing small about the potential profits you can make from small business. You can choose the way to invest in a small business that matches your skills and time. If you aspire to be the best boss you've ever had, here you can find the right ways to start your own or buy someone else's small business. Or maybe you'd like to try your hand at spotting up-and-comers but don't want to be on the front lines — try investing in someone else's small business.

Part V: Investing Resources

Click on your radio or television, crack open a magazine or newspaper, or go surfing on the Internet and you quickly discover that you can't escape investment advice. Surprisingly, each new guru you stumble upon contradicts the one who came before. Before you know it, although you've spent an avalanche of your valuable free time on all this investment stuff, you're no closer to making an informed decision. In fact, if you're like most people, you find yourself even more confused and paralyzed. Fear not! In this new and important section, I explain why many experts really aren't experts and why most try to make the world of investing so mysterious. I highlight experts worth listening to and those you should ignore.

Part VI: The Part of Tens

These shorter chapters build your investment knowledge further. You find advice about topics such as overcoming common psychological investment obstacles, issues to consider when selecting a broker, and points to ponder when you sell an investment.

You'll also be pleased to know that this book has a super-useful Index. If you're the kind of reader who jumps around from topic to topic instead of reading from cover to cover, you'll be pleased that the Index highlights the pages where investing terms are defined.

Icons Used in This Book

Throughout this book, icons help guide you through the maze of suggestions, solutions, and cautions. I hope you find that the following images make your journey through investment strategies smoother.

Denotes strategies that can enable you to build wealth faster and leap over tall obstacles in a single bound.

Indicates treacherous territory that has made mincemeat out of lesser mortals who have come before you. Skip this point at your own peril.

In the shark-infested investing waters, you'll find creatures who feast on novice waders, ready to take a bite out of a swimmer's savings. This icon notes when and where the sharks may be circling.

Points out companies, products, services, and resources that have proven to be exceptional over the years — in other words, resources that I would or do use personally or would recommend to my friends and family.

Skip it or read it, the choice is yours. You'll fill your head with more stuff that may prove valuable as you expand your investing know-how, but you risk overdosing on stuff that you may not need right away.

Demarcates an issue that requires more detective work on your part. Don't worry, I'll prepare you for your work so that you don't have to start out as a novice gumshoe.

I know this is something your parents always told you that promptly flew out your other ear, but this icon indicates something really, really important — don't you forget it!

Part I

Investing Fundamentals

The 5th Wave — By Rich Tennant

"We were told to put our money into something that got more interest, so we started sticking it into this mason jar that's got some dang thing in it we bought from a traveling freak show."

In this part . . .

Like a good map or aerial photograph, this part helps you see the big picture of the investment world. Here, I explain the different types of investments, which are good and bad for a variety of circumstances, what returns you can expect, and how to make wise investing decisions that fit with your overall financial situation.

Chapter 1

Investment Options

*I*f you succeed in accumulating some money to invest, congratulations! You've accomplished a feat that the majority of people in the world haven't yet done. If you decide to move to the next step — actually investing some of that money, you've come to the right place. *Investing For Dummies,* 2nd Edition, is your one-stop investment reference guide and counselor, ready to prepare you for the sometimes thrilling and sometimes dangerous (and hopefully rewarding) world of investing.

In many parts of the "developing" world, life's basic necessities — food, clothing, shelter, and taxes — gobble up people's earnings. In "advanced" countries, like the U.S., most Americans save little, if any, money despite considerably higher incomes. In recent years, Americans saved less than 5 percent of their take-home income, while people in other industrialized countries, such as Japan, Germany, and Switzerland, save two to three times this amount!

Some Americans share the same struggle for basic necessities with people in developing nations. But, for many others, everything — eating out, driving new cars, hopping on an airplane for vacation — is a necessity. I've taken it upon myself (using this book as my tool) to help you recognize that investing — that is, putting your money to work for you — is a necessity. If you want to accomplish important personal and financial goals such as owning a home, starting your own business, helping your kids through college, retiring, and so on, you must learn to invest well.

It has been said, and too often quoted, that the only certainties in life are death and taxes. To these two certainties I add one more: Being confused by and ignorant of investing is also certain. Because investing is a confusing activity, you may be tempted to look with anxiety-ridden eyes at those people in the world who appear to be savvy with money and investing. Remember that all of us start with the same level of financial knowledge — that is to say, with none! *No one* is born knowing this stuff! The only difference between those who know and those who don't is that those who know have invested their time and energy learning about the investment world.

Some of the people you think are investing wizards are in fact, investing fools. I know because I've witnessed professional athletes, movie stars, and business big shots make easily avoidable investing blunders. They all lost significant money through bad investments and flawed investment strategies. These wealthy people (and their advisors) made investment decisions that they could've and should've avoided.

What Is Investing?

Before I discuss investing options, I want to start with something that's quite basic, yet important. What exactly do I mean when I say "investing"?

Investing means that you have money and you put it away for future use. If you put your money in your mattress, you've chosen an investment that pays no interest and is subject to theft and fire! Many people chose to invest their money in their mattresses during the Great Depression in the U.S. in the early 1930s. Why, you ask? Banks were failing and the stock market fell off a cliff. Therefore, during the Great Depression, the mattress was a reasonable place to invest. (Although many didn't know it then, an even better place to invest their money was in government-backed bonds that appreciated in value as inflation ebbed.)

Investing is also a process of making choices. Whether you place your money in the bank, a mattress, or a relative's business, you ultimately decide where you invest it.

You may invest some, or even all of your money in things out of default or for reasons that don't match your current and long-term best interests. The following list contains examples of various places that you can hold your investment:

- ✔ Perhaps you hold your investment in a "parking place" until you figure out what to do with your money. Today, the equivalent of the Depression-era mattress is a bank account. When most people receive money, it goes into the local bank account where it may sit for years on end.

- ✔ Perhaps your investments were sold to you by a broker or financial advisor who was more interested in their profits than yours. Many people hold investments that they don't understand, and the investments may not be appropriate for their financial situation and goals. Perhaps you're already a student of the investing school of hard knocks and have lost money on poor investments ravaged by high commissions and fees.

✔ Your current investments may be based on your previous circumstances. Although your situation may change slowly from year to year, it
   may differ greatly from where you were five or ten years ago. Maybe you
   bought investments that made sense for you when you were in a much
   lower tax bracket. Perhaps your investment holdings require too much
   time to track and monitor.

✔ Perhaps you inherited your investments. What made a good investment
   for your parents, grandparents, and so on doesn't necessarily make
   sense for you, and who says that what they held is a good investment?
   You can love a person and honor her memory yet still be analytical
   about the investments that she left you.

This book, beginning with this chapter, helps you understand your best
investment options so that you may begin to choose and construct a portfolio
(collection of investments) that fits your financial situation and goals.

The Superiority of Simplicity

The first and only time that I met with George was at his home. (This was
back in the days when I made "house calls" for my financial counseling
clients, which I enjoyed doing because meeting people on their home turf
gave me a much better sense of a person's situation and personality.) George
kept a ledger of his investments on a sheet of paper that was faded and
smelled old. However, George was a millionaire, although you'd never know
it. I can best describe George's home furnishings as spartan — probably from
the years of family pets and children running around the house. The stuffing
of his living room couch was falling out and he had a Philco television set
that was probably black and white.

While I talked with George, the telephone rang, and after he said hello, he
waited to find out who called with all the anticipation of a young child in line
at an amusement park. Then his eyes really lit up as he realized it was his
granddaughter and she would soon be visiting.

George is a wealthy person in many ways. Nearly 80, he possesses great
health and appears to have lots of friends and family. He enjoyed his career
working in a manufacturing environment. George also served his country in
World War II and earned a Purple Heart.

Despite the fact that George never came close to earning a six-figure salary,
he was able to retire at the age of 50. In addition to being with his close-knit
family and friends, he spends his time volunteering and traveling. Although
George has significant financial wealth and the ability to save and invest
wisely, George says of his money: "I know that I can't take it with me."

George didn't have any advanced degrees in business or any other subject, and he never went to college. He accumulated his wealth the old-fashioned (and best) way — through hard work, savings, and commonsense investing.

In his 20s and 30s, George worked overtime to come up with the necessary cash to buy a couple of real estate properties. He's owned real estate ever since. George also took about 10 percent of each paycheck and invested it in stocks.

George also didn't follow any gurus to divine the right time to sell or trade his investments. He did some homework, bought sound investments, and turned, so to speak, into an investing couch potato. "After all the time, trouble, and work I spent to save up the money and then choose an investment, why would I want to sell it?" George asks. That's an excellent question that trigger-happy traders, especially those who predominate the world of Internet trading, may ask themselves too late in life.

George hired me to get my opinion on whether his portfolio was properly balanced and what mutual funds he should invest in, given his tax situation. Upon hearing about my book, *Mutual Funds For Dummies* (IDG Books Worldwide), George agreed that meeting with me (for advice) and reading that book and a couple of other books made the best use of his time, money, and educational needs. You see, George was also smart enough to realize that consultants cost money and that you can learn a lot on your own if you get pointed in the right direction!

Not everyone views financial advisors the way that George does, largely, I think, because too many advisors try to perpetuate the need for their services. I'll never forget the lunch that I had several years ago with a tax attorney, Larry, whom I had heard on a local radio station. On the air, he seemed well-spoken and knowledgeable. He called himself "The People's Attorney." I met with Larry because I was curious to learn more about tax attorneys and the world of radio.

After talking for a while, I asked Larry what his goals were. Without missing a beat, he said, "To make as much money as possible in as short a period of time as possible." He went on to explain that his practice didn't just focus on taxes, but that he would "help" his clients with many other legal matters.

"The key, Eric," Larry said with an almost paternalistic tone in his voice, "is to work on anything that's an urgent matter. That way, the customer is willing to pay my hourly fee of $275."

Gulp!

Larry then offered me a proposition. If I directed all my clients' legal needs to him, he'd put me on a retainer — in other words, kick back money that he was earning from clients I sent his way. Larry and I finished lunch and I went home with the beginnings of indigestion.

Over the next several weeks, I listened to Larry's radio show with fresh ears, and I noticed a repeated and disturbing pattern. "The People's Attorney" was short on specifics in response to callers' questions and often went out of his way to make his answers sound complicated.

One caller asked Larry about using a computer software program to create a will, to which Larry warned ominously, "Would you use a computer on yourself to perform brain surgery?! There are so many things that can go wrong."

Well, preparing a will and making most investments aren't even close to performing brain surgery. You can make intelligent, sound, wealth-building investment decisions using your common sense and some relatively simple strategies without obtaining input from financial advisors. Sadly, many advisors are only out to maximize their profits — by keeping you in the dark and dependent on them — rather than your profits. (Throughout this book, I explain when it may make sense for you to obtain professional advice and the best method for finding that help.)

The Major Choices

The investment field is filled with substantial jargon. Literally tens of thousands of different investments exist. Unfortunately for the novice, and even for experts who are honest with you, knowing the name of the investment or company is just the tip of the iceberg. Underneath each of these investments lurks a veritable mountain of details.

If you wanted to and had the ability, you could make a full-time endeavor out of analyzing financial statements, talking to the business's employees, customers, suppliers, and so on. That's why you must be realistic and selective about the investment spots that you choose. If you're like most people, your time on this Earth is limited.

I don't want to scare you from investing just because some people do it on a full-time basis. Making wise investments need not take a lot of your time. If you know where to get high-quality information and you purchase good, managed investments, you can do the work that you're best at and have more free time for other fun stuff.

An important part of the "making wise investments" process is knowing when you have enough information to do things well on your own versus when you should hire others to help you. For example, when investing in foreign stock markets, it makes far more sense to hire a good money manager, such as through a mutual fund, rather than going to all the time, trouble, and expense of trying to pick your own individual stocks.

So let's take a machete to all the high and dense foliage of the investment world. I'll clear a path so that you can identify the major and important landmarks and what each of the investments are good for.

Ownership investments

If you want your money to grow and you don't mind a bit of a roller coaster-type ride from time to time in your investment's values, ownership investments are for you. If you want to build wealth, observing how the world's wealthiest have built their wealth is enlightening.

Not surprisingly, the champions of wealth around the globe gained their fortunes largely through owning a piece (or all) of a successful company that they (or others) have built. Take the case of Bill Gates, founder and chief executive officer of Microsoft — and college dropout. Microsoft is the world's largest producer of personal computer software. DOS and Windows, the two primary PC operating systems, and Word, the word-processing software that I'm using to write this book, are all Microsoft products.

Every time I, or millions of other people, buy a personal computer with one of these Microsoft software packages, or simply buy or upgrade a Microsoft software package, Microsoft makes more money. As the largest stockholder in the company, Gates and other Microsoft shareholders stand to make more money as increasing sales and profits drive up the stock's price. Microsoft's profits and stock price have skyrocketed several thousand percent since the company first issued shares of stock in the company back in 1986.

In addition to their own businesses, many well-to-do people have also built their nest eggs investing in real estate and the stock market. And of course, some people come into wealth the old-fashioned way — they inherit it. Even if your parents are among the rare wealthy ones and you expect them to pass on big bucks to you, you need to learn how to invest your money intelligently. Investing like the big boys and girls is a smart move, as long as you understand and manage the risks.

If you understand and are comfortable with the risks and take sensible steps to diversify (don't put all your eggs in the same basket), ownership investments are the key to building wealth. In order to accomplish typical longer-term financial goals such as retiring, the money that you save and invest needs to grow at a healthy clip. If you dump all of your money in bank accounts that pay only a few percent interest per year, you're likely to fall short of your goals.

Not everyone needs to make his money grow, of course. For example, suppose you inherit a significant sum and/or maintain a restrained standard of living and work your whole life simply because you enjoy doing so. This situation makes it possible that you may not need to take the risks involved with a potentially faster-growth investment. You may be more comfortable with *safer* investments, such as paying off your mortgage faster than necessary. Chapter 3 helps you think through some of these issues.

The stock market

Stocks are an example of an ownership investment, because they represent shares of ownership in a company.

If you want to share in the growth and profits of companies like Microsoft, you can! You simply buy shares of their stock through a brokerage firm. However, just because Microsoft makes money in the future, there's no guarantee that the value of its stock will increase. In fact, the value of your Microsoft stock can decrease. But at least the next time you call Microsoft and fork over $35 for technical support, you'll have some small satisfaction knowing that you indirectly profit.

You can pick and choose the stocks that you want to own and buy them through a broker. Some companies today even sell their stock directly to investors, allowing you to bypass brokers altogether. You can also invest in stocks via a stock mutual fund, where a fund manager decides which stocks to buy. (I discuss the various methods for buying stock in Chapter 6.)

The stock market isn't a bad way to build wealth. In fact, Thomas has used the stock market to build his wealth over the years. At the age of 75, he is the proud owner of a more than $1.2 million portfolio. Thomas worked for 30 years as a pressman for a newspaper and retired in his early 50s. When he retired, he was making about $9,000 per year. "I never had a college education but always made sure to save and invest money each month and watch it grow," says Thomas.

B.A.s, M.B.A.s, M.D.s, or Ph.D.s are not required to make money in the stock market. If you can practice some simple lessons, such as making regular and systematic investments and investing in proven companies and funds while minimizing your investment expenses and taxes, you'll be a winner.

However, I don't believe that you can "beat the markets," and you certainly can't beat the best professional money managers at their own, full-time game. This book shows you time-proven, non-gimmicky methods to make your money grow in the stock market, as well as other financial markets. (I explain how in Part II.)

Real estate

Another method that people use to build wealth is to invest in real estate. Owning and managing real estate is like running a small business. You need to satisfy customers (tenants), manage your costs, keep an eye on the competition, and so on. Some methods of real estate investing require more time than others, but many are proven ways to build wealth.

John, who works for a city government, and his wife, Linda, a computer analyst, have built more than $2 million in investment real estate *equity* (the difference between the property's market value and debts owed) over the past three decades. "Our parents owned rental property, and we could see what it could do for you by providing income and building wealth," says John. Investing in real estate also appealed to John and Linda because they didn't know anything about the stock market, so they wanted to stay away from it. The idea of *leverage* — making money with borrowed money — on the real estate also appealed to them.

John and Linda bought their first property, a duplex, in 1971, when their combined income was $20,000 per year. Every time they moved to a new home, they kept the prior one and converted it to a rental. Now in their 50s, John and Linda own seven pieces of investment real estate and are millionaires. "It's like a second retirement, having several thousand in monthly income from the real estate," says John.

John readily admits that rental real estate isn't without its hassles. "We haven't enjoyed getting calls in the middle of the night, but now we have people who can help with this when we're not available. It's also a pain dealing with finding new tenants," he says.

Overall, John and Linda figure that they've been well rewarded for the time they spent and the money they invested. John and Linda's rental properties allow them to live in a nicer home than they otherwise could afford.

Ultimately, to make your money grow much faster than inflation and taxes, you must absolutely, positively do at least one thing — take some risk. Any investment that has real growth potential also has shrinkage potential! You may not want to, or have the stomach to take the risk. Don't despair: I discuss lower-risk investments in this book as well. You can find out about risks and returns in the next chapter.

Small business

I know people who have hit investing "home runs" by owning or buying a business. Unlike the stock market, most people work at running their business full time, increasing their chances of doing something big financially with it. If you try to invest in individual stocks, by contrast, you're likely to work at it part time and compete against professionals who invest practically around the clock.

A decade ago, Calvin set out to develop a corporate publishing firm. Because he took the risk of starting his business and has been successful in slowly building it, today in his early 40s, he enjoys a net worth in excess of $2 million and can retire if he wants.

Even more important to many business owners — and the reason that financially successful entrepreneurs such as Calvin don't call it quits once they've amassed a lot of cash — are the non-financial rewards of investing, including the challenge and fulfillment of operating a successful business.

Sandra has worked on her own as an interior designer for 18 years. She previously worked in fashion, as a model and then as a retail store manager. Her first taste of interior design was redesigning rooms at a condominium project. "I knew when I did that first building and turned it into something wonderful and profitable that I loved doing this kind of work," says Sandra.

Today, Sandra's firm specializes in the restoration of landmark hotels and her work has been written up in dozens of magazines. "The money is not of primary importance to me . . . my work is driven by a passion . . . but obviously it has to be profitable," she says. Sandra has also experienced the fun and enjoyment of designing hotels in many parts of the U.S. and overseas, including one in Japan.

Most small business owners (myself included) quickly point out that the entrepreneurial life is not a walk through the rose garden (although it does have its share of thorns). Emotionally and financially, entrepreneurship is sometimes a roller coaster. In addition to the financial rewards, however, small business owners can enjoy seeing the impact of their work and knowing that it makes a difference. Combined, Calvin's and Sandra's firms created 25 new jobs.

Not everyone needs to be sparked by the desire to start their own company to profit from small business. Other ways to get your foot in the entrepreneurial world include buying an existing business and investing in someone else's budding enterprise. I talk more about evaluating and buying a business in Part IV of this book.

Lending investments

The other major type of investments include those in which you lend your money. Suppose that, like most people, you keep some money in your local bank — most likely in a checking account, but perhaps also in a savings account or certificate of deposit (CD). No matter what type of bank account you place your money in, you lend your money to the bank.

How long and under what conditions you lend your bank the money depends on the specific bank and account that you use. With a CD, you commit to lend your money to the bank for a specific length of time — perhaps six months or even a year. In return, the bank probably pays you a higher rate of interest than if you put your money in a bank account offering immediate access. (You may demand termination of the CD early; however, you will be penalized.)

As I discuss later, you can also invest your money in bonds — another type of lending investment. When you purchase a bond that has been issued by the government or a company, you agree to lend your money for a predetermined period of time and receive a particular rate of interest. A bond may pay you 6 percent interest over the next five years, for example.

Lending investments are all the same in that, instead of directly sharing in the ownership of a company or other asset, such as real estate, you lend your money to some organization that in turn invests it. If you lend your money to Microsoft through one of its bonds that matures, say, in ten years, and Microsoft triples in size over the next decade, you won't share in its growth. Microsoft's stockholders and employees reap the rewards of the company's success, but as a bondholder, you don't.

Most people keep far too much of their money in lending investments where they effectively allow others to reap the rewards of economic growth. Although lending investments appear safer because you know in advance what return you will receive, they aren't that safe. The long-term risk of these seemingly safe money investments is that your money will grow too slowly to enable you to accomplish your personal financial goals.

Cash equivalents

Cash equivalents are any investment that you can quickly convert into cash without any cost to you. Of course, the cash in your wallet qualifies as a cash equivalent. With most checking accounts, for example, you can write a check or withdraw cash by visiting a teller — either the live or the mechanical automated type.

Money market mutual funds are another type of cash equivalent. Investors, both large and small, invest hundreds of billions of dollars in money market mutual funds because the best mutual funds produce higher yields than bank savings accounts. The yield advantage of a money market fund almost always widens when interest rates increase because banks move about as fast as molasses on a cold winter day to raise savings account rates.

Why should you sacrifice even 1 or 2 percent of "free" yield? Many bank savers sacrifice this yield because they think that money market funds are risky — but they're not. Money market mutual funds generally invest in ultra-safe things such as short-term bank certificates of deposit, U.S. government-issued Treasury bills, and commercial paper (short-term bonds) that the most creditworthy corporations issue.

WARNING!

The double whammy of inflation and taxes

Bank accounts and bonds that pay a decent return are reassuring to many investors. Earning a few percent interest sure beats losing some or all of your money in a risky investment.

The problem is that money in a savings account, for example, that pays 3 percent, is not actually yielding you 3 percent. It's not that the bank is lying — it's just that your investment bucket contains some not-so-obvious holes.

The first hole is taxes. When you earn interest, you must pay taxes on it (unless you invest the money in a retirement account, in which case you generally pay the taxes at a later date, when you withdraw the money). If you're a moderate income earner, you end up losing about a third of your interest to taxes. Your 3 percent return is now down to 2 percent.

But the second hole in your investment bucket is even bigger than taxes: inflation. Although a few products become cheaper over time (computers, for example), most goods and services increase in price. Inflation in the U.S. is running right around 2 percent per year. Inflation depresses the purchasing power of your investment's returns. If you subtract the 2 percent "cost" of inflation from the remaining 2 percent after payment of taxes, I'm sorry to say that you simply break even on your investment.

To recap: For every dollar you invested in the bank a year ago, despite the fact that the bank paid you your 3 pennies of interest, you have to pay a penny of that interest in taxes, and you lose another 2 pennies to inflation, so you're left with only one dollar of real purchasing power for every dollar you had a year ago. In other words, thanks to the inflation and tax holes in your investment bucket, you can buy the same with your money now as you did a year ago, even though you've invested your money for a year.

Another reason people keep too much money in traditional bank accounts is that the local bank branch office makes the cash seem more accessible. Money market mutual funds, however, offer many quick ways to get your cash. You can write a check (most funds stipulate the check must be for at least $250) or call the fund and request that it mail or wire you money.

By all means, keep your checking account at the local bank so that you can write smaller checks to pay your cable television, phone, and utility bills. Having local access to an ATM for fast cash withdrawals is also a plus. But move that extra money that's dozing away in your bank savings account, for example, into a higher-yielding money market mutual fund! Even if you have just a few thousand dollars, the extra yield more than pays for the cost of this book. If you're in a high tax bracket, you can also use tax-free money market funds (see Chapter 9 to find out more about money market funds).

Futures and options are not investments

Suppose you think that IBM's stock is a good investment. The direction that the management team is taking impresses you, and you like the new personal computers and other products and services that the company offers. Profits seem to be on a positive trend; everything's looking up.

You can go out and buy the stock — suppose it's currently trading at around $100 per share. If the price rises to $150 in the next six months, you've made yourself a 50 percent profit ($150–$100=$50) on your original $100 investment. (Of course, you have to pay some brokerage fees to buy and then sell the stock.)

But instead of buying the stock outright, you can buy what are known as call options on IBM. A *call option* gives you the right to buy shares of IBM under specified terms from the person who sells you the call option. You may be able to purchase a call option that allows you to exercise your right to buy IBM stock at, say, $120 per share in the next six months. For this privilege, you may pay $10 per share.

If IBM's stock price skyrockets to say, $150 in the next few months, the value of your options that allow you to buy the stock at $120 will be worth a lot — at least $30. You can then simply sell your options, which you bought for $10 in this example, at a huge profit — you've tripled your money.

Although this talk of fat profits sounds much more exciting than simply buying the stock directly and making far less money from a price increase, two big problems with options exist:

✔ If IBM's stock price goes nowhere or rises only a little during the six-month period when you hold the call option, the option expires as worthless, and you lose all — that is, 100 percent — of your investment. In fact, in my example, if IBM's stock trades at $120 or less at the time the option expires, the option is worthless.

✔ A call option represents a short-term gamble (in this example, over the next six months) on IBM's stock price. When you buy a call option, you're not investing in IBM as a long-term investment. IBM could expand its business and profits greatly in the years and decades ahead, but the value of the call option hinges on the ups and downs of IBM's stock price over a relatively short period of time. If the stock market happens to dip in the next six months, IBM may get pulled down as well, despite the company's improving financial health.

The way that most individuals use them, *futures* are a similar type of gambling instrument that deal mainly with the value of commodities such as heating oil, corn, wheat, gold, silver, and pork bellies. Futures have a delivery date that's in the not-too-distant future. (Do you really want 5,000 bushels of wheat delivered to your home? Or worse yet, 5,000 pork bellies!) You also can place a small down payment — around 10 percent — toward the purchase of futures, which greatly leverages your "investment." If prices fall, you need to put up more money to keep from having your position sold.

My advice: Don't gamble with futures and options. The only real use that you may (if ever) have for these *derivatives*, (so called because their value is "derived" from the price of other securities), is to hedge. Suppose you hold a lot of a stock, for example, that has greatly appreciated and you don't want to sell now because of the tax bite. Perhaps you want to postpone selling the stock until next year because you plan on not working, or you expect the government to lower the tax rate on capital gains. You can buy what's called a *put option,* which increases in value when a stock's price falls (because the put option grants you the right to sell your stock to the purchaser of the put option at a preset stock price). Thus, if the stock price does fall, the rising put option value offsets some of your losses. Using put options allows you to postpone selling your stock without exposing yourself to the risk of a falling stock price.

Precious metals

Over the millennia, gold and silver have served as mediums of exchange or currency because they have intrinsic value and cannot be debased the way that paper currencies can by printing more money. These precious metals are used in jewelry and manufacturing.

As investments, gold and silver perform well during bouts of inflation. For example, from 1972 to 1980, when inflation zoomed into the double-digit range in the U.S. and stocks and bonds went into the tank, gold and silver prices skyrocketed more than 500 percent. People were concerned that the U.S. government was going on a money-printing binge.

Generally over the long term, precious metals are lousy investments. They don't pay any dividends, and their price increases just keep you up with, but not ahead of, increases in the cost of living. Although investing in precious metals is better than keeping cash in a piggy bank or stuffing it in a mattress, the investment isn't as good as bonds, stocks, and real estate.

Collectibles

Collectibles are a catchall category for antiques, art, autographs, baseball cards, clocks, coins, comic books, diamonds, dolls, gems, photographs, rare books, rugs, stamps, vintage wine, writing utensils, and a whole host of other items. Although connoisseurs of fine art, antiques, and vintage wine wouldn't like the comparison of their pastime with buying old playing cards or chamber pots, the bottom line is that collectibles are all objects with little intrinsic value. Wine is just a bunch of old mushed-up grapes. A painting is simply a canvas and some paint that at retail would set you back a few bucks. Stamps are small pieces of paper, less than an inch square. Baseball cards — heck, my childhood friends and I used to, as kids, stick these between our bike spokes!

I'm not trying to diminish contributions that artists and others make to our culture. And I know that some people place a high value on some of these collectibles. But true investments that can make your money grow, such as stocks, real estate, or a small business, are assets that can produce income and profits. Collectibles have little intrinsic value and are thus subject to the whims and speculations of buyers and sellers. Here are some other major problems with collectibles:

- ✔ **Markups are huge.** The spread between the price that a dealer sells and then buys the same exact object back from you is often around 100 percent. Sometimes the difference is even greater, particularly if a dealer is the second or third middleman in the chain of purchase. So at a minimum, your purchase must typically double in value just to get you back to even. And that may take 10 to 20 years or more!

- ✔ **Lots of other costs add up.** If the markups aren't bad enough, with some collectibles, you incur all sorts of other costs. If you buy more-expensive pieces, you may need to have them appraised. You may have to pay storage and insurance costs as well. And, unlike the markup, you pay some of these fees year after year after year of ownership.

- ✔ **You can get stuck with a pig in a poke.** Sometimes, you may overpay even more for a collectible because you don't realize some imperfection or inferiority of an item. Worse, you may buy a forgery. Even reputable dealers have been duped by forgeries.

- ✔ **Your pride and joy can deteriorate over time.** Damage from sunlight, humidity, temperatures that are too high or too low, and a whole host of vagaries can ruin the quality of your collectible. Insurance doesn't cover this type of damage or negligence on your part.

- ✔ **The returns stink.** Even if you ignore the substantial costs of buying, holding, and selling, the average returns investors earn from collectibles barely keep up with inflation and are inferior to stock market, real estate, and small business investing. Objective collectible return data are hard to come by. Never, ever trust such "data" that dealers or the many collectible trade publications that boast of hefty annual returns provide. The best study I've seen comes from Salomon Brothers, an investment banking firm. During the past 20 years, while stocks returned investors an average 13.1 percent per year and conservative bonds returned 10.2 percent per year, the highest performing collectibles — and the only ones to produce inflation-beating returns — were stamps at 9.1 percent per year and diamonds at 7.9 percent per year. However, if you factor in the huge markups on buying and selling these collectibles, the returns don't even keep up with inflation.

The best returns that collectible investors enjoy come from the ability to identify, years in advance, items that will *become* popular. Do you think you can do that? You may be the smartest person in the world, but you should know that most dealers can't tell what's going to rocket to popularity in the next 20 years. Dealers make their profits the same way as other retailers, from the spread or markup on the merchandise that they sell. The public and collectors have fickle, quirky tastes that no one can predict. Did you know that Beanie Babies, Furbies, Pet Rocks, or Cabbage Patch Kids were going to be such hits?

You can learn enough about a specific type of collectible to become a better investor than the average person, but you're going to have to be among the best — perhaps the top 10 percent of such collectors — to have a shot at earning decent returns. To get to this level of expertise, you need to invest thousands of hours reading, researching, and educating yourself about your specific type of collectible.

Nothing is wrong with *spending* money on collectibles, but I don't want you to fool yourself into thinking that they're investments. You can sink lots of your money into these non-income producing, poor return "investments." At their best as investments, collectibles give the wealthy a way to buy quality stuff that doesn't depreciate.

If you must buy collectibles:

- ✔ Do so for your love of the collectible, your desire to enjoy it, or your interest to learn about or master an area, not because you expect high investment returns, because you probably won't get them.

- ✔ Keep quality items that you and your family have purchased and hope that someday they're worth something. Keeping these quality items is the simplest way to break into the collectible business. The complete sets of baseball cards I gathered as a youngster are now (20-plus years later) worth hundreds of dollars to, in one case, $1,000!

- ✔ Buy from the source and cut out the middlemen whenever possible. In some cases, you may be able to buy from the artist. (My brother purchases most of his pottery directly from artists.)

- ✔ Check collectibles that are comparable to the one you have your eye on, shop around, and don't be afraid to negotiate. An effective way to negotiate, once you decide what you like, is to make your offer to the dealer or artist by phone. Because the seller isn't standing right next to you, you don't feel pressure to decide immediately.

- ✔ Ask the dealer who thinks that the item is such a great investment for a written guarantee to rebuy the item from you, if you opt to sell, for at least the same price you paid or higher within five years.

- ✔ Use a comprehensive resource to research, buy, sell, maintain, and improve your collectible, such as *Kovels' Guide to Selling, Buying, and Fixing Your Antiques and Collectibles* (Crown) by Ralph and Terry Kovel.

Chapter 2

Risks and Returns

● ●

In This Chapter

▶ Determining risks

▶ Reducing risk and still earning good returns

▶ Figuring out how much you can expect your investments to return

▶ Deciding how much you want or need your investments to return

● ●

A woman passes up eating a hamburger at a picnic because she heard that she could contract a deadly e. coli infection from eating improperly cooked meat.

The next week, that same woman hops in the passenger's seat of her friend's car. Minutes later, the car is struck head on and the woman dies.

A young child is about to go for a bike ride when her parents notice that she left her bike helmet in the garage. The child rides off without her helmet and returns home unhurt.

The next day, that same girl goes to a friend's house to play with a boy who finds his parent's loaded gun, even though his older brother is at home. The older brother shoots the little girl in the chest and kills her.

I'm not trying to depress or frighten anyone. However, I am trying to make an important point about risk — something that we all deal with on a daily basis.

First things first: Risk is in the eye of the beholder. Many of us base our perception of risk, in large part, on our experiences and what we've been exposed to. Many people fret about relatively small risks while overlooking much larger risks.

Sure, a risk of an e. coli infection from eating poorly cooked meat exists, so the woman who was leery of eating the hamburger at the picnic had a legitimate concern. However, that same woman got into the friend's car without an airbag and placed herself at far greater risk of dying in that situation than if she had eaten the hamburger. Annually in the U.S., more than 40,000 people die in automobile accidents.

Likewise, although the parents had a right to be concerned about their young daughter suffering a head injury, should she fall off of her bike, they completely overlooked the significant risk of an improperly stored gun in other households. According to research conducted by the non-profit Center to Prevent Handgun Violence, an astounding 43 percent of U.S. households with children contain a firearm and 28 percent of these gun-owning parents do not keep the gun locked or otherwise secured.

Risks: Education Conquers Fear and Ignorance

Everywhere you turn, risks exist; some are just more apparent than others. Many people also misunderstand risks. With increased knowledge, you may be able to reduce or conquer some of your fears and make more sensible decisions about reducing risks. For example, some people who fear flying don't understand that statistically, flying is much safer than driving a car, because when a plane goes down, it's big news. Dozens and, in some cases, hundreds of people, who probably weren't under the influence or engaging in otherwise reckless behavior, perish. Meanwhile, the press seems to notice less the handfuls of people who die on the road every day. Statistically, you're approximately 40 times more likely to die in a motor vehicle than in an airplane.

Does this mean that you shouldn't drive or fly, or that you shouldn't drive to the airport? Of course not. However, you may consider steps you can take to reduce the significant risks you expose yourself to in a car. For example, you can get a car with more safety features, or you may bypass riding with reckless taxi drivers whose cars lack seat belts.

Although some of us like to live life to its fullest and take "fun" risks, — how else can you explain triathletes, mountain climbers, parachuters, and bungee jumpers — most people seek to minimize risk and maximize enjoyment in their lives. You'd be mighty unhappy living a life that sought to eliminate all risks, and you likely wouldn't succeed anyway. Likewise, if you attempt to avoid all the risks that investing involves, you won't succeed and you likely won't be happy with your investment results and lifestyle.

In the investment world, some people don't go near stocks or any investment that they perceive to be volatile. As a result, such investors often end up with lousy long-term returns, and they expose themselves to some high risks that they overlooked, such as the risk of inflation and taxes that erode the purchasing power of their money.

You can't live without taking risks. Risk-free activities or ways of living don't exist. You can minimize but never eliminate risks. Some methods of risk reduction aren't palatable because they reduce your quality of life. Risks are also composed of several factors. In the sections that follow, I discuss the various types of investment risks and methods that you can use to sensibly reduce these risks while not missing out on the upside that growth investments offer.

Market value risk

Although the stock market can help you build wealth, most people recognize that it can also plunge quite a bit — 10, 20, 30 percent or more in no time. In a mere six weeks (from mid-July 1998 to early September 1998), large company U.S. stocks plunged about 20 percent. An index of smaller company U.S. stocks plunged 33 percent over a slightly longer period of 2½ months. If you had invested $5,000 during this time period, your investment may have shrunk to $4,000 or less. Similarly, those who invested $50,000 saw it shrink to $40,000 or less. Although that loss doesn't feel good, it's the reality of risk. Your investment can shrink in value!

If you think that the U.S. stock market crash that occurred in the fall of 1987 was a big one (the market plunged 36 percent in a matter of weeks), consider these massive plunges in the U.S. stock market over the past 100-plus years. Table 2-1 lists plunges that were all *worse* than the 1987 crash.

Table 2-1	Most Depressing U.S. Stock Market Declines
Period	*Size of Fall*
1929-1932	89% (ouch!)
1937-1942	52%
1906-1907	49%
1890-1896	47%
1919-1921	47%
1901-1903	46%
1973-1974	45%
1916-1917	40%

Real estate exhibits similar unruly annoying tendencies. Although real estate has been a terrific long-term investment (like stocks), various real estate markets get clobbered from time to time.

U.S. housing prices took a near 25 percent tumble from the late 1920s to the mid-1930s. When the oil industry collapsed in the southeast in the early 1980s, real estate prices took a beating in that area. Later in the 1980s and early 1990s, the northeastern U.S. became mired in a severe recession, and real estate prices plummeted by 20 to 40 percent in many areas.

After peaking near 1990, many of the west coast housing markets, especially those in California, experienced falling prices — dropping 20 percent or more in most areas by the mid-1990s.

The Japanese real estate market crash also began around the time of the California market fall. Property prices in Japan collapsed more than 60 percent since that market's peak.

After reading this section, you may want to keep all your money in the bank — after all, you know you'll earn at least a few percent interest every year, and you won't have to be a non-stop worrier. No one has ever lost 20, 40, 60, or 80 percent of his bank-held savings vehicle in a few years!

However, if you pass up the stock and real estate markets simply because of the potential market value risk, you miss out on a historic, time-tested method of building substantial wealth. Later in this chapter, I show you the generous returns that these investments usually yield. The following sections suggest some simple things you can do to lower your investing risk and help prevent your portfolio from suffering a huge fall.

Diversify to smooth the bumpy ride

Individual stock markets may crash. However, the various stock markets around the world have never all crashed at the same time. For example, when the U.S. stock market crashed in the fall of 1987, many foreign stock markets dropped far less or not at all. So if you had spread your money across the many different stock markets, your portfolio wouldn't have suffered nearly as much as if you held all your stocks in the U.S. market.

You can invest overseas to reduce your investment risk if you worry about the health of the U.S. economy, the government, and the dollar. Most large U.S. companies do business overseas, so when you invest in larger U.S. company stocks, you get some international investment exposure. You can also invest in international company stocks, ideally via mutual funds (see Chapter 9).

TECHNICAL STUFF

Liquidity

The term *liquidity* refers to how long and at what cost you can convert an investment into cash. The money in your wallet is considered perfectly liquid — it's already cash.

Suppose you invested money in a handful of stocks. Although you can't easily sell these stocks on a Saturday night, you can sell most stocks quickly through a broker for a nominal fee any day that the financial markets are open (normal working days). You pay a higher percentage to sell your stocks if you use a high-cost broker or if you have a small number of stocks to sell.

Real estate is generally much less liquid than stock. Preparing your property for sale takes time, and if you want to get fair market value for your property, finding a buyer may take weeks or months. Selling costs (agent commissions, fix-up expenses, and closing costs) can easily approach 10 percent of the home's value.

A privately run small business is among the least liquid of the better growth investments that you can make. Selling such a business typically takes longer than selling most real estate.

So that you're not forced to sell one of your investments that you intend to hold for long-term purposes, keep an emergency reserve of three to six months' worth of living expenses in a money market account. Also consider investing some money in bonds (see Chapter 8), which pay higher than money market yields without the high risk or volatility that comes with the stock market.

Of course, investing overseas can't totally protect you. You can't do much about a global economic catastrophe. If you worry about the risk of such a calamity, you should probably also worry about a huge meteor crashing into Earth. Maybe there's a way to colonize outer space. . . .

Diversifying your investments can involve more than just your stock portfolio, however. You can also hold some real estate investments to diversify your investment portfolio. Some real estate markets actually appreciated in the late 1980s while the U.S. stock market was in the doghouse.

Check your time horizon

Investors who worry that the stock market may take a dive and take their capital down with it should first consider the time period that they plan to invest. In a one-year time period in the stock and bond markets, anything can happen (see Figure 2-1). History shows that once in every three years that you invest in the stock and bond markets, you lose money. However, stock market investors two-thirds of the time make money (sometimes substantial money), over a one-year time period. (Bond investors make money about two-thirds of the time, too, although they make a good deal less.)

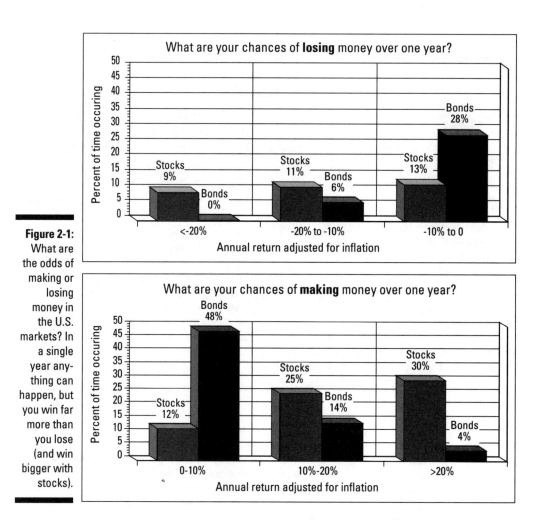

Figure 2-1:
What are the odds of making or losing money in the U.S. markets? In a single year anything can happen, but you win far more than you lose (and win bigger with stocks).

Although the stock market is more volatile in the short-term than the bond market, stock market investors earn far better long-term returns than do bond investors (see the "Stock returns" section later in this chapter). Remember, however, that bonds generally outperform keeping your money in a boring old bank account.

The risk of a stock or bond market fall becomes less of a concern the longer the time period that you plan to invest. As Figure 2-2 shows, as the holding period during which you own stocks increases from 1 year to 3 years to 5 years to 10 years, and then to 20 years, your likelihood of making a profit increases. In fact, over any 20-year time span, U.S. stock market investors have never lost money, even after you subtract for the effects of inflation.

Most stock market investors who I know are concerned about losing money. Figure 2-2 clearly shows that the key to minimizing the probability that you'll lose money in stocks is to hold them for the long term. As I discuss in great detail in Part II of this book, stocks are designed to be a long-term investment. If you want to invest in stocks, you should not do so unless you plan to hold them for at least five years — and preferably a decade or longer.

Pare down holdings in bloated markets

Perhaps you've heard the expression, "Buy low, sell high." Although I don't believe that you can time the markets (that is, predict the most profitable time to buy and sell), spotting a greatly overpriced market isn't too difficult. Throughout the book, I explain some simple yet powerful methods you can use to measure whether a particular investment market is of fair value, of good value, or overpriced.

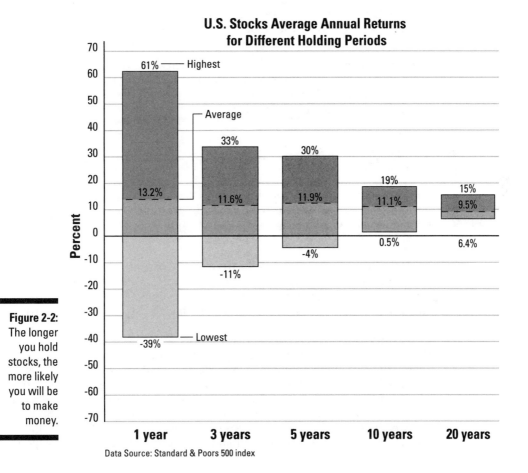

Figure 2-2: The longer you hold stocks, the more likely you will be to make money.

Data Source: Standard & Poors 500 index

You want to avoid overpriced investments for two important reasons. First, if and when these overpriced investments fall, they may fall farther and faster than more fairly priced investments. The second reason to avoid overpriced investments is that you can always find other investments that offer higher potential returns.

Ideally, you want to avoid having a lot of your money in markets that appear overvalued. Practically speaking, avoiding overvalued markets doesn't mean that you should try to sell all your holdings in such markets with the vain hope of buying them back at a much lower price. However, you may benefit from the following strategies:

- ✔ Focus investment of new money somewhere other than the overvalued market. As you save new investment money, put it into investments that offer you better values. Thus, without selling any of your seemingly expensive investments, they become a smaller portion of your total holdings. If you hold investments outside tax-sheltered retirement accounts, focusing your money elsewhere also offers the benefit of allowing you to avoid incurring taxes from selling appreciated investments.

- ✔ If you need to raise money to live on, such as for retirement, or for a major purchase, sell the expensive stuff. As long as the taxes aren't too troublesome, it's better to sell high and lock in your profits. Chapter 22 discusses issues to weigh when you contemplate selling an investment.

Individual investment risk

A downdraft can put an entire investment market on a roller-coaster ride, but healthy markets can also produce losers. Since the early 1980s, the U.S. stock market has had one of the greatest appreciating markets in history. You'd never know it, though, if you look at these losers.

Consider a company now called Navistar, which has undergone enormous transformations in the past two decades. This company used to be called International Harvester and manufactured farm equipment, trucks, and construction and other industrial equipment. Today, Navistar mostly makes trucks.

As recently as late 1983, this company's stock traded at more than $140 per share. It then plunged more than 90 percent over the ensuing decade (see Figure 2-3). Even with a rally in recent years, Navistar stock still trades at under $50 per share (after dipping below $10 per share). Lest you think that's a big drop, this company's stock traded as high as $455 per share in the early 1970s! If a worker retired from this company in the early 1970s with $200,000 invested in the company stock, the retiree's investment would be worth about $20,000 today! On the other hand, if the retiree had simply swapped his stock at retirement for a diversified portfolio of stocks, which I explain how to build in Part II, his or her $200,000 nest egg would've instead grown to more than $2,000,000!

"Okay," you say, "I would have been smart enough to avoid sinking my money into a company that made farm equipment — heck, I knew we were in the industrial age and heading into the information and technology age! Any old idiot could've made money by following the right trends."

How about Data General, a company that plays in the lucrative software industry, as well as the hardware part of the computer field? After trading as high as $76 in 1985, this stock fell off a cliff, plunging more than 95 percent to just $3 ½ per share by 1990, and has languished mostly below $20 per share since.

Likewise, more than a few investors, large and small, rode the Digital Equipment roller coaster. Once considered a blue chip company, Digital Equipment's share value has been clobbered in the years since 1987. From a high of nearly $200 per share, this stock dropped nearly 91 percent in the following seven years.

Just as individual stock prices can plummet, so too can individual real estate property prices. In California, for example, the prices of properties built on landfill were rocked by earthquakes during the 1990s. These quakes highlighted the dangers of building on poor soil. In the early 1980s, real estate values in the communities of Times Beach, Missouri, and Love Canal, New York, plunged due to carcinogenic toxic waste contamination. (Ultimately, many property owners in these areas were compensated for their losses by the federal government, as well as some real estate agencies that didn't disclose these known contaminations.)

Here are some simple steps you can take to lower the risk of individual investments that can upset your goals:

- **Do your homework.** When you purchase real estate, a whole host of inspections can save you from buying a money pit. With stocks, you can examine some measures of value and the company's financial condition and business strategy to reduce your chances of buying into an over-priced company or one on the verge of major problems. Parts II, III, and IV of this book give you more information on researching your investment.

- **Diversify.** Investors who seek growth invest in securities such as stocks. Placing significant amounts of your capital in one or a handful of securities is risky, particularly if the stocks are in the same type of industry. To reduce this risk, purchase stocks in a variety of industries and companies within each industry (see Part II for details).

- **Hire someone to invest for you.** Increasing numbers of investors turn to mutual funds (see Chapter 9) that offer professional management and oversight, as well as diversification. Stock mutual funds typically own 25 or more securities in a variety of companies in different industries. In Part III, I explain how you can invest in real estate in a similar way (that is, by leaving the driving to someone else).

Purchasing power risk

When Ethel retired at the age of 60, she was more than satisfied with her retirement income. She was receiving an $800-per-month pension and $1,200 per month from money that she had invested in long-term bonds. Her monthly expenditures amounted to about $1,500 so she was able to save a little money for an occasional trip.

Fast-forward 15 years. Ethel still receives $800 per month from her pension but now only $900 per month of investment income from some certificates of deposit. Ethel bailed out of bonds after she lost sleep over the sometimes roller coaster-like price movements in the bond market. Her monthly expenditures now amount to approximately $2,400 and she uses her investment principal (original investment) at a good clip. She's terrified of outliving her money.

Ethel has reason to worry. She has 100 percent of her money invested without protection against increases in the cost of living. Although her income felt comfortable in the beginning of her retirement, it doesn't at age 75, and Ethel can easily live another 15 or more years.

The erosion of the purchasing power of your investment dollar can, over longer time periods, be as bad as or worse than the effect of a major market crash. Table 2-2 shows the effective loss in purchasing power of your money at various rates of inflation and over differing time periods.

Table 2-2	Inflation's Corrosive Effect on Your Money's Purchasing Power			
Inflation rate	*10 years*	*15 years*	*25 years*	*40 years*
2%	−18%	−26%	−39%	−55%
4%	−32%	−44%	−62%	−81%
6%	−44%	−58%	−77%	−90%
8%	−54%	−68%	−85%	−95%
10%	−61%	−76%	−91%	−98%

As a financial counselor, I often see skittish investors who try to keep their money in bonds and money market accounts. The risk in this strategy is that your money won't grow enough over the years in order for you to accomplish your financial goals. In other words, the lower the return that you earn, the more you need to save to reach a particular financial goal. A 40-year-old wanting to accumulate $500,000 by age 65 would need to save $722 per month if she earns a 6 percent annual return but only needs to save $377 per month if she earns 10 percent return per year. Younger investors need to pay the most attention to the risk of generating low returns, but so too should younger senior citizens. At the age of 65, seniors need to recognize that a portion of their assets may not be used for a decade or more from the present.

Ironically, some people feel safe keeping much of their money in low yielding Treasury bonds issued by the U.S. federal government. Lending your money to the government has some patriotic value, but it certainly is not 100 percent risk free. Remember that the federal government has $5+ trillion total debt outstanding.

Career risk

Your ability to earn money is most likely your single biggest asset, or at least one of your biggest assets. Most people achieve what they do in the working world through education and hard work. By education, I'm not simply talking about what one learns in formal schooling. Education is a lifelong process. I've learned far more about business from my own front-line experiences and those of others than I've learned in educational settings. I also read a lot. Later in the book, I recommend books and other resources that I've found most useful.

Inflation ragin' outta control

You think 6, 8, or 10 percent annual inflation rates are bad? How would you like to live in a country that experienced that rate of inflation in a day?! As I discuss in Chapter 4, too much money in circulation chasing after too few goods causes high rates of inflation.

A government that runs amok with the nation's currency and money supply usually causes excessive rates of inflation — dubbed *hyperinflation.* Over the decades and centuries, hyperinflation has wreaked havoc in more than a few countries.

What happened in Germany in the late 1910s and early 1920s demonstrates how bad hyperinflation can get. Consider that during this time period, prices increased nearly one billion-fold!!! What cost 1 Reichsmark (the German currency in those days) at the beginning of this mess eventually cost nearly 1,000,000,000 Reichsmarks. People had to cart around so much currency that at times, they needed shopping-type carts to haul it! Ultimately, this inflationary burden was too much for the German society, fueling the rise of the Nazi party and Adolf Hitler.

In just the past decade, a number of countries, especially many that made up the former U.S.S.R. and others such as Brazil and Lithuania, have gotten themselves into a hyperinflationary mess with inflation rates of several hundred percent per year. In the mid-1980s, Bolivia's yearly inflation rate exceeded 10,000 percent.

Governments often try to slap on price controls to prevent runaway inflation (Richard Nixon did this in the U.S. in the 1970s), but the underground economy, known as the *black market,* usually prevails.

If you don't continually invest in your education, you risk losing your competitive edge. Your skills and perspectives can become dated and obsolete. Although that doesn't mean you should work 80 hours a week and never do anything fun, it does mean that part of your "work" time should always involve updating and building on your skills. The best organizations are those that recognize the need for continual knowledge and invest in their workforce through training and career development. Just remember to look at your own career objectives, which may not be the same as your company's.

Returns: How Much Can You Make?

The money that you invest is commonly referred to as *principal* (this has nothing to do with the quality, *principle*, lacking in disreputable financial advisors who sell inferior investments because it brings them hefty commissions, which is spelled *princip<u>le</u>*).

Return components

When you make investments, you have the potential to make money a variety of different ways. If you've ever had money in a bank account that pays *interest,* you know that the bank pays you a few percent in exchange for your allowing them to keep your money (which the bank turns around and lends to some other person or organization at a much higher rate of interest). The rate of interest is also known as the *yield.* So if a bank tells you that its savings account pays 3 percent interest, the bank may also say that it is yielding 3 percent. Banks usually quote interest rates or yields on an annual basis.

If a bank pays monthly interest for example, the bank also likely quotes a *compounded effective annual yield.* If the bank pays you interest each month instead of once per year, once the first month's interest is credited to your account, that *interest* starts earning interest as well. So, the bank may say that the account pays 3 percent, which compounds to an effective annual yield of 3.04 percent.

When you lend your money directly to a company — which is what you do when you invest in a bond that a corporation issues — you also receive interest. Bonds, as well as stocks (which are shares of ownership in a company) fluctuate in value once they are issued.

When you invest in a company's stock, you hope that the stock increases in value, that it appreciates. Of course, a stock can decline, or depreciate, in value. This change in market value is part of your return from a stock or bond investment:

$$\frac{\text{Current investment value} - \text{Original investment}}{\text{Original investment}} = \text{Appreciation or depreciation}$$

For example, if one year ago you invested $10,000 in a stock (you bought 1,000 shares at $10 per share) and the investment is now worth $11,000 (each share is worth $11), your investment's appreciation is

$$\frac{\$11,000 - \$10,000}{\$10,000} = 10\%$$

But stocks can also pay dividends, which are a bit like the interest you earn from a bank account. Dividends represent the company's way of sharing some of its profits with you as a stockholder. Some companies, particularly those that are small or growing rapidly, choose to reinvest all of their profits back into the company. (Of course, some companies don't turn a profit, so there's not much to pay out!) You need to factor these dividends into your return as well.

Suppose in the previous example that, in addition to your stock appreciating $1,000 to $11,000, it also paid you a dividend of $100 ($1 per share). Here's how you calculate your total return:

$$\frac{\text{Dividends} + \text{Current investment value} - \text{Original investment}}{\text{Original investment}} = \text{Total return}$$

Or, to apply it to the example

$$\frac{\$100 + \$11,000 - \$10,000}{\$10,000} = 11\%$$

Factoring in appreciation, dividends, interest, and so on, helps an investor calculate what her *total return* is. The total return figure tells you the grand total of what you made (or lost) on your investment.

After-tax returns

Although you may be happy that your stock has given you an 11 percent return on your invested dollars, remember: Unless you held your investment in a tax-sheltered retirement account, you owe taxes on your return. Specifically, the dividends and investment appreciations that you sell are taxed.

If you're in a moderate tax bracket, taxes on your investment probably run in the neighborhood of 30 percent (federal and state). So if your investment returned 7 percent before taxes, you're left with a return of 4.9 percent after taxes.

Often, people make investing decisions without considering the tax consequences of their moves. This is a big mistake. What good is making money if the federal and state government take a substantial portion of it away? In the next chapter, I explain how to make tax-wise investment decisions that fit with your overall personal financial situation and goals.

Psychological returns

Profits and tax avoidance can powerfully motivate you in the choice of your investments. However with investments, as with other life decisions, you need to consider more than the bottom line. Some people want to have fun with their investments. Of course, they don't want to lose money or sacrifice a lot of potential returns — less expensive ways to have fun do exist!

Psychological rewards compel some investors to choose particular investment vehicles such as individual stocks, real estate, or a small business. Why? Because, compared with other investments such as managed mutual funds, they see these investments as more tangible and, well, more fun.

Be honest with yourself about why you choose the investments that you do. Allowing your ego to get in the way can be dangerous. Do you invest in individual stocks because you really believe that you can do better than the best full-time professional money managers? Chances are high that you won't (see Chapter 6 for more details). Do you like investing in real estate more because of the gratification from driving by and showing off your properties to others than because of their investment rewards? I know that these aren't easy questions to answer, but they're worth considering as you contemplate what investments you want to make.

Savings and money market account returns

You need to keep your extra cash that awaits investment (or an emergency) in a safe place, preferably one that doesn't get hammered by the sea of changes in the financial markets. No reason exists why you shouldn't earn a healthier rate of return on such savings than the paltry amount of interest that most bank accounts pay. Ideally, you should keep as little money as possible in your bank checking account, for the simple reason that your bank likely pays you next to nothing (or actually nothing) in interest on this account.

By default and for convenience, many people keep their extra cash in a bank savings account. Although the bank offers the U.S. government's backing via the Federal Deposit Insurance Corporation (FDIC), it comes at a high price. Most banks pay a near microscopic 2 to 3 percent interest rate on their savings accounts.

A far better place to keep your liquid savings is in a money market mutual fund. These are the safest types of mutual funds around and, for all intents and purposes, equal a bank savings account's safety. However, the best money market funds pay higher yields than most bank savings accounts. Unlike a bank, money market mutual funds tell you how much they skim off for the cost of managing your money. If you're in a higher tax bracket, tax-free versions of money funds exist, as well. See Chapter 9 for more on money market funds.

If you don't need immediate access to your money, consider using Treasury bills or bank certificates of deposit. Usually issued for terms such as 3, 6, or 12 months, your money will surely earn more in one of these vehicles than a bank savings account. The drawback to Treasury bills and bank certificates of deposit is that you incur a penalty or fee if you get your investment back before the term expires. (See Chapter 8.)

Bond returns

When you buy a bond, you lend your money to the federal government or a corporation for a specific period of time. When you buy a bond, you expect to earn a higher yield than you would with a money market or savings account. You're taking more risk, after all. Companies can and do go bankrupt, in which case you may lose some or all of your investment.

Generally, you can expect to earn a higher return when you buy bonds that are

- ✔ Longer-term
- ✔ Lower credit quality

Wharton School of Business professor Jeremy Siegel has tracked the performance of bonds and stocks all the way back to 1802. Although you may say that what happened in the nineteenth century has little relevance to the financial markets and economy of today, the decades since the Great Depression, which most other return data track, are a relatively small slice of time. Figure 2-4 presents the data, so if you'd like to give more credibility to the recent numbers, you may.

Note that, although the rate of inflation has increased since the Great Depression, bond returns have not. Long-term bonds maintain slightly higher returns in recent years than short-term bonds. The bottom line: Bond investors typically earn about 4 to 5 percent per year.

Figure 2-4:
A historical view of bond performance: Inflation has eroded bond returns more in recent decades.

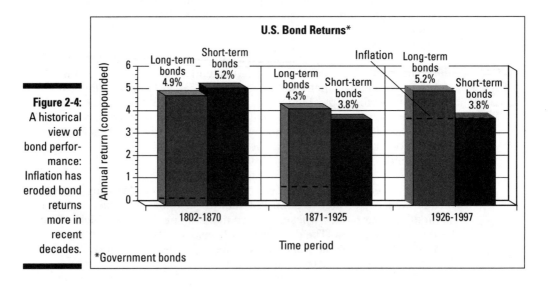

Stock returns

Let's face it: Most people are a little greedy (okay, some are a lot greedy). People who invest in the stock market are prime examples of those who want to make the most of a potentially good thing. Investors expect, indeed they demand, what they consider a fair return on investment. And if one investment doesn't offer a high enough rate of return, investors can choose to move their money into other investments that they believe will perform better. Rather than buying a sound stock and holding on to it, some investors frequently buy and sell, hoping to cash in on the latest superstar investment. This tactic seldom works out best in the long run.

Unfortunately, some of these investors use a rear view mirror when they purchase their stocks, chasing after investments that have recently performed strongly on the assumption (and the hope) that those investments will continue to earn strong returns. But chasing after the strongest performing investments can be dangerous if you catch the stock at its peak, ready to begin a downward spiral. You may have heard that the goal of investing is to buy low and sell high. Chasing high-flying investments can lead you to buy high, with the prospect of having to sell low if the stock has run out of steam. Even though stocks as a whole have proven to be a good long-term investment, picking individual stocks is a risky endeavor. See Chapter 5 for advice on making sound stock investment decisions.

A tremendous amount of data exists regarding stock market returns. In fact, in the U.S. markets, data going back nearly two full centuries documents the fact that stocks are a terrific long-term investment. The returns that investors have enjoyed, and continue to enjoy, from stocks have been remarkably constant from one generation to the next.

Going all the way back to 1802, the U.S. stock market has produced an annual return of 8.4 percent while inflation has grown at 1.3 percent per year. Thus, after subtracting for inflation, stocks have appreciated about 7.1 percent faster annually than the rate of inflation.

The U.S. stock market returns have consistently and substantially beaten the rate of inflation over the years (see Figure 2-5).

Stocks don't just exist in the U.S., of course (see Figure 2-6). More than a few U.S. investors seem to forget this fact, especially given the sizzling performance of the U.S. stock market during the late 1990s. As I discuss earlier in the chapter, one advantage of buying and holding overseas stocks is that they don't always fall when U.S. stocks drop. In other words, overseas stocks help to diversify your portfolio.

In addition to enabling U.S. investors to diversify, investing overseas has also proven profitable. The investment banking firm Morgan Stanley tracks the performance of stocks in both economically established countries and so-called emerging economies. As the name suggests, countries with emerging economies are "behind" economically but show promise of healthy rates of growth and progress.

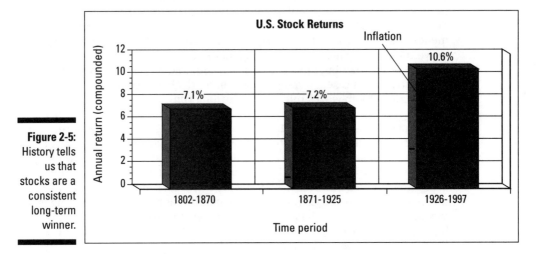

Figure 2-5:
History tells us that stocks are a consistent long-term winner.

Total Value of Stocks Worldwide

Figure 2-6:
Although the strong 1990s U.S. stock market increased the U.S. share of total stock market values worldwide, many investing opportunities exist outside the U.S.

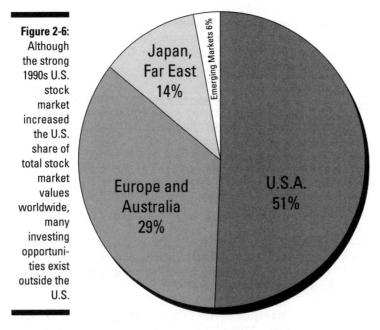

TECHNICAL STUFF

Are smaller company stock returns higher?

Stocks are generally classified by the size of the company. Small company stocks are not stocks that physically small companies issue — they are simply stocks issued by companies that haven't reached the size of corporate behemoths such as IBM, AT&T, or Coca-Cola. The Standard & Poor's 500 index tracks the performance of 500 large company stocks in the U.S. The Russell 2000 index tracks the performance of 2,000 smaller-company U.S. stocks.

Small company stocks have outperformed larger company stocks during the past seven decades. Historically, small company stocks have produced slightly higher compounded annual returns than large company stocks.

However, most of this extra performance is due to just one high-performance time period, from the mid-1970s to the early 1980s. If you eliminate this time period from the data, small stocks have actually under-performed larger company stocks.

Also, be aware that small company stocks can get hammered in down markets. For example, during the Great Depression, small company stocks plunged more than 85 percent between 1929 and 1932 while the S&P 500 fell only 64 percent. In 1937, small company stocks plummeted 58 percent; the S&P 500 fell 35 percent. And in 1969–1970, small company stocks fell 38 percent while the S&P 500 fell just 5 percent.

For example, between 1986 and 1995 Morgan Stanley's EAFE (which stands for Europe, Australia, and Far East) index of foreign stocks appreciated at a rate of 17.9 percent per year. Emerging market stocks performed even better. This compares quite favorably with the U.S. stock market, which averaged 13.9 percent per year during this time period.

Countries resemble companies in many ways. Smaller countries or companies can exhibit more explosive rates of growth. Once a company or country reaches a large scale, lower rates of growth prevail because of its sheer size. Faster-growing countries tend to have stock prices that rise faster.

Real estate returns

Over the years, real estate has proven to be about as lucrative as investing in the stock market. This fact makes sense because ultimately, growth in the economy, in jobs, and in population fuels the demand for real estate.

Consider what has happened to the U.S. population over the past two centuries. In 1800, a mere 5 million people lived within our borders. In 1900, that figure grew to 76.1 million and today it's more than 260 million. All of these people need a place to live, and as long as jobs exist, the income from jobs largely fuels the demand for housing.

Businesses and people have an annoying tendency to cluster in major cities and suburban towns. Although some people commute, most people and businesses locate near airports and major highways. Thus, real estate prices in and near major metropolises and suburbs appreciate the most. Consider the areas of the world that have the most expensive real estate prices: Hong Kong, Tokyo, San Francisco, Los Angeles, New York, Boston. . . . What all these areas have in common are lots of businesses and people and limited land.

Contrast these areas with the many rural parts of the U.S., such as those in the Midwest and South where real estate is a veritable bargain because of the abundant supply of buildable land and relatively low demand for housing.

Small-business returns

As I discuss in Part IV of this book, you have several choices for tapping into the exciting potential of the small-business world. If you have the drive and determination, you can start your own small business. Or, perhaps you may have what it takes to buy an existing small business. If you obtain the necessary capital and skills to assess opportunities and risk, you can invest in someone else's small business.

What potential returns can you get from small business? Small-business owners like myself who do something they really enjoy will tell you that the non-financial returns can be huge! The financial rewards can be handsome as well.

Every year, *Forbes* magazine publishes a list of the world's wealthiest individuals. As you see from perusing a sample page from the list (see Figure 2-7), most of these people built their wealth through a significant ownership stake from starting a small business that became large. These individuals achieved extraordinarily high effective returns (often in excess of hundreds of percent per year) on the amounts they invested to get their companies off the ground.

You may also achieve potentially high returns from buying and improving an existing small business. As I discuss in Part IV, such small business investment returns may be a good deal lower than the returns you may gain from starting a business from scratch.

Unlike the stock market, where plenty of historic rate of return data exists, data on the success, or lack thereof, that investors have had with investing in a small, private company is harder to come by. Smart venture capitalist firms operate a fun and lucrative business: They identify and invest money in smaller start-up companies that they hope will grow rapidly and eventually go public. Venture capitalists allow outsiders to invest with them via limited partnerships. To gain entry, you generally need $1 million to invest. (I never said this was equal opportunity investment club!)

Venture capitalists, also known as general partners, typically skim off 20 percent of the profits and also charge limited partnership investors a hefty 2 to 3 percent annual fee on the amount that they've invested. The return that's left over for the limited partnership investors isn't stupendous. According to Venture Economics, a firm that tracks limited partners' returns, over the past ten years, venture funds have averaged annual returns of 17.7 percent, almost exactly what stock market investors have earned on average this century. Over the last decade, U.S. stock market investors simply buying a Standard & Poor's 500 index fund earned 19.2 percent. (I discuss index funds in Chapter 9.)

The general partners that run venture capital funds make more than the limited partners. Estimates of the general partners' returns range from 17 or 18 percent to as high as 30 percent at the most successful firms.

You can attempt to do what the general partners do in venture capital firms and invest directly in small, private companies. You're quite likely to be investing in much smaller and simpler companies. Earning venture capitalist returns isn't easy to do. If you think you're up to the challenge, I explain the best ways to invest in small business in Chapter 16.

How Much Do You Need or Want to Earn?

This may seem like an extraordinarily stupid question for me to ask you! Who *doesn't* want to earn a high return? However, although investing in stocks, real estate, or small business can produce high long-term returns, you invest in these vehicles with greater risk, especially over the short term.

Some people can't stomach the risk. Others are at a time in their lives when they can't afford to take great risk. If you're near or in retirement, your portfolio and nerves may not be able to wait a decade for your riskier investments to recover after a major stumble. Perhaps you have sufficient assets to accomplish your financial goals and are more concerned with preserving what you do have, rather than risking it to grow more.

If you work for a living, odds are you need and want to make your investments grow at a healthy clip. If your investments grow slowly, you may fall short of your goals of owning a home or retiring or changing careers. The next chapter helps you with the important issue of making investing decisions that fit with your financial goals and situation.

NAME	PAGE	RESIDENCE	AGE	WORTH ($MIL)	PRIMARY SOURCE
DeVos, Richard M.	246	Ada, Michigan	72	1,500	Amway
Diller, Barry †	384	New York, New York	56	425	Television
Disney, Roy Edward	290	Los Angeles, California	68	900	Walt Disney Co.
Dolan, Charles Francis	236	Oyster Bay, New York	72	1,700	Cable TV
Donnelley family	370	Chicago, Illinois		1,400	R.R. Donnelley & Sons
Dorrance, Bennett	192	Paradise Valley, Arizona	51	2,700	Inheritance (Campbell Soup)
Douglas, Jean W.	332	Washington, D.C.	78	590	Pioneer Hi-Bred International
Drexler, Millard S. ★	326	San Francisco, California	54	615	The Gap
Druckenmiller, Stanley	296	New York, New York	45	850	Money management
Du Pont (Pierre Samuel II Heirs) family	370	Delaware, Virginia		13,000	Inheritance (Du Pont Co.)
Du Pont, Irénée Jr.	350	Montchanin, Delaware	78	525	Inheritance (Du Pont Co.)
Duffield, David A.	230	Danville, California	58	1,900	PeopleSoft Inc.
Duke, Jennifer Johnson ■	406	Jacksonville, Florida			Inheritance (Johnson & Johnson)
Durst family	371	New York City area		1,200	Real estate

E					
Earhart, Anne Catherine Getty	316	Laguna Beach, California	46	700	Inheritance (oil)
Ebbers, Bernard J. ★	316	Jackson, Mississippi	57	690	WorldCom Inc.
Edson, John Orin	288	Seattle, Washington	66	900	Manufacturing
Egan, Michael S. ■	406	Fort Lauderdale, Florida			Alamo Rent A Car
Egan, Richard J.	292	Hopkinton, Massachusetts	62	870	EMC Corp.
Eisner, Michael D.	312	Los Angeles, California	56	710	Walt Disney Co.
Ellison, Lawrence Joseph	182	Atherton, California	54	4,900	Oracle Corp.
Emmerson, Archie Aldis (Red)	268	Redding, California	69	1,100	Sierra Pacific Industries
Ergen, Charles	334	Denver, Colorado	45	570	Satellite television

F					
Farmer, Richard T.	254	Cincinnati, Ohio	64	1,300	Cintas Corp.
Feld, Kenneth	320	Potomac, Maryland	49	650	Circus
Field, Frederick Woodruff	262	Beverly Hills, California	46	1,200	Media
Filo, David ★	314	Mountain View, California	32	840	Yahoo! Inc.
Fireman, Paul Barry ■	410	Newton, Massachusetts			Reebok
Fisher family	371	New York, New York		1,300	Real estate
Fisher, Donald George	208	San Francisco, California	70	2,400	The Gap
Fisher, Doris Feigenbaum	208	San Francisco, California	67	2,300	The Gap
Fisher, John J.	208	San Francisco, California	37	1,000	Inheritance (The Gap)
Fisher, Max Martin	314	Franklin, Michigan	90	700	Oil, investments
Fisher, Robert J.	208	San Francisco, California	44	760	Inheritance (The Gap)
Fisher, William F.	208	San Francisco, California	41	810	Inheritance (The Gap)
Flatley, Thomas John	280	Milton, Massachusetts	66	975	Real estate
Flinn, Lawrence Jr.	288	Greenwich, Connecticut	62	900	United Video Satellite Group
Ford, Josephine F.	268	Grosse Pointe Farms, Michigan	75	760	Inheritance (Ford Motor Co.)
Ford, William Clay	268	Grosse Pointe Shores, Michigan	73	1,100	Inheritance (Ford Motor Co.)
Forstmann, Theodore ★	352	New York, New York	58	525	Leveraged buyouts
Fribourg, Michel	236	New York, New York	85	1,700	Grain trading
Frist, Thomas F. Jr.	325	Nashville, Tennessee	60	650	Columbia/HCA Healthcare

G					
Gallo, Ernest	358	Modesto, California	89	500	Wine
Galvin, Robert William	280	Barrington Hills, Illinois	76	975	Motorola, Inc.
Gates, Charles Cassius Jr.	264	Denver, Colorado	77	1,200	Gates Corp.
Gates, William H. III	166	Bellevue, Washington	42	58,400	Microsoft Corp.
Gaylord, Edward Lewis	272	Oklahoma City, Oklahoma	79	1,100	Media
Gebalie, Frances Koshland	228	San Francisco, California	77	820	Inheritance (Levi Strauss)
Geffen, David	204	Malibu, California	55	2,500	Music
George, Mari Hulman	360	Indianapolis, Indiana	63	500	Indianapolis 500, banking

★New entry.   ◇Returnee.   ■ Dropout.   †Near miss.

Figure 2-7:
A sampling of some of the world's wealthiest individuals and where their wealth comes from.

Reprinted by Permission of FORBES Magazine® Forbes Inc., 1998.

Chapter 3

Investing Prerequisites

*Y*ou want to know how to earn healthy returns on your investments without getting clobbered, right? Who doesn't? Although you generally must accept greater risk to have the potential for earning higher returns (see Chapter 2), in this chapter I tell you about some free lunches in the world of investing.

I know that you're eager to make some great, wealth-building investments. But if I told you to get your financial house in order first, you'd say "Forget it!" and likely close the book. The truth is that understanding and implementing some simple personal financial management concepts will pay off big for you in the decades ahead. You have a right to be skeptical about free lunches — but this chapter points out some easy-to-tap opportunities you likely have overlooked in managing your money.

Establish an Emergency Reserve

Warren owned his home as well as an investment property that he rented in the Pacific Northwest. He felt, and appeared to be, financially successful. But then Warren lost his job, a not-uncommon occurrence given corporate America's downsizing mood, accumulated sizable medical expenses, and had to sell his investment property to come up with cash to tide himself over.

Like Warren, you never know what life will bring, so it makes good financial sense to have a liquid reserve of cash to meet unexpected expenses. You likely don't have tens of thousands of dollars languishing in a low interest bank account. If you have a sister who works on Wall Street as an investment banker or a loaded and understanding parent, you can use them as your emergency reserve. (Ask them how they feel about that.)

If you don't have a financial safety net, you may be forced, as Warren was, into selling an investment that you've worked hard for. Selling some investments, such as real estate, costs big money (transaction costs, taxes, and so on). Warren wasn't able to purchase another investment property and missed out on 300 percent-plus appreciation over the subsequent two decades. Between the costs of selling and taxes, getting rid of the investment property cost Warren about 15 percent of its sales price. Ouch!

Should you invest emergency money in stocks?

As interest rates drifted lower during the 1990s, keeping emergency money in money market accounts became less and less rewarding. When interest rates were 8 or 10 percent, fewer people questioned the wisdom of an emergency reserve. However, in the late 1990s, with money market interest rates of 5 percent or less and stock market returns of 15 to 25 percent per year, more investors balked at keeping a low interest stash of cash.

Why not simply keep your emergency reserve in stocks? After all, you can easily sell stocks (especially those of larger companies) any day the financial markets are open. Why not treat yourself to the 20 percent annual returns that stock market investors enjoyed during the 1990s rather than earning a paltry 5 percent?

In general, I'm not enthusiastic about investors keeping their emergency money invested in stocks. Stock market investors shouldn't expect to earn such generous returns as they did during the early 1990s. As I discuss in Chapter 2, stocks historically have returned about 9 to 10 percent per year. In some years — in fact about one-third of the time — stocks decline in value, sometimes substantially.

Stocks can and have dropped 20, 30, or 50 percent or more over relatively short periods of time. Suppose such a drop coincides with an emergency — such as the loss of your job, major medical bills, and so on. Thus, your situation may force you to sell at a loss, perhaps a substantial one.

Keeping emergency money in stocks is also not a good idea because if your stocks appreciate and you need to sell some of them for emergency cash, you get stuck paying taxes on your gains.

I suggest that you invest your emergency money in stocks (ideally through well-diversified mutual funds), only if you have a relative or some other resource to tap for money in an emergency. Having a back-up resource for money minimizes your need to sell your stock holdings on short notice. As I discuss in Chapter 5, stocks are intended as a longer-term investment, not an investment that you expect (or need) to sell in the near future.

Make sure that you have quick access to about six months' worth of living expenses. Keep this emergency money in a high-yielding money market fund (see Chapter 9). You may also be able to borrow against your employer-based retirement account or against your home equity. Warren didn't have enough equity in his home to borrow. He didn't have other sources — a wealthy sister, for example — to borrow from either, so was stuck selling his investment property.

Evaluate Your Debts

Yes, paying down debts is boring, but it makes your investment decisions less difficult. Rather than spending so much of your time investigating specific investments, paying off your debts (if you have them) may be your best high-return, low-risk investment. Consider the interest rate you pay and your investing alternatives to determine which debts you should pay off.

Conquer consumer debt

Many folks have credit-card or other consumer debt, such as auto loans, that costs 8-, 10-, 12-, perhaps as much as 18-plus percent per year in interest. Paying off this debt with your savings is like putting your money in an investment with a guaranteed *tax-free* return equal to the rate that you pay on your debt.

For example, if you have outstanding credit-card debt at 15 percent interest, paying off that debt is the same as putting your money to work in an investment with a guaranteed 15 percent tax-free annual return. Because the interest on consumer debt is not tax deductible, you need to earn more than 15 percent investing your money elsewhere in order to net 15 percent *after* paying taxes. Earning such high investing returns is highly unlikely, and in order to even have a chance, you'll be forced to take great risk.

Consumer debt is hazardous to your long-term financial health because it encourages you to borrow against your future earnings. I often hear people say, "I can't afford to buy most new cars for cash — look at how expensive they are!" That's true, new cars are expensive, so set your sights lower and buy a good used car that you can afford. You can then invest the money that you'd otherwise spend on your auto loan.

Borrowing via credit cards, auto loans, and the like is also one of the most expensive ways to borrow. Banks and other lenders charge higher interest rates for consumer debt than for debt for investments, such as real estate and business. The reason: Consumer loans are the riskiest type of loan for a lender.

However, using consumer debt may make sense if you're financing a business. If you don't have home equity, personal loans (through a credit card or auto loan) may actually be your lowest-cost source of small-business financing (see Chapter 14 for more details). Again, for the loan to be worthwhile, you must expect to earn a higher return than the interest costs.

Mitigate your mortgage

Paying off your mortgage quicker may make sense for your financial situation, too. Making this financial move isn't as clear as paying off high-interest consumer debt because mortgage interest rates are generally lower and the interest is generally tax-deductible. When used properly, debt can help you accomplish your goals — such as buying a home or starting a business — and make you money in the long run. Borrowing to buy a home generally makes sense. Over the long term, homes generally appreciate in value.

If your financial situation has changed or improved since you first needed to borrow mortgage money, you need to reconsider how much mortgage debt you need or want. Even if your income hasn't escalated or you haven't inherited vast wealth, your frugality may allow you to pay down some of your debt sooner than the lender requires. Whether paying down your debt sooner makes sense for you depends on a number of factors, including your other investment options and goals.

Consider your investment opportunities

Financially, your mortgage interest rate versus your investments' rates of return (which I define in Chapter 2) is what matters when you decide whether to pay down your mortgage faster. Suppose you have a fixed-rate mortgage with an interest rate of 8 percent. If you decide to make investments instead of paying down your mortgage more quickly, your investments need to produce an average annual rate of return, before taxes, of 8 percent to come out ahead financially.

Besides the most common reason of lacking the funds to do so, other good reasons *not* to pay off your mortgage any quicker than necessary include the following:

> ✔ **You contribute instead to your retirement accounts, such as a 401(k), an IRA, or a Keogh.** Paying off your mortgage faster has no tax benefit. By contrast, putting additional money into a retirement plan can immediately reduce your federal and state income tax burdens. The more years you have until retirement, the greater the benefit you receive if you invest in your retirement accounts. Thanks to the compounding of your retirement account investments without the drain of taxes, you can actually earn a lower rate of return on your investments than you pay on your mortgage and still come out ahead. (I discuss the various retirement accounts in detail later in this chapter.)

✔ **You're willing to invest in more growth-oriented, volatile investments, such as stocks and real estate.** In order for you to have a reasonable chance of earning more on your investments than it costs you to borrow on your mortgage, you must be aggressive with your investments. As I discuss in Chapter 2, stocks and real estate have produced annual average rates of return of about 8 to 10 percent. You can earn even more with your own small business or investing in others' businesses. Some investors like to *leverage* (borrowing money to have more to invest) their investments. Paying down a mortgage ties up more of your capital, reducing your ability to make other attractive investments. To more aggressive investors, paying off the house seems downright boring — the financial equivalent of watching paint dry.

Remember that you have no guarantee of earning high returns from growth-type investments, which can easily drop 20 percent or more in value over a year or two.

✔ **Paying down the mortgage depletes your emergency reserves.** Psychologically, some people feel uncomfortable paying off debt more quickly if it diminishes their savings and investments. You probably don't want to pay down your debt if doing so depletes your financial safety cushion. Make sure that you have access — through a money market fund or other sources (a family member, for example) — to at least three months' living expenses.

Finally, don't be tripped up by the misconception that somehow you'll harm yourself more by a real estate market crash if you pay down your mortgage. Your home is worth what it's worth — its value has *nothing* to do with your debt load. Unless you're willing to walk away from your home and send the keys to the bank, (also known as *default*), you suffer the full effect of a price decline, regardless of your mortgage size, if real estate prices collapse.

Don't get hung up on mortgage tax deductions

Although it's true that mortgage interest is usually tax-deductible, don't forget (because if you do, you're sure to end up in trouble with the IRS) that you must also pay taxes on investment profits generated outside of retirement accounts. You can purchase tax-free investments like municipal bonds (see Chapter 8), but over the long haul, these investments won't earn a rate of return that's higher than the cost of your mortgage. Other types of lending investments, such as bank savings accounts, CDs, and other bonds, are unlikely to pay a high enough return either.

Don't assume that those mortgage interest deductions are that great. Just for being a living, breathing human being, you automatically qualify for the so-called "standard deduction" on your federal tax return. In 1999, this standard deduction was worth $4,300 for single filers and $7,200 for married people filing jointly. If you have no mortgage interest deductions — or less than you used to — you may not be missing out on as much of a write-off as you think. (Not to mention that joy of having one less schedule to complete on your tax return!)

If you earn a high income, you may not be able to fully deduct your mortgage interest on your tax returns. If your *adjusted gross income* (taxable income from all sources before subtracting itemized deductions and personal exemptions) exceeds $126,600 in 1999, you start to lose some of your mortgage interest deduction. You lose mortgage interest deductions by 3 percent times the amount that your adjusted gross income exceeds $126,600. In fact, you can lose up to 80 percent of your mortgage interest deduction. High-income couples are more likely to be affected by this provision because the $126,600 threshold is the same for couples as it is for single filers. This rule is another part of the so-called marriage tax penalty that you've perhaps heard about.

Establish Financial Goals

Although you may save money only because Mom and Dad told you it was the right thing to do, or because it makes you feel good, odds are that you save money with some purpose in mind. Common financial goals include saving for retirement, purchasing a home, starting your own business, and so on.

You may want to invest money for different purposes simultaneously. For example, when I was in my 20s, I put some money away toward retirement, but I also saved a stash so that I could hit the eject button from my job in management consulting. I knew that I wanted to pursue an entrepreneurial path and that in the early years of starting my own business, I couldn't count on as stable or as large an income as I had in consulting.

I invested my two "pots" of money — one for retirement, the other for my small business cushion — quite differently. As I discuss later in this chapter, you can afford to take more risk with the money that you don't plan on using in the near term. So, I invested the bulk of my retirement nest egg in stock mutual funds.

With the money I saved for the start-up of my small business, I took an entirely different track. I had zero desire to put this money in risky stocks — what if the market plummeted just as I was ready to leave the security of my full-time job? Thus, I kept this money safely invested in a money market fund that paid a healthy rate of interest but didn't fluctuate in value.

Are your savings on track?

In order to accomplish your financial and some personal goals, you need to save money. However, many people haven't a clue what their savings rate is. Your *savings rate* is the percentage of your past year's income that you saved and didn't spend. You may already know that your rate of savings is low, non-existent, or negative, and that you need to save more.

Part of being a smart investor involves figuring out how much you need to save to reach your goals. You're better able to make the most of your money after you figure out how much you *should* save and set some goals. Not knowing what you want to do a decade or more from now is perfectly normal — after all, your goals and needs evolve over the years. But that doesn't mean that you should just throw your hands in the air and not make an effort to see where you stand today and think about where you want to be in the future.

An important benefit of knowing your savings rate is that you'll know better how much risk you need to take to accomplish your goals. Seeing the amount that you need to save to achieve your dreams may encourage you to take more risk with your investments.

If you consistently save about 10 percent of your income during your working years, you're probably saving enough to meet your goals, unless you want to retire at a tender young age. On average, most people need about 75 percent of their pre-retirement income throughout retirement to maintain their standard of living.

If you're one of the many people who don't save enough, you need to do some homework. To save more, you need to reduce your spending, increase your income, or both.

For most people, reducing their spending is the more feasible option method to save more. But where do you begin? First, figure out where your money goes. You may have some general idea, but you need to have facts. Get out your checkbook register, credit card bills, and any other documentation that you have of your spending history and tally up how much you spend on dining out, operating your car(s), paying your taxes, and everything else. After you have this information, you can begin to prioritize and make the necessary tradeoffs to reduce your spending and increase your savings rate.

Earning more income may help boost your savings rate as well. Perhaps you can get a higher-paying job or increase the number of hours that you work. But if you already work a lot, reining in your spending is better for your emotional and economic well-being.

If you don't know how to evaluate and reduce your spending or haven't thought about your retirement goals, looked into what you can expect from Social Security, or calculated how much you should save for retirement, now's the time to do it. Pick up the latest edition of my first book, *Personal Finance For Dummies,* 2nd Edition, from IDG Books Worldwide, Inc., and find out all the necessary details for retirement planning and much more.

Determine your investment likes and dislikes

Many good investing options exist — you can invest in real estate, the stock market, mutual funds, in your own business or someone else's, or you can pay down mortgage debt more quickly. What makes sense for you depends on your goals, as well as your personal preferences. If you detest taking risks and volatile investments, paying down your mortgage, as recommended earlier in this chapter, may make better sense than investing in the stock market.

How do you deal with an investment that plunges 20 percent, 40 percent, or more in a few years or less? Some of the more aggressive investments that I discuss in this book can fall in a hurry (see Chapter 2 for examples). You shouldn't go into the stock market, real estate, or a small-business investment arena if such a drop is likely to cause you to sell low or make you a miserable wreck. If you haven't tried riskier investments yet, you may want to experiment a bit to see how you feel with your money invested in them.

A simple way to "mask" the risk of volatile investments is to _diversify_ your portfolio — that is, to put your money into different investments (see Chapter 2). Not watching prices too closely helps, too — that's one of the reasons real estate investors are less likely to bail out when the market declines. Stock market investors, unfortunately from my perspective, can get daily, even minute-by-minute price updates. Add that fact to the quick phone call or click of your computer mouse that it takes to dump a stock in a flash, and you have all the ingredients for short-sighted investing.

Fund Your Retirement Accounts

Saving money is difficult for most people. Don't make a tough job impossible by forsaking the terrific tax benefits that come from investing through most retirement accounts. Contributions to these plans are generally federally and state tax-deductible. And once you invest the money in these plans, the growth on your contributions is tax-sheltered as well.

Gaining those tax benefits

Retirement accounts should be called tax-reduction accounts — if they were, people may be more jazzed about contributing to them. Here's why: Suppose that you pay about 35 percent between federal and state income taxes on your last dollars of income (see the discussion later in this chapter to determine your tax bracket). With most of the retirement accounts that I describe in this chapter, you save yourself about $350 in taxes for every $1,000 that you contribute in the year that you make your contribution.

After your money is in a retirement account, any interest, dividends, and appreciation grow inside the account without taxation. With most retirement accounts, you defer taxes on all the accumulating gains and profits until you withdraw your money down the road, which you can do without penalty after age 59½. In the meantime, more of your money works for you over a long period of time.

The common mistake that investors make is neglecting to take advantage of these accounts because of their enthusiasm to either spend or invest in "non-retirement" accounts. Not investing in these tax-sheltered retirement accounts can cost you hundreds, perhaps thousands, of dollars per year in lost tax savings. Add that loss up over the many years that you work and save, and not taking advantage of these tax reduction accounts can easily cost you tens of thousands to hundreds of thousands of dollars in the long term. Ouch!

One of the "drawbacks" of investing heavily in real estate or small business is that you generally invest in real estate or small business outside your retirement accounts. Many people have made good money focusing on real estate and small-business investments — just ask Bill Gates or Ross Perot if they have any regrets about focusing on their own businesses. Lesser mortals need to be careful that they don't put too many of their investing eggs in non-retirement account baskets. Of the money that you don't earmark for real estate or a small-business investment, invest all that you can inside retirement accounts. In fact, taking advantage of saving and investing in tax-deductible retirement accounts should probably be your number one personal financial priority (unless you're still paying off high-interest consumer debt on credit cards or auto loans).

Delaying increases your pain

In order to take advantage of retirement savings plans and the tax savings that accompany them, you must first spend less than you earn. Only after you spend less than you earn can you afford to contribute to these retirement savings plans (unless you already happen to have a stash of cash from previous savings or inheritance).

The mistake that people of all income levels make is that they don't take advantage of retirement accounts at a younger age. The sooner you start to save, the less painful it is each year to save enough to reach your goals because your contributions have more years to compound.

Each decade you delay saving approximately doubles the percentage of your earnings that you need to save to meet your goals. For example, if saving 5 percent per year in your early 20s gets you to your retirement goal, waiting until your 30s may means socking away 10 percent; waiting until your 40s, 20 percent; and beyond that, the numbers get truly daunting.

If you enjoy spending money and living for today, you should be more motivated to start saving sooner. The longer that you wait to save, the more you ultimately need to save and therefore, the less you can spend today!

Retirement account options

If you earn employment income (or receive alimony), you have option(s) for putting money away in a retirement account that compounds without taxation until you withdraw the money. In most cases, your contributions to retirement accounts are tax-deductible.

Company-based plans

If you work for a for-profit company, you may have access to a *401(k)* plan that typically allows you to save up to $10,000 per year (for tax year 1999). Many non-profit organizations offer *403(b)* plans to their employees. As with a 401(k), your contributions to 403(b) plans are federal and state tax-deductible in the year that you make them. Non-profit employees can generally contribute up to 20 percent or $10,000 of their salaries, whichever is less. In addition to the up-front and ongoing tax benefits of such plans, some employers match your contributions.

If you're self-employed, you can establish your own retirement savings plans. *Simplified employee pension individual retirement account (SEP-IRA)* plans allow you to sock away about 13 percent (13.04 percent, to be exact) of your self-employment income (business revenue minus expenses), up to an annual maximum of $24,000 (for tax year 1999). Each year, *you* decide the amount you want to contribute — no minimums exist.

Keogh plans are another retirement savings option for the self-employed. Keogh plans require a bit more paperwork to set up and administer than SEP-IRAs. The appeal of certain types of Keoghs is that they allow you to put away a greater percentage (20 percent) of your *self-employment income* (revenue less your expenses), up to a maximum of $30,000 per year.

Unlike SEP-IRAs, Keogh plans allow *vesting schedules* that require employees to remain with the company a number of years before they earn the right to their retirement account balances. (If you're an employee in a small business, you *cannot* establish your own SEP-IRA or Keogh — that's up to your employer.)

If an employee leaves prior to being fully vested, his unvested balance reverts to the remaining Keogh plan participants. Keogh plans also allow for Social Security integration, which effectively allows those in the company who earn high incomes (usually the owners) to receive larger-percentage contributions for their accounts than the less-highly compensated employees. The logic behind this idea is that Social Security taxes and benefits top out after you earn $72,600 (for tax year 1999). Social Security integration allows higher-income earners to make up for this ceiling.

Please be advised that with all types of self-employed retirement plans, you need to cover your employees as well. As the owner of a small business, don't deter yourself from keeping such a plan because employees may receive contributions, too. If you take the time to educate employees about the value and importance of these plans in saving for the future and reducing taxes, they'll see it rightfully as part of their total compensation package. In addition to the vesting schedules and Social Security integration discussed earlier in this section, many plans allow you to exclude employees from receiving contributions until they complete a year or two of service.

IRAs

If you work for a company that doesn't offer a retirement savings plan or if you've exhausted contributing to your company's plan, consider funding an *individual retirement account (IRA)*. Anyone with employment (or alimony) income may contribute up to $2,000 each year to an IRA, or the amount of your employment or alimony income if it's less than $2,000 in a year. If you are a non-working spouse, you're eligible to put up to $2,000 per year into a spousal IRA.

Your contributions to an IRA may or may not be tax-deductible. For tax year 1999, if you're single and your adjusted gross income is $31,000 or less for the year, you can deduct your full IRA contribution. If you're married and you file your taxes jointly, you're entitled to a full IRA deduction if your AGI (adjusted gross income) is $51,000 per year or less. In 2000, these income limits bump up to $32,000 and $52,000 respectively. Whatever your income, you are entitled to an IRA deduction if neither you nor your spouse is covered by a company retirement plan.

If you can't deduct your contribution to a standard IRA account, consider making a contribution to a new type of non-deductible IRA account called the *Roth IRA* (or *IRA Plus*). Single taxpayers with an AGI less than $95,000 and joint filers with an AGI less than $150,000 can contribute up to $2,000 per year to a Roth IRA. Although the contribution is not deductible, earnings inside the account are shielded from tax, and unlike a standard IRA, qualified withdrawals from the account are free from income tax.

Consider a non-deductible IRA only *after* you've exhausted the possibilities of contributing to retirement accounts that do provide an immediate tax deduction, such as 401(k)s, SEP-IRAs, Keoghs, and so on.

Annuities

If you've exhausted contributing to IRA accounts and still want to put away more money into retirement accounts, consider *annuities*. Annuities are contracts that insurance companies back. If you, the *annuity holder* (investor), should die during the so-called *accumulation phase* (that is, prior to receiving payments from the annuity), your designated beneficiary is guaranteed reimbursement of the amount of your original investment.

Annuities, like IRAs, allow your capital to grow and compound tax-deferred. You defer taxes until you withdraw the money. However, unlike an IRA that has a $2,000 annual contribution limit, you can deposit as much as you want in any year into an annuity — even a million dollars if you've got it! However, as with a Roth IRA, you get no up-front tax deduction for your contributions.

Because annuity contributions aren't tax-deductible, and because annuities carry higher annual operating fees to pay for the small insurance that comes with them, don't consider contributing to one until you've fully exhausted your other retirement account investing options. Annuities generally make sense if you have 15 or more years to wait until you need the money because of their higher annual expenses.

Retirement account investing choices

When you establish a retirement account, you may not realize that the retirement account is simply a shell or shield that keeps the federal, state, and local governments from taxing your investment earnings each year. You still must choose what investments you want to hold inside your retirement account shell.

You may invest your IRA or other self-employed plan retirement account (SEP-IRAs, Keoghs) money into stocks, bonds, mutual funds, and even bank accounts. Mutual funds are an ideal choice, because they offer diversification and professional management (see Chapter 9).

Tame Your Taxes

Funding retirement accounts can help keep your income taxes lower. Maximizing the amount of investing that you do inside your retirement accounts is generally a wise strategy. By maximizing the amount of money that you invest in your retirement accounts, you reduce the amount of your income that's currently taxable and shelter your investments' profits from taxation over time.

Some of the investing that you need to do, however, happens outside retirement accounts. When you invest outside of tax-sheltered retirement accounts, the profits and distributions on your money are subject to taxation. So the type of non-retirement account investments that makes sense for you depends (at least partly) on your tax situation.

If you have money to invest, or if you're considering selling current investments that you hold, include taxes as an important factor in your decision. But tax considerations alone shouldn't dictate how and where you invest your money. You should also weigh investment options, your desire and the necessity to take risk, personal likes and dislikes, and the number of years you plan to hold the investment.

 Consider how taxes affect investing in stocks and bonds. If you're in a high tax bracket, you should give preference to investments such as tax-free bonds and stocks with low dividends. Real estate and small business investments that you expect to appreciate are also tax-wise choices. If you're in a lower tax bracket, avoid tax-free bonds because you'll end up with less of a return than in higher-yielding taxable bonds.

Determining your tax bracket

You may not know it but the government charges you different tax rates for different parts of your annual income. You pay less tax on the *first* dollars of your earnings and more tax on the *last* dollars of your earnings. For example, if you're single and your taxable income totaled $40,000 during 1999, you paid federal tax at the rate of 15 percent on the first $25,750 of taxable income and 28 percent on income above $25,750 up to $40,000.

Your *marginal tax rate* is the rate of tax that you pay on your *last* or so-called *highest* dollars of income. In the example of a single person with taxable income of $40,000, that person's federal marginal tax rate is 28 percent. In other words, he or she effectively pays a 28 percent federal tax on his or her last dollars of income — those dollars earned between $25,750 and $40,000. (Don't forget to factor in state income taxes that most states assess.)

Knowing your marginal tax rate allows you to quickly calculate any additional taxes that you would pay on additional income, or the amount of taxes that you save if you contribute more money into retirement accounts or reduce your taxable income (for example, if you choose investments that produce tax-free income).

Table 3-1 shows the 1999 federal tax rates for singles and for married households that file jointly.

Table 3-1	1999 Federal Income Tax Rates	
Singles Taxable Income	*Married Filing Jointly Taxable Income*	*Federal Tax Rate*
Less than $25,750	Less than $43,050	15%
$25,750 to $62,450	$43,050 to $104,050	28%
$62,450 to $130,250	$104,050 to $158,550	31%
$130,250 to $283,150	$158,550 to $283,150	36%
More than $283,150	More than $283,150	39.6%

Knowing what's taxed and when to worry

Interest that is paid on bank accounts, bonds, and dividends paid by stocks are all generally taxable. The exception is the interest that some types of bonds pay. U.S. Treasury bonds, for example, pay interest that is state tax-free. Municipal bonds, which state and local governments issue, pay interest that is federally tax-free and also state tax-free to residents in the state the bond is issued. (I discuss bonds in Chapter 8.)

If this sounds complicated, you may want to go ahead and pop an aspirin before I cover taxation on your *capital gains,* which is the *profit* (sales minus purchase price) on an investment. Investments held less than one year generate *short-term capital gains,* which are taxed at your normal marginal rate.

Profits from investments that you hold longer than 12 months are *long-term capital gains* that cap at 20 percent for those in a tax bracket of 28 percent or higher, and 10 percent for those in the 15 percent tax bracket.

For investments purchased after December 31, 2000, and then held longer than five years, the long-term capital gains rate drops to 18 percent for those in the 28 percent tax bracket or higher and 8 percent for those in the 15 percent bracket.

Avoid these supposed "tax savings" investments

Brokers and financial planners who work on commission try to sell you numerous investments that they claim offer big tax advantages. A limited partnership (LP) is a good example of a bad investment that these salespeople push. Limited partnerships invest in real estate and a variety of businesses, such as cable television, health care, and technology-related companies. Although some of the companies that LPs invest in are sound, the only sure thing about investing in LPs is that you won't earn the best possible returns for your money because of high sales commissions and ongoing management fees.

Commissions, which are immediately deducted from your investment, can run 10 percent or more. Annual management fees can also be steep, running up to 3 percent per year. The best *no-load* (commission-free) mutual funds, by comparison, charge 0.2 percent to 1 percent per year for similar investments.

LPs also have poor liquidity — you must typically wait 7 to 10 years until the partnership investments are sold to access your investment dollars. If you need to sell before then, you may be able to sell through the informal secondary market, but you'll receive pennies on the dollar.

Another investment that many salespeople love to pitch is cash value life insurance. Life insurance that combines life insurance protection with an account that has a cash value is usually known as *universal, whole,* or *variable life.*

Life insurance with a cash value is, at best, a mediocre way to invest money and at worst, a terrible mistake, especially if you haven't exhausted contributing money to retirement accounts. Retirement savings plans, such as 401(k)s, 403(b)s, SEP-IRAs, and Keoghs, give you an immediate tax deduction for your current contributions in addition to growth without taxation until withdrawal.

The only real advantage that cash value life insurance offers is that, if it's properly held in a trust for people who expect to have substantial estates at their death, the proceeds paid to your beneficiaries can be free of estate taxes. Cash value life insurance is one of many ways, and generally far from the best way, to reduce your estate tax problems. Pick up a copy of the latest edition of *Taxes For Dummies* (IDG Books Worldwide) to find out more about minimizing estate taxes.

Use these strategies to reduce the taxes on investments exposed to taxation:

✔ **Use tax-free money markets and bonds.** If you're in a high enough tax bracket (federal 28 percent to 31 percent, or higher), you may find that you come out ahead with tax-free investments. Tax-free investments yield less than comparable investments that produce taxable earnings, but because of the tax differences, the earnings from tax-free investments *can* end up being greater than what taxable investments leave you with. In order to do the comparison properly, subtract what you will pay in federal as well as state taxes from the taxable investment to see which investment nets you more.

✔ **Invest in tax-friendly stocks.** Companies that pay little in the way of dividends reinvest more of their profits back into the company. If you invest outside of a retirement account, unless you need income to live on, minimize your exposure to stocks with dividends. Be aware that low-dividend stocks tend to be more volatile.

Investing in index funds is a great way to include tax-friendly stocks in your portfolio. *Index funds* are mutual funds that invest in a relatively fixed portfolio of securities, such as stocks and bonds. They don't attempt to beat the market. Rather, they invest in the securities to mirror or match the performance of an underlying index, such as the Standard & Poor's 500 (see Chapter 5). Although index funds cannot beat the market, they have several advantages over actively managed funds. Because index funds trade less, they tend to produce lower capital gains distributions. For mutual funds held outside tax-sheltered retirement accounts, this reduced trading effectively increases an investor's total rate of return. See Chapter 9 to find out more about mutual funds and indexing.

✔ **Invest in small business and real estate.** The growth in value of a business and real estate asset isn't taxed until you sell the asset. Even then, with real estate you often can roll over the gain into another property as long as you comply with tax laws. However, the current income that a small business and real estate produces is taxed as ordinary income.

Short-term capital gains (investments held one year or less) are taxed at your ordinary income tax rate. This fact is another reason that you shouldn't be trading or flipping your investments quickly (within 12 months).

Protect Your Assets

If you're the thrifty, hard-working sort, you may actually be at risk of making a catastrophic investing mistake: not properly protecting your assets. That's the mistake that Manny, a successful entrepreneur, made. Starting from scratch, he built up a successful million-dollar manufacturing operation. He invested a lot of his own personal money and sweat into building the business over 15 years.

One day, catastrophe struck: An explosion ripped through the building, and the ensuing fire destroyed virtually all the firm's equipment and inventory, none of which was insured. The explosion also seriously injured several workers, including Manny, who didn't carry disability insurance. Ultimately, Manny had to file bankruptcy.

The decision as to what amount of insurance you need to carry is somewhat a matter of your desire and ability to accept financial risk. Some risks aren't worth taking. Don't overestimate your ability to predict in advance what accidents and other bad luck may befall you. Here's what you need to protect yourself and your assets:

- ✔ **Major medical health insurance.** I'm not talking about one of those policies that pays $100 a day if you need to go into the hospital, or cancer insurance, or that $5,000 medical expense rider on your auto insurance policy. I know it's unpleasant to consider, but you need a policy that pays for all types of major illnesses and major expenditures. A $5,000 rider may pay for the first day or two in the hospital and is hardly catastrophic coverage. Don't waste your money on these narrow, small-dollar coverage policies.

- ✔ **Adequate liability insurance on your home and car to guard your assets against lawsuits.** You should have at least enough liability insurance to protect your *net worth* (assets minus your liabilities/debts), or ideally, twice your net worth. If you run your own business, get insurance for your business assets if they are substantial, such as in Manny's case. Also consider professional liability insurance to protect against a lawsuit. You may also want to consider incorporating your business (see Chapter 15).

- ✔ **Long-term disability insurance.** What would you (and your family) do to replace your income if a major disability prevents you from working? Even if you don't have dependents, odds are that *you* are dependent on you. Most larger employers offer group plans that have good benefits and are much less expensive than coverage you'd buy on your own. Also, check with your professional association for a competitive group plan.

- ✔ **Life insurance if others are dependent on your income.** If you're single or your loved ones can live without your income, skip life insurance. If you need coverage, buy term insurance that, like your auto and home insurance, is pure insurance protection. The amount of term insurance you need to buy largely depends on how much of your income you want to replace.

- ✔ **Estate planning.** At a minimum, most people need a simple will to delineate to whom they would like to leave all their worldly possessions. If you hold significant assets outside retirement accounts, you may also benefit from establishing a living trust, which keeps your money from filtering through the hands and open wallets of probate lawyers. Living wills and medical powers of attorney are useful to have in case you're in a medically difficult state. If you have substantial assets, doing more involved estate planning is wise to minimize estate taxes and ensure the orderly passing of your assets to your heirs.

In my experience as a financial counselor, I've seen that whereas many people lack particular types of insurance, others possess unnecessary policies. Many people also keep very low deductibles. Remember to insure against potential losses that would be financially catastrophic for you — don't waste your money to protect against smaller losses. (See my book, *Personal Finance For Dummies,* 2nd Edition, to discover the right and wrong ways to buy insurance, what to look for in policies, and where to get good policies.)

Tread Carefully when Investing for College

Many well-intentioned parents want to save for the children's future educational expenses. The mistake that they often make, however, is putting money in accounts in their child's name (in so-called *custodial accounts*) or saving outside retirement accounts in general.

The more money you accumulate outside tax-sheltered retirement accounts, the less assistance you're likely to qualify for from federal and state financial aid sources. Don't make the additional error of assuming that financial aid is only for the poor. Many middle-income and even some modestly affluent families qualify for some aid, which can include grants and loans available, even if you're not deemed financially needy.

You receive no tax deduction on your contributions to non-retirement accounts, whereas your retirement account contributions not only are tax-deductible in the year that you make them but also compound tax-deferred.

Don't forgo contributing to your own retirement savings plan(s) in order to save money in a non-retirement account for your children's college expenses. When you do, you pay higher taxes both on your current income and on the interest and growth of this money. In addition to paying higher taxes, you are expected to contribute more to your child's educational expenses.

Under the current financial needs analysis that most colleges use in awarding financial aid, the value of your retirement plan is *not* considered an asset. Money that you save *outside* retirement accounts, including money in the child's name, is counted as an asset and reduces eligibility for financial aid.

If you're affluent enough that you expect to pay for your cherub's full educational costs, you can save a bit on taxes if you invest through custodial accounts. Prior to your child reaching age 14, the first $1,300 of interest and dividend income is taxed at your child's income tax rate rather than yours. After age 14, *all* income that the investments in your child's name generate is taxed at your child's rate.

If you plan to apply for financial aid, it's a good idea to save non-retirement account money in your name rather than in your children's names (custodial accounts). Colleges expect a greater percentage of money in your child's name (35 percent) to be used for college costs than money in your name (6 percent).

Hold off on putting any money into an Education IRA, a relatively new savings vehicle. In theory, Education IRAs sound like a great place to park some college savings: You can make non-deductible contributions of up to $500 per child per year, and investment earnings and account withdrawals are free of tax as long as you use the funds to pay for college costs. However, it's not yet clear how college financial aid officers will treat these accounts. College financial aid offices will probably treat the money either as a child's asset, which reduces financial aid by 35 percent for each dollar in the child's name, or as a prepaid tuition plan, which reduces aid dollar for dollar. In other words, funding an Education IRA can undermine your child's ability to qualify for financial aid. As with funding custodial accounts for your children, you should only consider funding an Education IRA if you expect to be able to pay for the full cost of your children's college education yourself and you expect them not to qualify for any type of financial aid.

Also, be aware that your family's assets, for purposes of financial aid determination, also generally include equity in real estate and businesses that you own. Although the federal financial aid analysis no longer counts equity in your primary residence as an asset, many private (independent) schools continue to ask parents for this information when they make their own financial aid determinations. Thus, paying down your home mortgage more quickly instead of funding retirement accounts can harm you financially. You may end up with less financial aid and pay more in taxes.

If you keep up to 80 percent of your investment money in stocks (diversified worldwide) with the remainder in bonds when your child is young, you can maximize the money's growth potential without taking extraordinary risk. As your child makes his or her way through the later years of elementary school, you need to begin to make the mix more conservative — scale back the stock percentage to 50 or 60 percent. Finally, in the years just before entering college, you need to whittle the stock portion down to no more than 20 percent or so.

Diversified mutual funds, which invest in stocks in the U.S. and internationally, and bonds are an ideal vehicle to use when you invest for college. Be sure to choose funds that fit your tax situation if you invest your funds in non-retirement accounts. See Chapter 9.

How to pay for college

If you keep stashing away money in retirement accounts, it's reasonable for you to wonder how you'll actually pay for education expenses when the momentous occasion arises. In most cases, even if you have some liquid assets that can be directed to your child's college bill, you will, in all likelihood, need to borrow some money. Only the affluent can truly afford to pay for college with cash.

One good source of money is your home's equity. You can borrow against your home at a relatively low interest rate, and the interest is generally tax-deductible. Some company retirement plans, (401 (k)s, for example) allow borrowing as well.

A plethora of financial aid programs allow you to borrow at reasonable interest rates. The Unsubsidized Stafford Loans and Parent Loans for Undergraduate Students (PLUS), for example, are available, even when your family isn't deemed financially needy.

In addition to loans, a number of grant programs are available through schools and the government, as well as through independent sources.

Complete the Free Application for Federal Student Aid (FAFSA) to apply for the federal government programs. Grants available through state government programs may require a separate application. Specific colleges and other private organizations, including employers, banks, credit unions, and community groups, also offer grants and scholarships.

Many scholarships and grants don't require any work on your part — simply apply for such financial aid through your college. However, you may need to seek out other programs — check directories and databases at your local library, your kid's school counseling department, and college financial aid offices. Also try local organizations, churches, employers, and so on because you have a better chance of getting scholarship money through these avenues than countrywide scholarship and grant databases.

Your child can work and save money during high school and college for school. In fact, if your child qualifies for financial aid, he or she is generally expected to contribute a certain amount to education costs from employment during the school year, summer breaks, and from savings. Besides giving your gangly teen a stake in his or her own future, this training encourages sound personal financial management down the road.

Choose the Right Investment Mix

A final and important consideration before I set you loose in the wild and woolly world of investing is how to mix up a great recipe of investments. Common sense suggests that you don't want to put all your eggs into one basket.

Diversifying your investments helps buffer your portfolio from being sunk by one or two poor performers: While some investments periodically visit the doghouse, others rise to the occasion.

Consider your age

The younger you are and the more years you have until you plan to use your money, the greater the amount of your longer-term investment money should be in growth (ownership) vehicles, such as stocks, real estate, and small business. As I discuss in Chapter 2, the attraction of these types of investments is the potential to really grow your money. The risk: The value of your portfolio can plunge from time to time.

The younger you are, the more time your investments have to recover from a bad fall. In this respect, investments are a bit like people. If a 30-year-old and an 80-year-old fall on a concrete sidewalk, odds are higher that the younger person will fully recover. Such falls sometimes disable older people.

An old rule of thumb says to subtract your age from 100 and invest the resulting number as a percentage of money to place in growth (ownership) investments. So if you're 35 years old

   100 − 35 = 65% of your investment money can be in growth investments.

If you want to be more aggressive, subtract your age from 120:

   120 − 35 = 85% of your investment money can be in growth investments.

Note that even for someone retired, they should still have a healthy chunk of their investment dollars in growth vehicles like stocks. A 70-year old person may want to totally avoid risk, but doing so is generally a mistake. Such a person can live another two or three decades. Living longer than anticipated can lead to running out of money if their money doesn't continue to grow.

 These tips are only rules of thumb and apply to money that you invest for the long term (ideally for 10 years or more). For money that you need to use in the shorter term, such as within the next several years, more-aggressive growth investments aren't appropriate. See Chapters 8 and 9 for more ideas.

Make the most of your investment options

No hard-and-fast rules exist that show you how to allocate the percentage that you've earmarked for growth investments among specific investments, like stocks and real estate. Part of how you decide to allocate your investments depends, for example, on the types of investments that you want to focus on. As I discuss in Chapter 5, diversifying in stocks worldwide can be prudent as well as profitable.

Here are some general guidelines to keep in mind:

✔ **Take advantage of your retirement accounts.** Unless you need accessible money for shorter-term non-retirement goals, why pass up the free extra returns from the tax benefits of retirement accounts?

✔ **Don't pile into investments that gain lots of attention.** Many investors make this mistake, especially those who lack a thought-out plan to buy stocks. In Chapter 5, I provide numerous illustrations of the perils of buying stocks garnering much attention.

✔ **Have the courage to be a contrarion.** No one likes to feel that they are jumping on board a sinking ship or a losing cause. However, just like shopping for something at retail stores, the best time to buy something is when it's on sale.

✔ **Diversify, diversify, diversify.** As I discuss in Chapter 2, different investments' value don't move in tandem. So, when you invest in growth investments such as stocks or real estate, your portfolio's value will have a smoother ride if you diversify properly.

✔ **Invest more in what you know.** Over the years, I've met successful investors who have built substantial wealth without spending gobs of free time. Some investors, for example, concentrate more on real estate because that's what they best understand and feel comfortable with. Others put more money in stocks for the same reason. No one-size-fits-all dress code exists for successful investors. Just be careful that you don't put all of your investing eggs in the same basket.

✔ **Don't invest in too many different things.** Diversification is good to a point. If you purchase so many investments that you can't perform a basic annual review of them (for example, with a mutual fund, reading the annual report), then you may have too many different investments.

✔ **Be more aggressive inside retirement accounts.** When you hit your retirement years, you'll probably begin to live off your non-retirement account investments first. Why? For the simple reason that allowing your retirement accounts to continue growing will save you tax dollars. Therefore, you should be relatively less aggressive with investments outside of retirement accounts since that money will be invested for a shorter time period.

Ease into risky investments with dollar cost averaging

With the continuing ascent of the U.S. stock market, increasing numbers of investors seek high potential returns but also fear high stock prices. In fact, high stock prices tempt many of us to wait to invest in stocks until prices dip.

However, holding money back for just the right moment isn't investing, but rather market timing, which even investment legends such as Warren Buffett and Peter Lynch say they can't do.

Enter *dollar cost averaging* (DCA), which is the practice of investing a regular amount of money at set time intervals, such as monthly or quarterly, into volatile investments, such as stocks and stock mutual funds. If you've ever deducted money from a paycheck and pumped it into a retirement savings plan investment account that holds stocks and bonds, you've done DCA.

Most of us invest a portion of our employment compensation as we earn it, but if you have extra cash sitting around you can choose to either invest that money in one fell swoop or invest it gradually via DCA. The biggest appeal of gradually feeding money into the market via DCA is that you don't dump all your money into a potentially overheated investment just before a major drop. Thus, DCA helps shy investors to psychologically ease into riskier investments.

DCA is made to order for skittish investors with a large lump of money sitting in safe investments like CDs or a savings account. For example, using DCA, an investor with $100,000 to invest in stock funds can feed her money into investments gradually — say at the rate of $12,500 or so quarterly over two years — rather than investing her entire $100,000 in stocks at once to avoid buying all her shares at a market peak.Most larger investment companies, especially mutual funds, allow investors to establish automatic investment plans so that the DCA occurs without an investor's ongoing involvement.

Of course, like any risk-reducing investment strategy, DCA has drawbacks. If growth investments appreciate (as they're supposed to), a DCA investor misses out on earning higher returns on his money awaiting investment. Richard E. Williams and Peter W. Bacon, finance professors at Wright State University, found that approximately 64 percent of the time, a lump sum stock market investor earned higher first year returns than an investor who fed the money in monthly over the first year (they studied data from the U.S. market over the past seven decades).

Knowing that you'll probably be ahead two-thirds of the time if you dump a lump sum into the stock market will be little solace if you happen to invest just before a major plunge in the stock market. In the fall of 1987, the U.S. stock market, as measured by the Dow Jones Industrial Average, plummeted 36 percent, and in 1973-74, the market shed 45 percent of its value.

So investors who fear that the U.S. market is due for such a major correction should DCA, right? Well, not so fast. Apprehensive investors who shun lump sum investments and use DCA are more likely to stop the DCA investment process if prices plunge, thereby defeating the benefit of doing DCA during a declining market.

So what's an investor with a lump sum of money to do? First, weigh the significance of the lump sum to you. Although $100,000 is a big chunk of most people's net worth, it's only 10 percent if your net worth is $1,000,000 and not worth a millionaire's time to DCA. If the cash that you have to invest is less than a quarter of your net worth, you may not want to bother with DCA.

Second, consider how aggressively you invest (or invested) your money. For example, if you aggressively invested your money through an employer's retirement plan that you roll over, don't waste your time on DCA.

DCA makes sense for investors with a large chunk of their net worth in cash who wish to minimize the risk of transferring that cash to riskier investments such as stocks. If you fashion yourself a market prognosticator, you can also assess the current valuation of stocks. Thinking that stocks are pricey increases the appeal of DCA.

Over how long a time period should you DCA? DCA too quickly and you may not give the market sufficient time for a correction to unfold during and after which some of the DCA purchases may take place. DCA over too long a period of time and you may miss a major upswing in stock prices. DCA over one to two years to strike a balance.

As for the times of the year that you DCA, mutual fund investors should DCA quarterly early in each calendar quarter because mutual funds that make taxable distributions tend to do so late in the quarter.

Your money that awaits investment should have a suitable parking place. Select a high-yielding money market fund that's appropriate for your tax situation. With rates on money funds just shy of those on more volatile bond funds, sitting on cash these days isn't so bad.

One last critical point: When you DCA, establish an automatic investment plan so that you are less likely to chicken out. And for the more courageous, you may want to try an alternative strategy to DCA — *value averaging* — which gets you to invest more if prices are falling and invest less if prices are rising.

Suppose that you want to value average $500 per quarter into an aggressive stock mutual fund. After your first quarterly $500 investment, the fund drops 10 percent, reducing your account balance to $450. Value averaging has you invest $500 the next quarter plus another $50 to make up the shortfall. (Conversely, if the fund value had increased to $550 after your first investment, you would only invest $450 in the second round). Increasing the amount that you invest requires confidence when prices fall, but doing so will magnify your returns when prices turn around.

Part II

Stocks, Bonds, and Wall Street

The 5th Wave   By Rich Tennant

"The first thing we should do is get you two into a good mutual fund. Let me get out the 'Magic 8-Ball' and we'll run some options."

In this part . . .

Stocks, bonds, and mutual funds are the core financial market instruments that investors play with these days. But what the heck *are* these devices, and how can you invest in them, make some decent money, and not lose your shirt? Here, you find out how and where to evaluate and buy these securities and how to comprehend the mind-numbing jargon the money pros use.

Chapter 4

How Financial Markets Function

*O*ne hot summer day when my wife and I were visiting New York, I dragged her to see the New York Stock Exchange in lower Manhattan. You can't actually go out onto the exchange floor, but you can view it from a visitor's observation deck. As with many popular things in the Big Apple, to get to the observation area you must wait in a long, single-file line. After enduring this ritual, you're then stuffed into a cramped elevator and transported to the viewing area. A maze of exhibits greets the elevator passengers, who, like hamsters, must first wander around the exhibits before finally reaching the narrow corridor that overlooks the floor. The corridor is glass enclosed to ensure that you don't toss a paper airplane or your gum onto this shrine of capitalism. There's enough space for people to stand half a dozen deep. If you're lucky, you may get to the front of the pack for a short time and actually see something — like a floor trader picking his nose!

After all this waiting and navigating, my wife says, "This is boring. . . ." As so often occurs in our marriage, she was right — you don't see a whole lot at this exchange or other stock exchanges, even on a day when the market plunges. The real action is at the companies that issue stocks and other securities, such as bonds. Our journey begins with these companies.

Public Companies

Imagine that you run your own business — many people do or want to. Suppose that you make something, anything at your business. A friend of mine, Liz, initially made necklaces and pins out of her home as a hobby. Her friends complimented her on the jewelry, so she began making some for them. Eventually, she started selling them to some local retail stores.

Suppose a large retail department store chain like Macy's contacts you to sell them thousands of necklaces and pins and you had to contract for big-time manufacturing help. Newspapers and magazines begin featuring your work, and lots of retailers line up for your creations.

The money begins rolling in and you're now in the big time. At some point, you may want to raise more money (known as *capital* in the financial world) to expand and afford your growing company's needs, such as hiring more employees, buying computer systems, and purchasing manufacturing equipment.

Why companies issue stocks versus bonds

Companies can choose between two major money-raising options when they go into the financial markets: issuing stocks or issuing bonds. A world of difference exists between these two major securities, both from the perspective of the investor as well as from the issuing company as the following explanations illustrate:

- ✔ **Bonds are loans that a company must pay back.** Rather than borrowing money from a bank, many companies elect to sell *bonds,* which are IOUs to investors. The primary disadvantage, from a company's perspective, is that the company must pay this money back with interest. On the other hand, the business doesn't have to relinquish ownership when it borrows money. Companies are also more likely to issue bonds if the stock market is depressed. A low stock market means that companies can't fetch as much for their stock.

- ✔ **Stocks are shares of ownership in a company.** Some companies choose to issue stock to raise money. Unlike bonds, the money that the company raises through a stock issue isn't paid back because it's not a loan. When the public (people like you and me) buys stock, outside investors continue to hold and trade it. (Although companies may occasionally choose to buy their own stock back, usually because they think it's a good investment, they are under no obligation to do so. If a company does a stock buyback, the price that the company pays is simply the price that the stock currently trades for.)

  Even though a company relinquishes some of its ownership when it issues stock, doing so allows its founders and owners to sell some of their relatively illiquid private stock and reap the rewards of their successful company. Many growing companies also favor stock issues because they don't want the cash drain that comes from paying loans (bonds) back.

Although many company owners like to take their companies public to cash in on their stake of the company, not all owners want to go public, and not all who do go public are happy that they did. One of the numerous drawbacks of establishing your company as public include the burdensome financial reporting requirements, such as production of quarterly earnings statements and annual reports. These documents not only take lots of time and money to produce but they can also reveal competitive secrets. Some companies also harm their long-term planning ability because of the pressure and focus on short-term corporate performance that comes with being a public company.

So how do companies decide whether to issue debt or equity? Companies that meet the requirements to sell stock on one of the exchanges try to do what is in their best interests. If the stock market is booming and new stock can sell at a premium price, companies opt to sell more stock. On the other hand, if investors don't believe that a company has good growth prospects and interest rates are relatively low, the company may lean toward selling bonds instead. Ultimately, companies seek to raise capital the lowest-cost way they can, so they'll elect to sell stocks or bonds based on what the finance folks tell them is the cheaper option.

From your perspective as a potential investor, you can make more money in stocks than bonds, but stocks are generally more volatile in the short-term (see Chapter 2).

What's an IPO?

Suppose that Liz's Distinctive Jewelry wants to issue stock for the first time, which is called an *initial public offering (IPO)*. If Liz decides to go public, she works with *investment bankers* who, like real estate agents trying to sell homes, help companies decide when and at what price to go public. (I need to note that most investment bankers don't like their comparison to real estate agents, but the successful ones in both professions make big bucks earning a percentage of every deal that they perform. Both investment bankers and real estate agents must determine their merchandise's asking price. Both sets of professionals also like to impress others driving expensive cars and dressing slickly.)

Suppose further that the investment bankers believe that Liz's Distinctive Jewelry can raise $50 million issuing stock. When a company issues stock, the price per share that the stock is sold for is somewhat arbitrary. The amount that a prospective investor will pay for a particular portion of the company's stock should depend upon the company's profits and future growth prospects. Companies that produce higher levels of profits and grow faster can generally command a higher sales price for a given portion of the company.

Consider the following ways that investment bankers can structure the IPO for Liz's Distinctive Jewelry:

Price of Stock	Number of Shares Issued
$5	10 million
$10	5 million
$20	2.5 million

In fact, Liz's Distinctive Jewelry can raise $50 million in an infinite number of ways, thanks to varying stock prices. If the company wants to issue the stock at a higher price the company sells fewer shares.

A stock's price per share by itself is meaningless in evaluating whether to buy a stock. Ultimately, the amount that investors will pay for a company's outstanding stock should depend greatly on the company's financial condition. If Liz's Distinctive Jewelry produces annual earnings (profits) of $3 million and companies comparable to Liz's include stock outstanding that sells at 10 times earnings, Liz's stock in the market is worth about $30 million.

$$\frac{\text{The value of a company's stock}}{\text{relative to (divided by) its earnings}} = \text{its } \textit{price-earnings ratio}$$

In the case of Liz's Distinctive Jewelry, here are the numbers:

$$\frac{\$30 \text{ million}}{\$3 \text{ million}} = 10$$

In the next chapter, I talk more about price earnings ratios and the factors that influence stock prices.

Understanding Financial Markets & Economics

We've made it to the moon, created powerful computer chips smaller than your fingernail, and cranked out $100 hightops with air-inflatable insoles that allow pimply-faced teenagers and wannabe athletes to aspire to Michael

Jordan's heights. But those advisors and money-savvy friends who are honest with you will admit that they still can't predict how the financial markets and the economy will perform in the years ahead.

Tens of thousands of books, millions of articles, and enough Ph.D. dissertations to fill a major landfill exist that explore these topics. You can spend the rest of your life reading all this stuff, and you still won't get through it. Don't try to read all of this information — it's an enormous waste of human potential! In this section I explain what you need to know about the factors that make the financial markets and economy work so that you can make informed investing decisions.

Capitalism makes money go 'round

In America, we live in a capitalistic (also known as free market) society. Have you ever stopped to think what that term means? Capitalism means that you have a tremendous (although not unlimited) amount of economic freedom.

If you want to start your own business, you can. However, that's not to say that you don't have to deal with obstacles, such as affording the start-up stages of your business and dealing with regulatory red tape. Most American entrepreneurs tell you that one of their greatest business frustrations is dealing with all the various government agencies. In addition to the long lists of licenses that you need to obtain for certain businesses, you may have to deal with zoning and planning offices regarding the use of the location of your business, other state and local agencies if you decide to incorporate, and still more government folks to comply with the myriad tax laws of the land.

Whine, whine, whine. Go to a socialist country if you want to see really red red tape and a lack of economic opportunity and mobility. Socialism, in contrast to capitalism, is an economic system that its nineteenth-century promoters, Karl Marx and Friedrich Engels, best sum up: "Abolish all private property."

Vladimir Lenin transformed Marx's and Engels' socialist theory into a political system known as communism. In communism, the government largely controls and owns the organizations that provide what people need. Over time, various countries in Europe, the former Soviet Union (Russia), and China have tried to make communism work. However, as is old news by now, increasing parts of the world continue to become more capitalistic. (Please note that just as the labels Republican and Democrat are somewhat meaningless, increasingly so too is the practice of labeling particular countries' economies as capitalistic or socialistic.) The low standard of living in communist countries, long waits in lines to purchase goods, poor health care, and so on all contributed to the downfall of communist systems.

What's good and not-so-good about capitalism

I came from a family that pulled itself up by its own bootstraps. My parents didn't have college educations, yet they were able to own a decent home and retire comfortably in their 60s after many years of hard work, which included raising three children who went to Ivy League colleges. Despite this fact, we all turned out all right, I think.

My brother, sister, and I are all entrepreneurs. My brother operates a thriving veterinary clinic, my sister operates a computer consulting firm, and then there's me. I continue to do what I love to do — teach others about sound financial management. Through books, teaching, and counseling work, I am able to fulfill my career dream.

I feel fortunate because if I were living in a country like Russia or China, I wouldn't be able to do the things that I like and have the enjoyment that my work and living in a free society bring me. That's the good side of capitalism — people who have some smarts and who roll up their sleeves and work hard can carve out a standard of living that many people around the world long for.

But, like any system, capitalism includes its warts. First, the free markets can be ruthless. People who lack particular skills (in some cases, through no fault of their own, but because of their lack of access to opportunities while growing up), get left behind or worse. Famous economist John Keynes, who is noted for clearly seeing some of the flaws of free markets, among other things, said, "The outstanding faults of the economic society in which we live are its failure to provide full employment and its arbitrary and inequitable distribution of wealth."

Another "problem" with capitalism is that, left to their own devices, some companies and their executives seek to maximize profits and ignore other important matters, such as ethics and the negative impact that their business practices may have on customers, the environment, and so on. In describing some of the less-savory businessmen of his time, Abraham Lincoln said in 1837, "These capitalists generally act harmoniously and in concert, to fleece the people."

Some companies do bad things in the pursuit of profits. Some opponents of any type of government regulation seem to forget about such companies. Some companies sell products that have been proven to harm users and other innocent bystanders. Tobacco, alcohol, and gun manufacturers come to mind. Even Malcolm Forbes, founder of one of the world's most pro-business, anti-big government magazines, said, "I'd say capitalism's worst excess is in the large number of crooks and tinhorns who get too much of the action."

But just because a company or person makes a great amount of money compared with others doesn't mean that they do less good than those who don't make as much money. I disagree with people such as Ayn Rand, author of *The Fountainhead,* who said, "Capitalism and altruism are incompatible; they are philosophical opposites; they cannot co-exist in the same man or in the same society." Baloney. My favorite examples of successful capitalists are those who succeed in business and accomplish a lot of good; you meet some of these people later in this book. When America is at its best as a country, we perform both capitalism and altruism well!

Profits drive stock prices

The goal of most companies is to make money, or *profits*. Profits result from the difference between what a company takes in, *revenue,* and what it expends, *costs.* I say *most* companies, because many organizations' primary purpose is not to maximize profits. Nonprofit organizations, such as colleges and universities, are a good example. But even nonprofits can't thrive and prosper without a steady flow of the green stuff.

Companies that trade publicly on the stock exchanges are supposed to maximize their profits — that's what their shareholders want. Higher profits make stock prices rise. Most private companies seek to maximize their profits as well but they contain much more latitude to pursue other goals.

So what's the secret to maximizing profits? The key is to produce products and services for which the demand (ideally) greatly exceeds the supply. If you made the mistake of majoring in economics like I did, one of the few useful things that you learned about are supply and demand curves. These important conceptual devices explain why products are priced the way that they are and why particular companies earn the profits that they do.

While profitable companies use a host of tactics to increase profits, the following are the major ways that successful companies increase profits:

- ✔ **Build a better mousetrap.** Some companies can develop or promote an invention or innovation that better meets customer needs. Consider the personal computer. In the "old days," if you wanted to write a business letter or report, you did it on a typewriter. Editing was a wearisome, time-consuming process. If you made a mistake, you either started the page over or retrieved the white correction fluid. Personal computers revolutionized the way that people write and edit their work. Of course, computers aren't better in all ways — you can possibly lose an entire document because of a major computer glitch. Your home has to burn to the ground or your dog has to go on a paper-eating rampage for that to happen with your typed papers!

- ✔ **Open new markets to your products.** Many successful U.S.-based companies, for example, have been stampeding into foreign countries to sell their products. Although some product adaptation is usually required to sell overseas, selling an already proven and developed product or service to new markets increases a company's chances for success.

- ✔ **Be in related businesses.** Being in a related business is what caused the Antitrust Division of the Justice Department to challenge Microsoft's business strategies. Microsoft develops operating systems, such as Windows and DOS, on which most personal computers run software. All the computer software, such as word-processing software, must run on and be compatible with the operating systems. Guess what — Microsoft is in the business of developing and selling "compatible" software as well.

✔ **Build a brand name.** Coca-Cola, for example, and many types of well-known beers rate comparably in blind taste tests to many generic colas and beers that are far cheaper. Yet, consumers (perhaps you) fork over more of their hard-earned loot because of the name and packaging. Companies build brand names largely through advertising and other promotions. (*...For Dummies* is a brand name, but *...For Dummies* books cost the same or less, in most cases, than the competition!)

✔ **Manage costs.** Smart companies control costs. Lowering the cost of manufacturing their products or providing their services allows companies to offer their products and services more cheaply. Managing costs may help fatten the bottom line (profit). Sometimes, though, companies try to cut too many corners and their cost-cutting ways come back to haunt them in the form of dissatisfied customers — or even lawsuits based on a faulty or dangerous product.

✔ **Watch the competition.** Successful companies don't necessarily mimic the competition but they do keep an eye on what their competition is up to. If lots of competitors target one part of the market, some companies target a less-pursued segment that, if they can capture it, may produce higher profits thanks to reduced competition. To avoid following the herd, companies must maintain courage and intelligence.

Efficient markets?

Companies generally seek to maximize profits and maintain a solid and healthy financial condition. Ultimately, the financial markets judge the worth of a company's stock or bond. Trying to predict in advance what happens to the stock and bond markets and individual securities consumes many a market prognosticator.

In the late 1960s, somewhat to the chagrin of market soothsayers, academic scholars developed a theory called the *efficient market hypothesis.* This theory basically maintains the following logic: Lots of investors collect and analyze all sorts of information about companies and their securities. If investors think that a security, such as a stock, is overpriced, they sell it or don't buy it. Conversely, if the investors believe that a security is underpriced, they buy it or hold what they already own. Because of the competition among all these investors, the price that a security trades at generally reflects what many informed smart people think it's worth.

Therefore, the efficient market theory implies that trading in and out of securities and the overall market in an attempt to obtain the right stocks at the right time is a futile endeavor. Buying or selling a security because of "new" news is also fruitless because the current market value of a stock reflects the news. As Burton Malkiel so eloquently said in his classic book, *A Random*

Walk Down Wall Street, this theory "Taken to its logical extreme . . . means that a blindfolded monkey throwing darts at a newspaper's financial pages could select a portfolio that would do just as well as one carefully selected by the experts."

Malkiel added, ". . . financial analysts in pin-striped suits don't like being compared with bare-assed apes." True enough, but since the 1980s, the *Wall Street Journal* actually has been running a contest where every three months several of their staff writers throw darts at the tacked up financial pages to "select" stocks to invest in. The writers then compare this randomly chosen portfolio to the stocks that esteemed money managers have selected. Over the 100 contests that have occurred, the dartboard-selected portfolio (which a computer now randomly chooses) has beaten the pros 39 times. In other words, the pros have won just 61 percent of the time — not very good considering that by chance alone they expect to win 50 percent of the time.

The real kicker to the *Journal* contest is that the writers leave the cost of hiring these professional money managers out of their comparison. Most professional money managers charge big bucks, and these fees erode the returns that your portfolio generates. If you factor in their hefty fees, the dartboard wins nearly half the time!

Some money managers have beaten the markets. In fact, beating the market over a year or three years isn't difficult, but few can beat the market over a decade or more. Efficient market supporters argue that some of those who beat the markets, even over a ten-year period, do so because of luck. Consider that if you flip a coin five times, on some occasions, you get five consecutive heads. This coincidence actually happens, on average, once every 32 times you do five coin-flip sequences because of random luck, not skill. Consistently identifying in advance which sequence gives you five consecutive heads is not possible.

Strict believers in the efficient market hypothesis say that it's equally impossible to identify the best money managers in advance. Some money managers, such as those who manage mutual funds, possess publicly available track records. Inspecting those track records and doing other common-sense things, such as investing in funds that minimize your expenses, improves your odds of performing a bit better than the market.

Various investment markets differ in how efficient (that is, that the current price of an investment accurately reflects its true value) they are. Although the stock market is reasonably efficient, many consider the bond market even more efficient. The real estate market is less efficient because properties are unique and sometimes less competition and access to information exist. If you can locate a seller who really needs to sell, you may be able to buy property at a discount from what it's really worth. Small business is also less efficient. Entrepreneurs with innovative ideas and approaches can earn enormous returns.

Specialists execute trades and make big bucks

Although not officially recognized until the Exchange Act passed after the Great Depression, the specialist system of trading actually began on the New York Stock Exchange around 1865. A *specialist* (and his or her firm) is a member of the exchange and is the focal point for trading a listed stock. Getting into this specialist's club requires a lot of money, in order to maintain a market in the securities the specialist is responsible for, and selection by the Board of Governors of the Exchange.

In most stocks, all trading centers around one specialist (several dozen stocks have two specialists). Specialists must maintain a continuous and stable market in the stocks that they handle. Specialists perform numerous functions that earn them megabucks. Specialists match up buy and sell orders to execute the trades that brokers place with them — in other words, they too earn a commission or cut on deals.

Specialists can also trade and hold stock positions in their own accounts. A few people and studies have raised questions about the specialist's potential for conflicts of interest in their work because of their capacity to maintain their own accounts. Specialists can only trade for their own accounts after they've fulfilled all the orders from other investors. Thus, specialists can only step in and buy or sell from their own accounts when an excess of sell or buy orders exists.

Although you may expect specialists to be decimated because they may buy and sell when others don't want them to, you'd be wrong. Although specialist firms aren't required to disclose the profits from their own investment accounts, several studies during periods of high market volatility demonstrate that specialists profit handsomely. For example, when President John F. Kennedy was assassinated on November 22, 1963, the stock market plunged. The next day, the market opened sharply higher. A House Subcommittee investigation found that specialists didn't step in to buy shares during the heavy selling on the 22nd until after they allowed prices to plummet, instead of attempting to support prices.

Prior to the 45 percent stock market drop in 1973 and 1974, specialists made near-record use of a trading technique known as *short-selling.* Short-selling enables an investor to profit by first selling the stock and later rebuying it when stock prices go down.

Economist Milton Friedman said the following in *Newsweek* in 1968: "Private monopolies seldom last long unless they can get governmental assistance in preserving their monopolistic position. In the stock market, the SEC both provides that assistance and shelters the industry from antitrust action." What Friedman said was more true then than today — retail brokerage firms in those days all charged the same commissions to the investing public. But the specialist system is still in place today, and recent data shows that specialists still make piles of money.

One of the keys to building wealth is to focus your time and investment strategies in a way that reflects the realities of the investment marketplaces that you invest in. If you desire to earn superior returns, you're better off trying to invest on your own in less-efficient markets like real estate and small business. On the other hand, trying to beat the market averages and the best professionals at picking stocks and bonds is a largely unproductive, but perhaps entertaining and addictive endeavor for most people.

Market overreactions can create buying opportunities. Efficiency notwithstanding, the financial markets that reflect the collective forces of millions of buyers and sellers can sometimes go to extremes. In the mid-1970s, pessimism ran rampant in this country. President Richard Nixon resigned in disgrace, inflation and unemployment spiraled upward, and the stock market fell out of bed. However, smart investors took advantage in this time period. Throughout this book, I show you how to evaluate different investment markets to identify if they've gone to extremes.

Interest rates, inflation, and the Federal Reserve

Although not as exciting to some as sex and rock and roll, the course of interest rates, inflation, and the monetary policies set forth by the Federal Reserve captivates the attention of many investors. For decades, economists, investment managers, and other often self-anointed gurus have attempted to understand these economic factors. Why? Because interest rates, inflation, and the Federal Reserves monetary policies seem to move the financial markets and the economy.

High interest rates are generally bad

Many businesses borrow money to expand. People like you and me, who are affectionately referred to as consumers, borrow money as well to buy things such as homes, cars, and educations.

Interest-rate increases tend to slow the economy. Businesses scale back on expansion plans, and some debt-laden businesses can't afford high interest rates and go under. Most individuals possess limited budgets as well and have to scale back some purchases because of higher interest rates. For example, higher interest rates translate into higher mortgage payments for homebuyers.

If high interest-rates choke business expansion and consumer spending, economic growth slows, or the economy shrinks in size — the economy possibly ends up in a *recession*. The government-sanctioned definition of a recession is two consecutive quarters (six months) of declining total economic output.

The stock market usually develops a case of the queasies as corporate profits shrink. High interest rates usually depress many investors' appetites for stocks, as the yields that certificates of deposit, Treasury bills, and other bonds pay increase.

Higher interest rates actually make some people happy. If you locked in a fixed-rate mortgage on your home or on a business loan, your loan looks much better than if you had a variable-rate mortgage. Some retirees and others who live off the interest income on their investments are happy with interest rate increases as well. Consider back in the early 1980s, for example, when a retiree received $10,000 per year in interest or dividends for each $100,000 that he or she invested in bonds or certificates of deposit (CDs) that paid 10 percent.

A retiree purchasing the same bonds and CDs in the late 1990s, however, saw dividend income slashed by about 50 percent, because rates on the same bonds and CDs were just 5 percent. So for every $100,000 invested, only $5,000 in dividend or interest income was paid.

If you try to live off the income that your investments produce, a 50 percent drop in that income is likely to cramp your lifestyle. So higher interest rates are better if you're living off of your investment income, right? Not necessarily.

The inflation and interest rate connection

Consider what happened to interest rates in the late 1970s and early 1980s. After the U.S. successfully emerged from a terrible recession in the mid-1970s, the economy seemed to be on the right track. But within just a few years, the economy was in turmoil again. The annual increase in the cost of living (known as the rate of inflation) burst through 10 percent on its way to 14 percent. The explosion in oil prices, which more than doubled in less than five years, was largely responsible for this increase. Interest rates, which are what bondholders receive when they lend their money to corporations and governments, followed inflation skyward.

Inflation and interest rates usually move in tandem. If you knew that, because of the ravages of inflation, your salary dollars for the next year would buy much less than they do in the present, wouldn't you too demand more interest? This reason is why interest rates soared along with inflation in the late 1970s and early 1980s, breaking 15 percent in 1981.

The primary driver of interest rates is the rate of inflation. Interest rates were much higher in the early 1980s because the U.S. had double-digit inflation. If the cost of living increases at the rate of 10 percent per year, why would you, as an investor, lend your money (which is what you do when you purchase a bond or CD) at 5 percent? Interest rates were so much higher in the early 1980s because you or I would never do such a thing.

In recent years, interest rates have been low because inflation has significantly declined since the early 1980s. Therefore, the rate of interest that investors could earn lending their money dropped accordingly. Although low interest rates reduce the interest income that comes in, the corresponding low rate of inflation doesn't devour the purchasing power of your principal balance. That's why higher interest rates aren't necessarily better if you try to live off your investment income.

So what's an investor, who's living off of the income he receives from his investments, but doesn't receive enough because of low interest rates, to do? A simple but psychologically difficult solution is to use up some of your principal to supplement your interest and dividend income. Using up your principal to supplement your income is what effectively happens anyway when inflation is higher — the purchasing power of your principal erodes more quickly. You may also not have saved enough money to meet your desired standard of living — that's why you may want to run a retirement analysis.

The role of the Federal Reserve

When the chairman of the Federal Reserve Bank Alan Greenspan speaks, an extraordinary number of people listen. When the 12 presidents from the respective Federal Reserve district banks and the 7 Federal Reserve governors conduct their Federal Open Market Committee meetings behind closed doors eight times a year, most financial market watchers and the media want to know what the Federal Reserve has decided to do about *monetary policy*.

What exactly is "the Fed," as it's known, and what does it do? The Federal Reserve tries to influence monetary policy. Yes, I know that's jargon, but that's the term that you often hear thrown around. All this jargon means is that the Fed tries to affect the amount of money or currency in circulation, known as the *money supply,* and the level of interest rates.

Before your eyes glaze over and you fall into a stupor like the one that I endured when I made the mistake of choosing economics as one of my two college majors (thankfully the other was in a real science: biology), let me quickly transport you to a point of light. Money is no different than lettuce, computers, or sneakers. All of these products and goods cost you dollars to buy them.

The cost of money is the interest rate that you must pay to borrow it. And the cost or interest rate of money is determined by many factors that ultimately influence the supply of and demand for money.

The Fed, from time to time and in different ways, attempts to influence the supply and demand for money and the cost of money: interest rates. The Fed raises or lowers the interest rates that they charge banks to borrow money in an attempt to influence the supply and demand for money. The Fed also buys or sells government bonds from time to time.

The senior officials at the Fed readily admit that the economy is quite complex and affected by so many things, so it's difficult to predict where the economy is heading. If it's so difficult to forecast and influence markets, then why does the Fed exist? The Fed officials believe that they can have a positive influence in creating a healthy overall economic environment: One in which inflation is low and growth proceeds at a modest pace. If the economy expands too rapidly, inflation can escalate. On the other hand, Fed officials believe that if the supply of money is too restricted and interest rates are too high, businesses won't be able to borrow and expand, and the economy will stagnate, or worse, actually shrink. So the Fed tries to keep everything just right!

Over the years, the Fed has come under attack for various reasons. Yale economist Edward Tufte's controversial book, *Political Control of the Economy,* argued that the Federal Reserve would, with a nudge of encouragement from the President, goose the economy. The Fed gooses the economy by loosening up on the money supply, which leads to a growth spurt in the economy, and a booming stock market, just in time to make the Prez look good just before an election. Conveniently, the consequences of inflation take longer to show up — not until after the election. In recent years, others have questioned the Fed's ability to largely do what they want without accountability.

The Greenspan obsession

During the latter half of the 1990s, the U.S. stock market continued to soar and more and more investors jumped into the market. Unfortunately, encouraged in large part by hyped media coverage that implies that Fed actions determine economic growth and future stock prices, some investors believed that they should move their money in and out of the market at particular times, based upon actions and statements that Federal Reserve officials made.

Perhaps you've read headlines that speculate about and document the Federal Reserve's moves to influence interest rates, inflation, and the economy. The stock market cable television channels are especially guilty of following every utterance that comes from Fed Chairman Alan Greenspan's mouth and trying to link the stock market's subsequent performance to what Greenspan said or didn't say.

If you've ever heard Fed officials speak, you know that they're always coy about tipping their hats and they rarely give specifics, even when they testify before Congress. Current Fed Chairman Alan Greenspan is widely considered a master of such verbal obfuscation. Most people can't understand half the often run-on sentences that this man speaks!

Here's a classic example of something that Greenspan said in a speech, that the media blew out of proportion:

> "Clearly, sustained low inflation implies less uncertainty about the future, and lower risk premiums imply higher prices of stocks and other earning assets. We can see that in the inverse relationship exhibited by price/earnings ratios and the rate of inflation in the past. But how do we know when irrational exuberance has unduly escalated asset values, which then become subject to unexpected and prolonged contractions as they have in Japan over the past decade? And, how do we factor that assessment into monetary policy? We as central bankers need not be concerned if a collapsing financial asset bubble does not threaten to impair the real economy, its production, jobs and price stability."

(I'm sure that you're grateful that Mr. Greenspan hasn't been retained to write Fed Policy Explained For Dummies!) Many in the media quickly focused on the sound bite "irrational exuberance" and linked it to the stock market. The morning after Greenspan's speech, stock prices dropped sharply and the same media attributed the drop to — you guessed it — his irrational exuberance comments. Turns out that investors who sold when Greenspan made this speech in early December 1996 at the American Enterprise Institute for Public Policy kick themselves because stocks prices have since soared.

Many, many factors influence the course of stock prices. Never, ever make a trade or investment based upon what someone at the Federal Reserve says or what someone in the media or some market pundit reads into the comments. The Fed simply doesn't have that much power or influence over the future. You need to make your investment plans based upon your needs and goals, not what the Fed does or doesn't do.

How do the Federal Reserve chiefs invest?

If Fed officials do have some insight into future interest rates and economic policy, wouldn't you like to know how the senior Fed officials invest their own personal money and when they refinance their mortgages and what type of mortgages they get? Inquiring minds like to know, and I was curious, so I started asking some questions.

Getting Fed officials, who don't generally see themselves as part of the government or accountable to the public, to return phone calls is a challenge. But persistence pays off. Bob Parry, president and CEO of one of the regional Federal Reserve banks, said to me of his investments, "It's pretty boring stuff. I don't have time to do research on individual securities, so I use mutual funds." Specifically, Parry says that he uses a lot of index funds (see Chapter 9), that hold a relatively fixed basket of stocks or bonds that mirror a broad market index, like the Standard & Poor's 500 index. Another Fed official that I spoke with also says he uses index funds because, as a former stock and bond analyst, he learned that, "You can't easily beat the market."

Somewhat to my surprise, I discovered that the top brass at the Fed have few restrictions on the types of investments that they may hold and when they can trade. The government prohibits Fed employees from owning individual stocks or bonds of banks or dealers in government securities and investing in government bonds. But no specific prohibitions prevent Fed officials, for example, from dumping their bond holdings if they think that interest rates are set to rise, loading up on them if the Fed enters a period of looser credit, or dumping stocks and bonds altogether.

Interestingly, most senior Fed officials come into the Fed from the private sector where they were forecasters. Greenspan, for example, was a partner in the Townsend and Greenspan economics forecasting firm. Surprisingly, despite earning a living for their predictions, most Fed officials dismiss their forecasting abilities *after* they join the Fed.

Some financial market pundits say not to underestimate the role of the Fed and its ability to signal its interest rate intentions to the financial markets. Others see the Fed as possessing less and less influence on the increasingly global financial markets and economy. Ultimately, some financial market pundits say, supply and demand determines interest rates, not the Fed.

How much Fed officials can divine the future remains an open question. If you can figure out a system for timing your investments and trying to buy and sell based on publicly available information and anticipated Federal Reserve moves, you should be a professional money manager! I don't know if Fed officials, who are privy to inside information, have been able to profit from their inside knowledge, but it seems prudent for them to set up safeguards to prevent such an occurrence or the likely outcry from the uncovering of past occurrences. Requiring public disclosure of their personal trades, as corporate executives must do when they trade their own companies' stock, is one solution. Another solution is for Fed officials to place their investments in a blind trust during their years of work at the Fed, as other senior government officials must do.

Chapter 5

The Stock Market and Valuations

*T*he stock market seems mysterious — it contains lots of jargon and sup-posed experts. When you want to buy stocks, you generally need a broker, and you may have heard about how you can seem like shark bait to these commission-hungry folks. Brokers and financial advisors possess many conflicts of interest. Most of them want to make the market seem compli-cated. If you understand the market and realize that their crystal ball has more than a few cracks in it, you can find other and better ways to invest your money in the stock market that don't involve their services.

Some people liken investing in the stock market to gambling. "I deal in a big floating crap game, one that is played every weekday in the richest and most exclusive casino in the world: the New York Stock Exchange," said Richard Ney, a veteran stock market prognosticator.

A real casino structures its games — slot machines, poker, roulette, and so on — so that in aggregate, the casino owners siphon off a healthy slab (40 percent) of the money that people brought with them. The vast majority of casino patrons lose money, in some cases all of it. The few who leave with more money than they came with are usually people who are lucky and are smart enough to quit while they're ahead.

I can understand why some individual investors, perhaps you, feel that the stock market resembles legalized gambling. So why bother with the stock market if it's so confusing and filled with people who are eager to separate you from your money? In Chapter 2, I discuss the potential risks and rewards of different investments. Shares of stock, which represent portions of owner-ship in companies, offer a way for people of modest and wealthy means and everybody in between, to invest in companies and build wealth.

The stock market isn't a casino — far from it. A casino is a zero-sum game where for every dollar you win or lose, that dollar comes from the casino. History shows that nearly all long-term investors can win in the stock market because it appreciates over the years. I say nearly because even some people who remain active in the market over many years manage to lose some money because of easily avoidable mistakes, that I can keep you from making in the future.

R. Foster Winans, a former writer for *Newsweek* and the *Wall Street Journal* said, "The only reason to invest in the market is because you think you know something others don't." Mr. Winans, who was later convicted of insider trading, was wrong.

You don't need any inside information to profit from stock investments. You simply need to understand this basic concept: The increasing profits that expanding companies will hopefully produce propel stock prices higher. As you can see in Figure 5-1, over the years, corporate profits continue on an upward trajectory. The trajectory path isn't a straight line up but more like the path that a small bird takes when it fights to gain altitude in a fierce head wind. Although the bird sometimes hits an air pocket or spot of bad weather and loses some altitude, the bird's aerodynamics win out. How many birds have you seen crash to Earth?

The same theory applies with corporate profits. Corporate profits also tend to trend up, but sometimes the economy hits a bad patch and profits fall. As with the bird, economies don't usually crash all the way back to ground zero. Yes, it's possible that if a huge meteor smashes into the Earth or a horrible, contagious virus spreads like wildfire, society may be done for — people and companies may cease to exist and make a profit. In the meantime, why not share in the expansion of the economy and keep an optimistic view on life?

What Is "The Market"?

So you invest in stocks to share in the spoils of capitalistic economies. When you invest in stocks, you do so through the stock market. What is the stock market? Everybody talks about The Market the same way they do a close personal friend. You know, they use the person's first name only, as if only one Tony exists in the world.

> "The Market is down 37 points today."

> "With The Market constantly hitting new highs, isn't now a bad time to invest in The Market?"

> "The Market's up more than 30 percent thus far this year. It seems ready for a fall."

If you've ever lived near New York or talked with New Yorkers, you've perhaps heard them refer to The City. New Yorkers use the term The City because they assume that you know what they're talking about: The City, as in New York City, or more specifically, Manhattan. Shame on anyone who thinks that you're referring to Brooklyn or Staten Island!

When people talk about The Market, they're usually referring to the U.S. stock market. Even more specifically, they're speaking about the Dow Jones Industrial Average, created by Charles Dow and Eddie Jones. Dow and Jones, two reporters in their 30s, started publishing a paper that you may have heard of — the *Wall Street Journal* — in 1889. Like its modern-day version, the nineteenth century *Wall Street Journal* reported current financial news. Dow and Jones also compiled stock prices of larger, important companies and created and calculated indexes to track the performance of the U.S. stock market.

The Dow Jones Industrial Average (DJIA) market index tracks the performance of 30 large companies that are headquartered in the U.S. The Dow 30 includes companies such as telecommunications giant AT&T, airplane manufacturer Boeing, soda maker Coca-Cola, oil giant Exxon, automaker General Motors, computer industry behemoth IBM, fast food king McDonald's, and retailers Sears and Wal-Mart.

The 30 stocks that make up the Dow aren't the 30 largest or the 30 best companies in America. They just so happen to be the 30 companies that senior staff members at the *Wall Street Journal* think reflect the diversity of the economy in the U.S. Some criticize the Dow index for encompassing so few companies and for a lack of diversity. The 30 stocks in the Dow change over time as companies merge, decline, and rise in importance.

Major stock market indexes

Just as Manhattan (thankfully) isn't the only city to visit or live in, the 30 stocks in the Dow Jones Industrial Average are far from representative of all the different types of stocks that you can invest in. Here are some other important market indexes and the types of stocks that they track:

✔ **Standard & Poor's 500.** Like the Dow Jones Industrial Average, the S&P 500 tracks the performance of larger-company U.S. stocks. As the name S&P 500 suggests, this index tracks the prices of 500 stocks. These 500 big companies account for nearly 80 percent of the total market value of the tens of thousands of stocks traded in the U.S. Thus, the S&P 500 is a much broader and more representative index of the larger company stocks in the U.S. than is the Dow Jones Industrial Average.

✓ **Russell 2000.** This index tracks the performance of 2,000 smaller U.S. company stocks of varying industries. While over the longer term, small company stocks tend to move in tandem with larger company stocks, it's not unusual for one to rise or fall more than the other or for one index to fall while the other rises in a given year. This situation did occur in 1998 when the S&P 500 was up 28.6 percent and the Russell 2000 was down 2.5 percent. As I discuss in Chapter 2, smaller company stocks tend to be more volatile, often rising more when the stock market increases and falling more precipitously when the market declines.

✓ **Wilshire 5000.** Despite its name, the Wilshire 5000 index actually tracks the prices of about 6,000 stocks of U.S. companies of all sizes — small, medium, and large. Thus, many consider this index the broadest and most representative of the overall U.S. stock market.

✓ **Morgan Stanley EAFE.** Stocks don't just exist in the United States. Morgan Stanley's EAFE index (EAFE stands for Europe, Australia, and Far East) tracks the prices of stocks in the other major countries of the world.

✓ **Morgan Stanley Emerging Markets.** This index follows the price movements of stocks in the less economically developed but "emerging" countries, which usually concentrate in Southeast Asia and Latin America. These stock markets tend to be more volatile than those in established economies. During good economic times, emerging markets usually reward investors with higher returns, but stocks can plunge farther and faster than stocks in developed markets.

Reasons to use indexes

Indexes serve several purposes. First, they can quickly give you an idea of how particular types of stocks fare and perform in comparison to other types of stocks. In 1993, for example, the S&P 500 was up 10.1 percent, but smaller company U.S. stocks, as measured by the Russell 2000 index, rose even more: 18.9 percent. The Morgan Stanley foreign stock EAFE index, by contrast, rose a whopping 33 percent, and its emerging markets index skyrocketed 74.9 percent in 1993! Every year is different: In 1998, the S&P 500 was up 28.6 percent whereas the EAFE was up 20.3 percent and the emerging markets index plunged 18.4 percent.

Indexes also allow you to compare or benchmark the performance of your stock market investments. If you invest primarily in large company U.S. stocks, for example, you should compare the overall return of the stocks in your portfolio to a comparable index — in this case, the S&P 500.

You may also hear about some other types of more narrowly focused indexes, such as those that track the performance of stocks in particular industries like advertising, banks, computers, drugs, restaurants, semiconductors, textiles, and utilities. Other countries, such as Japan, the United Kingdom, Germany, France, Canada, and Hong Kong, possess stock indexes that track the performance of their own stock markets. Focusing on your investments in the stocks of just one or two industries or smaller countries is dangerous. Thus I think you need to ignore these narrower indexes. Many companies, largely out of desire for publicity, develop their own indexes. If the news media reports on these indexes, the index developer effectively obtains free advertising. (In Chapter 9, I discuss investing strategies such as those that focus upon value stocks or growth stocks which also have market indexes.)

How Do I Buy Low and Sell High?

Now that you know about the different types of stock markets, you may wonder how you can get rich and not lose your shirt. Nobody wants to buy stocks before the markets take one of their big drops (which I discuss in Chapter 2). Thousands of books have been written about how to get rich in the stock market buying the best stocks cheaply and selling them when they become expensive.

As I discuss in Chapter 4, the stock market is reasonably efficient. A company's stock price normally reflects many smart people's assessments as to what is a fair price. Thus, it's not realistic for an investor to expect to discover a system for how to "buy low and sell high."

A few, rare professional investors may obtain an ability for spotting good times to buy and sell particular stocks, but consistently doing so is enormously difficult. In fact, the investing public doesn't possess a great track record with buying low and selling high. Smaller investors tend to sell heavily *after* major declines and step up buying *after* major price increases.

As a percentage of household assets, the American public's ownership of stocks fell below 20 percent after World War II before the stock market charged ahead on a bullish rampage. Stock ownership steadily increased until it peaked at about 36 percent of the public's financial assets in the late 1960s, when the market hit highs that it didn't break for nearly 15 years. When the market plunged in the mid-1970s, the public dumped stock and held less than 16 percent of its assets in stocks. During the 1980s and early 1990s, as the market boomed, the public has been slow to increase stock ownership. Today's stock ownership is close to the historic average.

The simplest and best way to make money in the stock market is to consistently and regularly feed new money into building a larger portfolio. If the market drops, you can use your purchases to buy more shares. The danger of trying to time the market is that you may be "out" of the market when it appreciates greatly and "in" the market when it plummets.

Calculate price-earnings ratios

Suppose I tell you that Liz's Distinctive Jewelry's stock sells for $50 per share and another stock in the same industry, The Jazzy Jeweler, sells for $100. Which would you rather buy?

If you answer, "I don't have a clue because you didn't give me enough information," go to the head of the class! On its own, the price per share of stock is meaningless.

Although The Jazzy Jeweler sells for twice as much per share, suppose that their profits are twice as much per share. The level of a company's stock price relative to its earnings or profits per share helps you calibrate how expensively, cheaply, or fairly a stock price is valued.

$$\frac{\text{Stock Price Per Share}}{\text{Annual Earnings Per Share}} = \text{Price-earnings (P/E) ratio}$$

Figure 5-1 shows you that stock prices and corporate profits tend to move in sync like good dance partners. The *price-earnings (P/E) ratio* (say PE — the "/" isn't pronounced) compares the level of stock prices to the level of corporate profits.

You can calculate P/E ratios for individual stocks as well as entire stock markets. Use this practical example to see how you can apply the use of P/Es.

In the late 1990s, many investors have been concerned that stock prices in the U.S. rose into the nosebleed area. The U.S. stock market continued to hit one new high after another. In March 1999, the most widely quoted stock market indicator, the Dow Jones Industrial Average, broke 10,000.

Because the U.S. stock market has had such a strong run throughout most of the 1980s and 1990s, I am concerned that the Dow's breaking 10,000 can make stock prices seem even more expensive. Some investors are rightfully concerned about the high level of stock prices in the U.S.

Over shorter periods of time, investors' emotions as well as fundamentals move stocks. Over longer terms, fundamentals possess a far greater influence on stock prices.

Longer-term investors such as myself who have invested since the early 1970s know that back then the Dow stood at a mere 1,000 or less. The Dow at 10,000 is ten times higher.

A particular price level in and of itself is meaningless, like a given stock such as IBM that rises above a specific price such as $100 per share. The level of a stock's price, or a stock market index, is important and meaningful when you compare it with earnings for the company or companies in the stock market index.

Examined on a price-earnings (P/E) basis, U.S. stocks are historically expensive. Over the past 100-plus years, the P/E ratio of the S&P 500 index has averaged about 14. In 1999, the S&P 500 P/E ratio was approximately 34, a historic high.

Corporate profits and inflation play major roles in the future of U.S. stock prices. If inflation remains low and corporate profits continue to grow at a healthy clip, the current P/E ratios may not be a problem. However, if profits stagnate or drop, U.S. stocks may suffer a significant fall. Likewise, increased inflation can throw a wrench in this bull market.

Just because the larger-company U.S. stocks (that make up the S&P 500 index) have historically averaged P/Es of about 14 doesn't mean that every individual stock will trade at such a P/E. Here's why: Suppose that you have a choice between investing in two companies, Superb Software, which makes computer software, and Tortoise Technologies, which makes typewriters. If both companies' stocks sell at a P/E of 15 and Superb Software's business and profits grow 40 percent per year and Tortoise's business and profits remain flat, which would you buy?

Because both stocks trade at a P/E of 15, Superb Software appears to be the better buy. Even if Superb's stock continues to sell at 15 times the earnings, its stock price should increase 40 percent per year as its profits increase. Faster-growing companies usually command higher price-earnings ratios, as shown in Table 5-1:

Table 5-1   Faster-Growing Companies Tend to Sell at Higher P/Es

Company	Recent P/E	Earnings Growth Past Five Years
Sears	17	3%
Gillette	43	16%
Microsoft	73	35%

What's a bull and a bear?

If you read magazines or newspapers or listen to people talk about the stock market, you often hear references to *bull* markets and *bear* markets. You may know which term means a good market and which term means a bad market for investors, but even if you do, you may wonder where these silly terms came from.

It's hard to find agreement on the origin of these terms, but my favorite description comes from Robert Claiborne's *Loose Cannons and Red Herrings — A Book of Lost Metaphors.* The term bear, according to Claiborne, originates from a proverb that mocks a man who "sells the bearskin before catching the bear." This is the connection to the stock market: When dealers in the stock market thought that the market became too pricey and speculative, these dealers sold stock that they hadn't yet "caught" (bought). These dealers were labeled "bearskin jobbers" and later, "bears."

The practice that these bearish dealers engaged in is *short selling.* They hoped that when they ultimately bought the stock that they had first sold, they could buy it back at a lower price. Their profit thus was the difference between the price that they originally sold it for and what they later bought it for. Short selling is simply investing in reverse: You sell first and buy back later. The worst situation for a bear is if prices go up, and he or she must buy back the stock at a high price. As Claiborne said, "He who sells what isn't his'n, must buy it back or go to prison."

The bulls, according to Claiborne, are those who work the "other side" of the street. Bulls buy stocks with the hope and expectation that they will rise in value. Ben Travato, a man whom Claiborne describes as one prone to inventing colorful, but often inaccurate, etymologies, said that bulls toss stocks up in the air with their horns.

Just because a stock price or an entire stock market seems to be at a high price level doesn't necessarily mean that the stock or market is overpriced. Always compare the price of a stock to that company's profits per share, or the overall market's price level to overall corporate profits. The price-earnings ratio captures this comparison. Faster-growing and more-profitable companies generally sell for a premium — higher P/Es. Also remember that future earnings, which are difficult to predict, influence stock prices more than current earnings, which are old news.

Don't get swept up in times of speculative excess

Because the financial markets move as much on the financial realities of the economy as well as people's expectations and emotions (particularly fear and greed), I don't believe that you should try to time the markets. Knowing when to buy and sell is much harder than you think.

You need to be careful that you don't get sucked into investing lots of your money into aggressive investments that seem to be in a hyped state. Many people go wrong when they begin to do this. In fact, many people don't become aware of an investment until it receives lots of attention. By the time everyone else talks about an investment, it's often nearing or at its peak. In the sections that follow, I walk you through some of the biggest speculative bubbles. Although some of these examples are from prior decades and even centuries, I chose these examples because I find that they best teach the warning signs and dangers of speculative fever times.

The 1920s consumer spending binge

The Dow Jones Industrial Average soared nearly 500 percent in a mere eight years from 1921 to 1929, one of the best bull market runs for the U.S. stock market. The country and investors had good reason for economic optimism. The "new" devices — telephones, cars, radios, and all sorts of electric appliances — were making their way into the mass market. The stock price of RCA, the radio manufacturer, for example, ballooned 5,700 percent during this great bull run.

Speculation in the stock market moved from Wall Street to Main Street. Investors during the 1920s were able to borrow lots of money to buy stock, through *margin borrowing*. You can still margin borrow today — for every dollar that you put up, you may borrow an additional dollar to buy stock with. At times during the 1920s, investors were able to borrow up to nine dollars for every dollar that they had in hand. The amount of margin loans outstanding swelled from $1 billion in the early 1920s to more than $8 billion in 1929. When the market plunged, margin calls forced margin borrowers to sell their stock, thus exacerbating the decline.

The steep run-up in stock prices was also due in part to market manipulation. Investment pools used to buy and sell stock amongst one another, thus generating high trading volume in a stock that made it appear that interest in the stock was great. Also in cahoots with pool operators were writers who dispensed enthusiastic prognostications about said stock. (Reforms later passed by the Securities and Exchange Commission addressed these problems.)

Not only were members of the public largely enthusiastic, so too were the supposed experts. After a small decline in September 1929, economist Irving Fisher said in mid-October, "Stock prices have reached what looks like a permanently high plateau." High? Yes! Permanent plateau? Investors wish!

On October 25, 1929, just days before all heck began breaking loose, President Herbert Hoover said, "The fundamental business of the country . . . is on a sound and prosperous basis." Days later, multimillionaire oil tycoon John D. Rockefeller said, "Believing that fundamental conditions of the country are sound . . . my son and I have for some days been purchasing sound common stocks."

Other maniacal manias in centuries long gone

I can fill an entire book with modern-day stock market manias. But bear with me as I roll back the clocks a couple of centuries to observe other market manias, the first being England's so-called South Sea bubble of 1719. South Seas wasn't the kind of company that would've met today's socially responsible investor's needs. Initially, the South Seas Company focused on the African slave trade, but too many slaves died in transit, so it wasn't a lucrative business.

If you think government corruption is a problem today, consider what politicians of those days did without the scrutiny of a widely read press. King George backed the South Seas Company and acted as its governor. Politicos in Parliament bought tons of stock in the South Seas Company and even rammed through Parliament a provision that allowed investors to buy stock on borrowed money. The stock of the South Seas Company soared from about £120 to more than £1000 in just the first six months in 1720.

After such an enormous run-up, insiders realized that the stock price was greatly inflated and quietly bailed. Citizens fell all over themselves to get into this surefire moneymaker. Other seafaring companies pursued the South Seas trade

business, so the greedy politicians passed a law that stated that only government-approved companies could pursue trade. The stocks of these other companies tumbled, and investor losses led to a chain reaction that prompted selling of the South Seas Company stock. South Seas Company stock plunged more than 80 percent by the fall of that same year.

Unfortunately, England wasn't the only European country that was swept up in an investment mania. Probably the most famous mania of them all was the tulip bulb (yes, those flowers that you can plant in your own home garden). A botany professor introduced tulips into Holland from Turkey in the late 1500s. Residents allowed a fascination with these bulbs turn into an investment feeding frenzy.

At their speculative peak, the price of a single tulip bulb was the equivalent of more than $10,000 in today's dollars. Many people sold their land holdings to buy more. Documented cases show that people traded a bulb for a dozen acres of land! Laborers cut back on their work to invest. Eventually, tulip bulb prices came crashing back to Earth. A trip to your local nursery shows you what a bulb sells for today.

By December of that same year, the stock market dropped by more than 35 percent. General Electric President Owen D. Young said at that time, "Those who voluntarily sell stocks at current prices are extremely foolish."

Well, actually not. By the time the crash had run its course, the market had plunged 89 percent in value in less than three years.

The magnitude of this steep decline in stock prices couldn't have been predicted or expected in the late 1920s. The economy went into a tailspin. Unemployment soared to more than 25 percent of the labor force. Companies entered this period with excess inventories, which mushroomed further once people slashed their spending. High overseas tariffs stifled American exports. Thousands of banks failed, as early bank failures triggered "runs" on other banks (no FDIC insurance existed in these days).

The 1960s weren't just about sex, drugs, and rock and roll

The U.S. stock market mirrored the climate of our country during this decade of change and upheaval. There were good years and bad years, but overall, the stock market gained. Unfortunately, most investors who were old enough to remember what happened to the stock market during the Great Depression were retired or had passed away. The new investors and the majority of the investors during the 1960s were born after the go-go years of the 1920s or were still sucking on a pacifier.

During the 1960s, consumer product companies' stocks were quite popular and were bid up to stratospheric valuations. When I say "stratospheric valuations," I mean that some stock prices were high relative to the company's earnings — our old friend, the price-earnings (P/E) ratio. Investors had seen such stocks' prices rise for many years and thought that the good times would never end.

Take the case of Avon Products, which sells cosmetics door-to-door primarily with an army of women. During the late 1960s, Avon's stock regularly sold at a P/E of 50 to 70 times earnings (remember, the market average is about 14). After trading as high as $140 per share in the early 1970s, Avon's stock took more than two decades to return to that price level. Remember that during this time period the overall U.S. stock market rose more than tenfold!

When a stock such as Avon's sells at such a high multiple of earnings, two factors can lead to a bloodletting. First, the company's profits may continue to grow, but investors may decide that the stock isn't such a great long-term investment after all and not worth, say, a P/E of 60. Consider that if investors decide it's only worth a P/E of 30 (still a hefty P/E), the stock price would drop 50 percent to cut the P/E in half.

The second shoe that can drop is the company's profits or earnings. If profits fall, say, 20 percent, as Avon's did during the 1974–75 recession, the stock price will fall 20 percent, even if it continued to sell for 60 times its earnings. But when earnings drop, investors' willingness to pay an inflated P/E plummets along with the earnings. So when Avon's profits finally did drop, the P/E that investors were willing to pay plunged to 9 — in less than two years, Avon's stock price thus dropped nearly 87 percent!

Avon was not alone in its stock price soaring to a rather high multiple of its earnings in the 1960s and early 1970s. Well-known companies such as Black & Decker, Eastman Kodak, Kmart (used to be called S. S. Kresge in those days), and Polaroid sold for 60 to as much as 100 times earnings. All these companies, like Avon, sell today at about the same or at a lower price than they achieved more than 20 years ago. Many other well-known and smaller companies sold at similar and even more outrageous premiums to earnings.

BEWARE

The *New York Times* and Merrill Lynch said buy at the highs

One of the reasons that otherwise intelligent people get sucked into grossly overpriced investments that are near their peak is because organizations they think are in the know encourage them to do so. In October 1989, the *New York Times*, the paper of record, weighed in with an article on the Japanese market entitled "Japanese Market Watchers Not Worried." The piece argued in a fairly one-sided fashion and quoted many supporting sources that said Japanese stock prices were on solid ground. The *New York Times* article said that Japanese financial executives didn't expect a sustained downturn in the Japanese stock market. The head of trading at Nikko Securities, a large Japanese brokerage firm, was quoted as saying, ". . . any drop would be temporary."

Of course, the people that the newspaper interviewed and what facts the paper uses have an enormous impact on the story that's told. What do you expect brokerage firms, which make all of their money encouraging stock market investing, to say? Duh.

U.S. economist James Grant pointed out in his newsletter a couple of years earlier that the silliness of high P/Es in some Japanese stocks were used to justify high P/Es elsewhere. Grant told of a Merrill Lynch brokerage analyst who recommended investing in Yasuda Trust, a Japanese bank. At the time, Yasuda's P/E was a modest 63 compared to other bank stocks, which weighed in at nearly 100 times earnings. Over the next five years, investors who followed Merrill's advice were greeted with a 70-plus percent decline. Being a U.S.-headquartered brokerage firm, Merrill should have known better. The desire to win more commissions clouded its judgment.

Less than three months after the *New York Times* wrote its "don't worry about high prices" piece on the Japanese stock market, the Japanese party ended with few of the invited guests ever told. The lights were shut off, the punch bowls emptied, and most people's cars stolen, so they couldn't even get home.

The Japanese stock market juggernaut

Lest you think that the U.S. and England cornered the market on manias, overseas examples abound. A rather extraordinary mania happened not so long ago — less than a decade — in the Japanese stock market.

After the crushing defeat suffered in World War II, Japan's economy was in shambles. Two major cities — Hiroshima and Nagasaki — were destroyed and more than 200,000 died when the U.S. dropped atomic bombs to "win" the war.

Out of the rubble, Japan emerged a strengthened nation that became an economic powerhouse. Over 22 years, from 1967 to 1989, Japanese stock prices rose an amazing 30-fold (3,000 percent) as the economy boomed. From 1983 to 1989 alone, Japanese stocks soared more than 500 percent.

In terms of the U.S. dollar, the Japanese stock market rise was all the more stunning, as the dollar lost value versus Japan's currency, the yen. The dollar lost about 65 percent of its value during the big run-up in Japanese stocks. In dollar terms, the Japanese stock market rose an astonishing 8,300 percent from 1967 to 1989.

Many considered investing in Japanese stocks close to a sure thing. Increasing numbers of people became full-time stock market investors in Japan. Many of these folks were actually speculators, as borrowed funds were used heavily. As the Japanese real estate market boomed in tandem with the stock market, real estate investors borrowed from their winnings to invest in stocks and vice versa.

Borrowing heavily was easy to do as Japan's banks were awash in cash, and it was cheap, cheap, cheap to borrow. Investors could borrow money for a mere few percent interest. "Established investors" could make property purchases with no money down. Cash abounded from real estate as the price of land in Tokyo, for example, soared 500 percent from 1985–1990. Despite having ⅕ as much land as the U.S., Japan's total land values at the close of the 1980s were four times that of all the land in the U.S.

Speculators also used futures and options (discussed in Chapter 1) to gamble on higher short-term Japanese stock market prices. Interestingly, Japan doesn't allow selling short. Likewise, given the strong Japanese currency, investors kept their money on their home turf, so they didn't lose out from devaluation of foreign currencies. Investing at home is one of the reasons why many Japanese investors had little sense (from other nation's stock markets) about what their investments were intrinsically worth.

Price-earnings ratios? Forget about it. Japanese market speculators pointed out that the real estate that many companies owned was soaring to the moon and making companies more valuable to justify the high prices that they paid for stocks.

Price-earnings ratios on the Japanese market soared during the early 1980s and ballooned to more than 60 times earnings by 1987. As I point out earlier in this chapter, such lofty P/Es were sometimes awarded hot stocks in the U.S. But the entire Japanese stock market, which included many mediocre and not-so-hot companies, possessed P/Es of 60-plus!

When Japan's version of AT&T, Nippon Telegraph and Telephone, went public in February 1987, it met such frenzied enthusiasm that its stock price was soon bid up to a stratospheric 300-plus price earnings ratio. At the close of 1989, Japan's stock market, for the first time in history unseated the U.S. stock market in total market value of all stocks. And this feat happened despite the fact that the total output of the Japanese economy was less than half that of the U.S.

Even some U.S. observers began to lose sight of the big picture and added to the rationalizations for why the high levels of Japanese stocks were justified. After all, it was reasoned, Japanese companies and executives were a tightly knit and "closed circle" investing heavily in the stocks of other companies that they did business with. The supply of stock for outside buyers was thus limited as companies sat on their shares.

Corporate stock ownership went further, though, as stock prices were sometimes manipulated as they had been in the U.S. in the earlier part of this century. Speculators gobbled up the bulk of outstanding shares of small companies and traded shares back and forth with others that they partnered with to drive up prices. Company pension plans began to place all (as in 100 percent) of their employees' retirement money into stocks with the expectation that stock prices would always keep going up. Surely someone else would always pay a higher price to buy stock.

The collapse of the Japanese stock market was swift. After peaking at the end of 1989, the Tokyo market plunged nearly 50 percent in the first nine months of 1990 alone. By the middle of 1992, the worst was over with Japanese stocks down nearly 65 percent — a plunge that the U.S. market hasn't experienced since the Great Depression. Japanese investors who borrowed lost everything and sometimes more. The total loss in stock market value was about $2.5 trillion, about the size of the entire Japanese annual output.

Several factors finally led to the pricking of the Japanese stock market bubble. Japanese monetary authorities tightened credit as inflation started to creep upward and concern increased over real estate market speculation. As interest rates began to rise, investors soon realized that they could earn 15 times more interest from a safe bond versus the paltry yield on stocks.

As interest rates rose and credit tightened, speculators were squeezed first. Real estate and stock market speculators began to sell their investments to pay off mounting debts. Higher interest rates, less available credit, and the already grossly inflated prices greatly limited the pool of potential stock buyers. The plunging stock and real estate markets fed off of one another. Investor losses in one market triggered more selling and price drops in the other. The real estate price drop was equally severe — registering 50 to 60 percent or more in most parts of Japan since the late 1980s.

The Internet and technology bubble

Unless you isolate yourself from what we call civilization, you've surely heard about the explosive growth in the Internet. In the mid-1990s, a number of Internet-based companies launched initial public offerings of stock (I discuss IPOs in Chapter 4). Most of the early Internet company stock offerings failed to really catch fire. By the late 1990s, however, some of these stocks began meteoric rises.

The bigger-name Internet stocks included companies such as Internet service provider America Online, bookseller and online retailer Amazon.com, Internet auctioneer eBay, and Internet portal Yahoo!. As with the leading new consumer product manufacturers of the 1920s that I discuss earlier in this chapter, many of the leading Internet company stocks zoomed to the moon.

An excellent starting point for understanding the valuation of a stock is the price earnings ratio (P/E). (See "Calculate price earnings ratio," earlier in this chapter.) Divide the stock price per share by the company's earnings per share to calculate the P/E ratio. Please note that the absolute stock price per share of the leading Internet companies in the late 1990s was meaningless. The P/E ratio is what mattered.

Valuing the Internet stocks based upon earnings posed a challenge because many of these Internet companies were losing money or just beginning to make money. Some Wall Street analysts, therefore, valued Internet stocks based upon revenue and not profits.

Valuing a stock based upon revenue and not profits can be highly dangerous. Revenues don't necessarily translate into high profits or any profits at all.

In the case of Amazon.com, its stock price soared in early 1999 to $221 per share, which gave the company's stock a total market valuation in excess of $35 billion, or more than 12 times that of competing bookseller Barnes & Noble. (B&N had prior year sales of nearly $3 billion compared with Amazon.com's approximate $400 million sales as it was losing money!)

Suppose that Amazon.com is successful many years down the road and builds the online equivalent of mass merchandiser Costco and sells lots of products to lots of customers. Consider this: Over the past year, Costco had revenue of more than $24 billion, net income of $460 million, and had a market value of just $13 billion, less than half that of Amazon.com's!

Now, Amazon.com, America Online, and other current leading Internet companies may go on to become some of the great companies and stocks of future decades. However, consider this perspective from veteran money manager David Dreman. "The Internet stocks are getting hundredfold more attention from investors than say a Ford Motor in chat rooms online and elsewhere. People are fascinated with the Internet — many individual investors have accounts on margin. Back in the early 1900s, there were hundreds of auto manufacturers and it was hard to know who the long-term survivors would be. The current leaders won't probably be long-term winners."

Internet stocks aren't the only stocks being swept to excessive prices relative to their earnings at the dawn of the new millenium. Various traditional retailers announced that they are opening Internet sites to sell their goods, and within days their stock prices doubled or tripled. Also, leading name brand technology companies such as Dell Computer, Cisco Systems, Lucent, and

PeopleSoft traded at P/E ratios in excess of 100. Companies in other industries like investment brokerage firm Charles Schwab, which expanded to offer Internet services, saw its stock price balloon to push its P/E ratio over 100. As during the 1960s and 1920s, name-brand growth companies soared to high P/E valuations. For example, coffee purveyor Starbucks at times had a P/E near 100.

What I find troubling about investors piling into the leading, name-brand stocks, especially in Internet and technology-related fields is that many of these investors don't even know what a price earnings ratio is and why it's important. Before you invest in any individual stock, no matter how great a company you think it is, you need to understand the company's line of business, strategies, competitors, financial statements, and price earnings ratio versus the competition, among many other issues. Selecting and monitoring good companies takes lots of research time and discipline.

Also, remember that if a company taps into a product line or way of doing business that proves highly successful, that company's success invites lots of competition. So, you need to understand the barriers to entry that a leading company has erected and how difficult or easy it is for competitors to join the fray. Also, be wary of analyst earnings and stock price predictions. As more and more investment banking analysts initiated coverage of Internet companies and issued buy ratings on said stocks, investors bought more shares. Analysts, who are too optimistic (as shown in numerous independent studies), have a conflict of interest because the investment banks that they work for seek to cultivate the business (new stock and bond issues) of the companies that they purport to rate and analyze. The analysts who say buy, buy, buy all the current market leaders are the same analysts who generate much new business for their investment banks and get the lucrative job offers and multi-million dollar annual salaries.

Simply buying today's rising and analyst-recommended stocks often leads to future investor disappointment. If the company's growth slows or the profits don't materialize as expected, the underlying stock price can nose-dive. This situation happened to investors who piled into computer disk drive maker Iomega's stock back in early 1996. After a spectacular rise to about $27½ per share (similarly touted on Internet message boards), the company fell on tough times. Iomega stock subsequently plunged to less than $3 per share. It will likely be many more years until this stock recovers to its early 1996 price levels.

Here are some other examples of supposed can't-lose technology that crashed and burned. Presstek, a company that uses computer technology for so-called direct imaging systems, rose from less than $10 per share in mid-1994 to nearly $100 per share just two years later. As was the case with Iomega, herds of novice investors jumped on the bandwagon simply because they believed that the stock price would keep rising. By 1999, less than three years after hitting nearly $100 per share, it plunged more than 90 percent to about $5 per share.

ATC Communications, which was, similar to Iomega, glowingly recommended by the Motley Fool Web site (see Chapter 20), plunged by more than 80 percent in a matter of months before the Fools recommended selling.

Psychologically, it's easier for many people to buy stocks *after* they've had a huge increase in price. Just as you shouldn't attempt to drive your car looking solely through your rearview mirror, basing investments solely on past performance usually leads novice investors into overpriced investments. If many people talk about the stunning rise in the market and new investors pile in based on the expectation of hefty profits, tread carefully.

I'm not saying that you need to sell your current stock holdings if you see an investment market getting frothy and speculative. As long as you diversify your stocks worldwide and hold other investments, such as real estate and bonds, the stocks that you hold in one market only need to be a fraction of your total holdings. Timing the markets is difficult: You can never know how high is high and when it's time to sell, and then how low is low and when it's time to buy. And if you sell non-retirement account investments at a profit, you end up sacrificing a lot of the profit to federal and state taxes.

Buy more when stocks are "on sale"

Along with speculative buying frenzies come valleys of pessimism. Having the courage to buy when stocks are "on sale" can pay bigger returns.

In the early 1970s, interest rates and inflation escalated. Oil prices shot up as the Arab oil embargo choked off supplies and Americans had to wait in long lines for gas. Gold prices soared, and the U.S. dollar plunged in value on foreign currency markets.

If the economic problems weren't enough to make most everyone gloomy, the U.S. political system hit an all-time low during this period as well. Vice President Spiro Agnew resigned in disgrace under a cloud of tax evasion charges, and then Watergate led to President Nixon's August 1974 resignation, the first presidential resignation in our history.

When all was sold and done, the Dow Jones Industrial Average plummeted more than 45 percent from early 1973 until late 1974. Among the stocks that fell the hardest and furthest included those that were most popular and selling at extreme multiples of earnings in the late 1960s and early 1970s. (See the section "The 1960s weren't just about sex, drugs, and rock and roll," earlier in this chapter.)

Take a gander in Table 5-2 at the drops in these well-known companies and how cheaply these stocks were valued relative to corporate profits (look at the P/Es) after the worst market drop since the Great Depression.

Table 5-2	Stock Bargains Galore in the Mid-1970s		
Company	*Industry*	*Stock Price Fall from Peak*	*1974 P/E*
Abbott Laboratories	Drugs	66%	8
AIG	Insurance	67%	10
H&R Block	Tax preparation	83%	6
Chemical Bank	Banking	64%	4
Coca-Cola	Beverages	70%	12
Dayton-Hudson	Department stores	86%	4
Disney	Entertainment	75%	11
Dun & Bradstreet	Business information	68%	9
General Dynamics	Military	81%	3
Hilton Hotels	Hotels	87%	4
Humana	Hospitals	91%	3
Intel	Semiconductors	76%	6
Kimberly-Clark	Consumer products	63%	4
McGraw-Hill	Publishing	90%	4
Mobil	Oil	60%	3
PepsiCo	Beverages	67%	8
Pitney Bowes	Postage meters	84%	6
Potlatch	Lumber and paper	66%	3
PPG Industries	Glass	60%	4
Quaker Oats	Packaged food	76%	6
Rite Aid	Drug stores	95%	4
Scientific-Atlanta	Communications Equipment	82%	4
Sprint	Telephone	67%	7
Tandy	Consumer electronic retailer	70%	5
Textron	Aerospace	80%	4
TRW	Electronics	83%	4
U.S. Shoe	Shoes	82%	4
Woolworth	Discount stores	86%	3

Those who were too terrified to buy stocks in the mid-1970s actually had plenty of time to get on board and take advantage of the buying opportunities. The stock market did have a powerful rally and, from its 1974 low, rose nearly 80 percent over the next two years. But over the next half dozen years, the market backpedaled, losing much of its gains.

In the late 1970s and early 1980s, inflation continued to escalate well into double digits. Corporate profits declined further and unemployment rose higher than in the 1974 recession. Although some stocks dropped, others simply treaded water and went sideways for years after major declines in the mid-1970s. As some companies' profits increased, P/E bargains abounded (see Table 5-3).

Table 5-3 More Stock Bargains in the Late 1970s and Early 1980s

Company	*Industry*	*Stock Price Fall from Peak*	*P/E Late 70s /Early 80s*
Anheuser-Busch	Beer	75%	8
Campbell Soup	Canned Foods	36%	6
Coca-Cola	Beverages	61%	8
Colgate-Palmolive	Personal care	69%	6
General Electric	Consumer /industrial products	44%	7
General Mills	Food	44%	6
Gillette	Shaving products	74%	5
McDonald's	Fast food	46%	9
MMM	Consumer/ industrial products	50%	8
Pacific Gas & Electric	Utility	52%	6
J.C. Penney	Department stores	80%	6
Procter & Gamble	Consumer products	46%	8
Ralston Purina	Pet food	49%	6
Rubbermaid	Rubber products	60%	7
Sara Lee	Food	60%	5
Schering Plough	Drugs	71%	7
Seagram	Alcohol	60%	7

Company	Industry	Stock Price Fall from Peak	P/E Late 70s /Early 80s
Tambrands	Feminine hygiene products	82%	7
Wells Fargo	Banking	50%	3
Whirlpool	Household appliances	63%	5
Xerox	Copiers	85%	5

When bad news and pessimism abound and the stock market has dropped, it's a much safer and better time to buy stocks by the truckload. You may even consider shifting some of your money out of your safer investments, such as bonds, and invest more aggressively in stocks. Investors feel during these times that prices can drop further, but if you buy and wait you'll be amply rewarded. Most of the stocks listed in the last several pages have appreciated 500 to 2,000-plus percent in the past 15 to 20 years.

Chapter 6

The Different Ways to Buy Stocks

• •

In This Chapter

▶ Buying stocks the smart way

▶ Sidestepping common stock shopping mistakes

▶ Understanding the keys to stock-investing success

• •

*W*hen it comes to investing in stocks, many (perhaps too many) options exist. Besides the tens of thousands of stocks from which you can choose, you can hire a mutual fund manager or stockbroker to pick for you. You can also pick your own stocks and even buy stock directly, in some cases, from the issuing company.

I remember that when I first moved to California and heard that you can go to a large farmers' market instead of going to the grocery store to buy fruits and vegetables. Farmers' markets brought the farmers to you. A number of California towns have small farming operations that set up shop for a few hours weekly and sell their stuff.

And if a farmers' market isn't direct enough, you can go straight to some farms and pick your own produce. I remember the first time that I did this — it was fun, but several weeks later I was mighty tired of eating the apples and berries that I had picked.

The next time I decided to drive out to these farms, the hour-plus drive in the hot, baking sun seemed a lot longer than I remembered. The produce prices, I noticed on this go-round, weren't that much less than our local supermarket, and I had to spend all my time and pick it myself, for goodness sakes — the farmers were saving on the labor costs! Then it dawned on me that the farm's fruit pickers probably weren't paid all that much and were likely ten times more efficient (okay, maybe a hundred times more) than I. When I factored the costs of driving my car out to buy the fruit, it ended up costing about the same or more as what I would've paid at the store five minutes from my home.

Some people may continue to drive out to the farms, perhaps even weekly, for the sheer joy and pleasure of selecting and picking their own produce in the heat and dust. But I've discovered that one of the values of the farmers and stores choosing and working for me is that they're better at their job than me.

Ways to Buy Stocks

When you invest in stocks, you have choices similar to those that you have when you go produce shopping. Picking your own stocks can be entertaining and educational, and few things are more gratifying and vindicating to the old ego than seeing your stock choice double (or better) in price after you purchase it. As with picking your own produce though, don't forget to factor your time and expertise into the equation and be realistic and honest about why you're buying stocks through the method you've chosen.

Acquiring stocks through funds

If you're busy and suffer no delusions about your expertise, you'll love the best stock mutual funds. Investing in stocks through mutual funds can be as simple as dialing an 800 number (or for you Net-heads, logging onto a fund company's Web site), obtaining and completing some application forms, and mailing a check.

Mutual funds are investment companies that invest money from people like you and me into securities, such as stocks and bonds. Stock mutual funds, as the name suggests, invest primarily or exclusively in stocks (some "stock" funds sometimes invest a bit in other stuff, such as bonds).

Stock mutual funds include many advantages:

- ✔ **Diversification.** Buying individual stocks on your own is prohibitively expensive, unless you buy reasonable chunks (100 shares or so) of each stock. But in order to buy 100 shares each in, say a dozen companies' stocks to ensure diversification, you need about $60,000 if the stocks that you buy average $50 per share in price.

- ✔ **Professional management.** Even if you have big bucks to invest, mutual funds offer something that you can't deliver: professional, full-time management. Look at it this way: Mutual funds are a huge time-saver. It's Friday night — would you rather go to the local library and do some research on semiconductor and toilet paper manufacturers or enjoy dinner or a movie with family and friends? (I guess that the answer to that question depends on who your family and friends are!)

Mutual fund managers peruse a company's financial statements and otherwise track and analyze a company's business strategy and market position. The best managers put in more than a 40-hour workweek and possess lots of expertise and experience in the field. (If you've been misled into believing that with minimal effort you can rack up market-beating returns, please be sure to read the rest of this chapter.)

✔ **Low costs — if you pick 'em right.** Those with a vested interest, such as stock-picking newsletter pundits, may point out the high fees that some funds charge to convince you that mutual funds aren't a good way for you to invest. An element of truth rings here: Some funds are expensive, charging you a couple percent or more per year in operating expenses on top of hefty sales commissions.

But just as you wouldn't want to invest in a fund that a novice with no track record manages, why would you want to invest in a high-cost fund? Contrary to the "You get what you pay for" notion often trumpeted by those trying to sell you something at an inflated price, many of the best managers are the cheapest to hire. Through a no-load (commission-free) mutual fund, you can hire a professional, full-time money manager to invest your $10,000 for a mere $20 to $100 per year. And if you have far less than this to invest, they'll still invest your money at a low cost: $2 to $10 per year if you invest $1,000.

As with all investments, mutual funds have drawbacks. The issue of control is a problem for some investors. If you're a controlaholic, turning over your investment stash to a seemingly black box process where others decide when and in what to invest your money may unnerve you. However, you need to be more concerned about the potential blunders that you may make investing in individual stocks of your own choosing or, even worse, those stocks pitched to you by a broker. (You might also seek a professional's perspective about why you are so control-oriented.)

Taxes are another concern for investing in mutual funds outside retirement accounts. Because the fund manager, and not you, decides when to sell specific stock holdings, some funds may produce somewhat high levels of taxable distributions. Fear not — simply select tax-friendly funds if taxes concern you.

In Chapter 9, I talk about investing in the best mutual funds that offer a time and cost-efficient, high-quality way to invest in stocks worldwide.

Buying individual stocks

More than a few investing books suggest and enthusiastically encourage that people like you do their own stock picking. However, the vast majority of people are better off *not* picking their own stocks.

Why do I make this statement? Not because I don't think highly of you and your capabilities; I do. I've long been an advocate of people educating themselves and taking responsibility for their own financial affairs, but taking responsibility for your own finances doesn't mean that you should do *everything* yourself. Remember my discussion in this chapter's introduction about picking your own produce in the fields versus buying it closer to home? I challenge you to consider why you might prefer to select your own individual stocks. Table 6-1 includes some of the thoughts that you may have on the subject:

Table 6-1	The Pros and Cons of Choosing Your Own Stocks
Good Reasons to Pick Your Own Stocks:	*Bad Reasons to Pick Your Own Stocks:*
You enjoy the challenge.	You think you can beat the best money managers. (If you can, you're in the wrong profession!)
You want to learn more about business.	You want more control over your investments, which you think may happen if you understand the companies that you invest in.
You possess a substantial amount of money to invest.	You think that mutual funds are for people who aren't smart enough to choose their own stocks.
You're a buy-and-hold investor.	You're attracted to the ability to trade your stocks anytime you want.

Several popular investing books have tried to convince investors that they can do a *better* job than the professionals at picking their own stocks. Former mutual fund manager Peter Lynch wrote a book entitled *Beating the Street.* This is a title designed to attract the greedy side of our personalities. (I should also note that the publisher, Simon & Schuster, also cranked out other financial titles, such as the oxymoronic *Wealth Without Risk.*)

Consider what Lynch says: ". . . an amateur who devotes a small amount of study to companies in an industry he or she knows something about can outperform 95 percent of the paid experts who manage the mutual funds. . ." Ninety-five percent, Mr. Lynch??? Quite a surprising statement from a man who made his living for more than a decade as a successful fund manager at Fidelity and today is a director at this largest of mutual fund companies. (Fidelity, I should note, also operates a brokerage division that earns hefty profits from stock traders.) You also need to invest more than "a small amount of study." Lynch worked 80 hours a week at investing!

A Midwest investment club that claims to have beaten the market's returns by a wide margin wrote an investing book, *The Beardstown Ladies' Common-Sense Investment Guide.* This club's philosophy, like Lynch's, is to invest in companies whose businesses you are familiar with and you can understand. (I discuss this book in Chapter 18.)

But such a simplistic investing approach can lead you to poor stock picks. For example, in his book, *Beating the Street,* published in 1993, Lynch advocated investing in restaurant chains' stocks: "Every region of the country has been the incubator for one of these small town successes that went on to capture the stomachs and wallets of the country: Luby's, Ryan's, and Chili's in the Southwest, Shoney's and Cracker Barrel in the Deep South, and Sizzler and Taco Bell in the Far West."

Students of the markets know that technology stocks led the stock market boom of recent years. If you bought into Lynch's methods, you may also have been more than disappointed with buying into the stocks of your favorite restaurant chain at the local strip mall. Sizzler, for example, has fallen on hard times with the heightened competition in the restaurant business. Sizzler stock has plunged 70 percent since 1993. Shoney's has plummeted from $25 down to $2. Remember that during this period the U.S. stock market has soared several hundred percent.

Although industry familiarity can, at times, supplement your choice of stocks, it's dangerous to base your investment decisions solely on your own knowledge and gut feelings. Allow me to introduce you to a company that attracted many people through this approach: Fresh Choice. The idea, and the restaurants based on it, is simple and understood by many. You enter the restaurants, which originated in California, and walk down a self-serving line, which offers salads and other fresh and healthy choices. A pasta bar, soups, breads, and even a self-service dessert bar greet hungry eyes. It's all you can eat for about seven bucks and because it's self-serve, you don't tip.

Fresh Choice went public in December 1992, with the cute trading symbol SALD. Over the next few months, it traded at around $23 per share, which represented a multiple of nearly 60 times earnings (P/E) — a whopping figure.

With Americans trying to eat healthier, how could you go wrong if you chose this stock? Brokerage analysts, many of whom work for firms that sold shares in Fresh Choice's initial public offering (IPO), engaged in a love fest for owning the stock. Almost every Wall Street analyst who followed the stock recommended buying it in the years following the (IPO), during which time its stock price bounced around between $25 to $30 per share while earnings steadily grew:

- Montgomery Securities said "buy."
- Morgan Grenfell called it a "must own."
- Dain Bosworth said to "buy."
- Rauscher Pierce Refsnes rated it a "buy" and one of their "two favorite picks" in the restaurant business. The firm said that the company was "uniquely positioned" and had a "unique concept."
- Seidler said, "We are excited by the growth prospects for Fresh Choice, and we project a five-year earnings per share growth rate of 35 percent. . . . We believe the stock represents a good value. . . ."
- Lead underwriter Alex Brown rated it a "strong buy" until July 1994, at which point it was merely downgraded to "buy." Prior to that time, Alex Brown said of Fresh Choice, ". . . an excellent company and an exciting concept."

In the second half of 1994, some major problems became apparent. Fresh Choice's expansion plan was poorly managed. Some new restaurants opened too close to existing ones and cannibalized sales. Even those new locations that weren't close seemed to cannibalize sales — it seemed that people who liked the idea had been driving a good distance to existing stores.

A warning sign that these analysts and investors should've heeded was that Fresh Choice refused to release same store sales, which would have allowed dissection of sales growth from existing stores versus the new locations that were opening. It's easy for an expanding company to increase sales by simply opening new locations. Meanwhile, existing locations can suffer declining revenue that is masked in the company's aggregate revenue figures. This is what happened at Fresh Choice.

Also, outside the confines of California, the chain met with an audience that wasn't as attuned to the type of food that Fresh Choice specialized in. The all-you-can-eat format, not surprisingly, attracted bigger eaters. People looking for less food, as many health-conscious eaters do, stayed away. As people tired of the same menu, the stores had difficulty retaining repeat customers.

As the company's profits sank, so too did the stock price. From a high of 32½ in March 1994, Fresh Choice's stock price plunged 84 percent in the next year and has continued to slide since — recently trading around $2 per share.

Although it may seem that I'm trying to scare you away from buying individual stocks, I'm not. But picking "good stocks," even those that seem easy to understand, isn't as easy as some people lead you to believe. Choosing a stock isn't as simple as visiting a restaurant chain, liking it, and then sitting back and getting rich watching your stock zoom to the moon.

If you invest in stocks, I think that you know by now that guarantees don't exist. But like many of life's endeavors, you can buy individual stocks in good and not-so-good ways. In the next chapter, I explain how to research and trade individual stocks.

Buying stock "direct" from companies

Over the years, increasing numbers of companies sell their stock directly to the public. For example, if you enjoy shopping at Home Depot and have researched the company and its stock, you may hold an interest in their direct stock purchase plan. Proponents of these direct stock purchase plans say that you can invest in stocks without paying any commissions. This isn't quite true and investing in such plans poses other challenges.

With Home Depot, for example, you need a minimum initial investment of $250. Buying stock "direct" isn't free — in the case of Home Depot, for example, you will be charged a $5 enrollment fee. Although that may not sound like much on a $250 investment, $5 represents 2 percent of your investment. For subsequent purchases, you pay the lesser of 5 percent of the amount invested or $2.50 plus 5 cents per share. And, although you can reinvest your dividends from Home Depot directly into buying more shares of its stock, you have to pay a fee for that as well — 5 percent of the amount that you invest (to a maximum of $2.50) plus 5 cents per share. If you want to sell your shares, you need to pay a fee to do that too — $5 plus 15 cents per share. Overall, these fees compare to what you would pay to buy stock through a discount broker (see Chapter 21). In fact, in some cases these fees are higher. For example, you can reinvest dividends at no cost through many discount brokers.

Some direct stock purchase plans entail even more hassle and cost than the type I just discussed. With other plans, you must buy your initial shares through a broker and then transfer your shares to the issuing company in order to buy more! Also, most direct stock purchase plans can't be done within retirement accounts.

Every time that you want to set up a stock purchase plan with a company, you must request and complete the company's application forms. If you go through the headache of doing so say, a dozen times, you're rewarded with receiving a dozen statements on a regular basis from each individual company. Frankly, because of this drawback alone, I prefer to buy stock through a discount brokerage account that allows centralized purchasing and holding of various stocks as well as consolidated tax-reporting statements.

A small number of companies offer investors the ability to reinvest dividends as well as make additional stock purchases at a discount of 1 to 5 percent from the current market price of their stock. Buying stock at a discount gets me more excited, but the previously listed drawbacks still apply. The companies that offer such plans tend to be smaller, run-of-the-mill utilities and banks, so you can't build a diversified, high-quality portfolio this way.

Skip direct stock purchase plans. If you want to buy good individual stocks, invest through your retirement accounts and in tax-friendly stocks outside your retirement accounts. In Chapter 7, I explain how to research for good companies. If you want to reinvest your dividends without cost, simply use one of the discount brokerage firms offering this service.

Ways Not to Buy Individual Stocks

You may be curious about other ways to buy individual stocks, but if I list those methods in this section, it's because I *don't* recommend using them. You can greatly increase your chances of success and earn higher returns if you avoid the commonly made stock investing mistakes that I present in this section.

Don't buy through commission-based brokers

Many investors make the mistake of investing in individual stocks through a broker who earns a living from commissions. Firms such as Prudential, Smith Barney, and Dean Witter employ armies of such brokers.

The standard pitch of these firms and their brokers is that they maintain research departments that monitor and report on stocks. Their brokers, using this research, tell you when to buy, sell, or hold. Sounds good in theory, but this "research" and system have significant problems.

Many brokerage firms happen to be in another business that creates enormous conflicts of interest in producing objective company reviews. You see, these investment firms also solicit companies to help them sell new stock and bond issues. To gain this business, the brokerage firms need to demonstrate enthusiasm and optimism for the company's future prospects.

Brokerage analysts who, with the best of intentions, write negative reports about a company find their careers hindered in a variety of ways. Some firms fire such analysts. Companies that the analysts criticize exclude the analysts from analyst meetings about the company. Analysts who know what's good for their career and their brokerage firm don't write disapproving reports.

Although investment insiders know that analysts are overly optimistic, little documented proof or people willing to talk on the record about this fact exist. One firm got caught encouraging its analysts via a memo not to say negative things about companies. As uncovered by *Wall Street Journal* reporter Michael Siconolfi, Morgan Stanley's head of new stock issues stated in a memo that the firm's policy needed to include "no negative comments about our clients." The memo also stated that any analyst's changes in a stock's rating or investment opinion, "which might be viewed negatively" by the firm's clients, had to be cleared through the company's corporate finance department head!

Various studies of the brokerage firm's stock ratings have conclusively demonstrated that, from a predictive perspective, most of their research is barely worth the cost of the paper that they print it on. In Chapter 7, I recommend independent research reports that beat the brokerage industry track record hands down. In Chapter 21, I cover the important issues that you need to consider when you select a good broker.

Pass on initial public offerings

As I explain in Chapter 4, an initial public offering (IPO) occurs when a company offers new stock to the investing public. If you bought Microsoft's IPO back in the spring of 1986 and held on to it until today, you'd be a mighty happy camper, having made about a 500-times return on your money. If you had invested $10,000 in Microsoft stock back then, it would have grown to approximately $5 million! Similar tales abound for investors who scooped up shares of McDonald's and other companies that have grown into behemoth, multibillion-dollar, worldwide enterprises.

So you'd like to buy shares of the next Microsoft and McDonald's. Who wouldn't? Investors and brokers who tell you that they bought IPOs that became big successes have a lot in common with some people who go fishing and tell you about the days that the fish were really biting and they landed some big catches. But you hear less or nothing at all about the hours and days that they caught nothing or small fry.

Even factoring in the Microsoft's and McDonald's of the world, IPOs as a group are poor investments. You read that right! Two university professors,

Jay Ritter and Timothy Loughran, went to the trouble of documenting the performance of the thousands of IPOs that have happened since 1970. Here's what they found:

Average annual return on the IPO stocks	5 percent per year
Average annual return on comparable stocks	12 percent per year

If you buy IPOs, you miss out on a lot of personal investing profits.

Consider what happened with Boston Chicken, which was touted as the next McDonald's. Boston Chicken went public with a bang in November 1993, less than a full year after commencing operations. Though the stock was to be originally issued for $10 per share, it soared to more than $25 per share and closed its first day of trading up more than 142 percent to $24¼ per share. At its high that first day of $25½ per share, the company's stock sold for astronomical 364 times earnings (P/E).

Boston Chicken is a chain of restaurants (now named Boston Market) that serves moderately priced, healthier home-cooked meals. The main menu offering is rotisserie chicken, which is supposedly lower in fat and calories than its fried counterpart. Dinner at Boston Market can also include veggies, salad, and the like.

The company's concept of food that's healthier than fast food is hardly unique (see my discussion of Fresh Choice earlier in this chapter), and their menu's healthy claim is open to debate. The restaurant industry trend is slowly moving away from fattier, cholesterol-laden foods — or at least dressing up the menu to make it appear healthier. Kentucky Fried Chicken changed its name to KFC in part to obfuscate the "fried" part of their offerings. My nutritionist friends tell me that chicken is still chicken, and many of the other Boston Market dishes are not so healthy. KFC, interestingly enough, copied Boston Chicken's chicken offerings. (Say that five times fast!)

In little more than a year, Boston Chicken's stock price declined 47 percent from its November 1993 high. Since then, it has struggled back to about the price where investors like you and me could first jump into it and now is languishing under $1 per share! During the same time that Boston Chicken's stock has plunged, the U.S. stock market has more than tripled.

If Boston Chicken experiences the kind of long-term growth and profitability that McDonald's has over the years, its stock may do well over the long term. Expecting this kind of success, however, is foolhardy. The company is on an aggressive growth plan and utilizes the team that built Blockbuster Video. Smart managers can replicate their success in different businesses, but running a video store is indeed different than a restaurant.

Is Netscape the next Microsoft?

In recent years, the hype over the Internet has reached a fevered pitch, and much like television and radio stocks in the late 1920s, technology stocks have been red hot in the late 1990s stock market. Before Netscape went public in August 1995, it was dubbed the next Microsoft. Netscape makes software that allows computer users to access the Web sites on the World Wide Web. The company boasts a 70 to 90 percent market share. Netscape also provides software to companies that put their stuff on the Internet. Netscape boasted former hotshot executives from Silicon Graphics and McCaw Cellular and a supposed Bill Gates-style technology wunderkind in Marc Andreessen, who was all of 23 when he joined Netscape.

Originally, the investment bankers who wanted to bring Netscape stock public planned to sell the company stock at $6.50 per share and later raised it to $14. On August 9, when the company went public, the demand to buy stock was stronger than the power of a 100-foot-high tidal wave. The stock opened at $35.50 per share and soon zoomed to more than $37. (Only large institutional investors that buy lots of other investment banker IPOs can get shares of a hot IPO at the offering price, which in this case was $28.) Within months it skyrocketed to $87.

At the time that it went public, Netscape was in business for less than a year and a half and had only $16 million in revenues for the first half of 1995. Furthermore, the company was losing money. When the stock traded at $174 per share, Netscape had a total stock market value of an unbelievable $6.5 billion. This amount exceeded the market value at that time of numerous companies — such as Quaker Oats, Charles Schwab, Clorox, Kmart, and Nordstrom — that had revenues of billions of dollars and profits of hundreds of millions of dollars and had been in business for a decade or more!

Unlike Netscape, most companies normally wait until they have several years under their belt and a track record of profits before going public. When Microsoft went public in 1986, it had turned a profit since 1982 and sold for a P/E of around 20. (Microsoft earned a profit of $24 million on sales of $140 million the prior year.) Although Microsoft's stock initially sold for about three times its annual revenue after its IPO, within months of its IPO Netscape sold for an astounding 198 times revenue. (And Netscape sold at a P/E of more than 400 times its 1996 estimated earnings.)

Many Netscape investors overlooked Netscape's formidable competitors, including Microsoft. As for the company's astronomical market share, many investors didn't know that these market share numbers were based partly upon the number of free copies of the company's software distributed via the Internet.

Only time will tell if Netscape is the next Microsoft. Since I wrote about Netscape in the first edition of this book, the stock has struggled to surpass the value that it achieved in those early initial months of trading. Not until early 1999 — more than three years after the IPO — did the stock price hit a new high. Netscape stock has performed worse than the average stock during this time period.

Don't invest in IPOs. Instead of IPO standing for initial public offering, it's more apt to mean, "it's probably overpriced." It's easy to see a decade later which companies dominate their industries and whose stock prices rocket skyward. However, picking these companies in advance is a difficult task. Investing in IPOs has proven to be a losing stock market investment strategy. Not surprisingly, most IPOs come to market when the market is high so that companies can maximize their take. Don't buy IPOs and run from them as fast as you can in an overheated market. If you can get in on the ground floor of an IPO (buy at the offering price), that's a sign that the stock is a turkey or a small, risky offering.

Don't day trade or short-term trade

Unfortunately (for themselves), some investors track their stock investments closely and believe that they need to sell after short holding periods — in months, weeks, or even days. With the growth of Internet and computerized trading, such shortsightedness has taken a turn for the worse as more investors now engage in a foolish process known as *day trading,* where you buy and sell a stock within the same day!

If you hold a stock only for a few hours or a few months, you're not investing but gambling. Specifically, the following lists the numerous drawbacks that I see to short-term trading:

- ✔ **Higher commissions.** Although the commission that you pay to trade stocks has declined greatly in recent years, especially through online trading (which I discuss in Chapter 19), the more you trade, the more of your investment dollars go into a broker's wallet. Commissions are like taxes — once collected, your dollars are forever gone and your return is reduced.

- ✔ **More taxes (and tax headaches).** When you invest outside of tax-sheltered retirement accounts, you must report every time that you buy and then sell a stock on your annual income tax return. After you make a profit, you must part with a good portion of it through the federal and state capital gains tax that you owe from the sale of your stock. If you sell a stock within one year of buying it, the IRS and most state tax authorities consider your profit short term and you owe a higher rate of tax than if you hold your stock for more than a year. Holding your stock for more than a year qualifies you for the favorable long-term capital gains tax rate (see Chapter 22). The return that you keep (after taxes) is more important than the return that you make (before taxes).

✔ **Lower returns.** If stocks increase in value over time, long-term buy-and-hold investors will enjoy the fruits of the stock's appreciation. However, when you jump in and then out of stocks, your money spends a good deal of time *not* invested in stocks. The overall level of stock prices in general and individual stocks in particular sometimes rise sharply during short periods of time. Thus, day-traders and other short-term traders inevitably miss stock run-ups. The best professional investors who I know don't engage in short-term trading for this reason (as well as because of the increased transaction costs and taxes that such trading inevitably generates).

✔ **Lost opportunities.** Most of the short-term traders that I've met over the years spend inordinate amounts of time researching and monitoring their investments. During the late 1990s, I began to hear of more and more people who quit their jobs so they could manage their investment portfolio full time! Some of the firms that sell day trading seminars advocate that you can make a living trading stocks. Your time is clearly worth something. Put your valuable time into working a little more on building your own business instead of wasting all those extra hours each day and week watching your investments like a hawk, which hampers rather than enhances your returns.

✔ **Poorer relationships.** Time is our most precious commodity. In addition to the financial opportunities that you lose when you indulge in unproductive trading, you need to consider the personal consequences. Like drinking and smoking, short-term trading is an addictive, gambling like behavior. Spouses of day-traders and other short-term traders report unhappiness over how much more time and attention their mates' place on their investments over themselves. And, what about the lack of attention that day-traders and short-term traders give friends and other relatives? (See the sidebar to help determine if you or a loved one has a gambling addiction.)

How a given stock performs in the next few hours, days, weeks, or even months may have little to do with the underlying financial health and vitality of the company's business. In addition to short-term swings in investor emotions, oftentimes unpredictable events (the emergence of a new technology or competitor, analyst predictions, changes in government regulation, and so on) push stocks one way or another for short periods of time.

As I say throughout this part of the book, stocks are intended as long-term holdings. You shouldn't buy into stocks if you don't plan on holding them for at least five, and preferably seven to ten years or more. When stocks suffer a setback, it may take months or even years for them to come back.

Do you or a loved one have an investment gambling problem?

Some gamblers spend their time at the racetrack, while you can find others in casinos. Increasingly though, you can find gamblers at their personal computers tracking and trading stocks.

In addition to the strong stock market performance in recent years, companies that often tout themselves as educational institutions suck legions of novice investors into dangerous practices. Masquerading under such pompous names as institutes or academies, these firms purport to teach you how to get rich day trading stocks. Perhaps you've heard their ads on the radio, seen them on stock market cable television channels, or on the Internet for "seminars" or other "training" methods. All you have to do is part with several thousand dollars for the training, but the only people getting rich are the owners of such seminar companies.

The non-profit organization Gamblers Anonymous developed the following 20 questions to help you identify if you or someone you know is a compulsive gambler that needs help:

1. Did you ever lose time from work or school due to gambling?

2. Has gambling ever made your home life unhappy?

3. Did gambling affect your reputation?

4. Have you ever felt remorse after gambling?

5. Did you ever gamble to get money with which to pay debts or otherwise solve financial difficulties?

6. Did gambling cause a decrease in your ambition or efficiency?

7. After losing did you feel you must return as soon as possible and win back your losses?

8. After a win did you have a strong urge to return and win more?

9. Did you often gamble until your last dollar was gone?

10. Did you ever borrow money to finance your gambling?

11. Have you ever sold anything to finance gambling?

12. Were you reluctant to use "gambling money" for normal expenditures?

13. Did gambling make you careless of the welfare of your family?

14. Did you ever gamble longer than you had planned?

15. Have you ever gambled to escape worry or trouble?

16. Have you ever committed, or considered committing, an illegal act to finance gambling?

17. Did gambling cause you to have difficulty in sleeping?

18. Do arguments, disappointments, or frustrations create within you an urge to gamble?

19. Did you ever have an urge to celebrate any good fortune by a few hours of gambling?

20. Have you ever considered self-destruction as a result of your gambling?

According to Gamblers Anonymous, compulsive gamblers typically answer yes to seven or more of these questions.

Don't buy penny stocks

Even worse than buying stocks through a broker whose compensation depends on what you buy and how often you trade is purchasing penny stocks through brokers that specialize in such stocks. As I explain in Chapter 4, tens of thousands of smaller-company stocks trade on the over-the-counter market. Some of these companies are quite small and sport low prices per share that range from pennies to several dollars, hence the name penny stocks.

Here's how penny stockbrokers typically work. Many of these firms purchase prospect lists of people who have demonstrated a propensity for buying other lousy investments by phone. Brokers are taught to first introduce themselves by phone and then call back shortly thereafter with a tremendous sense of urgency about a great opportunity to get in on the "ground floor" of a small, but soon to be stellar company. Not all of these companies and stocks have terrible prospects, but many do.

The biggest problem with buying penny stocks through such brokers is that they are grossly overpriced. Just as you don't make good investment returns purchasing jewelry that's marked up 100 percent, you don't have a fighting chance to make decent money on penny stocks that the broker may flog with similar markups. The individual broker that cons you into "investing" in such cheap stocks gains a big commission, which is why he continues to call you with "opportunities" until you send him a check. Many brokers in this business that possess records of securities' violations also possess an ability to sell, so they have no problem gaining employment with other penny stock peddlers.

A number of penny stock brokerage firms are known for engaging in manipulation of stock prices, driving up prices of selected shares to suck in gullible investors and then leaving the public holding the bag. These firms may also encourage companies to issue new overpriced stock that their brokers can then flog to people like you.

If you remember or know of a fellow by the name of Robert Brennan, then you know that he is the granddaddy of this reptilian business. I won't bore you with all the details, except to say that after more than a decade of financial shenanigans, Brennan was ordered by a judge to pay investors more than $70 million for all the bad stuff that he did. Pending suits may lead to hundreds of millions of dollars in additional judgments against Brennan's companies.

I remember when Brennan ran his infamous "Come Grow With Us" television ads in which he hopped out of a helicopter. Brennan was always nicely dressed and maintained a polished image. In addition to being in the penny stock trade, it's interesting to note that Brennan owned a horse race track and wanted to get into the casino business. All of these businesses share the same characteristics that they don't involve investments and they stack the deck against the gullible members of the public that they hoodwink.

Don't buy broker-sold limited partnerships

At their peak, brokers and brokers who masquerade as financial planners sold more than $10 billion per year of limited partnerships (LP). Prudential Securities sold more of these terrible investments than any other organization and has suffered the most pain as a result, having to cough up hundreds of millions of dollars as a result of lawsuits. I explain in Chapter 3 the fundamental problems (mainly outrageous commissions and fees) that drain your LP investment returns.

The Keys to Stock Market Success

Anybody, no matter what their educational background, IQ, occupation, income, or assets, can make good money through stock investments. Over long periods of time, you can expect to earn an average 10 percent per year total return by investing in stocks.

To maximize your chances of stock market investment success, do the following:

- ✔ **Don't try to time the markets.** Anticipating where the stock market and specific stocks are heading is next to impossible, especially over the short term. Economic factors, which are influenced by thousands of elements, as well as human emotions, determine stock market prices. Be a regular buyer of stocks with new savings. As I discuss in Chapter 5, buy more stocks when they are on sale and market pessimism is running high.

- ✔ **Diversify.** Invest in the stocks of different-size companies in varying industries around the world. When you assess the performance of your investments, look at your whole portfolio at least once a year and calculate your total return after expenses and trading fees.

- ✔ **Keep trading costs, management fees, and commissions to a minimum.** These represent a big drain on your returns. If you invest through a broker or "financial advisor" who earns a living on commissions, odds are high that you're paying far more than you need to be and you're likely receiving biased advice.

- ✔ **Pay attention to taxes.** Like commissions and fees, federal and state taxes are another major investment "expense" that you can minimize. Contribute most of your money to your tax-advantaged retirement accounts. You can invest your money outside of retirement accounts, but keep an eye on taxes (see Chapter 3). Calculate your annual returns on an *after*-tax basis.

✔ **Don't overestimate your ability to pick the big winning stocks.** One of the best ways to invest in stocks is through mutual funds (see Chapter 9), where you can hire an experienced, full-time money manager at a low cost to perform all the investing grunt work for you. If you want to invest in individual stocks, stay clear of initial public offerings, particularly trendy popular ones and ones that are issued during times of an overheated stock market.

Chapter 7

Researching Individual Stocks

• •

In This Chapter

▶ The inside scoop on *Value Line*

▶ What those annual reports really mean

▶ Deciphering 10-Ks, 10-Qs, and proxies

▶ Placing trades

• •

*I*n the earlier chapters in this part, I cover how the financial markets work and what drives stock prices. I also explain the different ways that you can buy stocks such as through stock mutual funds or on your own. This chapter provides a crash course in researching individual companies and their stocks. Be sure that you consider your reasons for taking this approach before you head down the path of picking and choosing your own stocks. If you haven't already done so, please read Chapter 6 now to help you better understand the process of purchasing stocks without the help of a broker or mutual fund.

If you decide to tackle the task of researching your own stocks, you don't need to worry about finding enough information to peruse. You will encounter the problem of information overload. You can literally spend hundreds of hours researching and reading information on one company alone. Therefore, unless you're financially independent and you wish to spend nearly all of your productive time investing, you need to focus on where you can get the best bang for your buck and time.

Leveraging from Others' Research

If you were going to build a house, I bet that you wouldn't literally try to do it on your own. You may likely see if you can obtain some sort of kit or plans drawn up by others who have built many houses. You can do the same when it comes to picking individual stocks.

The following publications offer useful columns and commentary, sometimes written by professional money managers, on individual stocks: *Barron's, Business Week, Forbes, Kiplinger's,* and the *Wall Street Journal.*

Another way to discern what smart money managers buy is to look at their portfolios. I'm not suggesting that you invade their privacy or ask rude questions. The best mutual fund managers are required to disclose at least twice a year what stocks they hold in their portfolio. You can call the fund companies and ask them to send their most recent semiannual reports that detail their stock holdings to request mutual fund manager information (see Chapter 9 for more information on stock mutual funds). Morningstar also offers a stock software program that allows you to see which mutual funds hold large portions of a given stock that you may be researching.

Value Line

You can also subscribe or borrow from your local library the *Value Line Investment Survey,* a helpful publication that I've been acquainted with for more than two decades. The beauty of *Value Line's* service is that it condenses the key information and statistics about a stock (and the company behind the stock) to a single page.

Value Line's securities analysts have tracked and researched stocks since the Great Depression. Their analysis and recommendation track record is quite good, and the analysts are beholden to no one. Many professional money managers use *Value Line* as a reference because of its comprehensiveness.

Suppose that you're interested in investing in Starbucks, the retail coffee house operator. You've seen their stores go up in strip malls around your neck of the woods and you figure that if you're going to shell out more than $3 for a cup of their flavored hot water, you may as well share in the profits and growth of the company. You look up the current stock price (I explain how to do that later in this chapter if you don't know how) and are happy to see that it's a mere $36 per share.

Take a look at the important elements of a *Value Line* page for Starbucks, shown in Figure 7-1.

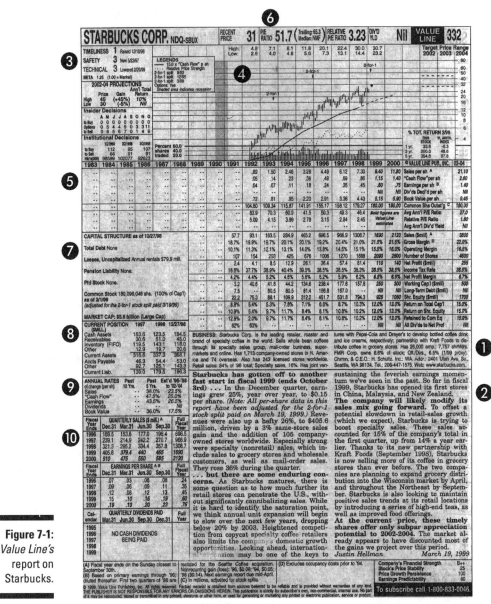

Figure 7-1:
Value Line's
report on
Starbucks.

1. **Business.** This section describes the business(es) that Starbucks partici-
   pates in. You can see that Starbucks is the largest retailer of specialty
   coffee in the world. Although 84 percent of the company's sales come
   from retail, note that 16 percent come from other avenues — such as mail
   order and supermarket sales. You also find details about joint ventures,

such as Starbucks' partnership with Pepsi to develop and sell a bottled coffee drink. In this section, you also can see that the senior executives and directors of the company own a decent share (6.5 percent) of the stock — it's good to see these folks have a financial stake in the success of the company and stock.

2. **Analyst assessment.** A securities analyst (in this case, Justin Hellman) follows each *Value Line* stock. An analyst focuses on specific industries and follows a few dozen stocks. This section provides the analyst's summary and commentary of the company's current situation and future plans. While Mr. Hellman makes note of the company's recent strong performance, he notes that growth of the U.S. retail stores is likely to slow in the next few years. Starbucks is expanding overseas, however, and is also seeking growth from specialty businesses. Adding it all up, Hellman notes that the stock price possesses a relatively high value, factoring in likely expected future growth.

3. ***Value Line's* rating.** *Value Line* provides a numerical ranking for each stock's timeliness (expected performance) over the next year. One is highest, five is lowest, and only about 5 percent of all stocks receive these extreme ratings. A two rating is above average and a four rating below average, and about one-sixth of the ranked stocks receive each of these ratings. All remaining stocks, a little more than half the total ranked, get the average three rating.

The safety rank works the same way as the timeliness rating, with one representing the best and least-volatile stocks and the most-financially stable companies. Five is the worst safety ranking and is given to the most-volatile stocks and least-financially stable companies.

Although I've never been a fan of predictions and short-term thinking (one year is a very short period of time for the stock market), historically, *Value Line's* system holds one of the best overall track records according to the *Hulbert Financial Digest,* which tracks the actual performance of investment newsletter recommendations. However, you shouldn't necessarily run out and buy Starbucks because of its high ranking. Just keep in mind that higher-ranked stocks within *Value Line* have historically outperformed those without such ratings.

4. **Stock price performance.** The graph shows you the stock price's performance over the past decade or so. The highest and lowest point of the line on the graph indicates the high and low stock price for each month. At the top of the graph you see the year's high and low prices. Starbucks stock has steadily risen since it first issued stock in 1992. (The small box in the lower right-hand corner of the graph shows you the total return that an investor in this stock earned over the previous 1, 3, and 5 years and how those returns compare with the average stock. This graph shows you that Starbucks has risen sharply and has beaten the average stock's return in recent years.)

The graph also shows how the price of the stock moves with changes in the company's cash flow. Cash flow is an important measure of a company's financial success and health — it's different than "net profits" that the company reports for tax purposes. For example, the tax laws allow companies to take a tax deduction each year for the depreciation (devaluation) of the company's equipment and other assets. Although depreciation is good because it helps lower a company's tax bill, subtracting it from the company's revenue gives an untrue picture of the company's cash flow (money coming in minus money going out). Thus, in calculating a company's cash flow, depreciation is not subtracted from revenue.

5. **Historic financials.** This section shows you up to 12 to 18 years of financial information on the company (in Starbuck's case, you get less information because the company went public just eight years ago).

   Book value per share indicates the value of the company's assets, including equipment, manufacturing plants, and real estate, minus any liabilities. Book value gives somewhat of a handle on the amount that the company can sell for if it has a "going out of business sale." I say somewhat because the value of some assets on a company's books isn't correct. For example, some companies own real estate, bought long ago, that is worth far more than the company's current financial statements indicate. Conversely, some manufacturers with equipment find that if they had to dump some equipment in a hurry, it's likely that they would need to sell the equipment at a discount to entice a buyer.

   The book value of a bank, for example, can mislead you if the bank makes loans that won't be paid back, and the bank's financial statements don't document this fact. All of these complications with book value are why full-time, professional money managers exist. (If you want to delve more into a company's book value, you need to look at other financial statements, such as the company's annual report that I discuss in the "Annual reports" section, later in this chapter.)

   For some companies (not Starbucks), *Value Line* also provides another useful number in this section — the *market share,* which indicates the portions of the industry that the company has captured in a given year. A sustained slide in a company's market share is a dangerous sign that may indicate its customers are leaving for other companies that presumably offer better products at lower prices. But that doesn't mean that you should avoid investing in a company that possesses such problems. You can produce big returns if you can identify companies that reposition and strengthen their product offerings to reverse a market share slide.

6. **P/E ratio.** This tells you that Starbuck's sells at a P/E of 51.7 because of its recent stock price and earnings. This P/E is quite high relative to the overall market (you can see that Starbuck's P/E is 3.23 times that of the overall market). To understand the importance of P/E in evaluating a stock, please refer to Chapter 5.

7. **Capital structure.** This section summarizes the amount of outstanding stocks and bonds that the company possesses. Remember that when a company issues these securities, it receives capital (money). What is

most useful to examine in this section is the company's debt. If a company accumulates a lot of debt (as many governments have), the burden of interest payments can create a real drag on profits. If profits stay down for too long, debt can even push some companies into bankruptcy.

Figure 7-1 shows you that Starbuck's has no outstanding debt. For most companies, this section delineates between short-term and long-term debt. *Short-term debt* is debt that is due within one year while *long-term* simply refers to debt that has to be paid back in more than a year. So how do you know if this is a lot, a little, or just the right amount of debt? For companies with debt, *Value Line* calculates "Long-term interest earned" that compares a company's annual profits to the yearly interest payments on its long-term debt. For example, if a company has long-term interest earned of 4.5x, that means that the company's most recent yearly profits can cover the interest payments on their long-term debt for about 4½ years.

Possessing a larger cushion to cover debt is more important when the company's business is volatile. Total interest coverage represents a similar comparison of profits to interest owed for all the debt that a company owes, not just long-term debt. This number tells you the number of years that the company's most recent annual profits can cover interest on all the company's debt. Warning signs for times interest earned numbers include a steep decline in this number over time and profits that cover less than one year's worth of interest.

8. **Current position.** This section provides a quick look at how the company's *current assets* (*current* meaning an asset that can be sold and converted into cash within a year relatively easily) compare with its *current liabilities* (debts due within the year). Trouble may be brewing if a company's current liabilities exceed or are approaching their current assets.

Some financial analysts calculate the *quick ratio*. The quick ratio ignores inventory when comparing current assets to current liabilities. A company may have to dump inventory at a relatively low price if it needs to raise cash quickly. Thus, some analysts argue, you need to ignore inventory as an asset.

9. **Annual rates.** This nifty section can save wear and tear on your calculator. The good folks at *Value Line* calculate rates of growth (or shrinkage) on important financial indicators, such as revenue and earnings (profits) over the past five and ten years. *Value Line* also lists their projects for the next five years.

Projections can prove highly unreliable, even from a research firm as good as *Value Line*. In most cases, the projections assume that the company continues as it has in the most recent couple of years.

How to obtain *Value Line* reports

The least costly way to obtain *Value Line* pages on stocks that interest you is to visit your local library. Most libraries that include decent business sections subscribe to it.

If you want your own copy of *Value Line* to read in the comfort of your home, *Value Line* (800-634-3583) offers a ten-week trial subscription to their *Value Line Investment Survey* for $55. An annual subscription costs $570. At the start of your subscription, you receive a rather large binder, divided into 13 sections, that includes the most recent reports on the 1,700 large- and medium-size company stocks that this publication tracks. Every week, you receive a new packet of reports that replaces one of the 13 sections. Thus, at the end of 13 weeks, you have new reports on all the stocks.

The trial subscription is a great place to start your research because you receive all the current reports plus the next ten weeks' worth of updates for a reasonable fee. You can also see

how much use you get out of the reports. The trial offer is only available to each household once every three years.

Value Line also offers an expanded investment survey that contains reports on 1,800 additional smaller companies. Unlike traditional *Value Line* pages, these pages include no analyst commentary or projections. You can't just subscribe to the expanded survey. A trial subscription to both surveys costs $100. A full-year subscription to both surveys costs $695.

If you simply want the Value Line report on one or two stocks, you can order single page reports from Value Line at a steep $30 each. Given the relatively low cost of the trial, you may as well order the trial and receive all 1,700 reports. Ordering copies of single pages only makes sense if you've purchased a trial within the last three years and you can't order another trial for a while. Or, you can try to interest a friend in the publication and have them order it for you!

10. **Quarterly financials.** For the most recent years, *Value Line* shows you an even more detailed quarterly breakout of sales and profits that may disclose changes that annual totals mask. You can also see the seasonality of some businesses. Starbucks, for example, tends to have its slowest quarter in the winter (quarter ending March 31). This makes sense if you figure that many of the customers who frequent Starbuck's coffee shops do so as they walk around town, which people tend to do less of on a blustery winter day.

The information in *Value Line* reports is in no way inside information. Look at these reports the same way that you review a history book — they're useful background information that can keep you from repeating common mistakes.

Annual reports

After you review the *Value Line* page on a company and you want to dig further into financial documents, the next step is to ask yourself why. Why do you want to torture yourself so?

I successfully completed one of the supposedly better M.B.A. programs (Stanford's) and took more than my fair share of accounting and finance courses. Over the years, I've gotten to know investment managers and financial analysts who research companies. Although some financial documents aren't that difficult to read (I show you how in this section), interpreting what they mean in respect to a company's future isn't easy. Identifying trouble *before* other investors do is a skill that many professional investors haven't mastered — if you can identify trouble early, go manage other people's money!

All publicly traded companies must annually file certain financial documents. Consider reviewing these documents to enhance your understanding of a company's businesses and strategies rather than for the predictive value that you hope they provide.

The first of such documents that companies produce that contain useful information is the *annual report.* This yearly report provides standardized financial statements as well as management's discussion about how the company has performed and how it plans to improve its performance in the future. If you're a bit of the skeptical sort like I am, you may think, "Aren't the company's officials going to make everything sound rosy and wonderful?"

To a certain extent yes, but not as badly as you may think. First, a large portion of annual reports include the company's financial statements, which an accounting firm must audit. However, audits don't mean that companies and their accounting firms can't legally structure the company's books to make them look rosier than they really are. And some companies have pulled the wool over their auditors' eyes who became unwitting accomplices in producing false financial figures.

Also keep in mind that more than a few companies have been sued for misleading shareholders with inflated forecasts or lack of disclosure of problems. Responsible companies try to present a balanced and, of course, hopeful perspective in their annual reports. Most companies' annual reports are written by non-techno geeks, so you have a decent chance of understanding them.

Financial and business highlights

The first section of most annual reports presents a description of a company's recent financial highlights and business strategies. You can use this information to learn about the businesses that the company is in and where the company is heading. For example, in Figure 7-1 *Value Line* mentioned that

Starbucks was also in the specialty sales business. The annual report can provide more detail about Starbucks' specialty business.

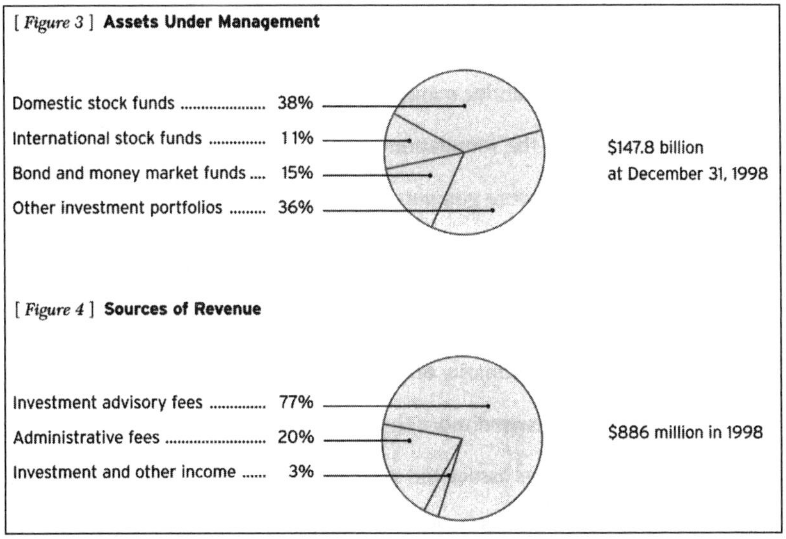

[*Figure 3*] **Assets Under Management**

Domestic stock funds 38%
International stock funds 11%
Bond and money market funds 15%
Other investment portfolios 36%

$147.8 billion
at December 31, 1998

[*Figure 4*] **Sources of Revenue**

Investment advisory fees 77%
Administrative fees 20%
Investment and other income 3%

$886 million in 1998

Figure 7-2:
T. Rowe Price's annual report shows where the company's revenues come from.

Source: T. Rowe Price Associates, Inc. 1998 Annual Report to Stockholders

Okay, enough about the coffee business — I want to expose you to another industry. T. Rowe Price is a publicly traded investment company that offers some decent mutual funds. In Figure 7-2, you can see that T. Rowe Price manages money in a variety of investment funds that provide investment advisory and other fees.

Balance sheet

You can find a company's hard-core financials in the back portion of most annual reports. You can find many of these same numbers in *Value Line* reports, except you get more specific details in the company's annual report. All annual reports contain a *balance sheet,* which is a snapshot summary of all the company's assets and liabilities. The balance sheet covers the company's assets and liabilities from the beginning of the year to the last day of the company's year-end, which is typically December 31. Some companies use a fiscal year that ends at other times of the year.

A company's balance sheet resembles a personal balance sheet. The entries, of course, look a little different because you likely don't own things like manufacturing equipment. And if you read my *Personal Finance For Dummies* book, you know that I'm against listing personal property, such as furniture and cars, as assets. (Do you plan to sell these things to raise money for retirement, home buying, and so on?) Figure 7-3 shows a typical corporate balance sheet.

Consolidated Balance Sheets

(in thousands)

	December 31,	
	1997	1998
ASSETS		
Cash and cash equivalents (Note 1)	$ 200,409	$ 283,838
Accounts receivable (Note 5)	86,795	100,702
Investments in sponsored mutual funds (Note 1)	173,729	192,914
Partnership and other investments (Note 7)	19,030	26,597
Property and equipment (Note 2)	142,497	166,612
Other assets (Note 6)	23,607	26,121
	$ 646,067	$ 796,784
LIABILITIES AND STOCKHOLDERS' EQUITY		
Liabilities		
Accounts payable and accrued expenses	$ 30,722	$ 45,737
Accrued compensation and retirement costs	49,694	56,757
Income taxes payable (Note 3)	19,102	15,308
Dividends payable	10,039	12,012
Minority interests in consolidated subsidiaries	49,837	52,666
Total liabilities	159,394	182,480
Commitments and contingent liabilities (Notes 2, 6 and 7)		
Stockholders' equity (Notes 1, 4 and 7)		
Preferred stock, undesignated, $.20 par value - authorized and unissued 20,000,000 shares	—	—
Common stock, $.20 par value - authorized 200,000,000 shares in 1997 and 500,000,000 shares in 1998; issued 59,097,705 shares in 1997 and 120,183,266 shares in 1998	11,819	24,037
Capital in excess of par value	30,707	41,073
Retained earnings	415,279	517,631
Accumulated other comprehensive income	28,868	31,563
Total stockholders' equity	486,673	614,304
	$ 646,067	$ 796,784

The accompanying notes are an integral part of the consolidated financial statements.

Figure 7-3:
The balance sheet from T. Rowe Price's annual report.

Source: T. Rowe Price Associates, Inc. 1998 Annual Report to Stockholders

Assets

The assets section lists the following items that the company holds or owns that are of significant value:

- ✔ **Cash.** I think that you know what cash is. Lest you think that there are stacks of green bills sitting around in corporate vaults, rest assured that companies invest this money to earn interest. Many items are explained in more detail in explanatory notes that follow these financial statements. Note 1 explains that T. Rowe Price eats its own cooking — the company keeps its extra cash in its own money market funds.

- ✔ **Accounts receivable.** This is money that is owed to the company. Figure 7-2 shows the note that explains that T. Rowe Price collects fees for the funds that it manages. Just as your employer pays you at the month's end for your work during the entire month, the company is paid for services previously provided. If you're paid $4,000 monthly at month's end and you prepare your own personal balance midmonth, you can list a salary of $2,000 as an asset because it's money due you that you haven't yet received.

  As companies grow, their accounts receivable usually do too. Watch out for cases where the receivables grow faster than the sales (revenue). This growth may indicate that the company is having problems with its products' quality or pricing. Unhappy customers pay more slowly or demand bigger price discounts.

- ✔ **Investments.** In addition to cash, some companies may invest in other securities, such as bonds and stocks. Just as with your own personal situation, companies usually invest money that they don't expect to use in the near future. (As with the company's cash investments, the explanatory note explains that T. Rowe Price invests in their own bond and stock funds.)

- ✔ **Property and equipment.** All companies need equipment to run their business. This equipment can include office furniture, computers, real estate they own, and manufacturing machinery that the company uses to make its products. Equipment becomes less valuable over time, so the company considers this depreciation as a cost of doing business each year. Therefore, if a company ceases buying new equipment, this entry on the balance sheet gradually decreases because the depreciation is subtracted from the value of the equipment.

- ✔ **Goodwill and other assets.** One of the assets that doesn't show up on most companies' balance sheets is their *goodwill*. Companies work hard through advertising, product development, and service to attract and retain customers. *Name-brand recognition* is a term that you sometimes hear thrown around. Companies can't put a value on the goodwill that they've generated, but when they purchase (acquire) another firm, some of the purchase price is considered goodwill. Specifically, if a company is acquired for $100 million but it has a net worth (assets minus liabilities) of just $50 million, the extra $50 million goes to goodwill. The goodwill then becomes an asset which, like equipment, is depreciated or amortized over the years ahead.

"Other assets" is a catchall category that can include some stuff that can make your eyes glaze over. For example, companies keep a different (yes, this is legal) set of books for tax purposes. Not surprisingly, companies do this because the IRS allows, in some cases, more deductions than what the company is required to show from an accounting standpoint on their financial statements. (If you were a company, wouldn't you want your shareholders, but not the IRS, to see gobs of profits?) Companies treat tax deferment as an asset until the IRS receives more of its share down the road.

Note: Manufacturing and retail companies also track and report *inventory* (the product that hasn't yet been sold) as an asset. Generally speaking, as a business grows, so too does its inventory. If inventory grows more quickly than revenue, such growth may be a warning sign. This growth can indicate that customers are scaling back purchases and that the company miscalculated and overproduced. It can also be a leading indicator of an obsolete or inferior product offering.

Liabilities

This section summarizes all the money that the company owes to others.

✔ **Accounts payable.** When companies make requests to purchase things for their business, they sometimes have time to pay the bills. As with inventory and accounts receivable, accounts payable generally increases with a company's increasing revenue.

If accounts payable increases faster than revenue, it can indicate a problem. On the other hand, that increase can also be a sign of good financial management. The longer that you take to pay your bills, the longer you have the money in your pocket working for you.

✔ **Accrued compensation and retirement costs.** This line tallies money that the company must someday pay to its employees. For example, many larger firms maintain pension plans. These plans promise workers who retire with at least five years of service a monthly income check in retirement. Thus, the company must reserve this money that they owe and list it as a liability or debt that they will someday have to pay.

✔ **Income taxes payable.** Companies are in business to make a profit and as they earn those profits, they need to reserve a portion to pay income taxes. As I explained earlier, some of the taxes that the company owes can be caused by accounting differences between the company's financial statements and those filed with the IRS.

✔ **Dividends payable.** Not all companies pay dividends (see Chapter 4) to their shareholders. But those companies that do pay dividends typically declare the dividend several weeks in advance of when they actually owe the dividend. During this interim period, the company lists the dividends that are promised but not yet paid as a liability.

Stockholders' equity

The difference between a company's assets and liabilities is known as *stockholders' equity*. Stockholders' equity is what makes balance sheets always balance. When companies issue stock, for example, they receive cash, which they then list as an asset, for the stock sold.

Companies divide stock proceeds between *par value* and *capital in excess of par value.* In the case of T. Rowe Price, the par value is $0.20 per share. Par values are arcane . . . and largely meaningless.

Income statement

The other big financial statement in an annual report is the income statement (see Figure 7-4).

Revenue

Revenue is simply the money that the company receives from its customers as compensation for its products or services. Just as you can earn income from your job(s) as well as investments and other sources, a company can make money from a variety of sources as well. In the case of mutual fund provider T. Rowe Price, the firm collects fees (investment advisory and administrative) for the mutual fund investments that it manages on behalf of its customers as well as privately managed money for wealthy individuals and institutions that are not its customers. The company also receives income from its own money that it has invested.

Ideally, you want to see a steady or accelerating rate of growth in a company's revenues. If a company's revenue grows more slowly, you need to inquire why. Is it because of poor service or product performance, better competitor offerings, ineffective marketing, or all of the above?

For companies with multiple divisions or product lines, the annual report may detail the revenue of each product line in a later section. If it doesn't, check out some of the other financial statements that the next section, "Other useful reports with quirky names," recommends. Examine what spurs or holds back the company's overall growth, and what different businesses the company operates in. Look for businesses that were acquired but don't really fit with the company's other business units as a red flag. Large companies that have experienced stalled revenue growth sometimes try to "enter" new businesses through acquisition but then don't manage them well because they don't understand the keys to their success.

Consolidated Statements of Income

(in thousands, except per-share amounts)

	Year ended December 31,		
	1996	1997	1998
REVENUES (NOTES 1 AND 5)			
Investment advisory fees	$ 451,307	$ 588,014	$ 684,296
Administrative fees	117,803	144,906	173,321
Investment and other income	16,960	22,037	28,525
	586,070	754,957	886,142
EXPENSES			
Compensation and related costs (Notes 4 and 6)	196,925	253,676	304,376
Advertising and promotion	58,291	66,954	73,044
Occupancy and equipment (Note 7)	51,850	68,018	83,374
International investment research fees	39,328	47,105	48,066
Other operating expenses (Note 7)	52,205	54,445	64,468
	398,599	490,198	573,328
Income before income taxes and minority interests	187,471	264,759	312,814
Provision for income taxes (Note 3)	72,608	101,208	118,676
Income from consolidated companies	114,863	163,551	194,138
Minority interests in consolidated subsidiaries	16,410	19,154	19,998
Net income	$ 98,453	$ 144,397	$ 174,140
Earnings per share			
Basic	$ 0.86	$ 1.24	$ 1.46
Diluted	$ 0.79	$ 1.13	$ 1.34

The accompanying notes are an integral part of the consolidated financial statements.

Figure 7-4:
T. Rowe
Price's
income
statement.

When researching retail stores, such as restaurant chains (for example, McDonald's) or clothing stores (such as The Gap), examine the revenue changes that come from opening new locations versus the changes at existing locations, sometimes referred to as *same stores*. Be concerned if you find that a company's revenue growth largely comes from opening new locations rather than growth at existing locations.

Expenses

If only you got to keep all the income that you make. Just as personal income taxes, housing, food, and clothing expenses gobble up much of your personal income, company expenses use up much and sometimes all of a company's revenue.

Even healthy, growing businesses can get into trouble if their expenses balloon faster than their revenue. Well-managed companies stay on top of their expenses during good and bad times. Unfortunately, it's easy for companies to get sloppy during good times.

It's particularly useful to examine each category of expenses relative to (in other words, as a percentage of) the company's revenue to see which grow or shrink. As a well-managed and financially healthy company grows, expenses as a percentage of revenue should decrease. As this happens, like in T. Rowe Price's case, profits as a percentage of revenue increase.

Not all expense categories necessarily decrease. As you can see from T. Rowe Price's expenses, the company's compensation costs to employees increased. Table 7-1 shows T. Rowe Price's expenses as a percentage of revenue during a recent three-year period.

Table 7-1   T. Rowe Price's Expenses as a Percentage of Revenue

Expense	1996	1997	1998
Compensation	33.6%	33.6%	34.3%
Advertising & Promotion	9.9%	8.9%	8.2%
Occupancy & Equipment	8.8%	9.0%	9.4%
Int'l investment research	6.7%	6.2%	5.4%
Other operating expenses	8.9%	7.2%	7.3%

Fundamental versus technical analysis

Throughout this chapter and the last, I talk a lot about the financial statements of a company — balance sheets, revenues, expenses, earnings, price-earnings ratios, and so on. Analyzing financial statements and making investing decisions based on them is known as *fundamental analysis.*

But another school of stock market analysis, known as *technical analysis,* exists. Folks who employ technical analysis like to examine chart patterns, volume, and all sorts of indicators that have little, if anything, to do with the underlying stock.

Technicians say things like, "Stock XYZ has a major support area at $20 per share" or "Stock ABC has broken out above $30 per share." Although it may be a bit extreme to say that all the technicians that have ever existed have never produced anything of value, you can

safely ignore this school of thinking. In fact, ignoring the technicians will likely *increase* your stock market profits. Why? Because technical analysis thinking encourages a trader's, not an investor's, mindset.

Not surprisingly, most technicians come from one of two camps. Many technical analysts work for brokerage firms and write daily, weekly, or monthly assessments of the entire stock market and some individual stocks. Recommendations and advice change over time, and the result is that you trade more. Curiously, these brokerage firms make more money the more you trade!

Investment newsletter writers are the other big advocates of this Ouija-board approach to investment management. Again, it's a great system for the newsletter writers that hook you on a $200-per-year monthly newsletter.

The net result of revenues increasing faster than expenses is a fatter bottom line. In T. Rowe Price's case, pre-tax income rose from 32.0 percent to 35.3 percent of revenue between 1996 and 1998. When you examine how a company's profits change relative to total revenue received, focus on operating income. Sometimes companies experience one-time events that can change profits temporarily. Companies usually list these one-time events in the section under expenses.

Last, but not least, and of great importance to shareholders, is the calculation of the earnings per share. Higher profits per share help fuel a higher stock price.

Other useful reports with quirky names

In addition to annual reports, companies produce other financial statements that you may want to peruse. You can generally obtain these from the company for free or from the Securities and Exchange Commission Web site (see Chapter 18).

10-Ks

10-Ks are an expanded version of an annual report. Most investment professionals read the 10-K instead of the annual report because the 10-K contains additional data and information, especially for a company's various divisions and product lines. Also, 10-Ks contain little of the verbal hype that you sometimes find in annual reports. The 10-K is probably one of the most objective reports that a company publishes. If you're not intimidated by annual reports, or you want more company meat, go for it!

Look at T. Rowe Price's 10-K (Figure 7-5) and consider how much more you can learn about a business. For example, the 10-K shows the amount of money that the company manages in various types of mutual funds.

10-Qs

10-Qs provide information similar to the 10-K but on a quarterly basis. 10-Qs are worthwhile if you like to read a reasonably detailed discussion by management of the latest business and financial developments at the company. However, I recommend leaving the research to *Value Line's* analysts.

The financial data in these reports is unaudited and not of great use for the long-term investor. If you want to watch your investments like a hawk and try to be among the first to detect indications of financial problems (easier said than done), this report is required reading.

Many companies go back to restate their quarterly financials. Remember that the accountants haven't approved these numbers. Sometimes companies take their financial lump in one quarter to get problems behind them, so one bad quarter doesn't necessarily indicate a harmful long-term trend.

Proxies

The final corporate document that you may want to review is the annual *proxy statement,* which is sent out in advance of a company's annual meeting. The proxy statement contains some of the more important financial information and discussions that you can find in the 10-K. It also contains information on other corporate matters, such as the election of the board of directors. Directors, who are usually corporate executives, lawyers, accountants, and other knowledgeable luminaries, serve as a sounding board, counselor, and sometimes overseer to the management team of a company.

The proxy statement becomes much more important when a company faces a takeover or some other controversial corporate matter, such as the election of an alternative board of directors.

The proxy tells you who serves on the board of directors as well as how much they and the executives of the company are paid. At annual meetings, where the board of directors discuss proxy statements, shareholders sometimes get angry and ask why the executives are paid so much when the company's stock price and business underperform the competition.

```
<PAGE> 6
  Balanced (1991)                                      $ 1,650
  Dividend Growth (1992)                                 1,338
  Mid-Cap Growth (1992)                                  3,310
  Small-Cap Stock (1992)                                 1,153
  Blue Chip Growth (1993)                                4,330
  Media & Telecommunications (1993)                        246
  Capital Opportunity (1994)                               125
  Personal Strategy - Balanced (1994)                      421
  Personal Strategy - Growth (1994)                        194
  Personal Strategy - Income (1994)                        213
  Value (1994)                                             775
  Health Sciences (1995)                                   317
  Financial Services (1996)                                224
  Mid-Cap Value (1996)                                     221
  Diversified Small-Cap Growth (1997)                       70
  Real Estate (1997)                                        28
  Tax-Efficient Balanced (1997)                             32
  Extended Equity Market Index (1998)                       21
  Total Equity Market Index (1998)                          61
 INTERNATIONAL:
  International Stock (1980)                             10,142
  International Discovery (1988)                            193
  European Stock (1990)                                  1,549
  New Asia (1990)                                          622
  Japan (1991)                                             181
  Latin America (1993)                                     182
  Emerging Markets Stock (1995)                             72
  Global Stock (1995)                                       49
  International Growth & Income (1998)                       2
 BOND AND MONEY MARKET FUNDS:
  New Income (1973)                                      2,103
  Prime Reserve (1976)                                   5,100
  Tax-Free Income (1976)                                 1,481
  Tax-Exempt Money (1981)                                  764
  U.S. Treasury Money (1982)                               927
  Tax-Free Short-Intermediate (1983)                       458
  High Yield (1984)                                      1,704
  Short-Term Bond (1984)                                   347
  GNMA (1985)                                            1,146
  Tax-Free High Yield (1985)                             1,344
  California Tax-Free Bond (1986)                          220
  California Tax-Free Money (1986)                         102
  International Bond (1986)                                926
  New York Tax-Free Bond (1986)                           210
  New York Tax-Free Money (1986)                          104
  Maryland Tax-Free Bond (1987)                          1,039
  U.S. Treasury Intermediate (1989)                        263
  U.S. Treasury Long-Term (1989)                           310
  Global Government Bond (1990)                             42
  New Jersey Tax-Free Bond (1991)                          118
  Short-Term U.S. Government (1991)                        136
```

Figure 7-5:
T. Rowe Price's 10-K details the company's business.

Source: T. Rowe Price Associates, Inc. 1998

Getting Ready to Invest in Stocks

Amidst the chorus of self-anointed gurus that tell you that you can make fat profits if you pick your own stocks, I sometimes think that I'm a lone voice that urges caution and sensible thinking. Unless you are extraordinarily lucky or unusually gifted at analyzing company's and investor behavior, you won't earn above average returns if you select your own stocks.

Keep to a minimum — ideally no more than 20 percent of your invested dollars — the amount that you dedicate to individual stock investments. I encourage you to do such investing for the educational value and enjoyment that you derive from it, not because you smugly think you're so much smarter than the best professional money managers. (If you want to learn more about analyzing companies, read the chapters in Part IV on small business as well as investing resource chapters in Part V.)

Understanding stock prices

Most major newspapers print a listing of the prior day's stock prices (unless you live in an area with a late afternoon paper that publishes that day's activity). Daily business papers such as the *Wall Street Journal* and *Investor's Business Daily* publish stock prices daily. Likewise, just about every major financial site on the Internet offers stock prices (usually for free as a lure to get you to visit their site). To view a stock price quote online, all you need is the security's trading symbol (which you look up the company's name to obtain, if you don't already know it).

For a real thrill, you can stop by a local brokerage office and see the current stock quotes whizzing by on a long, narrow screen on a wall. Stock market channels on cable television often have this ticker-tape screen running on the bottom of your television tube. Many brokerage firms also maintain publicly accessible terminals (that look a lot like a personal computer) on which you can obtain current quotes for free.

Figure 7-6 is a typical example of the kinds of information that you can find in daily price quotes in papers and online.

Figure 7-6:
An online stock quote for IBM.

| Stock | 52 Week | | Last Price | Change | High | Low | Open | Volume | Yield | PE |
	High	Low								
IBM	199 1/4	104 3/16	182 3/8	Down 3 15/16 (-2.1%)	183 5/8	181 1/16	183 1/2	4,366,600	0.5%	27.76

This listing examines the stock price information for the behemoth technology company, International Business Machines (also known as Big Blue or IBM). After the name of the company, you see the trading symbol, IBM, which is the code that you and brokers use to look up the price on computer-based quotation systems.

The next two lines indicate the high ($199¼) and low ($104⅜) trading prices for IBM during the past 52 weeks.

Last price indicates the most recent price that the stock traded at and "Change" indicates how that price differs from the previous day's close. In this case, you can see that the stock was down about 4 points (2 percent) from the prior day's close.

High, Low, and Open show, respectively, the highest and lowest prices that the stock traded at during the day and the opening trade price.

Volume indicates the number of shares that traded during the most recent trading day. (To conserve space, many newspapers indicate the volume in hundreds of shares — in other words, you must add two zeros to the end of the number to arrive at the actual number of shares).

Yield indicates the effective percentage yield that the stock's dividend produces. To calculate the effective yield, divide the dividend by the current stock price. Thus, IBM shareholders can expect to receive a dividend worth about 0.4 percent of the current stock value. (Some stock price listings will actually show you the current dividend, which in this case is $0.88 per share, that the company pays yearly to shareholders. Most companies actually pay out one-quarter of their total annual dividend every three months.)

The P/E ratio, as I explain in Chapters 4 and 5, measures the price of IBM's stock relative to the company's earnings or profits. Now you know how to read the stock pages!

Placing your trade through a broker

Once you decide to buy some stock, you generally need a broker (I explain in Chapter 6 a somewhat administratively hassled way to buy direct from some companies). As I explain in Chapter 10, discount brokers are the best way to go — they take your orders and charge far less than conventional brokers who pay their brokers on commission.

After you decide which discount broker you want to use, request (by phone or via the Internet) an account application package for the type of account that you desire (non-retirement, IRA, Keogh, and so on). Complete the forms (call the firm's 800 number or visit a branch office if you get stuck) and mail or bring them back to the discounter.

When it comes time to place your order, simply call the discount broker and tell them what you want to do (or use your touch-tone phone or computer to place your order). My advice is to place what's known as a *market order*. Such an order instructs your broker to buy you the amount of stock that you desire, 100 shares for example, at the current and best (lowest) price available.

Alternatively, you can try to buy a desired stock at a specific price — for example, you can place a purchase order at $32 per share when the stock's last trade was $33 per share. This type of order is known as a *limit order* and is good today, four months from now, or until you cancel it. I don't recommend that you try this tactic because it requires you to hope and gamble that the stock drops a little before it rises. If the stock simply rises from its current price of $33 per share or drops down to $32⅛ before it goes on a big increase, you'll kick yourself. If you think that the stock is a good buy for the long haul, then go buy it. If you don't think it's a good buy, then don't buy it.

One final word of advice. Try to buy stock in reasonable-size chunks, such as 100 shares. Otherwise, commissions gobble a large percentage of the small dollar amount that you invest. If you don't have enough money to build a diversified portfolio all at once, don't sweat it. Diversify over time. Purchase a chunk of one stock after you have enough money accumulated and then wait to buy the next stock until you've saved up another chunk to invest.

Chapter 8

Only Bankers Get Wealthy Lending Money

● ●

In This Chapter

▶ Getting the most out of a bank

▶ Going with bonds: Which type is best for you?

▶ Making the individual bond versus bond mutual fund choice

▶ Understanding guaranteed-investment contracts and private mortgages

● ●

*I*n Chapters 1 and 2, I discuss the major types of investments and their potential risks and returns. *Lending investments* are those in which you lend your money to an organization, such as a company or government, that typically pays you a set or fixed rate of interest.

If you really desire to make your money grow, lending investments aren't for you. However, even the most-aggressive investors possess a legitimate need for placing some of their money into lending investments. Table 8-1 shows some of the logic behind lending investments and when such investments make and don't make sense.

Table 8-1	The Logic of Lending Investments
Consider Lending Investments if . . .	*Consider Ownership Investments when . . .*
You need current income.	You don't need or want much current income.
You need to access money within five years.	You're investing for the long-term (seven to ten-plus years).
Investment volatility makes you a wreck or you just want to cushion some of the volatility of your other investments.	You don't mind/can ignore significant ups and downs.
You don't need to make your money grow after inflation and taxes.	You need more growth to reach your goals.

Lending investments are everywhere — at your local bank, brokerage, insurance, and mutual fund companies. Lending investments that you may have heard of include bank accounts (savings and certificates of deposit), Treasury bills and other bonds, bond mutual funds, mortgages, and guaranteed-investment contracts.

In this chapter, I walk you through these investments and explain what's good and bad about each of them and when you should and shouldn't use them. I also tell you what to look for and look out for when you compare them.

Banks: The Cost of Comfort

Putting your money in a bank may make you feel safe for a variety of reasons. If you're like most people, your first investing experience was at your neighborhood bank where you established a checking and savings account. Depending on your family, this event may have happened as early as elementary or junior high school or as late as college or post-college.

Part of the comfort of keeping money in the bank stems from the fact that the bank is where many of our parents first steered us financially. Also, at a relatively large branch, often within walking distance of your home or office, bank branches have vaults, security monitoring cameras, and barriers in front of the tellers. Most of these latter accoutrements shouldn't make you feel safer about leaving your money with the bank — they are needed because of bank robberies and the preponderance of guns in our society — think about that the next time you pay a visit to your local bank.

Large bank branches with all the trimmings cost a lot of money to operate. Guess where that money comes from? From you, of course! That's one of the reasons why the interest rates that banks pay is often so poor in comparison to equally safe alternatives.

The realities of bank insurance

Some people are consoled by the Federal Deposit Insurance Corporation insurance that comes with bank accounts. It's true that if your bank fails, your account is insured up to $100,000. So what, I say. Any Treasury bond is issued and backed by the federal government — the same, $5 trillion-debt-ridden organization that stands behind the FDIC. Plenty of other equally safe lending investments yield higher returns.

Just because the federal government stands behind the banking FDIC system doesn't mean, in the event of a bank failure, that a 100 percent certainty exists that you'll be paid back in full or paid back with dollars worth anywhere near what a dollar is worth today. Banks fail and will continue to fail. During the latter 1980s and early 1990s, hundreds of insured banks and savings and loans failed annually (more than 500 alone in 1989). Although you're insured for $100,000 in a bank, if the bank crashes, you'll likely wait quite a while to get your money back — and you may well get less interest than you thought you would.

Any investment that involves lending your money to someone else or to some organization carries risk. That includes putting your money into a bank or buying a Treasury bond that the federal government issues. Although I'm not a doomsayer, any student of history knows that governments and civilizations fail. It's not a matter of *whether* they will fail; it's a question of *when*.

The overused certificate of deposit (CD)

Other than savings accounts, banks also sell certificates of deposit (CDs). CDs are without a doubt the most overused bank investment around. The attraction is that you get a higher rate of return on a CD than on a bank savings or money market account. And unlike a bond, which I soon discuss, a CD's principal value does not fluctuate. Of course, CDs also give you the peace of mind afforded by the government's FDIC insurance program.

The reason that CDs pay higher interest rates than savings accounts is that you commit to tie up your money for a period of time, such as 6, 12, or 24 months. The bank pays you 5 to 6 percent and then turns around and lends your money to people through credit cards, auto loans, and the like and charges the borrower an interest rate of 10-plus percent. Not a bad business, eh?

When you tie up your money in a CD, you make a sacrifice. If you want it back before the CD matures, a hefty penalty (about six months' interest) is shaved from your return. With other lending investments, such as bonds and bond mutual funds, discussed later in this chapter, you can access your money without penalty and generally at little or no cost.

In addition to penalties for early withdrawal, CDs yield less than a high-quality bond with a comparable maturity (for example, two, five, or ten years). Often, the yield difference is 1 percent or more, especially if you don't shop around and simply buy CDs from your local bank where you keep your checking account.

A final and perhaps fatal flaw of CDs comes from high-tax bracket investors who purchase them outside of their retirement accounts. The interest on CDs is fully taxable at the federal and state levels. Bonds, by contrast, are available (if you desire) in tax-free (federal and/or state) versions.

You can earn higher returns and have better access to your money in bonds than in CDs. Bonds make especially good sense when you're in a higher tax bracket and would benefit from tax-free income on your non-retirement account investments. CDs make the most sense when you know, for example, that you can invest your money for one year, after which you need the money for some purchase that you expect to make. Just make sure that you shop around to get the best interest rate. If having the U.S. government insurance gives you peace of mind, take a look at Treasury bonds, which I discuss later in this chapter. Treasury bonds (also known as *Treasuries*) often pay more interest than the vast majority of CDs available.

The money fund alternative to savings accounts

I have a checking account at a local bank. I use that account to pay household bills and to access cash through automated teller machines. I keep enough money in my checking account to pay the bills but not a lot extra. I don't keep extra savings in the bank. You need to think long and hard about keeping extra savings in the bank (if you do). Bank savings accounts generally pay pretty crummy interest rates.

Keep your checking account at your local bank but not your extra savings. Money market funds, which are a type of mutual fund (other common funds focus on bonds or stocks), are a great place to keep your extra savings. Money market funds offer a higher yielding alternative to bank savings and bank money market deposit accounts.

Money market funds, which are offered by mutual fund companies, are unique among mutual funds because they don't fluctuate in value and maintain a fixed $1 per share price. As with a bank savings account, your principal investment in a money market fund does not change in value. While you invest your money in a money fund, it earns dividends (which is just another name for the interest you would receive in a bank account).

Money fund advantages

The best money market mutual funds offer several significant benefits over bank savings accounts. The biggest advantage is higher yields. Money market mutual funds pay higher yields because they don't have the high overhead that banks do. The most efficient mutual fund companies (I discuss them in the next chapter) don't have scads of branch offices on every street corner. Another reason that banks can get away with paying lower yields is that they know that many depositors, perhaps including you, believe that the FDIC insurance that comes with a bank savings account makes it safer than a money market mutual fund. Also, the FDIC insurance is an expense that banks ultimately pass onto their customers.

Another advantage of money funds over bank accounts is that money funds come in a variety of tax-free versions. So if you're in a high tax bracket (see Chapter 3), tax-free money funds offer you something that bank accounts don't.

Another useful feature of money market mutual funds is the ability to write checks, without charge, against your account. Most mutual fund companies require that the checks that you write be for larger amounts — typically at least $250. They don't want you using these accounts to pay all your small household bills because checks cost money to process.

Money market funds are a good place to keep your emergency cash reserve of at least three to six months' living expenses. They're also a great place to keep money awaiting investment elsewhere in the near future. If you're saving money for a home that you expect to purchase soon (in the next year or so), a money fund can be a safe place to accumulate and grow the down payment. You don't want to risk placing such money in the stock market, because the market can plunge in a relatively short period of time.

Just as you can use a money market fund for your personal purposes, you can open a money market fund for your business. I have one for my business. You can use this account to deposit checks that you receive from customers, to hold excess funds, and to pay bills via the check-writing feature.

A few money funds, such as those that brokerage cash management accounts at firms such as Charles Schwab, Jack White, and Fidelity offer, allow you to write for any size amount and can completely replace a bank checking account. You can also establish money market funds that allow unlimited check writing and that you can use for household checking purposes as well. (The brokerage firms that offer accounts with this capability downplay your ability to do this.) With these types of money market funds, you can leave your bank altogether because these brokerage accounts often come with debit cards that you can use at bank ATMs for a nominal fee.

Money funds lack insurance

Higher yields, tax-free alternatives, and check writing. It almost sounds too good to be true. What's the catch? Good money market funds really don't have any, but you need to know about an important difference between bank accounts and money market mutual funds. Money funds are not insured. As I discuss earlier in this chapter, bank accounts come with FDIC insurance that protects your deposited money up to $100,000. So, if a bank fails because it lends too much money to people and companies that go bankrupt or abscond with the funds, you should get your money back from the FDIC.

The lack of FDIC insurance on a money fund shouldn't trouble you. Mutual fund companies can't fail because they have a dollar invested in securities for every dollar that you deposit in their money fund. By contrast, banks are required to have available just 12 cents for every dollar that you hand over to them.

A money market fund's investments could decline slightly in value, which can cause the money fund's share price to fall below a dollar. A few cases have occurred where money market funds bought some bad investments. However, in each and every case except one, the parent company running the money fund infused cash into the affected fund, thus enabling it to maintain the $1 per share price.

One money market fund did "break the buck." It didn't take money in from people like you or me, but was run by a bunch of small banks for themselves. This money market fund made some bone-headed investments. The share price of the fund declined by 6 percent, and the fund owners decided to disband the fund; they didn't bail it out, because they would be repaying themselves.

Stick with larger mutual fund companies if you're worried about the lack of FDIC insurance. They have the financial wherewithal and the largest incentive to save a floundering money fund. Fortunately, the larger fund companies have the best money funds anyway. You can find more details about money funds in the next chapter.

Bonds: Jargon for IOU

In the 1920s, Andrew Mellon said, "Gentlemen prefer bonds." I've never figured out why, and I'm convinced that Mr. Mellon wasn't serious or sober when he said this. My observation is that conservative investors prefer bonds. (That is conservative when it comes to taking risk, not politics.) Otherwise aggressive investors that seek diversification or investments for shorter-term financial goals also prefer bonds. The reason: Bonds offer higher yields than bank accounts without as much volatility as the stock market.

A bond is similar to a certificate of deposit (CD). With a five-year CD, for example, a bank agrees to pay you a set interest rate, say, 6 percent. If all goes according to plan, at the end of five years of earning the 6 percent annual interest, you get back the principal that you originally invested.

Bonds work in a similar fashion. For example, you can purchase a bond, scheduled to mature five years from now, that a company such as the retailing behemoth Wal-Mart issues. A Wal-Mart five-year bond may pay you 7 percent interest. As long as Wal-Mart doesn't have a financial catastrophe and after five years of receiving interest payments on the bond, Wal-Mart returns your original investment to you. So, in effect, you're loaning your money to Wal-Mart (instead of the bank when you deposit money in a bank account).

The worst that can happen to your bond investment is that Wal-Mart's business goes into a tailspin and the company ends up in financial ruin — also known as bankruptcy. If that happens, you may lose all of your original investment and miss out on some of the expected interest.

But bonds that high-quality companies such as Wal-Mart issue are quite safe — they rarely default. Heck, many companies have been around longer than you've been alive. Besides, even if every now and then a big company goes under, you don't have to invest all of your money in just one or two bonds. If you own bonds in many companies (which you can easily do through a good bond mutual fund) and one bond unexpectedly takes a hit, it affects only a small portion of your portfolio. And, unlike a CD which comes with stiff early withdrawal penalties, you can generally sell your bonds anytime you desire at minimal cost.

Bond investors accept the risk of default because bonds pay higher interest rates than the bank. If you take extra risk and forsake the FDIC insurance, you should receive a higher rate of interest investing in bonds. Remember that when you invest in bank savings accounts and CDs, you're paid less interest in part because of the overhead of the bank branches as well as the cost of the FDIC insurance.

The uses for bonds

Investing in bonds is a time-honored way to earn a better rate of return on money that you don't plan to use within the next couple of years or more. As with stocks, bonds can generally be sold any day that the financial markets are open. Because their value fluctuates though, you're more likely to lose money if you're forced to sell your bonds sooner rather than later. In the short term, the bond market can bounce every which way; but in the longer term you're more likely to receive your money back with interest.

Bonds generally pay you more than bank savings and money market mutual funds, but with a catch. As I discuss later in this chapter, bonds are riskier than money market funds and savings accounts because their value can fall if interest rates rise. However, bonds tend to be more stable in value than stocks (I cover the risk and return of bonds and stocks in Chapter 2).

Don't put your emergency cash reserve into bonds — that's what a money market fund or bank savings account is for. But don't put too much of your longer-term investment money in bonds, either. As I show in Chapter 2, bonds are lousy investments for making your money grow. Growth-oriented investments, such as stocks, real estate, and your own business, hold the potential to build real wealth.

The following list provides some common financial goals and reasons why investing some money in bonds can make sense:

- ✔ **A major purchase** that won't happen for at least two years, such as the purchase of a home or some other major expenditure. Shorter-term bonds may work for you as a higher-yielding and slightly riskier alternative to money market funds.

- ✔ **Diversification.** Bonds don't move in tandem with the performance of other types of investments, such as stocks. In fact, in a terrible economic environment (such as occurred during the Great Depression), bonds may appreciate in value while riskier investments such as stocks plunge.

- ✔ **Retirement investments.** You may invest some of your money in bonds as part of a longer-term investment strategy, such as for retirement. You need to have an overall plan about how you want to invest your money, sometimes referred to as an *asset allocation strategy* (see Chapter 3). Aggressive, younger investors should keep less of their retirement money in bonds than older folks who are nearing retirement.

- ✔ **Income-producing investments.** If you're retired or not working, bonds can be useful because they are better at producing current income than many other investments.

The differences among bonds

Bonds aren't as complicated and unique as people, but they're certainly more complex than a bank savings account. And, thanks to some shady marketing practices by some investing companies and salespeople who sell bonds, you have your work cut out for you while trying to get a handle on what many bonds really are and how they differ from their peers. The major ways that bonds differ from one another follow so that you can make educated bond purchases.

To whom are you lending your money?

Bonds differ from one another according to the type of organization that issues them — in other words, what kind of organization you lend your money to. The following lists the major options and when each option may make sense for you.

Treasury bonds

Treasuries are IOUs from the biggest debtor of them all, the U.S. Federal Government. The types of Treasury bonds include Treasury bills (which mature within a year), Treasury notes (which mature between one and ten years), and Treasury bonds (which mature in more than ten years). These distinctions and delineations are arbitrary — you don't need to know them for an exam.

Treasuries pay interest that is state tax-free but federally taxable. Thus, they make sense if you want to avoid a high state income tax but not a high federal income tax bracket. However, most people in a high state income tax bracket also happen to be in a high federal income tax bracket. Such high tax bracket investors may be better off in municipal bonds (explained in the next section), which are both federal and state tax-free.

The best use of Treasuries is in place of bank CDs. If you feel secure with the federal government insurance that a bank CD provides, check out a Treasury bond. Treasuries that mature in the same length of time as a CD almost always pay the same or better interest rate. If you hunt around, you may stumble upon a bank that pays a slightly higher interest rate than a comparable Treasury bond. Just remember that bank CD interest is fully taxable, whereas a Treasury's interest is state tax-free. Unless you really shop for a bank CD, you will likely earn a lower return on a CD than on a Treasury. I explain later in the chapter how to purchase Treasury bonds.

Municipal bonds

Municipal bonds are state and local government bonds that pay interest that's federally tax-free and state tax-free to residents in the state of issue. For example, if you live in California and buy a bond issued by a California government agency, you don't owe California state or federal income tax on the interest.

The government organizations that issue municipal bonds know that the investors who buy municipals don't have to pay most or any of the income tax that is normally required on other bonds — which means that the issuing governments can get away with paying a lower rate of interest.

If you're in a high tax bracket (31 percent or higher for federal tax) and you want to invest in bonds outside tax-sheltered retirement accounts, you can end up with a higher after-tax yield from a municipal bond (often called *muni*) than a comparable bond that pays taxable interest. If you're in the 28 percent federal bracket, you may still come out ahead with munis (you need to compare the yield on a given municipal bond to the after-tax yield on a comparable taxable bond). At less than 28 percent, don't invest in munis because you should net more interest, even after paying taxes, from a taxable bond.

International bonds

You can buy bonds outside the country that you call home. If you live in the U.S. for example, you can buy most of the bonds that I describe in this chapter from foreign issuers as well. International bonds are riskier to you because their interest payments can be offset by currency price changes.

Although the prices of foreign bonds tend not to move in tandem with U.S. bonds and protect against a declining U.S. dollar and therefore offer some diversification value, foreign bonds are not a vital holding for a diversified portfolio. Foreign bonds are generally more expensive to purchase and hold than comparable domestic bonds.

Some people worry about the impact that passage of a flat tax on their municipal bonds may impose. Under some of the proposed versions of the flat tax, all interest earned on investments wouldn't be taxed. Thus, muni bonds would lose their tax-free advantage versus other bonds. If such a flat tax were to pass, the price of municipal bonds, particularly longer-term ones, could fall significantly. Unless a Republican wins the White House at the same time that Republicans control Congress, the passage of such a measure is remote. Even then, municipal bond holders aren't likely to take such a change lying down. That's why, like many radically proposed reforms in the tax laws, a flat tax is likely to end up in the scrap heap.

Corporate bonds

Companies such as McDonald's, Macy's, and IBM issue corporate bonds. Corporate bonds pay interest that's fully taxable. Thus, they're appropriate for investing inside retirement accounts. Only lower tax bracket investors should consider buying such bonds outside a tax-sheltered retirement account (higher-bracket investors should instead consider municipal bonds). Later in the chapter, I show you how to read the newspaper listings for such bonds. If you buy corporate bonds through a well-managed mutual fund, an approach I advocate, you don't need to read the newspaper listings.

Mortgage bonds

Remember that mortgage you took out when you purchased your home? Well, you can actually purchase a bond to invest in your mortgage! Many banks actually sell their mortgages as bonds in the financial markets to allow other investors to invest in them. The repayment of principal on such bonds is usually guaranteed at the bond's maturity by a government agency, such as the Government National Mortgage Association (GNMA, also known as. Ginnie Mae) or the Federal National Mortgage Association (FNMA, also known as Fannie Mae).

Convertible bonds

Convertible bonds are hybrid securities — they're bonds that you can convert under specified circumstance into a preset number of shares of stock in the company that issued the bond. Although these bonds do pay interest, their yield is lower than non-convertible bonds because convertibles offer you the upside potential of being able to make more money if the underlying stock rises.

Likelihood of default

In addition to who issues them, bonds differ from one another in terms of the creditworthiness of the issuer. Every year, billions of dollars worth of bonds default. To minimize investing in bonds that default, purchase high-credit quality bonds. Credit rating agencies, such as Moody's, Standard & Poor's, and Duff & Phelps rate the credit quality and likelihood of default of bonds.

The credit rating of a bond depends on the issuer's (company or government) ability to pay back its debt. Bond credit ratings are usually done on some sort of a letter-grade scale where AAA is the highest rating, with ratings descending through AA and A, followed by BBB, BB, B, CCC, CC , C, and so on. AAA- and AA-rated bonds are considered "high-grade" or "high-credit quality." Such bonds possess little chance — a fraction of 1 percent — of default.

Bonds rated A and BBB are considered "general" grade or quality. Junk bonds (known more by their marketed name, *high yield*) are rated BB or lower. Junk bonds are more likely to default — perhaps as many as a couple of percent per year actually default.

You may ask yourself why any right-minded investor would buy a bond with a low credit rating. Companies pay a higher interest rate on lower-quality bonds to attract investors. The lower a bond's credit rating and quality, the higher the yield you can and should expect from such a bond. Poorer quality bonds though, are not for the faint of heart because they are generally more volatile in value.

 In addition to paying attention to the credit quality of the bonds that you buy, make sure that you diversify. Don't put all your money earmarked for corporate bonds into just one or two corporate bonds. Bond mutual funds are a great way to invest in bonds because they typically invest in dozens of bonds. I don't recommend buying individual junk bonds — only consider investing in these through a junk bond fund (see Chapter 9).

Maturity

Maturity simply means the time at which the bond pays you back — next year, in 5 years, in 30 years, and so on. You need to care how long it takes a bond to mature. Why? Because a bond's maturity gives you a good (although far from perfect) sense of how volatile a bond may be if interest rates change.

Suppose that you're considering investing in two bonds that the same organization issues and both yield 7 percent. The bonds differ from one another only in when they will mature: One is a 2-year bond and the other a 20-year bond. If interest rates were to rise just 1 percent (from 7 percent to 8 percent), the 2-year bond might fall about 2 percent in value whereas the 20-year bond could fall approximately 5 times as much — 10 percent.

If you hold a bond until it matures, you get your principal back unless the issuer defaults. In the meantime, however, if interest rates fall, bond prices rise. The reason is simple: If the bond that you hold is issued at, say, 7 percent and interest rates on similar bonds rise to 8 percent, no one (unless they don't know any better) wants to purchase your 7 percent bond. The value of your bond has to decrease enough so that it effectively yields 8 percent.

Not all bonds make regular interest payments. Zero coupon bonds are sold at a substantial discount to its future maturity value. Thus, an investor in a zero-coupon bond implicitly earns interest as the value of the bond should rise over time to reach full value by maturity. Zero-coupon bonds are highly sensitive to interest rate changes, which is why I don't recommend them.

Bonds are generally classified by the length of time until maturity:

- **Short-term bonds** mature in the next few years.
- **Intermediate-term bonds** come due within three to ten years.
- **Long-term bonds** mature in more than 10 years and generally up to 30 years. Although rare, a number of companies issue 100-year bonds! A number of railroads did, as well as Disney and Coca-Cola in recent years. Such bonds are quite dangerous to purchase, especially if they are issued during a period of relatively low interest rates. As I explain earlier in this section, longer-term bonds fall more in price when the overall level of interest rates rise.

Most of the time, longer-term bonds pay higher yields than short-term bonds. You can look at a chart of the current yield of similar bonds plotted against when they mature — such a chart is known as a *yield curve*. At most times, this curve slopes upward. Investors generally demand a higher rate of interest for taking the risk of holding longer-term bonds. Most financial newspapers and magazines carry a current chart of the yield curve.

Individual bonds or bond mutual funds?

You can invest in bonds in one of two major ways: You can purchase individual bonds or you can invest in a professionally selected and managed portfolio of bonds via a bond mutual fund.

Assessing individual bonds that you already own

If you already own individual bonds and they fit your financial objectives and tax situation, you can hold them until maturity because you've already incurred a commission when they were purchased; selling them now would just create an additional fee. When the bonds mature, the broker who sold them to you will probably be more than happy to sell you some more. That's the time to check out good bond mutual funds (see Chapter 9).

Don't mistakenly think that your current individual bonds pay the yield that they had when they were originally issued (that yield is the number listed in the name of the bond on your brokerage account statement). As the market level of interest rates changes, the *effective yield* (the interest payment divided by the bond's price) on your bonds fluctuates as well to rise and fall with the market level of rates. So if rates have fallen since you bought your bonds, the value of those bonds has increased — which in turn reduces the effective yield that you currently earn.

Unless the bonds you are considering purchasing are easy to analyze and homogeneous (such as Treasury bonds), you're generally better off investing in bonds through a mutual fund. The first reason is diversification. You shouldn't put your money into a small number of bonds that companies in the same industry issue or that mature at the same time. It's difficult to cost effectively build a diversified bond portfolio with individual issues unless you have several hundred thousand dollars that you want to invest in bonds.

If you purchase individual bonds through a broker, you're going to pay a commission. In most cases, the commission cost is hidden — the broker quotes you a price for the bond that includes the commission. Even if you use a discount broker though, these fees take a healthy bite out of your investment. The smaller the amount that you invest, the bigger the bite. On a $1,000 bond, the commission fee can equal up to 5 percent. Commissions take a smaller bite out of larger bonds — perhaps less than 0.5 percent if you use discount brokers.

The best reason to invest in bond funds instead of individual bonds is that you've got better things to do with your time. Do you really want to research bonds and go bond shopping? Bonds are boring! And bonds and the companies that stand behind them aren't that simple to understand. For example, did you know that some bonds can be "called" before their maturity date? Companies often call bonds (repay the principal before maturity) to save money if interest rates drop significantly. After you purchase a bond, you need to do the same things that a good bond mutual fund portfolio manager needs to do, such as track the issuer's creditworthiness and monitor other important financial developments.

A final reason to invest in bonds through a mutual fund is that it's cost-effective. Great bond funds are yours for less than 0.5 percent per year in operating expenses. Selecting good bond funds isn't hard, as I explain in Chapter 9.

How to buy individual bonds

If you want to purchase a Treasury bond, buying them through the Federal Reserve is the lowest-cost method. The Federal Reserve doesn't charge for accounts with less than $100,000 and charges $25 annually for accounts with more than $100,000 in Treasury bonds. Contact a Federal Reserve branch near you (check the government section of your local phone directory) and ask them to mail you information to purchase Treasury bonds through their Treasury Direct program or visit the US Department of Treasury's Web site (http://www.ustreas.gov).

You may also purchase and hold Treasury bonds through brokerage firms and mutual funds. Brokers typically charge a flat fee for buying a Treasury bond. Buying Treasuries through a brokerage account makes sense if you hold other securities through the brokerage account, and you like the ability to quickly sell a Treasury bond that you hold.

Selling Treasury bonds held through the Federal Reserve isn't easy nor cost-free. In the past, you had to transfer them to a broker. Now, you can sell your Treasury bonds through the Fed rather than transferring them out, which eliminates that hassle. However, selling Treasury bonds through the Fed isn't easy.

Here's what you have to do. First, you have to obtain and complete a form, get a certified signature, and then mail the form to the Chicago Federal Reserve. The Chicago Fed will then get in touch with you and provide you with three bids from dealers and you can then select the best one. After the transaction is completed, which you will be charged $34 for, you then must wait a couple of business days for the proceeds to be placed into your account.

The advantage of a mutual fund that invests in Treasuries is that it typically holds Treasuries of differing maturities to diversify. You can generally buy and sell no-load (commission-free) Treasury bond mutual funds easily and without fees. Funds, however, do charge an ongoing management fee. The Vanguard Group of mutual funds offers Treasury mutual funds with good track records and low management fees (see Chapter 9).

Purchasing other types of individual bonds, such as corporate and mortgage bonds, is a much more treacherous and time-consuming undertaking. Here's my advice for doing it right and minimizing the chance of a catastrophic mistake:

✔ **Don't buy through salespeople.** Brokerage firms that employ representatives on commission are in the sales business. Many of the worst bond investing disasters have befallen customers of such brokerage firms. Your best bet is to purchase individual bonds through discount brokers (see Chapter 21).

✔ **Don't be suckered into high yields — buy quality.** Yes, junk bonds pay higher yields, but they also have a much higher chance of default. Nothing personal, but you're not going to do as good a job as a professional money manager at spotting problems and red flags with a bond's issuing company. Thus, you're more likely to be left holding the bag when some of your junk bond purchases don't work out the way you expect. Stick with highly rated bonds so that you don't have to worry about and suffer through these unfortunate consequences.

✔ **Understand callability.** Many bonds, especially corporate bonds, can legally be called before maturity. This means that the bond issuer pays you back early, either because they don't need to borrow as much money or because interest rates have fallen and the borrower wants to reissue new bonds at a lower interest rate. Be especially careful about purchasing bonds that were issued at higher interest rates than those that currently prevail. Borrowers pay off such bonds first.

✔ **Diversify.** Invest and hold bonds from a variety of companies in different industries to buffer changes in the economy that adversely affect one or a few industries more than others. Of the money that you want to invest in bonds, don't put more than 5 percent into any one bond. That means that you need to hold at least 20 bonds. Diversification requires a good chunk of change to invest, given the size of most bonds, and because high fees erode your investment balance if you invest too little.

✔ **Shop around.** Just like when you buy a car, you need to shop around for good prices on the bonds that you have in mind. The hard part is doing an apples-to-apples comparison as different brokers may not be able to offer the same exact bond as other brokers. Remember that the two biggest determinants of what a bond should yield are when it matures and its credit rating.

Unless you invest in boring, simple-to-understand bonds such as Treasuries, you're better off investing in bonds via mutual funds. One exception is if you absolutely, positively must receive your principal back on a certain date. Because bond funds don't mature, individual bonds with the correct maturity for you may best suit your needs. Consider Treasuries because they carry little, if any, default risk. Otherwise, you need a lot of time, money, and patience to invest well in individual bonds.

Understanding individual bond prices

Most daily newspapers don't publish the prices of individual bonds. Newspapers don't possess a lot of interest in devoting what space they do have for for bonds. More business-focused publications, such as the *Wall Street Journal,* provide daily bond pricing. You may also call a broker or browse Internet sites to obtain bond prices. The following steps walk you through the bond listing for PhilEl (Philadelphia Electric) in Figure 8-1:

Bonds	Cur Yld	Vol	Close	Net Chg.
PacTT 7¼08	7.3	30	100	...
ParCm 7s03A	7.5	30	93⅛	– ¾
ParCm 7s03B	7.5	5	93⅞	+ ⅞
Pathmk zr03	...	20	66½	– ⅜
Paten 8¼12	cv	69	88½	+ 2
PaylCsh 9⅛03	12.1	1128	75¾	– 1
PennTr 9⅝05	11.6	291	82¾	– ⅛
Pennzl 6½03	5.5	15	119¼	...
Pepsic 7⅝98	7.4	5	103⅝	– ⅛
PhilEl 7⅛23	7.7	15	93	+ 2⅛
PhilPt 7.92s23	8.0	75	99½	+ 1
Pier1 6⅞02	cv	80	104	+ 2½
PionFn 8s00	cv	10	128½	+ ¼
PotEl 5s02	cv	57	90	...
Primark 8¾00	8.6	15	101⅞	+ 1
PSEG 6½04	6.7	25	97¼	– ½
PSEG 7½23	7.6	102	99	+ 1⅜
RJR Nb 8s00	7.8	47	102½	+ ¾
RJR Nb 8⅝02	8.4	25	103⅛	...
RJR Nb 7⅝03	7.9	224	96¾	+ ¼
RJR Nb 8¾05	8.6	5	101⅞	+ ½
RJR Nb 8⅞07	8.7	52	101½	+ ½
RJR Nb 9¼13	9.1	84	101⅞	+ ½
RJR Nb 8.3s99	8.1	34	103	...
RJR Nb 8¾04	8.5	43	102½	+ ¼
Rallys 9⅞00	16.7	395	59	– 1
RalsP 9½16	9.1	34	103⅞	+ ⅛
RalsP 9⅜16	9.0	10	103¾	– ⅝
RalsP 8⅝22	8.0	40	108⅜	+ ⅞

Philadelphia Electric

Figure 8-1: Sample bond listings.

1. **Bond name.** This tells you who issued the bond. In this case, the issuer is a large utility company, Philadelphia Electric.

2. **Funny numbers after company name.** The first part of the numerical sequence here — 7⅛— refers to the original interest rate (7.125 percent) that this bond paid when it was issued. This interest rate is known as the *coupon rate.* The second part of the numbers —23 — refers to the year that the bond matures, 2023 in this case.

3. **Current Yield.** Divide the interest paid, 7.125, by the current price per share, $93 to arrive at the current yield. In this case it equals (rounded off) 7.7 percent.

4. **Volume.** Indicates the number of bonds that traded on this day.

5. **Close.** Shows the last price that the bond traded.

6. **Change.** Indicates how this day's close compares with the previous day's. In this case, this bond rose 2⅛ points, a pretty healthy gain on a day that the overall bond market was up only modestly. Some bonds don't trade all that often. Notice that some bonds were up and others were down on this day. The demand of new buyers and the supply of interested sellers influences the price movement of a given bond.

In addition to the direction of overall interest rates, changes in the financial health of the company that stands behind the bond most affects the price of an individual bond.

Other Lending Investments

Bonds, money market funds, and bank savings vehicles are hardly the only lending investments that exist. A variety of other companies are more than willing to have you lend them your investment dollars and pay you a relatively fixed rate of interest. In most cases, you're better off staying away from the following investments.

Too many investors get sucked into lending investments that offer higher yields. Remember, remember, remember: Risk and return go hand in hand. Higher yields mean greater risk and vice versa.

Guaranteed-investment contracts

Insurance companies sell and back guaranteed-investment contracts (GICs). The allure of GICs is that your account value doesn't appear to fluctuate. Like a one-year bank certificate of deposit, GICs generally quote you an interest rate for the next year. Some GICs lock in the rate for longer periods of time, whereas others may change the interest rate several times per year.

The insurance company that issues the GIC actually invests your money, mostly in bonds and maybe a bit in stocks. Like other bonds and stocks, these investments fluctuate in value — you just don't see it.

Typically once a year, you receive a new statement that shows that your GIC is worth more, thanks to the newly added interest. This statement makes nervous investors who can't stand volatile investments feel all warm and fuzzy.

The yield on a GIC is usually comparable to those available on shorter-term, high-quality bonds. Yet, the insurer invests in longer-term bonds and some stocks. The difference between what these investments generate for the insurer and what the GIC pays you in interest goes to the insurer.

The insurer's take can be huge and is generally hidden. Unlike a mutual fund, which is required to report the management fee that it collects and subtracts it before paying your return, GIC insurers have no such obligations. By having a return guaranteed in advance, you pay heavily — an effective fee of 2 to 4 percent per year — for the peace of mind in the form of lower long-term returns.

Why companies offer GICs in their retirement plans

In their retirement plans, more than a few companies offer GICs as an investment option. You may rightfully ask why because, as I discuss in this chapter, GICs are investments that leave much to be desired. I see GICs most often in companies where an insurer is already entrenched as the provider of the company's retirement plan investment options. Insurers love GICs because they're so profitable — for them, that is.

But in some company retirement plans, GICs are the one and only investment option that an insurance company offers. Historically, companies were attracted to GICs as a defensive measure. GICs seemed so safe and conservative. Therefore, GICs made company officials who selected their retirement plan investment options feel safe. (More than a few benefits and other corporate personnel who establish and maintain these plans aren't exactly investing geniuses.)

Over the years, as more insurers have failed (including ones that appeared to be financially sound), the true risk of GICs is more apparent. Because more people and companies have discovered attractive alternative investment options such as mutual funds that offer higher returns and low expenses, the popularity of GICs wanes. If your company's retirement plan doesn't offer good investment choices and has too many GIC-like investments, talk to your benefits department. You can also anonymously leave them a copy of this book so they can better educate themselves!

The high effective fees that you pay to have an insurer manage your money in a GIC aren't the only drawbacks. When you invest in a GIC, your assets are part of the insurer's general assets. Insurance companies sometimes fail, and although they often merge with a healthy insurer, you can still lose money. The rate of return on GICs from a failed insurance company is often slashed to help restore financial soundness to the company. So the only "guarantee" that comes with a GIC is that the insurer agrees to pay you the promised rate of interest (as long as they are able)!

Private mortgages

Earlier in the chapter, I discuss investing in mortgages that resemble the one that you take out to purchase a home. To directly invest in mortgages, you can loan your money to people who need money to buy or refinance real estate. Such loans are known as mortgages or second mortgages.

Private mortgage investments appeal to investors who don't like the volatility of the stock and bond markets but aren't satisfied with the seemingly paltry returns on bonds or other common lending investments. Private mortgages seem to offer the best of both worlds — stock market like 10-plus percent returns without volatility.

Mortgage and real estate brokers often arrange mortgage investments, so you must tread carefully because these people have a vested interest in seeing the deal done. Otherwise, the mortgage broker doesn't get paid for closing the loan and the real estate broker doesn't get a commission for selling a property.

One broker who also happens to write about real estate wrote a newspaper column describing mortgages as the "perfect real estate investment" and added that mortgages are a "high-yield, low-risk investment." If that wasn't enough to get you to whip out your checkbook, the writer/broker further gushed that mortgages are great investments because you have ". . . little or no management, no physical labor. . . ."

You know by now that a low-risk, high-yield investment does not exist. Earning a relatively high interest rate goes hand in hand with accepting relatively high risk. The risk is that the borrower can default — which leaves you holding the bag. More specifically, you can get stuck with a property that you may need to foreclose on, and if you don't hold the first mortgage, you're not first in line with a claim on the property.

The fact that private mortgages are high risk should be obvious when you consider why the borrower elects to obtain needed funds privately rather than through a bank. Put yourself in the borrower's shoes. As a property buyer or owner, if you can obtain a mortgage through a conventional lender, such as a bank, wouldn't you do so because banks generally give better interest rates? If a mortgage broker offers you a deal where you can borrow money at 11 percent when the going bank rate is 8 percent, the deal must carry a fair amount of risk.

I would avoid these investments. If you must invest in such mortgages, you must do some time-consuming homework on the borrower's financial situation. A banker doesn't lend someone money without examining a borrower's assets, liabilities, and monthly expenses and you shouldn't either. Be careful to check the borrower's credit and get a large down payment (at least 20 percent). The best case to be a lender is if and when you sell some of your own real estate and you're willing to act as the bank and provide the financing to the buyer in the form of a first mortgage.

Also recognize that your mortgage investment carries interest rate risk: If you need to "sell" it early, you'd have to discount it, perhaps substantially if interest rates have increased since you purchased it. Try not to lend so much money on one mortgage so that it represents more than 5 percent of your total investments.

If you're willing to lend your money to borrowers who carry a relatively high risk of defaulting, consider investing in high-yield (junk) bond mutual funds instead. With these funds, you can at least diversify your money across many borrowers, and you benefit from the professional review and due diligence of the fund management team. You can also consider lending money to family members.

Mortgages, GICs, and CDs really do fluctuate in value

One of the allures of non-bond investments, such as private mortgages, GICs, and CDs, is that they don't fluctuate in value — at least not that you can see. Such investments appear safer and less volatile. You can't watch your principal fluctuate in value because you can't look up the value daily the way you can with bonds and stocks.

But the principal values of your mortgage, GIC, and CD investments really do fluctuate; you just don't see the fluctuations! As I explain earlier in this chapter, just as the market value of a bond drops when interest rates rise, so too does the market value of these investments, and for the

same reasons. At higher interest rates, investors expect a discounted price on your fixed-interest rate investment because they always have the alternative of purchasing a new mortgage, GIC, or CD at the higher prevailing rates. Some of these investments are actually bought and sold (and behave just like bonds) among investors on what's known as a secondary market.

If the normal volatility of a bond's principal value makes you queasy, try not to follow your investments so closely!

Chapter 9

Mutual Funds

• •

In This Chapter

▶ When and why you should invest in funds

▶ The secrets of successful fund investing

▶ Creating your fund portfolio

▶ The best stock, bond, and money market funds

• •

*I*n the earlier chapters of this part, I explain all about stocks, bonds, and other common securities. If you understand these securities, you can understand mutual funds. A *mutual fund* is simply a big pool of money from lots of investors like you and me that a mutual fund manager uses to buy a bunch of stocks, bonds, and/or other assets that meet the fund's investment criteria.

When you invest in a fund, you buy shares and become a shareholder of the fund. Good mutual funds enable you to give your money to some of the best money managers in the country. Because efficient funds take most of the hassle and cost out of figuring out which companies to invest in, they are one of the finest investment vehicles available today. They allow you to diversify your investments — that is, invest in many different industries and companies.

Different types of mutual funds can help you meet various financial goals — that's one of the reasons that investors have more than $5 trillion invested in funds! You can use money market funds for something most everybody needs — an emergency savings stash of three to six months' living expenses. Or, perhaps you're thinking about saving for a home purchase, retirement, or future educational costs. If so you can consider some stock and bond mutual funds.

Many people plunge into mutual funds without looking at their overall financial situation. In their haste, such investors end up paying more taxes and neglect considering other valuable financial strategies. If you haven't taken a comprehensive look at your personal finances, you're not alone. Read Chapter 3 to begin this important process.

The Benefits of the Best Funds

ERIC'S PICKS

The best mutual funds are superior investment vehicles for people of all economic means and for accomplishing many financial objectives. Following are the main reasons why investing in mutual funds rather than individual securities best serves you.

Professional management

Mutual funds are investment companies that pool your money with the money of hundreds, thousands, or even millions of other investors. The investment company hires a portfolio manager and researchers whose full-time jobs are to research and purchase suitable investments for the fund. These people screen the universe of investments for those that meet the fund's stated objectives.

Typically, fund managers are graduates of the top business and finance schools in the country, where they learned portfolio management and securities valuation and selection. Many have additional investing credentials, such as the Chartered Financial Analyst's (CFA) degree. In addition to their educational training, the best fund managers typically possess ten or more years of experience in analyzing and selecting investments.

For most fund managers and researchers, finding the best investments is more than a full-time job. Fund managers do tons of stuff that you probably lack the time or expertise to do. For example, fund managers analyze company financial statements; interview a company's managers to get a sense of the company's business strategies and vision; examine competitor strategies; speak with company customers, suppliers, and industry consultants; and attend trade shows and read industry periodicals.

In short, a mutual fund management team does more research, number crunching, and due diligence than you could ever have the energy or expertise to do in what little free time you have. Investing in mutual funds frees up time for friendships, family relationships, and maybe even your sex life — don't miss the terrific time-saving benefits of fund investing!

Cost efficiency

Mutual funds are a cheaper, more communal way of getting your investment work done. When you invest your money in an efficiently managed mutual fund, it likely costs you less than trading individual securities on your own. Fund managers can buy and sell securities for a fraction of the cost that you would pay to buy and sell them yourself.

Funds also spread the cost of research over thousands of investors. The most efficiently managed mutual funds cost less than 1 percent per year in fees (bonds and money market funds cost much less — in the neighborhood of 0.5 percent per year or less). Some of the larger and more established funds can charge annual fees as low as 0.2 percent per year — a mere $2 annual charge per $1,000 you invest. Such a deal!

Diversification

Diversification is a big attraction for many investors who choose mutual funds. Most funds own stocks or bonds from dozens of companies, thus diversifying against the risk of bad news from any single company or sector. Achieving such diversification on your own is difficult and expensive unless you have a few hundred thousand dollars and a great deal of time to invest.

Mutual funds typically invest in 25 to 100 securities, or more. Proper diversification increases the chances of the fund earning higher returns with less risk.

Although most mutual funds are diversified, some aren't. For example, some stock funds invest exclusively in stocks of a single industry (food and agriculture, for example) or country (such as Mexico). I'm not a fan of these funds because of the narrowness of their investments and their typically higher operating fees.

For richer and poorer . . .

Most funds have low minimum investment requirements. Many funds have minimums of $500 or $1,000 or less. Retirement account investors can often invest with even less. Some funds even offer monthly investment plans, so you can start with as little as $50 per month.

Even if you have lots of money to invest, you also should consider mutual funds. Join the increasing number of companies with millions to invest that use the low-cost, high-quality money management services that you can get from a mutual fund.

Different funds for different folks

Many people, including some financial writers, think that mutual funds = stock market investing = risky. Wrong. The majority of money in mutual funds is not in the stock market. You may select the funds that take on the kinds of risks that you're comfortable with and that meet your financial goals. Following is a list of the three major types of mutual funds:

- ✔ **Stock funds.** If you want your money to grow over a long period of time (and you can handle down as well as up years), select funds that invest more heavily in stocks.

- ✔ **Bond funds.** If you need current income and don't want investments that fluctuate as widely in value as stocks do, consider some bond funds.

- ✔ **Money market funds.** If you want to be sure that your invested principal does not decline in value because you may need to use your money in the short term, choose a money market fund.

Most investors choose a combination of these three types of funds to diversify and help accomplish different financial goals.

High financial safety

Thousands of banks and insurance companies have failed in recent decades. Banks and insurers can fail because their *liabilities* (the money that customers give them to invest) can exceed their *assets* (the money that they've invested or lent). For example, when a big chunk of a bank's loans go sour at the same time that its depositors want their money, the bank fails because banks typically have less than 15 cents on deposit for every dollar that you and I place with them. Likewise, if an insurance company makes several poor investments or underestimates the number of insurance policyholder claims, it too can fail.

Such failures can't happen with a mutual fund. The situation in which the investors' demand for their investments (the fund's liabilities) exceeds the value of a fund's investments (its assets) simply cannot occur. Mutual funds can't fail because the value of the fund's shares fluctuate as the securities in the fund fluctuate in value. For every dollar of securities they hold for their customers, mutual funds have a dollar's worth of securities. The worst that can happen with a fund is that if you want your money, you may get less cash than you originally put into the fund — but you won't lose all of your investment.

The specific stocks, bonds, and other securities that a mutual fund buys are held at a *custodian,* a separate organization independent of the mutual fund company. A custodian ensures that the fund management company can't embezzle your funds or use assets from a better-performing fund to subsidize a poor performer.

Accessibility

What's really terrific about dealing with mutual funds is that they're set up for people who value their time and don't like going to a local branch office and standing in long lines. With funds, you can fill out a simple form and write a check in the comfort of your living room to make your initial investment. You can then typically make subsequent investments by mailing in a check or authorizing money transfers by phone from your other accounts, such as at a bank.

Additionally, most money market funds offer check-writing privileges. Many mutual fund companies also allow you to wire money back and forth from your local bank account; you can access your money almost as quickly through a money market fund as you can through your local bank.

Selling shares of your mutual fund is usually simple. Generally, all you need to do is call the fund company's toll-free 800 number. Some companies have representatives available around the clock, all year round. Most of the larger fund companies also offer online account access and trading capabilities as well (although as I discuss in Chapter 21, some people are prone to over-trading online).

The Keys to Successful Fund Investing

This chapter helps explain why funds are a good investment vehicle to use, but not all funds are worthy of your investment dollars. Would you, for example, invest in a mutual fund run by an 18-year-old who has never invested in his or her life? How about a fund that charges high fees and produces inferior returns in comparison to other similar funds? These are common-sense questions, aren't they? You don't have to be an investing wizard to know the correct answers.

When you select a fund, you can use a number of simple, common-sense criteria to greatly increase your chances of investment success.

Minimize those fees

For a particular type of mutual fund (U.S. stock funds, for example), dozens to sometimes hundreds of choices are available. The charges that you pay to buy or sell a fund, as well as the ongoing fund operating expenses, have a big impact on the rate of return that you earn on your investments.

Fund costs are an important factor in the return that you earn from a mutual fund. Why? Fees are deducted from your investment returns and can attack a fund from many angles. All other things being equal, high fees and other charges depress your returns.

Avoid load funds

The first such fee that you need to minimize are *sales loads,* which are commissions paid to brokers and "financial planners" who work on commission and sell mutual funds. Commissions or loads generally range from 4 to 8.5 percent of the amount that you invest.

Sales loads are an additional and unnecessary cost that is deducted from your investment money. You can find plenty of outstanding no-load (commission-free) funds.

Brokers, being brokers, of course, sing the praises of buying a load fund, the pitfalls of no-loads, and they even sometimes try to obscure the load altogether. For example, brokers may tell you that the commission doesn't cost you because the mutual fund company pays them. Remember that the commission always comes out of your investment dollars regardless of how cleverly some load funds and brokers disguise the commission.

Brokers also may say that load funds perform better than no-load funds. One reason, brokers claim, is that load funds supposedly hire better fund managers. Absolutely no relationship exists between paying a sales charge to buy a fund and gaining access to better investment managers. Remember that the sales commission goes to the selling broker, *not* to the management of the fund. Objective studies demonstrate time and again that load funds not only don't outperform, but in fact underperform no-loads. Common sense suggests why — when you factor in the higher commission and the higher average ongoing operating expenses charged on load funds, you pay more to own a load fund, so your returns are less.

Another problem with commission-driven load fund sellers is the power of self-interest. This issue is rarely talked about, but it's even more important than the extra costs that you pay with load funds. When you buy a load fund through a salesperson, you miss out on the chance to get holistic advice on other personal finance strategies. For example, you may be better off paying down your debts or investing in something entirely different than a mutual fund. But, in my experience, salespeople almost never advise you to pay off your credit cards or your mortgage — or to invest through your company's retirement plan — instead of buying an investment through them.

Some mutual fund companies try to play it both ways: They sell load as well as no-load funds. Fidelity and Dreyfus, for example, sell both types of funds. Fidelity goes a step further: On many of their better stock funds, they levy a sales charge for non-retirement account investments. The logic behind this approach, from Fidelity's perspective, is that they expect retirement account investors to stay in a fund longer, thus providing a steady stream of fund management fees and profits. If you invest outside a tax-sheltered retirement account, I wouldn't purchase Fidelity's funds with sales charges. They're simply not worth it because plenty of other good alternatives exist. Also, beware that Fidelity funds do lots of trading, so they tend to produce high rates of capital gains distributions — increasing the tax burden for non-retirement account investors.

Beware of high operating expenses

In addition to loads, the other costs of owning funds are the ongoing *operating expenses.* All mutual funds charge fees as long as you keep your money in the fund. The fees pay for the costs of running a fund, such as employees' salaries, marketing, toll-free phone lines, printing and mailing prospectuses (legal disclosure of the fund's operations and fees), and so on.

A mutual fund's operating expenses are essentially invisible to you because they're deducted before you're paid any return. Companies charge operating expenses on a daily basis, so you don't need to worry about trying to get out of a fund at a particular time of the year before the company deducts these fees. They're invisible, but their impact on your returns is very real.

Expenses make a return difference on all types of funds, but they matter more on some and less on others. Expenses are critical on money market mutual funds and bond funds because these funds buy securities that are so similar and so efficiently priced in the financial markets that most fund managers in a given type of money market or bond fund earn quite similar returns before expenses.

With stock funds, expenses may play less of an important role in your fund decision. However, don't forget that over time stocks have averaged returns of about 10 percent per year. So if one stock fund charges 1.5 percent more in operating expenses than another, you give up an extra 15 percent of your expected annual returns.

All types of funds with higher operating expenses tend to produce lower rates of return, on average. Conversely, funds with lower operating costs can more easily produce higher returns for you than a comparable type of fund with high costs. This effect makes sense because companies deduct operating expenses from the returns that your fund generates. Higher expenses mean a lower return to you.

Fund companies quote a fund's operating expenses as a percentage of your investment. The percentage represents an annual fee or charge. You can find this number in a fund's prospectus, in the fund expenses section, usually in a line that says something like "Total Fund Operating Expenses." Or you can call the mutual fund's 800 number and ask a representative. Make sure that a fund doesn't appear to have low expenses simply because it's temporarily waiving them (you can ask the fund or look in their prospectus at their fees to find out this information).

Hiding loads

Unfortunately, in recent years fund companies have come up with craftier ways of hiding sales loads. Increasing numbers of brokers and "financial planners" sell funds that they *call* no-loads, but these funds are *not* no-loads.

In back-end or deferred sales load funds, the commission is hidden, thanks to the different classes of shares, known as A, B, C, and D classes. Salespeople tell you that as long as you stay in a fund for five to seven years, you need not pay the back-end sales charge that applies when you sell the investment. This claim may be true, but it's also true that these funds pay investment salespeople a hefty commission.

The salespeople can receive their commissions because the fund company charges you exorbitant continuing operating expenses (which are usually 1 percent more per year than the best funds). So, one way or another, they get their commissions from your investment dollars.

Stick with funds that maintain low total operating expenses and that don't charge sales loads (commissions). Both types of fees come out of your pocket and reduce your rate of return. You don't need to pay a lot for the best funds. Many excellent commission-free money market, bond, and stock funds from leading fund companies "cost" less than 1 percent per year. Plenty of funds are available for less than 0.5 percent per year in terms of their annual operating expense ratio. See my recommendations later in this chapter.

Consider performance and risk

A fund's historic rate of return or *performance* is another important factor to weigh when you select a mutual fund. Keep in mind, however, as all mutual fund materials must tell you, past performance is no guarantee of future results. In fact, many former high-return funds achieved their results only by taking on high risk. Funds that assume higher risk should produce higher rates of return. But high-risk funds usually decline in price faster during major market declines. Thus, a good fund should consistently deliver a favorable rate of return given the level of risk that it takes.

A big mistake that many investors make when they choose a mutual fund is over-emphasizing the importance of past performance numbers. The shorter the time period, the greater the danger of misusing high performance as an indicator for a good future fund.

Although past performance *can* be a good sign, high returns for a fund, relative to its peers, are largely possible only if a fund takes more risk. The danger of taking more risk is that it doesn't always work the way you'd like.

The odds are high that you won't be able to pick the next star before it vaults to prominence in the investing sky. You have a far greater chance of boarding that star when it's ready to plummet back to Earth.

In fact, if you had invested in the annual #1 top performing stock and bond funds over the last 15 years, 80 percent of those top performers subsequently performed worse, over the next 3 to 10 years, than the average fund in their peer group! Two of these former #1 funds are actually the worst performing funds in their particular category.

One clever way that mutual funds make themselves look better than other comparable funds is to compare themselves to funds that aren't really comparable. The most common ploy is for a fund to invest in riskier types of securities and then compare their performance to funds that invest in less risky securities.

A classic example of this false marketing is the Fidelity Magellan fund that, during Peter Lynch's tenure, invested in smaller company stocks as well as international stocks. Yet, in Magellan's annual reports to its shareholders, the fund's performance was compared to the Standard & Poor's 500 index of 500 large company U.S. stocks. This wasn't a fair comparison because smaller company stocks and international stocks are riskier and had outperformed the larger company U.S. stocks in the S&P 500 index during the time of Lynch's management.

Magellan's not a bad fund, but it certainly wasn't as stellar as Fidelity's performance comparisons made it out to be. Many other funds with mediocre or worse performance records have made themselves appear near the top of their class through similar comparison games.

Examine the types of securities that a fund invests in and make sure that the comparison funds or indexes invest in similar securities.

Stick with experience

A great deal of importance is made of who manages a specific mutual fund. Although the individual fund manager is important, a manager isn't an island unto himself or herself. The resources and capabilities of the parent company are equally, if not more, important. Managers come and go, but fund companies don't.

Different companies maintain different capabilities and levels of expertise with different types of funds. Vanguard, for example, is terrific at money market, bond, and conservative stock funds, thanks to their low operating expenses. Fidelity has significant experience with investing in U.S. stocks.

A fund company gains more or less experience than others, not only from the direct management of certain fund types, but also through hiring out. For example, some fund families contract with private money management firms that possess significant experience. In other cases, private money management firms, such as PIMCO, Neuberger & Berman, and Dodge & Cox, with long histories in private money management, offer mutual funds.

Buy index funds

Unlike other mutual funds, in which the portfolio manager and a team of analysts scour the market for the best securities, an index fund manager simply invests to match the performance of an index such as Standard & Poor's 500 index of 500 large U.S. company stocks. Index funds are funds that are mostly managed by a computer.

Index funds deliver relatively good returns by keeping expenses low, staying invested, and not trying to jump around. Over ten years or more, index funds typically outperform about three-quarters of their peers! Most other so-called actively managed funds cannot overcome the handicap of high operating expenses that pulls down their funds' rates of return. Index funds can run with far lower operating expenses because significant ongoing research doesn't need to be conducted to identify companies to invest in.

The average U.S. stock mutual fund, for example, has an operating expense ratio of 1.4 percent per year (some funds charge expenses as high as 2 percent or more per year). That being the case, a U.S. stock index fund with an expense ratio of just 0.2 percent per year has an advantage of 1.2 percent per year over the average fund. A 1.2 percent difference may not seem like much, but in fact it is a significant difference. Because stocks tend to return about 10 percent per year, you end up throwing away about 12 percent of your expected stock fund returns. (Factoring in the taxes that you pay on your fund profits, these higher expenses gobble up perhaps a quarter of your after-tax profits.)

With actively managed stock funds, a fund manager can make costly mistakes, such as not being invested when the market goes up, being too aggressive when the market plummets, or just being in the wrong stocks. An actively managed fund can easily underperform the overall market index that it's competing against. An index fund, by definition, can't. Index funds make great sense for investors who fear that fund managers may make mistakes and underperform the market.

Don't overestimate your ability to pick *in advance* the few elite money managers who manage to beat the market averages by a few percentage points per year in the long run. Also, don't overestimate the pros' ability to consistently

pick the right stocks. Index funds make sense for a portion of your investments, especially when you invest in bonds and larger, more conservative
stocks, where beating the market is difficult for portfolio managers.

In addition to lower operating expenses, which help boost your returns,
index mutual funds are tax-friendlier to invest in when you invest outside
retirement accounts. Mutual fund managers of actively managed portfolios, in
their attempts to increase returns, buy and sell securities more frequently.
However, this trading increases a fund's taxable capital gains distributions
and reduces a fund's after-tax return.

Vanguard is the largest and best mutual fund provider of index funds because
they maintain the lowest annual operating fees in the business. Vanguard has
all types of bond and stock (both U.S. and international) index mutual funds.

Creating Your Fund Portfolio

When you invest money for the longer term, such as for retirement, you can
choose among the various types of funds that I discuss in this chapter. Most
people get a big headache when they try to decide how to spread their
money across the choices. The specific amount that you decide to invest in
each of the major types of securities is known as *asset allocation*. Asset allocation simply means that you decide what percentage of your investments
you place — or *allocate* — into bonds versus stocks and into international
versus U.S. stocks. (Before you invest in funds, you should take a big-picture
look at the rest of your finances — see Chapter 3.)

Many working folks have time on their side, and they need to use that time to
make their money grow. You may have two or more decades before you need
to draw on some portion of your retirement account assets. If some of your
investments drop a bit over a year or two — or even over five years — the
value of your investments has plenty of time to recover before you spend the
money in retirement.

Your current age and the number of years until you retire should be the
biggest factors in your allocation decision. The younger you are and the more
years that you have before retirement, the more comfortable you should be
with growth-oriented (and more volatile) investments, such as stock funds.
(See Chapter 2 for the risks and historic returns of different investments.)

Table 9-1 lists guidelines for allocating money that you've earmarked for long-
term purposes, such as retirement. You don't need an M.B.A. or Ph. D. to
decide your asset allocation — all you need to know is how old you are and
the level of risk that you desire!

Table 9-1	Asset Allocation for the Long Haul	
Your Investment Attitude	*Bond Allocation (%)*	*Stock Allocation (%)*
Play it safe	= Age	= 100 – age
Middle of the road	= Age – 10	= 110 – age
Aggressive	= Age – 20	= 120 – age

What's it all mean, you ask? Consider this example: If you're a conservative sort who doesn't like a lot of risk, but you recognize the value of striving for some growth to make your money work harder, you're a middle-of-the-road type. Using Table 9-1 if you're 35 years old, you may consider putting 25 percent (35 – 10) into bonds and 75 percent (110 – 35) into stocks.

Now divvy up your stock investment money between U.S. and international funds. Here's what portion of your "stock allocation" I recommend investing in overseas stocks:

✔ 20 percent (for play it safe)

✔ 35 percent (for middle-of-the-road)

✔ 50 percent (for aggressive)

If, for example, in Table 9-1, the 35-year-old, middle-of-the-road type invests 75 percent in stocks, he or she can then invest about 35 percent of the stock fund investments (which works out to be around 25 percent of the total) in international stock funds.

So here's what the 35-year-old, middle-of-the-road investor's portfolio asset allocation looks like so far:

Bonds	25%
U.S. Stocks	50%
International Stocks	25%

Now let's take things a step further. Suppose that your investment allocation decisions make you to want to invest 50 percent in U.S. stock funds. Which ones do you choose? As I explain later in this chapter, stock funds differ from one another on a number of levels. There are growth-oriented stocks and funds and those that focus on value stocks. Small-, medium-, and large-company stocks and funds also invest in such stocks. I explain these types of stocks and funds later in the chapter. You also need to decide about whether you want to invest in index funds (that I discuss in the previous "Buy index funds" section) versus actively managed funds that try to beat the market.

Generally, it's a good idea to diversify into different types of funds. You can diversify in one of two ways. Your first option is to purchase several individual funds, each of which focuses on a different style. For example, you can invest in a large-company value stock fund and in a small-company growth fund. I find this approach somewhat tedious. Granted, it does allow a fund manager to specialize and gain greater knowledge about a particular type of stock. But many of the best managers invest in more than one narrow range of security.

A second approach is to invest in a handful of funds (5 – 10), each of which covers several bases, and that together cover them all. Remember, the investment delineations are somewhat arbitrary, and most funds do more than just one type of investment. For example, a fund may focus on small-company value stocks but also invest in medium-size company stocks, as well as in some that are more growth-oriented.

As for how much you should use index versus actively managed funds, it's really a matter of personal taste. If you're happy knowing that you'll get the market rate of return and that you can't underperform the market, there's no reason why you can't index your entire portfolio. On the other hand, if you enjoy the challenge of trying to pick the better managers and want the potential to earn better than the market level of returns, don't use index funds at all. A happy medium is to do both. (You may be interested in knowing that John Bogle, founder of Vanguard and pioneer of index investment funds, has about half of his money invested in index funds.)

If you haven't experienced the sometimes significant plummets in stock prices that occur, you may feel queasy when it next happens and you've got a chunk of your nest egg in stocks. Be sure to read Chapters 2 and 5 to understand the risk in stocks and what you can and can't do to reduce the volatility of your stock holdings.

The Best Stock Mutual Funds

Earlier in this book, I made the case for investing in stocks (also known as equities) to make your money grow. However, stock market investing carries risk because stocks sometimes plummet or can otherwise depress for a few years. Thus, stock mutual funds (also known as equity funds), as their name suggests investment in stocks, are not a place for money that you know you may need to protect in the next few years.

Unless you possess a lot of money to invest, you're likely to buy only a handful of stocks. If you end up with a lemon in your portfolio, it can devastate your other good choices. If such a stock represents 20 percent of your holdings, the rest of your stock selections need to increase about 25 percent in value just to get you back to even.

Stock mutual funds reduce your risk because they invest in dozens of stocks. For example, if a fund holds 50 stocks and one goes to zero, you lose only 2 percent of the fund value if the stock was an average holding. If the fund holds 100 stocks, you lose just 1 percent. Remember that a good fund manager is more likely to sidestep disasters than you.

Another way that stock funds reduce risk (and thus their volatility) is that they invest in different types of stocks, such as growth stocks, or in the stocks of larger, established companies. Some funds also invest in U.S. and international stocks. Different types of stocks don't always move in tandem. So if smaller-company stocks get beat up, larger-company stocks may fare better. If international stocks are in the tank, U.S. stocks may be fine.

Making money with stock funds

When you invest in stock mutual funds, you can make money in three ways. First, most stocks pay dividends. Companies hopefully make some profits during the year. Some high-growth companies reinvest most or all of their profits right back into the business. Many companies, however, pay out some of their profits to shareholders in the form of dividends. As a mutual fund investor, you can choose to receive these dividends as cash or reinvest them into purchasing more shares in the fund.

Unless you need the income to live on (if, for example, you're already retired), reinvest your dividends into buying more shares in the fund. If you do this outside a retirement account, keep a record of those reinvestments because you need to factor those additional purchases into the tax calculations that you make when you sell your shares.

The second way you can make money with a stock fund is through capital gains distributions. When a fund manager sells stocks for more than he or she paid, the resulting profits, known as *capital gains,* must be netted against losses and paid out to the fund's shareholders. Just as with dividends, you can reinvest your capital gains distributions in the fund.

The final way that you can make money with stock funds is via appreciation. The fund manager isn't going to sell all the stocks that have gone up in value. Thus, the price per share of the fund increases to reflect the gains in its stock holdings. For you, these profits are on paper until you sell the fund and lock them in. Of course, if a fund's stocks decline in value, the share price depreciates.

If you add together dividends, capital gains distributions, and appreciation, you arrive at the *total return* of a fund. Stocks, and the funds that invest in them, differ in the dimensions of these three possible returns, particularly with respect to dividends. Utility companies, for example, tend to pay out more of their profits as dividends. But don't buy utility stocks thinking you'll make more money because of the heftier dividends. Utilities and other companies paying high dividends tend not to appreciate as much over time because they don't reinvest as much in their businesses, and they're not growing.

Bond funds, as I discuss later in this chapter, can make you money like all the three ways that a stock fund can. However most of the time, the bulk of your return in a bond fund comes from dividends. With money market funds (that I also discuss later in this chapter), all your return comes from dividends.

The different types of stock funds

Stock funds and the stocks that they invest in are usually pigeonholed into particular categories, based on the types of stocks that they focus on. Categorizing stock funds is often tidier in theory than in practice though, because some funds invest in an eclectic mix of stocks. Don't get bogged down with the names of funds — funds sometimes have misleading names and don't necessarily do what their names imply. The investment strategies of the fund and the fund's typical investments are what matter.

The first dimension on which a stock fund's stock selection differs is based on the size of the company — small, medium, and large companies — in which the fund invests. The total market value (*capitalization*) of a company's outstanding stock defines the categories that define the stocks that the fund invests in. Small-company stocks, for example, are usually defined as stocks of companies that possess total market capitalization of less than $2 billion. Medium-capitalization stocks have market values between $2 billion and $10 billion. Large-capitalization stocks (also known as large caps) are those of companies with market values greater than $10 billion. These dollar amounts are arbitrary and as stock prices increase over time, investment market analysts have moved up their cutoffs.

Why care what about the size of the companies that a fund holds? Historically, smaller companies pay less dividends but appreciate more. They have more-volatile share prices but tend to produce slightly higher total returns. Larger companies' stocks tend to pay greater dividends and on average are less volatile and produce slightly lower total returns than small company stocks. Medium-size, as you may suspect, falls between the two. So investors looking for income as well as appreciation from their stock market investments can focus more on larger-company stocks. Also, since smaller-company stocks don't move in lockstep with larger-company stocks, investing in both reduces a portfolio's volatility.

Stock fund managers and their funds are further categorized by whether they invest in growth or value stocks. *Growth stocks* are companies that experience rapidly expanding revenues and profits. These companies tend to reinvest most of their earnings in the company to fuel future expansion; thus, these stocks pay low dividends. Microsoft, for example, pays no dividends and reinvests most of its profits back into its business.

Value stocks are priced cheaply in relation to the company's assets, profits, and potential profits. It's possible that such a company is a growth company, but that's unlikely because growth companies' stock prices tend to sell at a bigger premium compared to what the company's assets are worth.

Mutual fund companies sometimes use other terms to describe other types of stock funds. Aggressive growth funds tend to invest in the most growth-oriented companies and may undertake riskier investment practices, such as frequent trading. Growth and income funds tend to invest in stocks that pay decent dividends, thus offering the investor the potential for growth and income. Income funds tend to invest more in higher-yielding stocks. Bonds usually make up the other portion of income funds.

Stocks and the companies that issue them are also divvied up based upon the location of their main operations and headquarters. Funds that specialize in U.S. stocks are not surprisingly called U.S. stock funds; those focusing overseas are typically called international or overseas funds.

Putting together two or three of these major classifications, you can start to comprehend all those silly and lengthy names that mutual funds give to their stock funds. You can have funds that focus on large-company value stocks or small-company growth stocks. You can add in U.S., international, and world-wide finds to further subdivide these categories into more fund types. So you can have international stock funds that focus on small-company stocks or growth stocks.

You can purchase several stock funds, each focusing on a different type of stock, to diversify into different types of stocks. Two potential advantages result from doing so. First, not all of your money rides in one stock fund and with one fund manager. Second, each of the different fund managers can look at and track particular stock investment possibilities.

Using the selection criteria I outline earlier in this chapter, the following sections describe the best stock funds that are worthy of your consideration. The funds differ from one another primarily in terms of the types of stocks that they invest in. Keep in mind as you read through these funds that they also differ from each other in their tax-friendliness (see Chapter 3). If you invest inside a retirement account, you don't need to worry about tax-friendliness.

All-in-one funds

Balanced and asset allocation mutual funds, also known as *hybrid funds,* invest in a mixture of different types of securities. Most commonly, they invest in both bonds and stocks. These funds are usually less risky and less volatile than funds that invest exclusively in stocks; in an economic downturn, bonds usually hold value better than stocks.

Hybrid funds make it easier for investors who are skittish about investing in stocks to hold stocks because they avoid the high volatility that normally comes with pure stock funds. Because of their extensive diversification, hybrid funds are excellent choices for an investor who doesn't have much money to start with.

Balanced funds generally try to maintain a fairly constant percentage of investment in stocks and bonds. Asset allocation funds, in contrast, normally adjust the mix of different investments according to the portfolio manager's expectations. Some asset allocation funds, however tend to keep more of a fixed mix of stocks and bonds whereas some balanced funds shift the mix around quite frequently. Although the concept of a manager being in the right place at the right time and beating the market averages sounds good in theory, most of these funds fail to outperform a buy-and-hold approach.

Because hybrid funds pay decent dividends from the bonds that they hold, they're not appropriate for some investors who purchase funds outside tax-sheltered retirement accounts. If you're in a higher tax bracket (that is, a federal tax bracket of 31 percent and higher), bonds that you purchase outside a retirement account need to be tax-free. With the exception of the Vanguard Tax-Managed Balanced Fund, which holds federally tax-free bonds, avoid hybrid funds if you're in a higher tax bracket. You should instead buy separate tax-friendly stock funds and tax-free bond funds (both discussed later in the chapter) to create your own hybrid portfolio.

Here's my recommended short list of great balanced-type mutual funds (I've also placed a list of phone numbers for the mutual funds that I recommended in this chapter at the end of the chapter):

Dodge & Cox Balanced

Fidelity Asset Manager

Fidelity Puritan

Lindner Dividend

T. Rowe Price Balanced

Vanguard LifeStrategy Funds

Vanguard Wellesley Income

Vanguard Wellington

U.S. stock funds

Of all the different types of funds offered, U.S. stock funds are the largest category. To see the forest amidst the trees, refer to the classifications that I cover earlier in this section. Stock funds differ mainly in terms of the size of the companies that they invest in and in whether the funds focus on growth or value companies. Some funds do all these things, and some funds may even invest a bit overseas.

The only way to know for sure where a fund currently invests (or where the fund may invest in the future) is to ask. You can call the 800 number of the mutual fund company that you're interested in to start your information search. You can also read the fund's annual report. Don't waste your time looking for this information in the fund's prospectus, because it doesn't give you anything beyond general parameters that guide the range of investments. The prospectus doesn't tell you what the fund currently invests in or has invested in.

For mutual funds that you hold outside of retirement accounts, you gotta pay current income tax on distributed dividends and capital gains. (This is another reason that most investors, during their working years, are best off sheltering more money into retirement accounts.) If your circumstances allow you to invest money in stock funds outside retirement accounts, then by all means do it. But pay close attention to the dividend and capital gains distributions that funds make. In the following list I indicate which funds are tax-friendly.

Here's my short list of U.S. stock funds:

Columbia Growth

Dodge & Cox Stock

Fidelity

Fidelity Disciplined Equity

Fidelity Equity-Income (buy only for retirement accounts)

Fidelity Equity-Income II

Fidelity Low Priced Stock (buy only for retirement accounts)

Neuberger & Berman: Partners, and Focus

T. Rowe Price Spectrum Growth

Vanguard Index 500 (tax-friendly)

Vanguard Index Total Stock Market (tax-friendly)

Vanguard Primecap

Vanguard's Tax-Managed Capital Appreciation (tax-friendly)

Vanguard's Tax-Managed Small Capitalization (tax-friendly)

International stock funds

For diversification and growth potential, you should include stock funds that invest overseas as part of your portfolio. Normally, you can tell that you're looking at a fund that focuses its investments overseas if its name contains words such as international (foreign only), global (foreign and U.S.), or world-wide (foreign and U.S.).

As a general rule, avoid foreign funds that invest in just one country, regardless of whether that country is Australia, Zimbabwe, or anywhere in between. As with investing in a sector fund that specializes in a particular industry, this lack of diversification defeats the whole purpose of investing in funds. Funds that focus on specific regions, such as Southeast Asia, are better but still generally problematic because of poor diversification and higher expenses than other, more-diversified international funds.

If you want to invest in more geographically-limiting international funds, take a look at T. Rowe Price's and Vanguard's offerings, which invest in broader regions, such as investing just in Europe, Asia, and the volatile but higher-growth-potential emerging markets in Southeast Asia and Latin America.

In addition to the risks normally inherent with stock fund investing, changes in the value of foreign currencies relative to the U.S. dollar can also subject international securities and funds to buffeting. A decline in the value of the U.S. dollar helps the value of foreign stock funds. Some foreign stock funds hedge against currency changes. Although this hedging helps reduce volatility a bit, it does cost money.

Here are my picks for diversified international funds that may meet your needs:

Schwab International Index (tax-friendly)

T. Rowe Price International Stock

Tweedy Browne Global Value (note: this fund invests in the U.S. as well)

USAA Investment International

Vanguard International Growth (tax-friendly)

Vanguard Total International (tax-friendly)

Sector funds

Sector funds invest in securities in specific industries. In most cases, you should avoid sector funds. Investing in stocks of a single industry defeats a major purpose of investing in mutual funds — you give up the benefits of diversification. Also, just because the fund may from time to time be dedicated to a "hot" sector (different examples of these sector funds are often at the top of short-term performance charts), you can't assume that the fund will pick the right securities within that sector.

Another good reason to avoid sector funds is that they tend to carry much higher fees than other mutual funds. Many sector funds also have high rates of trading or turnover of their investment holdings. Investors who use these funds outside of retirement accounts have to face the IRS for the likely greater capital gains distributions that this trading produces.

The only types of specialty funds that may make sense for a small portion (10 percent or less) of your investment portfolio are funds that invest in real estate or precious metals. These funds can help diversify your portfolio because they can perform better during times of higher inflation — which often depresses bond and stock prices. You can comfortably skip these funds because diversified stock funds tend to hold some of the same stocks as these specialty funds.

Real estate investment trusts (REITs) are stocks of companies that invest in real estate. REITs typically invest in properties such as apartment buildings, shopping centers, and other rental properties. REITs allow you to invest in real estate without the hassle of being a landlord. Just as it's a hassle to evaluate REIT stocks, you can always invest in a mutual fund of REITs.

REITs usually pay decent dividends. As such, they are not appropriate for people in a higher tax bracket that invest money outside retirement accounts. Some good no-load REIT funds include Fidelity Real Estate, Vanguard REIT Index, and Cohen & Steers Realty Shares. (You can purchase the latter fund with a lower minimum initial investment through discount brokers.)

If you expect high inflation, consider a gold fund. But know that these funds swing wildly in value and are not for the faint of heart or for the majority of your portfolio. A good precious metals fund is the Vanguard Gold Fund. Don't buy the bullion itself; storage costs and the concerns over whether you're dealing with a reputable company make buying gold bars a pain. Also avoid futures and options, which are gambles on short-term price movements.

The Best Bond Funds

In the previous chapter, I discuss what bonds are and how different bonds vary from one another. Make sure that you read that material before you venture into bonds.

When selecting bond funds to invest in, investors are often led astray as to how much they can expect to make in a bond fund. The first mistake is to look at recent performance and assume that you'll get that return in the future. Investing in bond funds based only on recent performance is tempting right after a period where interest rates have declined, because declines in interest rates pump up bond prices and, therefore, bond fund total returns. Remember that an equal but opposite force waits to counteract pumped-up bond returns — bond prices fall when interest rates rise.

Don't get me wrong: Past performance is an important issue to consider. In order for performance numbers to be meaningful and useful, you must compare bond funds that are comparable to each other (such as intermediate-term funds that invest exclusively in high-grade corporate bonds).

The importance and dangers of yield

Bond mutual funds calculate their yield after they subtract their operating expenses. When you call a mutual fund company to ask for a fund's current yield, make sure that you understand what time period the yield covers. Fund companies are supposed to give you the *SEC yield,* which is a standard yield calculation that allows for fairer comparisons among bond funds. The SEC yield reflects the bond fund's so-called yield to maturity. The SEC yield is the best yield to utilize when you compare funds because it captures the effective rate of interest that an investor can receive in the future.

Unfortunately, if you select bond funds based on advertised yield, you're almost guaranteed to purchase the wrong bond funds. Bond funds and the mutual fund companies that sell them can play more than a few games of creative accounting to fatten a fund's yield. Such sleights of hand make a fund's marketing and advertising departments happy because higher yields make it easier for salespeople and funds to hawk their bond funds. But remember that yield-enhancing shenanigans can leave you poorer. Here's what you need to watch out for:

✔ **Lower quality**. You may compare one short-term bond fund to another and discover that one pays 0.5 percent more and decide that it therefore looks better. However, it turns out that the higher-yielding fund invests 20 percent of its money in junk bonds, whereas the other fund fully invests in high-quality bonds.

✔ **Longer maturities.** Bond funds can usually increase their yield just by increasing their maturity a bit. If one long-term bond fund invests in bonds that mature in an average of 17 years, while another fund possesses an average maturity of 12 years, comparing the two is a classic case of comparing apples to oranges.

✔ **Giving your money back without you knowing it.** Some funds return a portion of your principal in the form of dividends. This move artificially pumps up a fund's yield but depresses its total return. When you compare bond funds to each other, make sure that you compare their total return over time (in addition to making sure that the funds have comparable portfolios of bonds).

✔ **Waiving of expenses.** Some bond funds, particularly newer ones, waive a portion or even all their operating expenses to temporarily inflate the fund's yield. Yes, you can invest in a fund that has a sale on its operating fees, but you'd also buy yourself the bother of monitoring things to determine when the sale is over. Bond funds that engage in this practice often end sales quietly when the bond market is performing well. Don't forget that if you sell a bond fund (held outside of a retirement account) that has appreciated in value, you owe taxes on your profits.

You can earn a higher yield from investing in a bond fund that — holds longer-term bonds, holds lower-quality bonds, or that has lower operating expenses. After you settle on the type of bonds that you want, a bond fund's costs — its sales commissions and annual operating fees — are a huge consideration. Stick with no-load funds that maintain lower annual operating expenses.

Although hundreds of bond funds exist (an overwhelming number of choices), not that many remain after you eliminate high-cost funds (those with loads and high ongoing fees), low-performance funds (which are often the high-cost funds), and funds managed by fund companies and fund managers with minimal experience investing in bonds.

Although it's not difficult to tell a good bond fund from a bad one, remember that it's important to make sure that you're in the right category. Bond fund objectives and names usually fit one of three maturity categories — short, intermediate, and long term.

Also pay attention to the taxability of the dividends that bonds pay. If you're investing in bonds inside retirement accounts, you want taxable bonds. If you invest in bonds outside retirement accounts, the choice between taxable versus tax-free depends on your tax bracket (see Chapter 3).

The riskier the bonds that a fund holds, the higher the yield that fund should be. Generally speaking, the longer their maturity and the lower their issuer's credit rating, the riskier the bond. A higher yield is the bond market's way of compensating you for taking greater risk.

Invest in bond funds only if you have sufficient money in an emergency reserve. If you invest money for longer-term purposes, particularly retirement, you need to come up with an overall plan for allocating your money among a variety of different funds, including bond funds (see my asset allocation discussion, earlier in this chapter).

Tread carefully with actively managed funds

Some bond funds are aggressively managed funds. Managers of these funds possess a fair degree of latitude to purchase and trade bonds that they think will perform best in the future. For example, if a fund manager thinks that interest rates will rise, he or she usually buys shorter-term bonds and keeps more of a fund's assets in cash. The fund manager may invest more in lower-credit-quality bonds if he or she thinks that the economy is improving and that more companies will prosper and improve their credit standing.

Aggressively managed funds are a gamble. If interest rates fall instead of rise, the fund manager who moved into shorter-term bonds and cash suffers worse performance. If interest rates fall because the economy sinks into recession, the lower-credit-quality bonds will likely suffer from a higher default rate and depress the fund's performance even further.

Some people think that it's not difficult for the "experts" to predict which way interest rates or the economy is heading. The truth is that economic predictions are difficult, and the experts are often wrong. Few bond fund managers have been able to beat a buy and hold approach. William Gross, who manages the PIMCO bond funds, is one fund manager who has pretty consistently beaten the market averages by a bit.

But, remember that trying to beat the market can lead to getting beaten! Increasing numbers of examples have occurred in recent years of bond funds that fall on their face after risky investing strategies backfire. Interestingly, bond funds that charge sales commissions (loads) and higher ongoing operating fees are the bonds that are more likely to blow up perhaps because these fund managers are under more pressure to pump up returns to make up for higher operating fees.

It's fine to invest some of your bond fund money in funds that try to hold the best position for changes in the economy and interest rates, but remember that if these fund managers are wrong, you can lose more money. Over the long term, you'll probably do best with efficiently managed funds that stick with an investment objective and that don't try to time and predict the bond market. Index funds that invest in a relatively fixed basket of bonds so as to track a market index of bond prices are a good example of this passive approach.

Short-term bond funds

Of all bond funds, short-term bond funds are the least sensitive to interest rate fluctuations. The stability of short-term bond funds makes them appropriate investments for money which you seek a better rate of return on than a money market fund could produce for you. But, with short-term bond funds, you also have to tolerate the risk of losing a percent or two in principal value if interest rates rise.

Short-term bonds work well for money that you earmark for use in a few years, such as the purchase of a home or a car, or for money that you plan to withdraw from your retirement account in the near future.

Taxable, short-term bond funds

Bond funds that pay taxable dividends are appropriate when you're not in a high tax bracket (less than or equal to 28 percent federal) and for investing inside retirement accounts. Good funds to consider include:

Vanguard Short-Term Corporate Portfolio

PIMCO Low Duration (purchase through discount broker Jack White)

U.S. Treasury short-term bond funds

U.S. Treasury bond funds are appropriate if you prefer a bond fund that invests in U.S. Treasuries (which possess the safety of government backing) or if you're not in a high federal tax bracket (less than or equal to 28 percent), but you *are* in a high state tax bracket (5 percent or higher). I don't recommend Treasuries for retirement accounts because they pay less interest than fully taxable bond funds:

Vanguard Short-Term Treasury

Vanguard Admiral Short-Term U.S. Treasury (higher yields if you have $50,000 to invest)

Federally tax-free short-term bond funds

State and federally tax-free short-term bond funds are scarce. If you want shorter-term bonds, invest in these *federally* tax-free bond funds (their dividends are state taxable) if you're in a high federal bracket (31 percent and up) but in a low state bracket (less than 5 percent). If you live in a state with high taxes, also consider checking out the state and federal tax-free intermediate-term bond funds — if you can withstand their volatility (see the next section). Another option is to use a state money market fund, covered later in this chapter in "The Best Money Market Funds."

Vanguard Municipal Short-Term Portfolio

Vanguard Municipal Limited-Term

Intermediate-term bond funds

Intermediate-term bond funds hold bonds that typically mature in a decade or so. They are more volatile than shorter-term bonds but can also prove more rewarding. The longer that you can own an intermediate-term bond fund, the more likely you are to earn a higher return on it than on a short-term fund, unless interest rates continue to rise over many years.

As an absolute minimum, don't purchase an intermediate-term fund unless you expect to hold it for three to five years — or even longer, if you can. Therefore, you need to make sure that the money that you put into an immediate-term fund is money that you don't expect to use in the near future.

Taxable intermediate-term bond funds

Taxable intermediate-term bond funds to consider include:

> American Century-Benham GNMA
>
> Dodge & Cox Income
>
> PIMCO Total Return & Total Return III
>
> USAA GNMA
>
> Vanguard GNMA
>
> Vanguard Index Total Bond Market

U.S. Treasury intermediate-term bond funds

U.S. Treasury bond funds are appropriate if you prefer a bond fund that invests in U.S. Treasuries (which maintain the safety of government backing) or if you're not in a high federal tax bracket (less than or equal to 28 percent), but you *are* in a high state tax bracket (5 percent or higher). I don't recommend Treasuries for retirement accounts because they pay less interest than fully taxable bond funds.

> Vanguard Intermediate-Term Treasury
>
> Vanguard Admiral Intermediate-Term U.S. Treasury (higher yields if you have $50,000 to invest)

Federally tax-free intermediate-term bond funds

You should consider *federally* tax-free bond funds if you're in a high federal bracket (31 percent and up) but a relatively low state bracket (less than 5 percent). If you're in a high federal and state tax bracket, refer to the state and federally tax-free bonds that I mention later in this section.

> Vanguard Municipal Intermediate-Term

State and federally tax-free intermediate-term bond funds

You may find *state and federally* tax-free bond funds appropriate when you're in high federal (31 percent and up) *and* state (5 percent or higher) tax brackets. (If a tax-free bond is not listed for your state or if you're only in a high federal tax bracket, remember that you can use the nationwide Vanguard municipal bond fund that I listed in the last section.)

The following list shows you some good state and federally tax-free intermediate-term bond funds:

> American-Century CA Tax-Free Intermediate-Term
>
> Vanguard CA Tax-Free Insured Intermediate Term

Long-term bond funds

Long-term bond funds are the most aggressive and volatile bond funds around. If interest rates on long-term bonds increase substantially, you can easily see the principal value of your investment decline 10 percent or more. (See the discussion in Chapter 8 of how interest rate changes impact bond prices.)

Long-term bond funds are generally used for retirement investing in one of two situations: (1) where investors don't expect to tap their investment money for a decade or more, or (2) where investors want to maximize current dividend income and are willing to tolerate volatility. Don't use these funds to invest money that you plan to use within the next five years because a bond market drop can leave your portfolio short of your monetary goal.

Taxable long-term bond funds

Taxable long-term bond funds to consider include:

> PIMCO High Yield
>
> Vanguard Long-Term Corporate
>
> Vanguard High Yield Corporate

U.S. Treasury long-term bond funds

U.S. Treasury bond funds are advantageous if you desire a bond fund that invests in U.S. Treasuries or if you're not in a high federal tax bracket (less than or equal to 28 percent), but you *are* in a high state tax bracket (5 percent or higher). I recommend Treasuries for non-retirement accounts only because Treasuries pay less interest than fully taxable bond funds.

I recommend the following:

Vanguard Long-Term Treasury

Vanguard Admiral Long-Term U.S. Treasury (higher yields if you have $50,000 to invest)

Federally tax-free long-term bond funds

Municipal (federally tax-free) long-term bond funds to consider include:

Vanguard Municipal Long-Term

Vanguard Municipal Insured Long-Term

State and federally tax-free long-term bond funds

State and federally tax-free bond funds may be appropriate when you're in high federal (31 percent and up) *and* high state (5 percent or higher) tax brackets. (If a fund isn't listed for your state or if you're only in a high federal tax bracket, you can use the nationwide Vanguard Municipal bond funds.)

State and federally tax-free long-term bond funds to consider include:

American Century-Benham CA Tax-Free Long-Term

Vanguard CA Tax-Free Insured Long-Term

Fidelity Spartan CT Muni Income

Fidelity Spartan FL Muni Income

USAA FL Tax-Free Income

Vanguard FL Insured Tax-Free

Fidelity Spartan MA Muni Income

Fidelity Spartan MD Muni Income

Fidelity Spartan MI Muni Income

Fidelity Spartan MN Muni Income

Vanguard NJ Tax-Free Insured Long-Term

Vanguard NY Insured Tax-Free

USAA NY Tax-Free Bond

Vanguard OH Tax-Free Insured Long-Term

Vanguard PA Tax-Free Insured Long-Term

USAA TX Tax-Free Income

USAA VA Tax-Free Income

The Best Money Market Funds

As I explain in Chapter 8, money market funds are a safe, higher yielding alternative to bank accounts. (If you're in a higher tax bracket, money funds have even more appeal because you can get tax-free versions of money market funds.) Under Securities and Exchange Commission regulations, money market funds can invest only in the most creditworthy securities, and their investments must have an average maturity of less than 120 days. The short-term nature of these securities effectively eliminates the risk of money market funds being sensitive to changes in interest rates.

The securities that money market funds use are extremely safe. General-purpose money market funds invest in government-backed securities, bank certificates of deposit, and short-term corporate debt that the largest and most creditworthy companies and the U.S. government issue (although the latter may not be much comfort to you).

The main motivation for investing in a money market fund instead of a bank savings account is that you earn a greater rate of return, or yield. In addition to higher yields, good money market funds offer other useful services, such as free check writing, telephone exchange and redemptions, and automated, electronic exchange services with your bank account.

Within a given category of money market funds (general, Treasury, municipal, and so on), money market fund managers invest in the same basic securities. The market for these securities is pretty darn efficient, so "superstar" money market fund managers may eke out an extra 0.1 percent per year in yield, but not much more.

Select a money market fund that does a good job controlling its expenses. The operating expenses that the fund deducts before payment of dividends are the single biggest determinant of yield. All other things being equal (which they usually are with different money market funds), lower operating expenses translate into higher yields for you.

You have no need or reason to tolerate annual operating expenses of greater than 0.5 percent. Some top-quality funds charge a quarter of 1 percent or less annually. Remember, lower expenses don't mean that a fund company cuts corners or provides poor service. Lower expenses are possible in most cases because a fund company is successful in attracting much money to invest.

Expenses are important, but so, too, are the consequences of taxes. What you actually get to keep of your investment returns (on non-retirement account investments) is what is left over after the federal and state governments take their cut of your investment income. If you invest money that's held outside of a retirement account and you're in a high tax bracket (particularly the federal 31 percent or higher bracket), you can come out ahead if you invest in *tax-free* money market funds. If you're in a high-tax state, a *state* money market fund, if good ones exist for your state, may be a sound move.

Tax-free refers to the taxability of the dividends that the fund pays. You don't get a tax deduction for money that you put into the fund as you do with 401(k) or other retirement-type accounts.

Another factor that may be important to you in determining which money fund to use is what other investing you plan to do at the fund company where you establish a money market fund. For example, if you decide to make other mutual fund investments in stocks and bonds at T. Rowe Price, then keeping a money market fund at a different firm that offers a slightly higher yield may not be worth the time and administrative hassle, especially if you don't plan on keeping much cash in your money market fund.

Most mutual fund companies don't have many local branch offices. Generally, this fact helps fund companies keep their expenses low and pay you greater yields on their money market funds. As I discussed previously, you may open and maintain your mutual fund account via the fund's toll-free 800 phone line and the mail. You don't really get much benefit, except psychological, if you select a fund company with an office in your area. But I don't want to diminish the importance of your emotional comfort level.

Using the criteria that I just discussed, this section recommends the best money market funds: those that offer competitive yields, check writing, access to other excellent mutual funds, and other commonly needed money market services.

Taxable money market funds

Money market funds that pay taxable dividends are appropriate for retirement account funds that await investment as well as non-retirement account money when you're not in a high federal tax bracket (less than or equal to 31 percent federal) *and* are not in a high state tax bracket (less than 5 percent). Here are the best taxable money market funds to consider:

Vanguard's Money Market Reserves Prime Portfolio

Fidelity Cash Reserves and Fidelity Daily Income Trust

Fidelity's Spartan Money Market (higher yields if you invest $20,000)

Schwab Value Advantage Money Market (higher yields if you invest $25,000)

USAA Mutual Money Market

T. Rowe Price Summit Cash Reserves (higher yields if you invest $25,000)

U.S. Treasury money market funds

U.S. Treasury money market funds are appropriate if you prefer a money market fund that invests in U.S. Treasuries, which maintain the safety of government backing, or if you're not in a high federal tax bracket (less than or equal to 28 percent) but *are* in a high state tax bracket (5 percent or higher). The following lists U.S. Treasury funds that I recommend:

Vanguard Money Market Reserves U.S. Treasury Portfolio

Vanguard's Admiral U.S. Treasury Money Market Portfolio (higher yields if you invest $50,000)

American Century Benham Capital Preservation & Government Agency Funds

USAA's Treasury Money Market.

Fidelity's Spartan U.S. Treasury Money Market ($20,000 minimum)

Municipal money market funds

Municipal (also known as muni) money market funds invest in short-term debt that state and local governments issue. A municipal money market fund, which pays you federally tax-free dividends, invests in munis issued by state and local governments throughout the country. A state-specific municipal fund invests in state and local government-issued munis for one state, such as New York. So if you live in New York and buy a New York municipal fund, the dividends on that fund are federal and New York state tax-free.

So how do you decide whether to buy a nationwide or state-specific municipal money market fund? Federally tax-free-only money market funds are appropriate when you're in a high federal (31 percent and up) but *not* a high state bracket (less than 5 percent).

If you're in a higher state tax bracket, your state may not have good (or any) state tax-free money market funds available. If you live in any of those states, you're likely best off with one of the following national money market funds:

Vanguard Municipal Money Market

Fidelity Spartan Municipal Money Market ($25,000 minimum)

USAA Tax-Exempt Money Market

The state tax-free money market funds in the following list are appropriate when you're in a high federal (31 percent and up) *and* a high state tax bracket (5 percent or higher). If none are listed for your state or you're only in a high federal tax bracket, remember that you need to use one of the nationwide muni money markets that I described in the previous paragraph.

How to contact fund providers

The following list provides the phone numbers that you can use to contact mutual fund companies and discount brokers that sell the mutual funds that I discuss in this chapter. To learn more about selecting and investing in mutual funds, pick up a copy of my book, *Mutual Funds For Dummies* (IDG Books Worldwide, Inc.).

American Century-Benham Funds: 800-345-2021

Cohen & Steers Realty Shares, Inc.: 800-437-9912

Columbia Funds: 800-547-1707

Dodge & Cox Funds: 800-621-3979

Fidelity Funds: 800-544-8888

Lindner Funds: 800-995-7777

Neuberger & Berman Funds: 800-877-9700

PIMCO Funds: 800-927-4648

Schwab Funds: 800-435-4000

T. Rowe Price Funds: 800-638-5660

Tweedy Browne Funds: 800-432-4789

USAA Funds: 800-382-8722

The Vanguard Group: 800-662-7447

Warburg Pincus Funds: 800-927-2874

Jack White & Company: 800-323-3263

State and federally tax-free money market funds to examine include:

Fidelity Spartan AZ Muni Money Market

USAA Tax-Exempt CA Money Market

Vanguard CA Tax-Free Money Market

Fidelity Spartan FL Muni Money Market

USAA Tax-Exempt FL Money Market

Fidelity Spartan MA Muni Money Market

Vanguard NJ Tax-Free Money Market

USAA Tax-Exempt NY Money Market

Vanguard NY Tax-Free Money Market

Vanguard OH Tax-Free Money Market

Vanguard PA Tax-Free Money Market

USAA Tax-Exempt TX Money Market

USAA Tax-Exempt VA Money Market

Chapter 10

Selecting a Brokerage Firm

. . . .

. . . .

*I*n this part of the book, I discuss the different types of securities investments — stocks and bonds — that you can make. I think that investors are
better served making such investments through the best mutual funds.
Selecting one of the premier fund companies that I recommend in Chapter 9
as your base for making fund investments makes good sense.

That said, you need to consider setting up a brokerage account for one or
both of the following reasons:

✔ If you hold or invest in individual stocks and bonds.

✔ If you seek to invest in and hold mutual funds from a variety of fund
companies through a single account.

Considering Discount Brokers

Prior to 1975, all brokerage firms charged the same fee, known as a *commission,* to trade stocks and bonds. The Securities and Exchange Commission
(SEC), the federal government agency responsible for overseeing investment
firms and their services, regulated commissions.

Beginning May 1, 1975 — May Day — brokerage firms were free to compete
with one another on price, like companies in almost all other industries. Most
of the firms in existence at that time, such as Prudential, Merrill Lynch, E.F.
Hutton, and Smith Barney, largely continued with business as usual, charging
relatively high commissions.

However, a new type of brokerage firm, the *discount broker,* was born. Discount
brokerage firms charge substantially lower commissions — typically 50 to 75

percent lower — than the other firms. Today, discount brokers, which include many online brokers, abound and continue to capture the lion's share of new business.

In this chapter, I explain the ins and outs of discount brokers and online brokers to help you find the right broker for your investment needs.

When you hear the word "discount," you probably think of adjectives like cheap, inferior quality, and such. However, when it comes to the securities brokerage field, the discount brokers who place your trades at substantial discounts can offer you even better value and service than high-cost brokers.

Why discount brokers?

Discount brokers can place your trades at a substantially lower price because they have much lower overhead. Discount brokers tend not to rent the most posh, downtown office space — complete with mahogany-paneled conference rooms — that they can find in order to impress customers. Discounters also don't waste tons of money employing economists and research analysts to produce forecasts and predictive reports.

In addition to lower commissions, another major benefit of using a discount broker is that their brokers generally work on salary. Working on salary removes a significant conflict of interest that continues to get commission-paid brokers and firms, such as Prudential, Smith Barney Shearson, Merrill Lynch, and Dean Witter, into trouble. Although many of these firms today claim to offer financial planning, the reality is that commission-paid brokers aren't any different than other salespeople, whether the product is cars, copy machines, or computers. People who sell on commission to make a living aren't inherently evil, but don't expect to receive holistic, in-your-best-interest, investing counsel.

One of the many sales tactics of high-commission brokerage firms is to try to disparage discounters by saying things such as, "You'll receive poor service from discounters." My own experience, as well as that of others, suggests that in many cases, discounters actually offer better service. High-commission firms, for example, used to argue that discount brokerage customers received worse trade prices when they bought and sold. This assertion is a bogus argument, because all brokerage firms use a computer-based trading system for smaller retail trades. Trades are processed in seconds.

High-commission brokers also say that discounters are only "for people who know exactly what they're doing and don't need any help." This statement is also false. Many of the larger discounters with branch offices offer help that includes assistance with filling out paperwork and access to independent research reports. And, as I discuss in Chapter 9, you can buy no-load (commission-free) mutual funds that make investment decisions for you.

Choosing a discount broker

Which discount broker is best for you depends on what your needs are. In addition to fees, consider how important having a local branch office is to you. If you want to invest in some mutual funds as well, the firms that I list later in this section also offer access to good funds. In addition, these firms offer money market funds into which you can deposit money awaiting investment or proceeds from a sale.

Within the discount brokerage business, *deep discounters* are known as firms that offer the lowest rates but fewer frills and other services. Generally, deep discounters don't have local branch offices like big discounters, or offer money market funds with the highest yields. Be careful of some deep discounters that offer bargain commissions but stick it to you in other ways, such as high fees for other services or low interest rates on money awaiting investment.

The best discount brokers

Here are my top picks for discount brokers, as well as the pros and cons of each:

- ✔ **T. Rowe Price (800-225-5132).** T. Rowe Price offers a solid family of no-load mutual funds that you can also purchase through its discount brokerage division. The company's brokerage fees are competitive but not among the cheapest discounters. Branch offices are in Baltimore, Colorado Springs, Los Angeles, Tampa, and Washington, D.C., and hours are weekdays 8 a.m. to 10 p.m. EST.

- ✔ **Vanguard (800-992-8327).** Vanguard is best known for its excellent family of no-load (commission-free) mutual funds, but its discount brokerage services have improved in recent years. Vanguard has also reduced its brokerage fees in recent years, and it's near the low end of discount brokers. I sometimes find its service a bit bureaucratic when I try to resolve problems.

- ✔ **Waterhouse (800-233-3411).** Waterhouse Securities recently merged with Jack White and Company to form T.D. Waterhouse. White was a minimal-frills, deep-discounter with only one branch office. Waterhouse offered competitive, but slightly higher, commission rates and nearly 200 branch offices. The new company offers round-the-clock customer assistance.

All the preceding firms offer mutual funds from many fund companies in addition to their family of funds, if they have one. In other words, you may purchase non-T. Rowe Price mutual funds through T. Rowe Price's brokerage department. There are certainly other discounters with good service and competitive rates, such as Muriel Siebert, so shop around if you desire. Note, however, that you generally pay a transaction fee to buy funds from firms that don't offer their own family of funds.

Is keeping your securities in a brokerage account better?

When most investors purchase stocks or bonds today, they don't receive the actual paper certificate demonstrating ownership. Brokerage accounts often hold the certificate for your stocks and bonds on your behalf. Holding your securities through a brokerage account is beneficial because most brokers charge an extra fee to issue certificates.

Sometimes people hold stock and bond certificates themselves — this practice was more common among your parents' and grandparents' generations. The reason: During the Great Depression, many brokerage firms failed and took people's assets down with their sinking ships. Since then, various reforms have greatly strengthened the safety of money and the securities that you hold in a brokerage account.

Just as the FDIC insurance system backs up money in bank accounts, the SIPC (Securities Investor Protection Corporation) provides insurance to investment brokerage firm customers. The base level of insurance is $500,000 per account. However, many firms purchase additional protection — some as high as $100 million total!

Brokerage firms don't often fail these days, but unlike during the Depression, the SIPC protects you if they do. However, the SIPC coverage doesn't protect you against a falling stock market. If you invest your money in stocks, bonds, or whatever that plunge in value, that's your own problem!

Besides not having to worry about losing your securities if a brokerage firm fails, another good reason to hold securities with a broker is so you don't lose them — literally! Surprising numbers of people — the exact number is unknown — have lost their stock and bond certificates. Those who realize their loss can contact the issuing firms to replace them, but doing so takes a good deal of time. However, just like future goals and plans, some certificates are simply lost, and owners never realize their loss. This financial fiasco sometimes happens when people die and their heirs don't know where to look for the certificates or the securities that their loved ones held.

Another reason to hold your securities in a brokerage account is that doing so cuts down on processing all those dividend checks. For example, if you own a dozen stocks that each pay you a quarterly dividend, you must receive, endorse, and otherwise deal with 48 separate checks. Some people enjoy this practice — they say that doing so is part of the "fun" of owning securities. My advice: Stick all your securities into one brokerage account that holds your paid dividends. Brokerage accounts offer you the ability to move these payments into a reasonably good yielding money market fund. Most of the better discount brokers even allow you to reinvest stock dividends into the purchase of more shares of that stock at no extra charge.

One final recommendation: If you want a cut-rate discounter for stock and other securities trading, consider Brown & Company (800-822-2021). The company charges a mere $12 for stock trades that you place via a market order for up to 5,000 shares ($5 if you trade through their Web site that I mention, later in this chapter). Brown & Company doesn't offer mutual funds and is a horrible place to keep cash awaiting investment, because its money market yields are abysmal. Also beware of the sometimes-hefty fees that the company levies for special services.

Absent from my list are the large discounters Fidelity and Schwab. The simple reason is that those companies now charge significantly more than the competition does, especially for transaction fee mutual funds. These firms can get away with premium pricing, despite comparable services, because enough investors prefer to do business with name-brand companies. Although I think that both companies can offer investors a fine base from which to do their investing, I don't feel that their fees are justified unless you wish to do business with a broker that maintains a branch office in your area.

Considering Online Brokers

Today, to get the lowest trading commissions, you generally must place your trades online. Even if you've never visited an online brokerage site, ads for them online, in print publications, and even on national television have surely bombarded you. Visit any Web site that's remotely related to investing in stocks and you're sure to find ads for eTrade, Ameritrade, eSchwab, SureTrade, ProTrade, First Flushing Securities, Bidwell & Co., Cutter & Co., or Crazy Eddie's Online Brokers.

Okay, I was kidding about that last one, but the number of online brokers and investors interested in trading online is skyrocketing. In less than a decade, the number of online brokerage firms, which are generally discount brokers, increased to more than 100.

In the following sections, I offer suggestions for finding the best online broker for your investing needs.

Don't shop on price alone

Anyone familiar with the economics of running a brokerage firm can tell you that technology, properly applied, cuts a broker's labor costs. Some brokerages now perform market orders for a mere five bucks. Hence the attraction of online trading.

Before you jump at the chance to save a few bucks, read the following sections for other considerations that should factor into your choice of an online broker — or your decision to trade online at all.

Examine your motivations for trading online

If trading online attracts you, first examine why you are motivated to do so. Tracking prices daily or, even worse, hourly, and frequently checking your account balances leads to addictive trading. A low $5 or $10 per trade fee makes little difference if you trade a lot and rack up significant total commissions, and you pay more in capital gains taxes. Don't forget that, as with trading through a regular brokerage firm, you also lose the "spread" (difference between the bid and ask prices when you trade), in addition to the explicit commission rates that online brokers charge. Likewise, more online brokers share in the spread on NASDAQ stocks, which is how they can offer some trades for "free."

Investment Web sites also push the surging interest in online trading with the pitch that you can beat the market averages and professionals at their own game if you do your research and trade online. Although beating the market and professionals is highly unlikely, you can save some money trading online, but probably not as much as the hype has you believe.

Consider other costs

Online brokerage customers shop for low costs. In a recent American Assocation of Individual Investors survey of online investors, about half of respondents said that commission rates were the primary factor in their selection of a specific online discount broker. However, review of online message boards where customers speak their minds clearly shows that shopping merely for low-cost trading prices often leads to the investor overlooking other important issues.

For starters, there's more to your costs of trading online than simply the commission on a trade. Unless you use your employer's computer or work for or attend a university, you must pay online fees for Internet access (including relevant local phone charges), as well as connect-time fees in some cases. Some discounters don't provide 800 numbers, so bear this in mind if you need to call with questions and service problems. Others charge fees for real-time stock quotes.

When you buy or sell an investment, you may have cash sitting around in your brokerage account. Not surprisingly, the online brokers pitching their cheap online trading rates in 3-inch-high numbers don't reveal their money market rates in such large type (if at all). Some don't pay interest on the first $1,000 or so of your cash balance, and even then some companies only pay about 3 percent. Others pay low rates — such as 2 percent. Under those terms, you'd earn up to $150 less in interest per year if you average a $5,000 cash balance during the year, versus keeping your money in an account that pays just 5 percent on your entire cash balance.

Finally, some brokers whack you $20 here and $50 there for services such as wiring money or simply closing your account. So, before you sign up with any broker, make sure that you examine its entire fee schedule.

Examine service quality

When you establish a brokerage account, the last thing that you're likely to consider is the quality of your year-end account statement, but you should. "I have found that most brokers give little information about year-end account information in writing, and when you call to get details, they promise everything and don't deliver," says David Wright, an online trader who fired three brokerages over four years due to problems with year-end statements and poor customer service.

Other common complaints among customers of online brokers are slow responses to e-mail queries, long dead-time as you wait to speak with a live person to answer questions or resolve problems, delays in opening accounts and receiving literature, unclear statements, incorrect processing of trading requests, and the fact that the Web sometimes is slow to respond during periods of heavy traffic. With a number of firms that I called such as Datek, Discover, and National Discount Brokers, I experienced phone waits of up to 10 minutes and was transferred several times to retrieve answers to simple questions, such as whether the firm carried a specific family of mutual funds.

When you shop for an online broker, check your prospects thoroughly. Call for literature and see how long reaching a live human being takes. Ask some questions and see how knowledgeable and helpful the representatives are. For non-retirement accounts, if the quality of the firm's year-end account statements concern you, ask prospective brokerages to send you a sample. Try sending some questions to the broker's Web site and see how accurate and timely they respond. If you're a mutual fund investor, check out the quality of the funds that the company offers — don't allow the sheer number of funds that the company offers impress you. Also, inquire about the interest rates that the company pays on cash balances, as well as the rates that the company charges on margin loans, if you want such borrowing services.

Consider checking online message boards to see what current and past customers of the firm say about the firms that you're considering. Most online brokers that have been around for more than six months lay claim to a #1 rating with some survey or ranking of online brokers. Place little value on such claims.

Also, examine what the firm did before it got into the online brokerage business. Would you rather put your money and trust in the hands of an established and respected financial service company that has been around for a number of years or an upstart firm run by a couple of people hoping to strike it rich on the Net? Only transact business with firms that offer sufficient account insurance through SIPC — the online industry will inevitably have a shakeout, and you need to protect yourself against it.

Abuses and uses for online brokerage accounts

Frankly, trading online is an unfortunately easy way for people to act impulsively and emotionally when the make important investment decisions. Use the Internet to check account information and gather factual information online rather than telephoning someone. Also, know that most of the best investment firms now allow you to trade via touch-tone phone. In most cases, touch-tone phone trading is discounted when you compare it to trading through a live broker, although it is admittedly less glitzy than trading through an Internet site.

Some brokers also offer account information and trading capabilities via personal digital assistants, which, of course, add to your costs. Digital assistants can also promote addictive investment behaviors.

The best online brokers

Among the e-brokers I reviewed, my top picks are:

Broker	Phone Number	Web Site
DLJ Direct	800-825-5723	dljdirect.com
Muriel Siebert	800-872-0711	siebertnet.com
T. Rowe Price	800-638-5660	troweprice.com
Vanguard	800-992-8327	vanguard.com
Waterhouse	800-934-4443	waterhouse.com

As I mention earlier in this chapter, use Brown & Company (www.brownco.com) for a cut-rate discounter for stock and other securities trading. This company charges a mere $5 for market order stock trades of up to 5000 shares that you place via the Internet.

No matter how you trade, keep track of your overall annual returns, minus trading costs, and see how your performance compares to the market averages. Unless you invest purely for thrill and education, consider tossing in your modem for some well-managed mutual funds that won't glue you to your computer screen.

Part III
Real Estate

The 5th Wave — By Rich Tennant

"I'm well aware that we ask for a lot from our home mortgage applicants, Mr. Harvey. However, sarcasm is rarely required."

In this part . . .

Owning a home and investing in real estate are time-proven methods for building wealth. However, if you're not careful, you can easily fall prey to a number of pitfalls. In this part, you discover the right and wrong ways to purchase real estate and how to build your real estate empire. Even if you don't want to be a real estate tycoon, you'll also see how simply owning your own home can help build your net worth and accomplish future financial goals.

Chapter 11

Investing at Home

1 hesitate somewhat to call the home in which you live an investment. Homes suck up money the same way most politicians do. And most people don't view their homes as a ticket to important financial goals such as retirement.

You may also feel that calling a home an investment is potentially problematic for another reason. Perhaps you've owned a home or seen others who own homes that have declined in value. All investments, however, go through up and down periods. Over the long term, you should see a lot more up than down in home values, so those who stick with homeownership profit. Over the decades, the rate of home investment return has been comparable to the rates of return that stock market investments achieve (see Chapter 2).

For most people, buying a home in which to live is their first, best, and only real estate investment. Homes may require a lot of financial feeding, but over the course of your life, owning a home (instead of renting) can make and save you money. And while the pile of mortgage debt seems daunting in the years just after your purchase, someday your home may well be among your biggest assets.

Even though your home consumes a lot of dough while you own it, it can help you accomplish important financial goals, such as:

✔ **Retiring.** By the time you hit your 50s and 60s, the size of your monthly mortgage payment should start to look small or non-existent. Relatively low housing costs can help you afford to retire or cut back from a full-time workweek. Increasingly, people are choosing to sell their homes and buy less-costly ones or even rent and use some or even all the cash to live on in retirement. Some homeowners enhance their retirement income by taking out a reverse mortgage to tap the *equity* (market value your home minus the outstanding mortgage debt) that they've built up in their properties.

✔ **Pursuing your small-business dreams.** Running your own business can be a source of great satisfaction. Financial barriers, however, prevent many people from pulling the plug on a regular job and taking the entre-preneurial plunge. You may be able to borrow against the equity that you've built up in your home to get the cash you need to start up your own business. Depending upon what type of business you have in mind, you may even be able to run your enterprise from your home.

✔ **Financing college.** When your kids are old enough to vote and head off to war, they're also ready for an expensive four-year undertaking: col-lege. Borrowing against the equity in your home is a viable way to help pay for your kids' educational costs.

Perhaps you won't use your home's equity for retirement, a small business, educational expenses, or other important financial goals. But even if you decide to pass your home on to your children, charity, or a long-lost relative, it's still a valuable asset and a worthwhile investment.

The Buying Decision

Most people approach property ownership with trepidation — and with good reason. Because buying a home is probably the largest financial transaction of your life, it ranks high on the stress-o-meter.

Who wants stress? Why not keep renting and be happy? Actually, some people may be better off doing just that. More than a few couples have landed in divorce court thanks to squabbles over homeownership. Remodeling debates and arguments can drain your savings and your psyche.

I'm not trying to scare you off from buying a home — I believe that most people should buy and own a home. But homeownership isn't for everybody and certainly not at all times in your adult life.

The decision about if and when to buy a home may be complex. Money mat-ters, but so do personal and emotional issues. Buying a home is a big deal — you're settling down. Can you really see yourself coming home to this same place day after day, year after year? Of course you can always move, but now you've got a financial obligation to deal with.

Financially speaking, I advise that you wait to buy a home until you can see yourself staying put for a minimum of three years. Ideally, I'd like you to think that you have a solid chance of staying with the home for five or more years. Why? Buying and selling a home cost big bucks:

- ✔ **Inspection fees.** You shouldn't buy a property without checking it out, so you'll have to pay some inspection expenses. Good inspectors can help you identify problems with the plumbing, heating, and electrical systems, as well as the foundation, roof, termites, and so on.

- ✔ **Loan costs.** The costs of getting a mortgage include such items as the *points* (up-front interest that can run 1 to 2 percent of the loan amount), application and credit report fees, and appraisal fees.

- ✔ **Title insurance.** When you buy a home, you and your lender need to protect yourselves against the chance — albeit small — that the property seller doesn't actually legally own the home that you're buying. That's where title insurance comes in — it protects you financially from unscrupulous sellers.

- ✔ **Moving costs.** You can lug all that furniture, clothing, and other personal belongings, but your time is worth something and your moving skills are likely limited. Besides, do you want to end up in a hospital emergency room after you're pinned by a runaway couch at the bottom of a stairwell?

- ✔ **Real estate agents' commissions.** A commission of 5 to 7 percent of the purchase price of most homes goes into the pockets of real estate salespeople and the companies they work for.

To cover all these costs plus the additional costs of homeownership, such as maintenance (for example, fixing leaky pipes and painting), the value of your home needs to appreciate about 15 percent over the years that you own it just for you to be as well off financially as if you had continued renting. Fifteen percent! If you need or want to move elsewhere in a couple of years, it's risky to count on that kind of appreciation in those few years. If you happen to buy just before a sharp upturn in housing prices, you may get this much appreciation in a short time. But you can't count on this upswing — you'll probably lose money on such a short-term deal.

Some people invest in real estate even when they don't expect to live in it for long and may consider turning their home into a rental if they move within a few years. Doing so can work well financially in the long haul, but don't underestimate the responsibilities that come with rental property, which I discuss in the next chapter.

Weighing the pros and cons

To hear some people — particularly enthusiastic salespeople in the real estate business — everybody should own a home. You may hear them say things like

"Renting is like throwing your money away."

"Buy a home for the tax breaks."

As I discuss later in this chapter, it's true that the bulk of the costs of home-ownership — namely mortgage interest and property taxes — are tax-deductible. However, these tax breaks are already largely factored into the higher cost of owning a home. Don't buy a home just because of the tax breaks.

Renting is not throwing your money away, and you're not a failure if you do rent. Renting has emotional and psychological rewards. First is the not-so-inconsequential fact that you have more flexibility to pack up and move on. You may have a lease to fulfill, but you can renegotiate it if you need to move on. As a homeowner, you have a large monthly payment to take care of — to some people, this responsibility feels like a financial ball and chain. With a home, you have no guarantee that you can sell your home in a timely fashion or at the price you desire if you want to move.

In some areas, you can get more for your money by renting, thus enabling you to keep your housing expenses lower than if you did buy. Happy and successful renters that I've seen include people who pay low rent, perhaps because they've made housing sacrifices. If you live in a shared rental home, you likely get more living space for your money than if you lived alone in a small property that you've purchased. If you're able to sock away 10 percent or more of your earnings while renting, you're probably well on your way to accomplishing your future financial goals.

Another benefit of renting is that, as a renter, the money that you save and hopefully invest is placed in financial assets, such as stocks, bonds, and mutual funds, which are quite accessible. Most homeowners, by contrast, have a substantial portion of their wealth tied up in their homes. (Accessibility is a double-edged sword, because it may tempt you as a cash-rich renter to blow the money in the short term.)

Although renting has its benefits, renting has at least one big drawback: exposure to inflation. As the cost of living increases, your landlord can (unless you live in a rent-controlled unit) keep jacking up your rent. As a homeowner, the big monthly expense of the mortgage payment does not increase, assuming that you buy your home with a fixed-rate mortgage. However, your property taxes, homeowners insurance, and maintenance expenses are exposed to inflation, although these expenses are usually much smaller in comparison to your monthly mortgage payment or rent.

Here's a quick example to show you how inflation can work against you as a long-term renter. Suppose that you are comparing the costs of owning a home that costs $160,000 to renting a similar property for $800 a month. Buying at $160,000 sounds a lot more expensive than renting, doesn't it? But this isn't a fair apples-to-apples comparison. You must compare the monthly cost of owning to the monthly cost of renting. You must also factor in the tax benefits of homeownership (mortgage interest and property taxes are tax-deductible) to your comparison so that you compare the after-tax monthly cost of owning versus renting. Figure 11-1 does just that for a 30-year example.

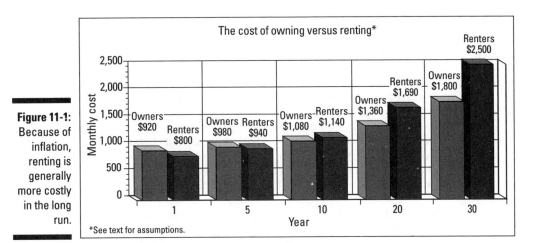

The cost of owning versus renting*

Owners $920 / Renters $800 (Year 1)
Owners $980 / Renters $940 (Year 5)
Owners $1,080 / Renters $1,140 (Year 10)
Owners $1,360 / Renters $1,690 (Year 20)
Owners $1,800 / Renters $2,500 (Year 30)

Monthly cost

Year

*See text for assumptions.

Figure 11-1: Because of inflation, renting is generally more costly in the long run.

As you can see in Figure 11-1, although it costs more in the early years to own, owning should be less expensive in the long run. Renting is higher in the long term because all your rental expenses increase with inflation. (***Note:*** I haven't factored in the potential change in the value of your home over time. Over long periods of time, home prices tend to appreciate, which makes owning even more attractive.)

The example in Figure 11-1 assumes that you make a 20 percent down payment and take out a 7 percent fixed-rate mortgage to purchase the property. I also assume that the rate of inflation of your homeowners insurance, property taxes, maintenance, and rent is 4 percent per year. If inflation is lower, renting doesn't necessarily become cheaper in the long term. In the absence of inflation, your rent should escalate less, but your homeownership expenses, which are subject to inflation (property taxes, maintenance, and insurance), should increase less too. And with low inflation, you can probably refinance your mortgage at a lower interest rate, which reduces your monthly mortgage payments. With low or no inflation, owning can still cost less, but the savings versus renting aren't as dramatic as when inflation is greater.

Deciding how much to spend

Buying a home is a long-term financial commitment. You'll probably take out a 15- to 30-year mortgage to finance your purchase, and the home that you buy will need all sorts of maintenance over the years. So, before you make a decision to buy, take stock of your overall financial health.

If you have good credit and a reliable source of employment, lenders will eagerly offer to loan you money. They'll tell you how much you may borrow from them — the maximum that you are qualified to borrow. But that doesn't mean that you should borrow the maximum. What about your other financial options and goals? The most common mistake that I see people make when they buy a home is that they ignore their overall financial situation.

If you buy a home without considering your other monthly expenditures and long-term goals, you may end up with a home that dictates much of your future spending. Have you considered, for example, how much you need to save monthly to reach your retirement goals? How about the amount that you want to spend on recreation and entertainment?

If you want to continue your current lifestyle, you have to be honest with yourself about how much you can really afford to spend as a homeowner. First-time homebuyers in particular run into financial trouble when they don't understand their current spending. Buying a home can be a wise decision, but it can also be a huge burden. And, there are all sorts of nifty things to buy for a home. Some people prop up their spending habits with credit cards — a dangerous practice.

Don't let your home control your financial future. Take stock of your overall financial health, especially where you stand in terms of retirement planning (if you hope to someday retire), before you buy property or agree to a particular mortgage. Start by reading Chapter 3.

The lender's perspective on borrowing

All mortgage lenders want to know your ability to repay the money that you borrow, so you have to pass a few tests. Mortgage lenders calculate the maximum amount that you can borrow to buy a piece of real estate.

For a home in which you will reside, lenders total up your monthly housing expense. They define your housing costs as:

Mortgage Payment + Property Taxes + Insurance

A lender does not consider maintenance and upkeep expenses in owning a home. (You shouldn't ignore this important issue in your budget, however.) Lenders typically loan you *up to* an amount so that no more than 28 percent (33 percent for so-called jumbo loans) of your monthly gross (pre-tax) income goes toward housing expense. (If you're self-employed, lenders use the net income from the bottom line of your federal tax form Schedule C rather than gross monthly income.) Lending ratios vary slightly from lender to lender.

Homeownership tax savings

Your mortgage interest and property taxes are tax-deductible on Form 1040, Schedule A of your personal tax return. When you calculate the costs of owning a home, subtract the tax savings to get a more complete and accurate sense of what homeownership will cost you.

When you finally buy a home, be sure to refigure how much you need to pay in income tax, because your mortgage interest and property tax deductions can help lower your tax bill. If you work for an employer, ask your payroll/benefits department for Form W-4. If you're self-employed, you can complete a worksheet that comes with Form 1040-ES (call 800-TAX-FORM for a copy). Many new homebuyers don't bother with this step, and they receive a big tax refund the next year. Although getting money back from the IRS may feel good, it means that

at a minimum, you gave the IRS an interest-free loan. In the worst case scenario, the reduced cash flow during the year may cause you to accumulate debt or miss out on contributing to tax-deductible retirement accounts.

If you want a more precise estimate as to how homeownership may affect your tax situation, get out your tax return and plug in some reasonable numbers to "guesstimate" how your taxes may change. You can also speak with a tax advisor.

Last but not least, eligible homeowners can exclude from taxable income a significant portion of their gain on the sale of a principal residence: up to $250,000 for single taxpayers and $500,000 for married couples filing jointly.

Although lenders may not care where you spend money outside your home, they do care about your other debt. A lot of other debt, such as credit cards or auto loans, diminishes the funds that are available to pay your housing expenses. Lenders know that having other debt increases the possibility that you may fall behind or actually default on your mortgage payments.

If you have consumer debt that requires monthly payments, lenders calculate another ratio to determine the maximum that you can borrow. Lenders add the amount that you need to pay down your other consumer debt to your monthly housing expense. These total costs typically cannot exceed 36 percent (38 percent for jumbo loans) of your income.

Consumer debt is bad news even without considering that it hurts your qualification for a mortgage. Consumer debt is costly and encourages you to live beyond your means. Unlike the interest on mortgage debt, consumer debt interest is not tax-deductible. Get rid of it — curtail your spending and adjust to living within your means. If you can't live within your means as a renter, it's going to be even harder as a homeowner.

Determining your down payment

Another factor to consider when you decide how much you should borrow is that most lenders require you to purchase *private mortgage insurance* (PMI) if your down payment is less than 20 percent of your home's purchase price. PMI protects the lender from getting stuck with a property that may be worth less than the mortgage you owe, in the event that you default on your loan. On a moderate-size loan, PMI can add hundreds of dollars per year to your payments.

If you have to take PMI to buy a home with less than 20 percent down, keep an eye on your home's value and your loan balance. Over time, your property should appreciate and your loan balance should decrease as you make monthly payments. After your mortgage represents 80 percent or less of the market value of the home you can, with an appraisal that provides proof of the value of your property, get rid of the PMI.

What if you have so much money that you can afford to put down more than a 20 percent down payment? This problem doesn't usually arise — most buyers, especially first-time buyers, struggle to get a 20 percent down payment together. How much should you put down then? The answer depends on what else you can or want to do with the money. If you're considering other investment opportunities, determine whether you can expect to earn a higher rate of return on those other investments versus the interest rate that you'll pay on the mortgage. Forget about the tax deduction for your mortgage interest. Yes, the interest is deductible, but don't forget that the earnings from your investments are taxable.

During this century, stock market and real estate investors have enjoyed average annual returns of around 10 percent per year. So if you borrow mortgage money at around 7 to 8 percent today, in the long term you should come out ahead if you invest in such growth investments. You aren't guaranteed, of course, that you can earn 10 percent yearly (past returns don't guarantee the future). And don't forget that all investments come with risk. The advantage of putting more money down for a home and borrowing less is that it's essentially a risk-free investment (as long as you have adequate insurance on your property).

If you prefer to put down just 20 percent and invest more money elsewhere, that's fine. Just don't keep the extra money (beyond an emergency reserve) under the mattress, in a savings account, or in bonds that pay less interest than your mortgage costs you in interest. Go for growth by investing in stocks, real estate, or a small business. Otherwise, you don't have a chance at earning a higher return than the cost of your mortgage, and you're therefore better off paying down your mortgage.

Is this a good or bad time to buy?

If you're thinking about buying a home, you may be concerned whether home prices are poised to rise or fall. No one wants to purchase a home that then plummets in value. And who wouldn't like to buy just before prices go on an upward trajectory?

It's not easy to predict what's going to happen with real estate prices in a particular city, state, or country over the next one, two, or three or more years. Ultimately, the economic health and vitality of an area drive the demand and prices for homes in that area. An increase in jobs, particularly ones that pay well, increases the demand for housing.

If you first buy a home when you're in your 20s, 30s, or even your 40s, you may end up as a homeowner for several or more decades. Over such a long time, you'll experience lots of ups and downs, but most likely more ups than downs, so I wouldn't be too concerned about trying to predict what's going to happen to the real estate market in the near term. I know

people who avoided buying homes years ago because they thought that prices were expensive. Investors make the same mistake when they avoid investing in stocks because of price.

That said, you may be, at particular times in your life, ambivalent about buying a home. Perhaps you're not sure that you'll stay put for more than three to five years. Therefore, part of your home-buying decision may hinge on whether current home prices in your local area offer you a good value. Examining the level of real estate prices as compared to rent, the state of the job market, and the number of home listings for sale are useful indicators of the housing market's health. Trying to time your purchase has more importance if you think that you may move in less than five years. In that case, avoid buying in a high market. If you expect to move so soon, renting generally makes more sense as I said earlier in this chapter because of the high transaction costs of buying and selling real estate.

Selecting Your Property Type

If you're ready to buy a home, you must make some decisions about what and where to buy. If you grew up in the suburbs, your image of a home may include the traditional single-family home with a lawn, a couple of kids, and a dog or a cat. But single-family homes, of course, aren't the only or even the main types of residential housing in many areas, especially in some higher-cost, urban neighborhoods. Other common types of higher-density housing include:

 ✔ **Condominiums.** These are generally apartment-style units that are stacked on top of and side by side one another. Many condo buildings were originally apartments that were converted — through the sale of ownership of separate units — into condos. When you purchase a condominium, you purchase a specific unit as well as a share of the common areas (for example, the pool, grass and other plantings, entry and hallways, laundry room, and so on).

✔ **Townhomes.** Townhomes are just a fancy way of saying attached or row homes. Think of townhomes as a cross between a condominium and a single-family house. Townhomes are condolike because they're attached (generally sharing walls and a roof) and are homelike because they're often two-story buildings that come with a small yard.

✔ **Cooperatives.** Cooperatives resemble apartment and condominium buildings. When you buy a share in a cooperative, you own a share of the entire building, including some living space. Unlike a condo, you generally need to get approval from the cooperative association if you want to remodel or rent your unit to a tenant. In some co-ops, you must even gain approval from the association for the sale of your unit to a proposed buyer. Co-ops are generally much harder to obtain loans for and to sell, so I don't recommend that you buy one unless you get a deal and you can easily obtain a loan.

All types of shared housing offer two potential advantages. First, this type of housing generally gives you more living space for your dollars. This value makes sense because with a single-family home, a good chunk of the cost for the property is for the land that the home sits upon. Land is good for decks, recreation, and playing children, but you don't live "in" it the way you do with your home. Shared housing maximizes living space for the housing dollars that you spend.

Another benefit of shared housing is that in many situations, you're not personally responsible for general maintenance because the homeowners association (which you pay into) takes care of it. If you don't have the time, energy, or desire to keep up a property, shared housing can make sense. Shared housing units may also provide you with better safety than a stand-alone home and may give you access to shared recreation facilities, such as a pool, tennis courts, and exercise equipment.

So why doesn't everyone purchase shared housing? As an investment, single-family homes generally perform better in the long run. In a good real estate market, single-family homes and other types of housing appreciate, but single-family homes tend to outperform other housing types. Likewise, shared housing is easier to build (and to overbuild) — the greater supply tends to keep its prices depressed. Single-family homes tend to attract more potential buyers — most people, when they can afford it, prefer a stand-alone home, especially for the increased privacy.

If you can afford a smaller single-family home instead of a larger shared-housing unit, buy the single-family home. Shared housing makes more sense for people who don't want to deal with building maintenance and who value the security of living in a larger building with other people. Also know that shared-housing prices tend to hold up better in developed urban environments. If possible, avoid shared housing units in suburban areas where the availability of developable land makes building many more units possible.

If shared housing interests you, make sure that you have the property well inspected. Also, examine the trend in maintenance fees over time to ensure that these costs are under control (see Chapter 12 for more specifics on how to check out property).

Finding the Right Property and Location

Some people know where they want to live so they look at a handful of properties and then buy. Most people take much more time — finding the right house in a desired area at a fair price can take a lot of time. Buying a home can also entail much compromise when you buy with other family members (particularly spouses).

Be realistic about how long it may take you to get up to speed about different areas and to find a home that meets your many needs and concerns. If you're a normal person with a full-time job and you're confined to occasional weekends and evenings to look for a house, three to six months is a short amount of time to settle on an area and actually find and negotiate successfully on a property. Six months to a year is not unusual or slow. Remember that you're talking about spending tens, if not hundreds, of thousands of dollars on a place that you'll come home to every day until you move or sell it.

The biggest barrier to taking your time is real estate agents. Some agents are pushy and want to make a sale and get their commission. Don't work with such agents as a buyer — they can make you miserable, unhappy, and broke. If necessary, begin your search without an agent to avoid this outside pressure.

Be open-minded

Before you start your search, you may have an idea about the type of property and location that interests you or that you think you can afford. You may think, for example, that you can afford only a condominium in the neighborhood that you want. But if you take the time to check out other communities, you may find another area that meets most of your needs and has affordable single-family homes. You'd never know that, though, if you narrowed your search too quickly.

Even if you've lived in an area for a while and think that you know it well, look at different types of properties in a variety of locations before you start to narrow your search. Be open-minded and make sure that you know which of your many criteria for a home you *really* care about. You may have to be flexible with some of your preferences.

After you focus on a particular area or neighborhood, make sure that you see the full range of properties available. If you want to spend $200,000 on a home, look at properties that are more expensive. Most real estate sells for less than its listing price, and you may feel comfortable spending a little bit more if you see what you can purchase if you stretch your budget a little bit. Also, if you work with an agent, make sure that you don't overlook homes that are for sale by their owners (that is, not listed with real estate agents). Otherwise, you may miss out on some good properties.

Research, research, research

Assuming what an area is like from anecdotes or from a small number of personal experiences is a mistake. You may have read or heard that someone was mugged or shot in a particular area. That doesn't make that area dangerous or more dangerous than others. *Get the facts.* Anecdotes and people's perceptions often are not accurate reflections of the facts. Check out the following key items:

✔ **Amenities.** Hopefully, you won't spend all your time at work, slaving away to make your monthly mortgage payment. I hope that you have time to use parks, sports and recreation facilities, and so on. You can drive around the neighborhood to get a sense of these attractions. Most real estate agents just love to show off their favorite neighborhoods. Cities and towns can also mail you information booklets that detail what their town has to offer and where you can find it.

✔ **Schools.** If you have kids, you care about this issue a lot. Unfortunately, many people make snap judgments about school quality without doing their homework. Visit the schools and don't blindly rely on test scores. Talk to parents and teachers and discover what goes on at the school.

If you don't have (or want!) school-age children, you may be tempted to say, "What the heck do I care about the quality of the schools?" You need to care about the schools because even if you don't have kids, the quality of the local schools has direct bearing on the value of your property. Consider these issues even if they're not important to you, because they can affect the resale value of your property.

✔ **Property taxes.** What will your property taxes be? Property tax rates vary from community to community. Check with the town's assessment office or with a good real estate agent.

✔ **Crime.** Call the local police department or visit your public library to get the facts on crime. Cities and towns keep all sorts of crime statistics for neighborhoods — use them!

✔ **Future development.** Check with the planning department in towns that you're considering living in to find out what types of new development and major renovations are in the works. Planning people may also be aware of problems in particular areas.

✔ **Catastrophic risks.** Are the neighborhoods that you're considering buying a home in susceptible to major risks, such as floods, tornadoes, mud slides, fires, or earthquakes? Although proper homeowners insurance can protect you financially, you need to consider how you may deal with such catastrophes emotionally — insurance eases only the financial pain of a home loss. All areas have some risk, and a home in the safest of areas can burn to the ground. Although you can't eliminate all risks, you can at least educate yourself about the potential catastrophic risks in various areas.

If you're new to an area or don't have a handle on an area's risks, try a number of different sources. Knowledgeable and honest real estate agents may help, but you can also dig for primary information. For example, the U.S. Geologic Survey puts together maps that help you see the differences of potential earthquake risks by area. The USGS maintains offices all around the country — check your local phone directory in the government white pages section. The Federal Emergency Management Agency (FEMA) provides maps that show flood risk areas (800-358-9616). Insurance companies and agencies can also tell you what they know of risks in particular areas.

Understand market value

Over many months, you'll look at lots of properties for sale, perhaps dozens or even hundreds. Use these viewings as an opportunity to find out what places are worth. The listing price is not what a house is worth — it may be, but odds are it's not. Property that is priced to sell usually does just that — sell. Properties left on the market are often overpriced. The listing price on such properties may reflect what an otherwise greedy or uninformed seller and his or her agent hope that some fool will pay.

Of the properties that you see, keep track of the price that it ends up selling for (good agents can help). Properties often sell for less than the listed price. Keeping track of selling prices gives you a better sense of what you can afford and gives you a good handle on what properties are really worth.

Pound the pavement

After you set your sights on that special home, thoroughly check out the surroundings that you'll live near, should you decide to buy. You need to know what you're getting yourself into.

Go back to the neighborhood in which the property is located at different times of the day and on different days of the week. Knock on a few doors and meet your potential neighbors. Ask questions. Talk to property owners as well as renters. Because they don't have a financial stake in the area, renters are often more forthcoming with negative information about an area.

Once you decide where and what to buy, you're ready to try to put a deal together. I cover issues common to both home and investment property purchases — such as mortgages, negotiations, inspections, and so on — in Chapter 12.

Chapter 12

Investing in Real Estate

· ·

· ·

*I*f you've already bought your own home (and even if you haven't), using real estate as an investment may interest you. Over the years, decades, and centuries, real estate investing, like the stock market and small-business investments, has generated vast wealth for participants. As I discuss in Chapters 2 and 11, the rate of return from good real estate investments is comparable to that available from investing in the stock market.

Real estate is like other types of ownership investments, such as stocks, where you have an ownership stake in an asset. Although you have the potential for significant profits, don't forget that you also accept more risk. Real estate is not a gravy train or a simple way to get wealthy. Like stocks, real estate goes through good and bad performance periods. Most people who make money investing in real estate do so because they invest and hold property over many years. The vast majority of people who don't make money in real estate make easily avoidable mistakes, which I discuss in this chapter.

Real Estate Investment Attractions

As I discuss in Chapter 1, in addition to those who built their wealth by focusing on real estate investments, many others who built their wealth through the companies that they started or through other avenues also diversified into real estate investments. What do these wealthy folks know, and why do they choose to invest in real estate? The following are some of real estate's attractions:

✔ **Limited land.** Short of using landfill to build buildings over water, the supply of land on planet Earth is fixed, thanks in part to water that covers about 70 percent of our globe. And because people are prone to reproduce (I must confess to being party to this as well), demand for land and housing continues to grow. Land, and what you can do with it, is what makes real estate valuable. Cities and islands, such as Hawaii, Tokyo, San Francisco, Los Angeles, and New York City, have the highest housing costs around because land is limited.

✔ **Leverage.** Real estate is different from most other investments in that you can borrow up to 80 to 90 percent or more of the value of the property. Thus, you can use your small down payment of 10 to 20 percent of the purchase price to buy, own, and control a much larger investment. Of course, you hope that the value of your real estate goes up — if it does, you make money on your investment as well as on the money that you borrowed.

Here's a quick example to illustrate. Suppose that you purchase a property for $100,000 and make a $20,000 down payment. Over the next three years, imagine that the property appreciates to $120,000. Thus, you have a profit (on paper at least) of $20,000 on an investment of just $20,000. In other words, you've made a 100 percent return on your investment. (Note that in this scenario I ignore whether your expenses from the property exceed the rental income that you collect.)

Leverage is good for you if property prices appreciate, but leverage can also work against you. If your $100,000 property decreases in value to $80,000, even though it's only dropped 20 percent in value, you actually lose (on paper) 100 percent of your original $20,000 investment. If you have an outstanding mortgage of $80,000 on this property and you need to sell, you actually must pay money into the sale to cover selling costs, in addition to losing your entire original investment. Ouch!

✔ **Growth and income.** Another reason that real estate is a popular investment is that you can make money from it in two major ways. First, you hope and expect over the years that your real estate investments appreciate in value. The appreciation of your properties compounds tax-deferred during your years of ownership. You don't pay tax on this profit until you sell your property — and even then you can roll over your gain into another investment property and avoid paying tax. (See the "Roll over those rental property profits" sidebar for details on tax-deferred exchanges of investment properties.)

In addition to making money from your properties' increase in value, you can also make money from the ongoing business that you run. You rent out investment property to make a profit based on the property's rental income that (hopefully) exceeds your expenses (mortgage, property taxes, insurance, maintenance, and so on). Unless you make a large down payment, your monthly operating profit is small or non-existent in the early years of rental property ownership. Over time, your operating profit, which is subject to ordinary income tax, should rise as you increase your rental prices faster than your expenses. During soft periods in the local economy, however, rents may rise slower than your expenses (rents may even fall).

✔ **Diversification.** An advantage of holding some investment real estate is that its value doesn't necessarily move in tandem with other investments, such as stocks or small-business investments that you hold.

✔ **Ability to "add value."** Unlike investing in the stock market, you may have some good ideas about how to improve a property and make it more valuable. Perhaps you can fix up a property or develop it further and raise the rental income accordingly. Perhaps through legwork, persistence, and good negotiating skills, you can purchase a property below its fair market value.

Relative to investing in the stock market, persistent and savvy real estate investors can more easily buy property below its fair market value. You can do the same in the stock market, but the scores of professional, full-time money managers who analyze stocks make finding bargains more difficult.

✔ **Ego gratification.** Face it, investing in real estate appeals to some investors because it's one of the few investments that's tangible. Although few admit it, some real estate investors get an ego rush from a tangible display of their wealth. You can drive past investment real estate and show it off to others. In "What My Ego Wants, My Ego Gets,"a piece appropriately written for the *New York Times,* "Donald Trump publicly admitted what most everyone else knew long ago: He holds his real estate investments partly for his ego. Trump confessed of his purchase of the famed Plaza Hotel in the Big Apple, ". . . I realized it was 100 percent true — ego did play a large role in the Plaza purchase and is, in fact, a significant factor in all of my deals."

✔ **Less emotionally based decisions.** One of the problems with investing in the securities markets, such as the stock market, is that prices are constantly changing. Newspapers, television news programs, and online computer services dutifully report the latest price quotes. From my observations and my work with individual investors, I've seen the constant changes in the financial markets and the constant reports on those changes cause some investors to lose sight of the long-term and the big picture. In the worst cases, large short-term drops lead investors to panic and sell at what end up being bargain prices. Or, headlines about big increases pull investors in lemminglike fashion into an overheated and peaking market. Because all you need to do is pick up a telephone and place your sell or buy order, some stock market investors fall prey to snap, irrational judgments.

Roll over those rental property profits

When you sell a stock or mutual fund investment that you hold outside a retirement account, you must pay tax on your profits. By contrast, you can avoid paying tax on your profit when you sell a rental property if you roll over your gain into another *like kind* investment real estate property.

The rules for properly making one of these 1031 exchanges (also called *Starker exchanges*) are complex and usually involve third parties. With like-kind transactions, you don't receive the proceeds of the sale — they must go into an escrow account. You must complete the rollover within a 6 month time limit, and you must also identify a replacement property within 45 days of the sale of the first property. Make sure that you find an attorney and/or tax advisor who is an expert at these transactions to ensure that everything goes smoothly (and legally).

If you don't roll over your gain, you may owe significant taxes because of how the IRS defines your gain. For example, if you buy a property for $200,000 and sell it for $250,000, you not only owe tax on that difference, but you also owe tax on an additional amount, depending on the property's depreciation. The amount of depreciation that you deducted on your tax returns reduces the original $200,000 purchase price, making the taxable difference that much larger. For example, if you deducted $25,000 for depreciation over the years that you owned the property, you owe tax on the difference between the sale price of $250,000 and $175,000 ($200,000 purchase price minus $25,000 depreciation).

Like the stock market, the real estate market is constantly changing. However, to a real estate investor, short-term, day-to-day, and week-to-week changes are transparent. Publications don't report the value of your real estate holdings daily, weekly, or even monthly, which is good because you can focus more on the longer term. If prices do decline over the months and years, you're much less likely to sell in a panic with real estate. Preparing a property for sale and eventually getting it sold takes a good deal of time, and this added time helps keep your vision in focus.

Who Should Avoid Real Estate Investing?

Real estate investing isn't for everyone, not even close. Most people perform better when they invest their ownership holdings in a diversified portfolio of stocks, such as through stock mutual funds. You should shy away from real estate investments that involve managing property if any of the following traits describe you:

✔ **Time starved.** Buying and owning investment real estate and being a landlord takes a lot of time. If you fail to do your homework before purchasing property, you can end up overpaying or buying a heap of trouble. As for managing a property, you can hire a property manager to help with screening and finding good tenants and troubleshooting problems with the building, but this step costs money and still requires some time involvement. Also, remember that most tenants don't care for a property the same way property owners do. If every little scratch or carpet stain sends your blood pressure skyward, avoid distressing yourself as a landlord.

✔ **Not funding your retirement accounts.** Exhaust contributions to retirement accounts such as 401(k)s, SEP-IRAs, Keoghs, and so on (see Chapter 3), before you seriously invest in real estate. Funding retirement accounts gives you an immediate tax deduction when you contribute money to them. And after the money is inside a retirement account, all the growth and income from your investments compounds without taxation. However, you derive no tax benefits while you accumulate your down payment for an investment real estate purchase. Furthermore, the operating profit or income from your real estate investment is subject to taxes as you earn it.

✔ **Real estate doesn't interest you.** Some people simply don't feel comfortable and informed when it comes to investing in real estate. If you've had experience and success with stock market investing, that's a good reason to stick with it and avoid real estate. Over long periods of time, both stocks and real estate provide comparable returns.

Simple, Profitable Real Estate Investments

Investing in rental real estate that you're responsible for can be a lot of work. With rental properties, you have all the headaches of maintaining a property, including finding and dealing with tenants, without the benefits of living in and enjoying the property.

Unless you're extraordinarily interested in and motivated to own investment real estate, start with, and perhaps limit your real estate investing to a couple of much simpler yet still profitable methods that I discuss in this section.

A place to call home

During your adult life, you need to provide a roof over your head. You may be able to sponge off your folks or some other relative for a number of years, and if you're content with this, good for you! By minimizing your housing costs, you may be able to save and invest more, and you can save more for a down payment. Go for it, if your relatives will!

But what if neither you nor your relatives are up for the challenge? For the long term, because you need a place to live, why not own real estate instead of renting it? Real estate is the only investment that you can live in or rent to produce income. You can't live in a stock, bond, or mutual fund! Unless you expect to move within the next few years, buying a place probably makes good long-term financial sense. In the long term, owning usually costs less than renting and allows you to build equity in an asset. Read Chapter 11 to find out more about buying and profiting from a home.

Real estate investment trusts

Real estate investment trusts (REITs) are entities that generally invest in different types of property, such as shopping centers, apartments, and other rental buildings. For a fee, REIT managers identify and negotiate the purchase of properties that they believe are good investments and manage these properties, including all tenant relations. Thus, REITs are a good way to invest in real estate for people who don't want the hassles and headaches that come with directly owning and managing rental property.

Surprisingly, most books that focus on real estate investing neglect REITs. Why? I have come to the conclusion they do so for three major reasons. First, if you invest in real estate through REITs, you don't need to read a long, complicated book on real estate investment. Second, real estate brokers write many of these books. Not surprisingly, the real estate investment strategies touted in these books include and advocate the use of brokers. You can buy REITs without real estate brokers. Finally, a certain snobbishness prevails among people who consider themselves to be "serious" real estate investors. One real estate writer/investor went so far as to say that REITs aren't "real" real estate investments.

Please. No, you can't drive your friends by a REIT and show it off. But those who put their egos aside when making real estate investments are happy that they considered REITs and have enjoyed double-digit annual gains over the decades.

You can research and purchase shares in individual REITs, which trade as securities on the major stock exchanges (see Chapter 7 for more information). An even better approach is to buy a mutual fund that invests in a diversified mixture of REITs (see Chapter 9). Unlike direct real estate investments, investments in REITs are generally easy to sell.

In addition to providing you with a diversified, low-hassle real estate investment, REITs offer an additional advantage that traditional rental real estate does not. You can easily invest in REITs through a retirement account (for example, IRA or Keogh). As with traditional real estate investments, you can even buy REITs and mutual fund REITs with borrowed money. You can buy with 50 percent down when you purchase such investments through a brokerage account. (You can only buy with 50 percent down, called buying on margin, through a non-retirement account.)

Generally Lousy Real Estate "Investments"

Some "simple" ways to invest in real estate rarely make sense because they're near-certain money losers. Others may work for you, depending on the investments that you're looking for.

Second/vacation homes

A sometimes idyllic notion and expanded part of the American dream is the weekend cottage or condo — a place that you can retreat to when crowded urban or suburban living conditions get on your nerves. When it's not in use, you may rent out your vacation home and earn some income to help defray part of the maintenance expenses.

If you can realistically afford the additional costs of a second, or vacation, home, I'm not going to tell you how to spend your extra cash. Investment real estate is property that you rent out 90 percent or more of the time. Most second-home owners that I know rent their property out very little — 10 percent or less of the time. As a result, second homes are usually money drains. Even if you do rent your second home most of the time, high tenant turnover decreases your net rental income.

Part of the allure of a second home is the supposed tax benefits. Even when you qualify for some or all of them, tax benefits only partially reduce the cost of owning a property. I've seen more than a few cases in which the second home is such a cash drain that it prevents its owners from contributing to and taking advantage of tax-deductible retirement savings plans.

If you don't rent out a second home property most of the time, ask yourself whether you can afford such a luxury. Can you accomplish your other financial goals — saving for retirement, paying for the home in which you live, and so on — with this added expense? Keeping a second home is more of a consumption than an investment decision.

Time-shares

Time-shares are near-certain money losers. With a time-share, you buy a week or two of ownership or usage of a particular unit, usually a condominium, in a resort location. If you pay $8,000 for a week of "ownership" (in addition to ongoing maintenance fees, which can easily run $200 per year or more), you pay the equivalent of more than $400,000 a year for the whole unit ($8,000/week x 52 weeks), but a comparable unit nearby may sell for only $150,000. All the extra markup pays the salespeople's commissions, administrative expenses, and profits for the time-share development company.

People usually get hoodwinked into buying a time-share when they're enjoying a vacation someplace. Vacationers are easy prey for salespeople who, often using high-pressure sales tactics, want to sell them a souvenir of the trip. The cheese in the mousetrap is an offer of something free (for example, a free night's stay in a unit) for going through the sales presentation.

The time-share concept unfortunately, was imported into the U.S. in the early 1970s and has stuck ever since. Even large and otherwise reputable companies, such as Disney, Marriott, and Hilton, have moved into this business in recent years. It's a good business for them — selling lousy time-share investments to the public — but now you won't become one more of their victims!

If you can't live without a time-share, consider buying a used one. Many previous buyers, who almost always have lost much of their original investment, try to dump their time-shares. This fact tells you something about time-shares. You may be able to buy a time-share from an existing owner at a fair price, but why commit yourself to taking a vacation in the same location and building at the same time each year? Many time-shares let you trade your weeks; however, doing so is a hassle, and you're limited by what time slots you can trade for, which are typically dates that other people don't want. Most of these open time slots are undesirable — that's why people trade them!

Limited partnerships

In Chapter 1, I give you good reasons to avoid limited partnerships. Limited partnerships sold through stockbrokers and financial planners who work on commission are burdened by high sales commissions and ongoing management fees. Good real estate investment trusts, which I discuss earlier in this chapter, are infinitely better alternatives. REITs, unlike limited partnerships, are also completely liquid.

Scams

Wanting to make a lot of money in a hurry is very American. Real estate investors with lofty expectations for high returns become bait for various hucksters who promise these investors great riches. As I've discussed already in the section on crummy real estate investments, it's bad enough when the deck is stacked against you. Even worse is to put your money into scams.

First Pension was an outfit run by loan broker William Cooper that bilked investors out of more than $100 million. First Pension was sold as a limited partnership that invested in mortgages. Using a Ponzi-type (pyramid) scheme, Cooper used the money from new investors to pay dividends to earlier investors.

Another way that some investors invest in real estate is to invest in second mortgages. The allure of lending your money to a property buyer is the double-digit returns. As I discuss in Chapter 8, the only way to charge interest rates of 10 percent or higher is to lend your money to higher-risk borrowers.

Even worse than the high risk that comes with higher interest rates is the problem that some second mortgage investments are hypes and scams. Liz Pulliam reported in the *Orange County Register* that Irvine Mortgage Corporation promised second mortgage investors 14 percent returns by investing in properties with at least 30 percent equity. It also boasted no investor losses over 25 years.

When the real estate market softened in California in the early 1990s, some of these second mortgages defaulted. Investors, many of whom placed their retirement dollars with the Irvine Mortgage Corporation, later discovered that some of the properties that they had lent money on never had their mortgage recorded against it. These properties ended up in default.

Time-shares, a truly terrible investment that I discuss in this chapter, have also been subject to bankruptcy and fraud problems.

Hundreds of thousands of viewers fall prey annually to infomercial hucksters. Among the more infamous real estate infomercial promoters is Tom Vu. At his seminars, according to the *Los Angeles Times*, he says, "Well, if you make no money with me, you a loser." Vu, who came to the U.S. from Vietnam in the mid-1970s, claims to have made a fortune investing in real estate using a fairly simple system. He says that he searches for property owners who are in debt up to their eyeballs and offers to buy their properties with no money down. By finding desperate buyers, he says, you can buy real estate at a big discount from its fair market value.

Vu makes his money from running high-priced seminars to teach you basic real estate techniques that you can read in a book for about $20. Vu, however, charges up to $15,000 for a five-day seminar! As if overpaying this much isn't enough, Vu's former "students," who have filed a number of lawsuits that include a class action suit, say that his methods don't work and that he reneged on his promises to go into partnership on properties that they identified. A number of states have and are currently investigating Vu's practices, have barred further Vu seminars in their state, and are seeking compensation for victims. Unfortunately, Vu appears to have moved much of his money overseas. Other real estate seminar hucksters such as Robert Allen and Ed Buckley saw their seminar enterprises end up in bankruptcy, sunk by the claims of their unhappy students.

Other scams also abound. Stephen Murphy was a real estate investor who claimed to make a fortune buying foreclosed commercial real estate and wrote and self-published a book to share his techniques with the public. Murphy's organization called the people who bought his book and pitched them into collaborating with him on property purchases that supposedly would return upwards of 100 percent or more per year. However, Murphy had other ideas, and he siphoned off nearly two-thirds of the money for himself and for promotion of his books! He even hoodwinked Donald Trump to write praise for his book and work saying, "I really admire Steve Murphy. . . . Steve commands some very wise, intelligent . . . and unique purchasing strategies." I'll say!

New York attorney Alan Harris also defrauded real estate investors out of millions of dollars (including actress Shirley Jones) when he pocketed money that was set aside for property investments. The lure: Harris promised investors far higher yields than they could get elsewhere.

If an investment "opportunity" sounds too good to be true, it is. If you want to invest in real estate, avoid the hucksters and either invest directly in properties that you can control or invest through reputable REITs.

Advanced (Direct) Real Estate Investments

Every year *Forbes* magazine publishes a special issue that profiles the 400 wealthiest Americans, known as the Forbes 400. Forbes leaves out mobsters and drug kingpins — to get on the list, you must make the money through seemingly legitimate and legal channels. Numerous people made the most recent list primarily because of their real estate investments. For others on the list, real estate was an important secondary factor that contributed to their wealth.

Consider the case of Thomas Flatley. An Irish immigrant, he was practically broke when he came to America at age 18. After dabbling at his own small business, he got into real estate development. Today he owns more than 5,000 apartments, 14 hotels, and more than 6 million square feet of office and retail space, and his net worth is hundreds of millions of dollars. That's a lot of property and tenants to manage!

If you think you're cut out to be a landlord and are ready for the responsibility of buying, owning, and managing rental real estate, you have literally millions of direct real estate investment options from which to choose.

Before you begin this potentially treacherous journey, I strongly recommend that you read Chapter 11. Many concepts that you need to know to be a successful real estate investor are similar to those that you need when you buy a home. However, the rest of this chapter focuses on issues that are more unique to real estate investing.

Have realistic expectations

If you've attempted to read or have read some of the many real estate investment books that have been published over the years, you may need to slightly deprogram yourself. Too often, authors attempt to make real estate investments sound like the one and only sure way to become a multimillionaire with little effort. Consider the following statements made by real estate book authors. My rebuttals to their claims follow:

> **"Rather than yielding only a small interest payment or dividend, real estate in prime locations can appreciate 20 percent a year or more."**

Bank accounts, bonds, and stocks pay interest or dividends that typically amount to 2 to 6 percent per year. However, bank accounts and bonds aren't comparable investments — they're far more conservative and liquid and therefore, don't offer the potential for double-digit returns. Stock market investing is comparable to investing in real estate, but you shouldn't go into real estate investments expecting annual returns of 20 percent or more. Those who purchased good Los Angeles real estate in the 1950s and held onto it for the next three decades earned handsome returns as the population of this area boomed. Finding areas like Los Angeles and knowing how long to hold onto investments in these areas is easier said than done. With real estate investments, you can expect to earn 8 to 12 percent per year, but not 20 percent or more.

> **"A good piece of property can't do anything but go up."**

Any city, town, or community has good pieces of real estate. But that doesn't mean that communities can't and won't have slow or depressed years. Real estate in some parts of the Midwest and South, for example, has appreciated quite slowly — at or just above the rate of inflation — for periods as long as a generation or more.

> **"Real estate is the best way of preserving and enhancing wealth. . . . [it] stands head and shoulders above any other form of investment."**

Investing in stocks or in a small business is every bit as profitable as investing in real estate. In fact, more great fortunes have been built in small business than in any other form of investment. Over the long term, stock market investors have enjoyed (with far less hassle) average annual rates of return comparable to real estate investor's returns.

Real estate, like all investments, has its pros and cons. Investing in real estate is time intensive, carries investment risks, and, as you can see later in this chapter, comes with other risks. Invest in real estate because you enjoy the challenge of the business and because you want to diversify your portfolio, not because you want a get-rich-quick outlet.

Evaluate your options

As I discuss in Chapter 11, purchasing real estate if you don't intend to hold it over a number of years — preferably at least five — doesn't make a whole lot of sense. Even if you're lucky enough to buy your property right before big price increases, you're not likely to make an immediate profit. All the costs associated with buying and then selling a property can easily gobble up your profit and sometimes can cause you to lose money. If prices hold steady or decline during your short period of ownership, you'll lose money. Ideally, you should plan to make real estate investments that you hold until, and perhaps through, your retirement years.

But what should you buy? The following is my take on various potential real estate investments.

Residential housing

Your best bet for real estate investing is to purchase residential property. People always need a place to live. Residential housing is easier to understand, purchase, and manage than most other types of property, such as office and retail property. If you're a homeowner, you already have experience locating, purchasing, and maintaining residential property.

The most common residential housing options are single-family homes, condominiums, and townhouses. You can also purchase multi-unit buildings. In addition to the considerations that I address in Chapter 11, from an investment and rental perspective, consider these issues when you decide what type of property to buy:

✔ **Tenants.** Single-family homes that require just one tenant are simpler to deal with than a multi-unit apartment building that requires the management and maintenance of multiple renters and units.

✔ **Maintenance.** For individual owners, condominiums are generally the lowest-maintenance properties because most condominium associations deal with issues such as roofing, gardening, and so on for the entire building. Note that you're still responsible for maintenance that is needed inside your unit, such as servicing appliances, interior painting, and so on. Beware, though, that some condo complexes don't allow you to rent your unit. With a single-family home or apartment building, you're responsible for all the maintenance. Of course, you can hire someone to do the work, but you still have to find the contractors and coordinate and oversee the work.

✔ **Appreciation potential.** Look for property where simple cosmetic and other fixes may allow you to increase rents. Such improvements can increase the market value of the property. Although condos may be somewhat easier to keep up, they tend to appreciate less than homes or apartment buildings, unless the condos are located in a desirable urban area. One way to add value to some larger properties is to "condo-ize" them. In some areas, if zoning allows, you can convert a single-family home or multi-unit apartment building into condominiums. Keep in mind, however, that this metamorphization requires significant research, both on the zoning front as well as with estimating remodeling and construction costs.

✔ **Cash flow.** As I discuss later in the chapter, your rental property brings in rental income that you hope covers and exceeds your expenses. The difference between the rental income that you collect and the expenses that you pay out is known as your *cash flow.*

Unless you can afford a large down payment (25 percent or more), the early years of rental property ownership may financially challenge you. Making a profit in the early years from the monthly cash flow with a single-family home is generally the hardest stage of owning rental property because such properties usually sell at a premium price relative to the rent that they can command (you pay extra for the land, which you can't rent). Also, the downside to having just one tenant is that when you have a vacancy, you have no rental income. Apartment buildings, particularly those with more units, can generally produce a small positive cash flow, even in the early years of rental ownership. With all properties, as time goes on, generating a positive cash flow gets easier as you pay down your mortgage debt and hopefully increase your rents.

Unless you really want to minimize maintenance responsibilities, I would avoid condominium investments. Single-family home investments are generally more straightforward for most people. Just make sure that you run the numbers (I show you how in the "Cash flow" section of this chapter) on your rental income and expenses to see if you can afford the negative cash flow that often occurs in the early years of ownership. Apartment building investments are best left to sophisticated investors who like a challenge and can manage more-complex properties. As I discuss in the next chapter, make sure that you do thorough inspections before you buy any rental property.

Land

If tenants are a hassle and maintaining a building is a never-ending pain, why not invest in land? You can simply buy land in an area that will soon experience a building boom, hold onto it until prices soar, and then cash in.

Such an investment idea sounds good in theory. In practice, however, making the big bucks through land investments isn't easy. Although land doesn't require upkeep and tenants, it does require financial feeding. Investing in land is a cash drain, and because it costs money to purchase land, you also have a mortgage payment to make. Mortgage lenders charge higher interest rates on loans to purchase land because they see it as a more speculative investment. You also don't get depreciation tax write-offs because land isn't depreciable. You also have property tax payments to meet, as well as other expenses. However, with land investments, you don't receive income from the property to offset these expenses.

If you decide that you someday want to develop the property, that will also cost you a hefty chunk of money. Obtaining a loan for development is challenging and more expensive than obtaining a loan for a developed property.

What about converting your current home into a rental when you move?

If you move into another home, turning your current home into a rental property may make sense. After all, it saves you the time and cost of finding a separate rental property.

Unfortunately, many people make the mistake of holding onto their current home for the wrong reasons when they buy another. This situation often happens when homeowners must sell their home in a depressed market. Nobody likes to lose money and sell their home for less than they paid for it. Thus, some owners hold onto their homes until prices recover.

If you plan to move and want to keep your current home as a long-term investment property,

you can. But turning your home into a short-term rental is usually a bad move. First, you may not want the responsibilities of a landlord, yet you force yourself into the landlord business when you convert your home into a rental.

Second, if the home eventually does rebound in value, you owe tax on the profit if your property is a rental when you sell it and don't buy another rental property. You can purchase another rental property through a 1031 exchange to defer paying taxes on your profit. (See the discussion earlier in this chapter.)

Identifying many years in advance which communities will experience rapid population and job growth is not easy. Land prices in those areas that people believe will be the next hot spot already sell at a premium price. If property growth doesn't meet expectations, appreciation will be low or non-existent.

If you decide to invest in land, be sure that you:

- ✔ **Can afford it.** Tally up your annual carrying costs so that you can see what your annual cash drain may be. What are the financial consequences of this cash outflow — for example, will you be able to fully fund your tax-advantaged retirement accounts? If you can't, count the lost tax benefits as another cost of owning land.

- ✔ **Understand what further improvements the land needs.** Running utility lines, building roads, landscaping, and so on, all cost money. If you plan to develop and build on the land that you purchase, research what these things may cost. Make sure that you don't make these estimates with your rose-tinted sunglasses on — improvements almost always cost more than you expect.

- ✔ **Know its zoning status.** The value of land is heavily dependent upon what you can develop on it. Never, ever purchase land without thoroughly understanding its zoning status and what you can and can't build on it. Also research the disposition of the planning department and nearby communities. Areas that are antigrowth and antidevelopment are less likely to be good places for you to invest in land, especially if you need permission to do the type of project that you have in mind. Beware that zoning can change for the worse — sometimes a zoning alteration can reduce what you can develop on a property and therefore the property's value.

- ✔ **Are familiar with the local economic and housing situations.** In the best of all worlds, you want to buy land in an area that is home to rapidly expanding companies and that has a shortage of housing and developable land.

Commercial real estate

Ever thought about owning and renting out a small office building or strip mall? If you're really motivated and willing to roll up your sleeves, you may want to consider commercial real estate investments. Generally, you're better off not investing in such real estate because it's much more complicated than investing in residential real estate. It's also riskier from an investment and tenant-turnover perspective. When tenants move out, new tenants sometimes require extensive and costly improvements, which you'll likely need to provide to compete with other building owners.

If you're a knowledgeable real estate investor and you like a challenge, there are two good reasons to invest in commercial real estate. First, is if your analysis of your local market suggests that it's a good time to buy.

Another reason to consider buying commercial real estate is that you can use some of the space if you own your own small business. Just as it's generally more cost-effective to own your home rather than rent over the years, so it is with commercial real estate if — and this is a big if — you buy at a reasonably good time and hold the property for many years.

So how do you evaluate the state of your local commercial real estate market? You must check out, over a number of years, the supply and demand statistics. How much space is available for rent, and how has that changed in recent years? What is the vacancy rate, and how has that changed over time? Also, examine the rental rates, usually quoted as a price per square foot.

One warning sign that purchasing a commercial property in an area is a bad idea is a market where the supply of available space has increased faster than demand, leading to falling rental rates and higher vacancies. A slowing local economy and a higher unemployment rate also spell trouble for commercial real estate prices. Each market is different, so make sure that you check out the details of your area. In the next section, I explain where you can find such information.

Decide where and what to buy

If you're going to invest in real estate, you can do tons of research to decide where and what to buy. In the sections that follow, I explain what to look for in a community and area that you want to invest in. Keep in mind, though, that as in other aspects of life, you can spend the rest of your life looking for the perfect real estate investment, never find it, never invest, and miss out on lots of opportunities, profit, and even fun.

Tax credits for low-income housing and old buildings

If you invest in low-income housing or particularly old commercial buildings, you can gain special tax credits. The credits represent a direct reduction in your tax bill because you spend money to rehabilitate and improve such properties. These tax credits exist to encourage investors to invest in and fix up old or run-down buildings that likely would continue to deteriorate otherwise.

The tax credits range from as little as 10 percent of the expenditures to as much as 90 percent, depending on the property type. The IRS has strict rules governing what types of properties qualify. You may earn tax credits for rehabilitating certain older nonresidential buildings. *Certified historic structures,* both residential and nonresidential, also qualify for tax credits. See IRS Form 3468 to find out more about these credits.

TECHNICAL STUFF

> # Should you form a real estate corporation?
>
> When you invest in and manage real estate with at least one other partner, you can set up a company through which both of you collectively own the property.
>
> The main reason that you may want to consider forming a real estate corporation is liability protection. A corporation can reduce the chances of lenders or tenants suing you.
>
> To find out more about the pros and cons of incorporating and the different entities under which you can do business, see Chapter 15.

Economic issues

INVESTIGATE

People need a place to live, but an area doesn't generally attract people to buy homes if no jobs exist. Ideally, look to invest in real estate in communities that maintain diverse job bases. If the local economy is heavily reliant on jobs in a small number of industries, that dependence increases the risk of your real estate investments. The U.S. Bureau of Labor Statistics compiles this data for metropolitan areas and counties. A good local library should have this data. You can also visit the Bureau's Web site at www.bls.gov.

Also, consider which industries are more heavily represented in the local economy. If most of the jobs come from slow-growing or shrinking employment sectors, such as farming, small retail, shoe and apparel manufacturing, and government, real estate prices are unlikely to rise quickly in the years ahead. On the other hand, areas with a greater preponderance of high-growth industries, such as technology, stand a greater chance of faster price appreciation.

Also, check out the unemployment situation and examine how the jobless rate has changed in recent years. Good signs to look for are declining unemployment and increasing job growth. The Bureau of Labor Statistics also tracks this data.

I'm not suggesting that you need to conduct a nationwide search for the best areas. In fact, investing in real estate closer to home is best, because you're probably more familiar with the local area and you should have an easier time researching and managing local property. If you live in or near a major metropolitan area, you can find some areas that easily fit the bill.

Real estate market

The price of real estate, like the price of anything else, is driven by supply and demand. The smaller the supply and the greater the demand, the higher prices climb.

John Reed, a real estate investor and writer, learned this the hard way: "I personally lost all the money I had made in 15 years of apartment investing as a result of owning apartments in Texas when the overbuilding occurred in the mid-'80s," Reed says.

Ouch! Imagine investing for 15 years and then losing it all! Credit was loose in some areas during the 1980s, which led to a building boom. But in many parts of Texas, as in some other parts of the country, a ton of buildable land existed. This abundance of land and available credit inevitably led to over-building. When the supply of anything expands at a much faster rate than demand, prices usually fall.

Upward pressure on real estate prices tends to be greatest in areas with little buildable land. This characteristic was one of the things that attracted me to real estate in the San Francisco Bay Area when I moved there in the mid-1980s. If you look at a map of this area, you can see that the city of San Francisco and the communities to the south are on a peninsula. Ocean, bay inlets, and mountains bound the rest of the Bay Area. Eighty-two percent of the land in the greater Bay Area isn't available for development because state and federal government parks, preserves, and other areas protect the land from development, or the land is impossible to develop. Of the land available for development, about 98 percent of it in San Francisco, and two-thirds of the land in nearby counties, had already been developed.

In the long term, the lack of buildable land in an area can prove a problem. Real estate prices that are too high may cause employers and employees to relocate to less-expensive areas. If you want to invest in real estate in an area with little buildable land and sky-high prices, run the numbers to see if the deal makes economic sense. (I explain how to do this later in this section.)

In addition to buildable land, consider these other important real estate market indicators to get a sense of the health, or lack thereof, of a particular market:

- **Building permits.** The trend in the number of building permits tells you how the supply of real estate properties may soon change. A long and sustained rise in permits over several years can indicate that the supply of new property may dampen future price appreciation. Many areas experienced enormous increases in new building during the late-1980s, right before prices peaked due to excess inventory. Conversely, new building dried up in many areas in the late 1970s and early 1980s as onerous interest rates strangled builders and developers.

- **Vacancy rates.** As with building permits, low vacancy rates generally foretell future real estate price appreciation. If few rentals are vacant, that means more competition and demand for existing units, which is a good sign for investors. Conversely, high vacancy rates indicate an excess supply of real estate, which may put downward pressure on rental rates as many landlords compete to attract tenants.

✔ **Listings of property for sale and number of sales.** Just as the building of many new buildings is bad for future real estate price appreciation, increasing numbers of property listings is also an indication of future trouble. As property prices reach high levels, some investors decide that they can make more money cashing in and investing elsewhere. When the market is flooded with listings, prospective buyers can be choosier, exerting downward pressure on prices. At high prices (relative to the cost of renting), more prospective buyers elect to rent and the number of sales relative to listings drops.

A sign of a healthy real estate market is a decreasing and low level of property listings, which indicates that the demand from buyers meets or exceeds the supply of property for sale from sellers. When the cost of buying is relatively low compared with the cost of renting, more renters elect and can afford to purchase, thus increasing the number of sales.

✔ **Rents.** The trend in rental rates that renters are willing and able to pay over the years gives a good indication as to the demand for housing. When the demand for housing keeps up with the supply of housing and the local economy continues to grow, rents generally increase. This increase is a positive sign for continued real estate price appreciation. Beware buying rental property subject to rent control — the property's expenses may rise faster than you can raise the rents.

Property valuation and financial projections

How do you know what a property is really worth? Some say it's worth what a ready, willing, and financially able buyer is willing to pay. But some buyers pay more than what a property is truly worth. And sometimes buyers who are patient, do their homework, and bargain hard are able to buy property for less than its fair market value.

Crunching some numbers to figure what revenue and expenses a rental property may bring is one of the most important exercises that you can go through when you decide whether you should buy a property and determine the property's worth. In the sections that follow, I walk you through these important calculations.

Cash flow

Cash flow is the difference between the money that a property brings in minus what you pay out for expenses. If you pay so much for a property that its expenses (including the mortgage payment and property taxes) consistently exceed its income, you have a money drain on your hands. Maybe you have the financial reserves to withstand the temporary drain for the first few years, but you need to know what you're getting yourself into up front.

One of the biggest mistakes that novice rental property investors make is not realizing all the costs associated with investment property. In the worst cases, some investors end up in personal bankruptcy from the drain of *negative cash flow* (expenses exceeding income). In other cases, I've seen negative cash flow hamper people's ability to accomplish important financial goals.

The second biggest mistake rental property investors make is believing the financial statements that sellers and their real estate agents prepare. Just as an employer views a resumé, you should always view such financial statements as advertisements rather than sources of objective information. In some cases, sellers and agents lie. In most cases, these statements contain lots of projections and best-case scenarios.

For property that you're considering purchasing, ask for a copy of Schedule E (Supplemental Income and Losses) from the property seller's federal income tax return. When most people complete their tax returns, they try to minimize their revenue and maximize their expenses — the opposite of what they and their agents normally do on the statements they sometimes compile to hype the property sale. Confidentiality and privacy aren't an issue when you ask for Schedule E because you're only asking for this one schedule and not the person's entire income tax return. (If the seller owns more than one rental property for which financial data is compiled on Schedule E, he can simply black out this other information if he doesn't want you to see it.)

You should prepare financial statements based on facts and a realistic assessment of a property (see Table 12-1). There's a time and a place for unbridled optimism and positive thinking, such as when you're lost in a major snowstorm. If you think pessimistically, you may not make it out alive! But deciding whether to buy a rental property is not a life-or-death situation. Take your time and do it with your eyes and ears open and with a healthy degree of skepticism.

The monthly rental property financial statement that you prepare in Table 12-1 is for the present. Over time, you hope and expect that your rental income will increase faster than the property's expenses, thus increasing the cash flow. If you want, you can use Table 12-1 for future years' projections as well.

Table 12-1   Monthly Rental Property Financial Statement

(*Note:* If you're purchasing a simple residential rental property, such as a single-family home, some of the following does not apply.)

	$ per month
Rents: Ask for copies of current lease agreements and also check comparable unit rental rates in the local market. Ask if the owner made any concessions (such as a month or two of free rent), which may make rental rates appear inflated. Make your offer contingent on the accuracy of the rental rates.	$_____

$ per month

Garage rentals: Some properties come with parking spaces that the tenants rent. As with unit rental income, make sure that you know what the spaces really rent for.   +$_____

Laundry income: Dirty laundry isn't just on the evening news — it can make you wealthier! Don't underestimate or neglect to include the cost of laundry machine maintenance when you figure the expenses of your rental building.   +$_____

Other income: $_____

Vacancy allowance: Keeping any rental occupied all the time is difficult, and finding a good tenant who is looking for the type of unit(s) that you have to offer may take some time. You can do occasional maintenance and refurbishing work in between tenants. Allow for a vacancy rate of 5 to 10 percent (multiply 5 to 10 percent by the rent figured in the first line). $_____

Total income: =$_____

Mortgage: Enter your expected mortgage payment. $_____

Property taxes: Ask a real estate person, mortgage lender, or your local assessor's office what your annual property tax bill would be for a rental property of comparable value to the one that you're considering buying. Divide this annual amount by 12 to arrive at your monthly property tax bill.   +$_____

Utilities: Get copies of utility bills from the current owner. Get bills over the previous 12-month period — a few months won't cut it because utility usage may vary greatly during different times of the year. (In a multi-unit building, it's a plus for each unit to have a separate utility meter so that you can bill each tenant for what he/she uses.)   +$_____

Insurance: Ask for a copy of the current insurance coverage and billing statement from the current owner. If you're considering buying a building in an area that has floods, earthquakes, and so on, make sure that the cost of the policy includes these coverages. Although you can insure against most catastrophes, I would avoid buying property in a flood-prone area. Flood insurance does not cover lost rental income.   +$_____

Water: Again, ask the current owner for statements that document the water bill over the past 12 months.   +$_____

Garbage: Get the bills for the last 12 months from the owner.   +$_____

(continued)

Table 12-1 (continued)

	$ per month

Repairs/maintenance/cleaning: You can ask the current owner what to expect and check the tax return, but even doing this may provide an inaccurate answer. Some building owners defer maintenance. (A good property inspector can help to ferret out problem areas before you commit to buy a property.) Estimate that you'll spend at least 1 to 2 percent of the purchase price per year on maintenance, repairs, and cleaning. Remember to divide by 12! +$_____

Rental advertising/management expenses: Finding good tenants takes time and promotion. If you list your rental through rental brokers, they normally take one month's rent as their cut. Owners of larger buildings sometimes have an on-site manager to show vacant units and deal with maintenance and repairs. Put the monthly pay for that person on this line or the preceding line. If you provide a below-market rental rate for an on-site manager, make sure that you factor this into the rental income section. +$_____

Extermination/pest control: Once a year or every few years, you likely need to take care of pest control. Spraying and/or inspections generally start at $200 for small buildings. +$_____

Legal, accounting, and other professional services: Especially with larger rental properties, you'll likely need to consult with lawyers and tax advisors from time to time. +$_____

Total expenses =$_____

Total income (from preceding page) $_____

Total expenses (from above) –$_____

Pretax profit or loss =$_____

Depreciation: The tax law allows you to claim a yearly tax deduction for depreciation, but remember that you can't depreciate land. Break down the purchase of your rental property between the building and land. You can make this allocation based on the assessed value for the land and the building or on a real estate appraisal. Residential property is depreciated over 27 ½ years (3.64 percent of the building value per year) and non-residential property is depreciated over 39 years (2.56 percent of the building value per year). For example, if you buy a residential rental property for $300,000 and $200,000 of that is allocated to the building, that means that you can take $7,273 per year as a depreciation tax deduction ($200,000 x .0364). –$_____

	$ per month
Net income	=$_____

Important note: Although depreciation is a deduction that helps you reduce your profit for tax purposes, it doesn't actually cost you money. Your cash flow from a rental property is the revenue minus your out-of-pocket expenses.

Valuing property

Examining and estimating a property's cash flow is an important first step to deciding a property's ultimate worth. But on its own, examining and estimating a building's cash flow doesn't provide enough information to intelligently decide whether to buy a particular real estate investment. Just because a property has a positive cash flow doesn't mean that you should buy it. Real estate generally sells for less, and therefore has better cash flow in areas that investors expect to earn lower rates of appreciation.

In the stock market, you have more clues about a specific security's worth. Most companies' stocks trade on a daily basis, so you at least have a recent sales price to start with. Of course, just because a stock recently traded at $20 per share doesn't mean that it's worth $20 per share. Investors may be overly optimistic or pessimistic.

Just as you should compare a stock to other comparable stocks, so too should you compare the value of real estate with other comparable real estate. But what if all real estate is overvalued — such a comparison doesn't necessarily reveal the state of inflated prices. In addition to comparing a real estate investment property to comparable properties, you need to also perform some global evaluations of whether prices from a historic perspective appear too high, too low, or just right. To answer this last question, see "Is this a good or bad time to buy?" in Chapter 11.

To value a piece of property, you can try one of three approaches. You can hire an appraiser, enlist the help of a real estate agent, or crunch the numbers yourself. These approaches aren't mutually exclusive — you probably want to at least review the numbers and analysis that an appraiser or real estate agent puts together. Here are the pros and cons of the different approaches that you can use to value property:

✓ **Appraisers.** The biggest advantage of hiring an appraiser is that he or she values property for a living. An appraisal also gives you some hard numbers to use for negotiating with a seller. Make sure that you hire an appraiser who works at it full time and has experience valuing the type of property that you're considering. Ask for examples of a dozen similar properties that he or she has appraised in the past three months in the area.

The drawback of appraisers is that they cost money. A small home may cost several hundred dollars to appraise and a larger multi-unit building may cost $1,000 or more. The danger is that you spend money on an appraisal for a building that you don't end up buying.

✔ **Real estate agents.** If you work with a good real estate agent (I discuss how to find one in the next chapter), ask him or her to draw up a list of comparable properties and help you estimate the value of the property that you're considering buying. The advantage of having your agent help with this analysis is that you don't pay extra for this service.

The drawback of asking an agent what to pay for a property is that his/her commission depends on your buying a property and the amount that you pay for that property. The more you're willing to pay for a property, the more likely the deal flies and the more the agent makes on commission.

✔ **Do-it-yourself.** If you're comfortable with numbers and analysis, you can try to estimate the value of the property yourself. The hard part is identifying comparable properties. It's usually impossible to find identical properties, so you need to find similar properties and then make adjustments to their selling price so that you can do an apples-to-apples comparison.

Among the factors that should influence your analysis of comparable properties are the date the properties sold; the quality of their location; lot size; building age and condition; the number of units; the number of rooms, bedrooms, and bathrooms; garages; fireplaces; and yard. A real estate agent can provide this information, or you can track it down for properties that you've seen or that you know have recently sold.

For example, if a similar property sold six months ago for $250,000 but prices overall have declined 5 percent in the last six months, subtract 5 percent from the sales price. Ultimately, you have to attach a value or price to differences between comparable properties and the one that you're considering buying. Through a series of adjustments, you can then compare the value of your target property to others that have recently sold.

Information sources

When you evaluate properties, you need to put on your detective hat. If you're creative and inquisitive, you'll soon realize that this isn't a hard game to play. You can collect useful information about a property and the area in which it's located in many ways.

The first place to begin your inquiries is with the real estate agent who listed the property for sale. One thing that most agents love to do is talk and schmooze. Try to understand why the seller is selling. This knowledge helps you negotiate an offer that's appealing to the seller.

As for specifics on the property's financial situation, as I explain earlier in this chapter, ask the sellers for specific independent documents, including Schedule E from their tax return. Hire inspectors (I explain hiring inspectors in Chapter 13) to investigate the property's physical condition.

Local government organizations have treasure troves of details about their communities. You can also see the other recommended sources in Chapter 11, as well as some other sources that I recommend earlier in this chapter.

Dig for a deal

Everyone likes to get a deal or feel like they bought something at a really good price. How else can you explain the American retail practice of sales? Merchandise is overpriced so that store owners can then mark it down to create the illusion that you're getting a bargain! Some real estate sellers and agents do the same thing. They list property for sale at an inflated price and then mark it down after they realize that no one will pay the freight. "$30,000 price reduction!" the new listing screams. Of course, this reduction isn't a deal.

Purchasing a piece of real estate at a discount to what it's really worth is possible. Without doing a lick of work, purchasing a property at a discount means that you've made money — one of the ultimate thrills of being a capitalist!

The wisdom of buying in the "best" areas

Some people, particularly those in the real estate business, say, "Buy real estate in the best school districts." Or, "Buy the worst home in the best neighborhood." Conventional wisdom is often wrong, and these examples are yet another case.

Remember that as a real estate investor, you hope to profit from selling your properties, many years in the future, for a much higher price than you purchased them. If you buy into the "best," there's not much room for growth.

Take school districts, for example. Conventional wisdom says that you should look at the test scores of different districts and buy real estate in the best (that is, highest score) districts. But odds are that real estate in those areas is probably already priced at a premium level. If things deteriorate, such an area may experience more decline than an area where property buyers haven't bid prices up into the stratosphere.

The biggest appreciation often comes from those areas and properties that benefit the most from improvement. Identifying these in advance isn't easy, but look for communities where the trend in recent years has been positive. Even many "average" areas perform better in terms of property value appreciation than today's "best" areas.

Scores of books claim to have the real estate investment strategy that can beat the system. Often these promoters claim that you can become a multi-millionaire through investing in some sort of distressed property. A common strategy is to purchase property that a seller has defaulted on or is about to default on. Or how about buying a property in someone's estate through probate court? Maybe you'd like to try your hand at investing in a property that has been condemned or has toxic waste contamination!

It is possible to get a good buy and purchase a problem property at a discount larger than the cost of fixing the property. However, these opportunities are hard to find, and sellers of such properties are often unwilling to sell at a discount that's big enough to leave you much room for profit. If you don't know how to thoroughly and correctly evaluate the problems of the property, you can end up overpaying.

In some cases, the strategies that these real estate gurus advocate involve taking advantage of people's lack of knowledge. For example, some people don't know that they can protect the equity in their home through filing personal bankruptcy. If you can find a seller in such dire financial straits and desperate for cash, you may get a bargain buy on the home. (You may or may not struggle with the moral issues of buying property cheaply this way, but that's one of the not-so-ultimate thrills of capitalism.)

Other methods of finding discounted property take lots of time and digging. Some involve cold-calling property owners to see if they're interested in selling. This method is a little bit like trying to fill a job opening by interviewing people you run into on a street corner. Although you may eventually find a good candidate this way, if you factor in the value of your time, deals turn from bargains to a pig in a poke.

Without making things complicated or too risky, you can use some of the following time-tested and proven ways to buy real estate at a discount to its fair market value:

- ✔ **Find a motivated seller.** Be patient and look at lots of properties, and sooner or later you'll come across one that someone needs to sell. Perhaps the seller has bought another property and needs the money out of his or her other property to close on the recent purchase. Having access to sufficient financing can help secure such deals.

- ✔ **Buy unwanted properties with fixable flaws.** The easiest problems to correct are cosmetic. Some sellers and their agents are lazy and don't even bother to clean a property. One single-family home that I bought had probably three years' worth of cobwebs and dust accumulated. It seemed like a dungeon at night because half the light bulbs were burned out.

Painting, tearing up old, ugly carpeting, refinishing hardwood floors, and putting new plantings in a yard are relatively easy-to-fix problems. It makes the property worth more and makes renters willing to pay higher rent. Of course, these things take money and time, and many buyers aren't interested in dealing with problems. If you have an eye for improving property and are willing to invest the time that coordinating the fix-up work requires, go for it! Just make sure that you hire someone to conduct a thorough property inspection before you buy (see the next chapter for more details).

Be sure to factor in the loss of rental income if you can't rent a portion of the property during the fix-up period. Many investors have gone belly-up from the double cash drain of fix-up expenses and lost rents.

✔ **Buy when the real estate market is depressed.** When the economy takes a few knocks and investors rush for the exits, it's time to wheel out your shopping cart of cash. Buy real estate when prices and investor interest are down. During times of depressed markets, obtaining properties that produce a positive cash flow (even in the early years) is easier. In Chapter 11, I explain how to spot a depressed market.

✔ **Check for zoning opportunities.** Sometimes, you can make more productive use of a property. For example, you can legally convert some multi-unit apartment buildings into condominiums. Some single-family residences may include a rental unit if local zoning allows for it. A good real estate agent, contractor, and the local planning office in the town or city where you're looking at the property can help you identify properties that you can convert. If you're not a proponent of development, then you probably won't like this strategy.

If you buy good real estate and hold it for the long term, you can earn a healthy return from your investment. Over the long haul, having bought a property at a discount becomes an insignificant issue. You make money from your real estate investments as the market appreciates and your ability to manage your property well.

Chapter 13

Real Estate Dilemmas and Decisions

• •

In This Chapter

▶ Selecting the best way to finance your real estate investment

▶ Working with and without real estate agents

▶ Negotiating and inspecting your deals

▶ Making smart selling decisions

• •

*I*n Chapter 11, I cover what you need to know to purchase a home, and in Chapter 12, I review the fundamentals of investing in real estate. In this chapter, I discuss issues such as understanding and selecting mortgages, working with real estate agents, negotiating, and other important details that help you actually put a real estate deal together. I also provide some words of wisdom about taxes and selling your property that may come in handy down the road.

Financing 101

Unless you're affluent or buying a low-cost property, you likely need to borrow some money, via a mortgage, to finance your property acquisition. If you can't line up financing, your deal may fall apart. If you don't shop correctly for a good mortgage, you can spend thousands, perhaps even tens of thousands, of dollars in extra interest and fees. Even worse, you can get saddled with a loan that you someday can't afford and you may end up in bankruptcy.

Understanding the differences between fixed-rate and adjustable-rate mortgages

Two major types of mortgages exist: those with a fixed interest rate and those with an adjustable rate (known as *ARMs* for adjustable-rate mortgages). When you buy real estate, you have to choose the one that best fits your needs. Your choice depends on your financial situation, how much risk you're willing to accept, and the type of property that you want to purchase. For example, obtaining a fixed-rate loan on a property that lenders perceive as a riskier investment is more difficult than getting an ARM for the same property.

Fixed-rate mortgages

Fixed-rate mortgages, which are typically for a 15- or 30-year term, have interest rates that stay fixed or level. With a fixed-rate mortgage, you lock in an interest rate that doesn't change over the life of your loan. Because the interest rate stays the same, your monthly mortgage payment stays the same. You have nothing complicated to track and no uncertainty. Fixed-rate loans give people peace of mind and payment stability.

Fixed-rate loans aren't without risks however. If interest rates fall significantly after you obtain your mortgage and you're unable to refinance, you face the danger of being stuck with a higher-cost mortgage. This scenario may happen, for example, if you lose your job or the value of your property decreases. Even if you're able to refinance, you'll probably have to spend significant time and money to complete the paperwork.

Adjustable-rate mortgages (ARMs)

In contrast to a fixed-rate mortgage, an adjustable-rate mortgage (ARM) carries an interest rate that varies. You can start with one interest rate this year and pay different rates for every year, possibly even every month, during a 30-year mortgage. Thus the size of your monthly payment fluctuates. Because a mortgage payment makes an unusually large dent in most property owners' checkbooks, signing up for an ARM without fully understanding it is fiscally foolish.

The advantage of an ARM is that if you purchase your property during a period of high interest rates, you can start paying your mortgage with a relatively low initial interest rate (compared with fixed-rate loans). And if interest rates decline, you can capture many of the benefits of lower rates without the cost and hassle of refinancing.

Balloon loans

Balloon loans generally start the way traditional fixed-rate mortgages start. You make level payments based on a long-term payment schedule, over 15 or 30 years, for example. But at a predetermined time, usually three to ten years from the loan's inception, the remaining loan balance becomes fully due.

Balloon loans may save you money because they have a lower interest rate than a longer-term fixed-rate mortgage. Sometimes, balloon loans may be the only option for the buyer (or so the buyer thinks). Buyers are more commonly backed into these loans during periods of high interest rates. When a buyer can't afford the payments on a conventional mortgage and really wants a particular property, a seller may offer a balloon loan.

Balloon loans are dangerous — your financial situation can change, and you may not be able to refinance when your balloon loan is due. What if you lose your job or your income drops? What if the value of your property drops and the appraisal comes in too low to qualify you for a new loan? What if interest rates rise and you can't qualify at the higher rate on a new loan?

I recommend avoiding balloon loans. You should take such a loan if, and only if, such a loan is your only financing option, you've really done your homework to exhaust other financing options, and you're certain that you can refinance when the balloon comes due. If you take a balloon loan, get one with as much time as possible, preferably seven to ten years, before it becomes due.

Choosing between a fixed-rate or adjustable-rate mortgage

Choosing between a fixed-rate or adjustable-rate loan is an important decision in the real estate buying process. You need to weigh the pros and cons of each mortgage type and decide what's best for your situation *before* you go out to purchase real estate or refinance.

In the real world, most people ignore this sensible advice. The excitement of purchasing a home or other piece of real estate tends to cloud judgment. My experience has been that few people look at their entire financial picture before they make major real estate decisions.

Unfortunately, too many real estate buyers try to let their interest rate crystal ball dictate whether they should take an adjustable- or fixed-rate mortgage. For example, people who think interest rates can only go up find fixed-rate mortgages attractive.

You can't predict the future course of interest rates. Even the professional financial market soothsayers and investors can't predict where rates are heading. If you could foretell this information, you could make a fortune investing in bonds and interest-rate futures and options. So cast aside your crystal ball and ask yourself the following two vital questions to help you decide whether a fixed or adjustable mortgage will work best for you.

How comfortable are you with taking risk?

How much of a gamble can you take with the size of your monthly mortgage payment? For example, if your job and income are unstable and you need to borrow an amount that stretches your monthly budget, you can't afford much risk. If you're in this situation, stick with fixed-rate mortgages.

If you're in a position to take the financial risks that come with an adjustable-rate mortgage, you have a better chance of saving money with an adjustable- rather than a fixed-rate loan. Your interest rate starts lower and stays lower if the overall level of interest rates stays unchanged. Even if rates go up, they'll likely come back down over the life of your loan. If you can stick with your adjustable-rate loan for better and for worse, you may come out ahead in the long run.

Adjustables make more sense if you borrow less than you're qualified for. Or perhaps you can save a sizable chunk — more than 10 percent — of your monthly income. If your income significantly exceeds your spending patterns, you may feel less anxiety about fluctuating interest rates. If you do choose an adjustable loan, you may feel more financially secure if you have a hefty financial cushion (at least six months' to as much as a year's worth of expenses reserved) that you can access if rates go up.

Too many people take adjustables when they can't really afford them. Those who can afford adjustables can save money but sooner or later, interest rates go up (sometimes significantly). When rates rise, property owners who can't afford much higher payments face a financial crisis. If you don't have emergency savings that you can tap into to make the higher payments, how can you afford the monthly payments — much less all the other expenses of real estate ownership?

If you can't afford the highest-allowed payment on an adjustable-rate mortgage, don't take one. You shouldn't take the chance that the rate may not rise that high — it can, and you could lose the property. Ask your lender to calculate the highest possible monthly payment that your loan allows. The number that the lender comes up with is the payment that you face if the interest rate on your loan goes to the highest level allowed, or the *lifetime cap*.

Almost all adjustables limit, or *cap*, the rise in the interest rate that your loan allows. Typical caps are 2 percent per year and 6 percent over the life of the loan.

Don't take an adjustable mortgage because the lower initial interest rates allow you to afford the property that you want to buy (unless you're absolutely certain that your income will rise to meet future payment increases). Try setting your sights on a property that you can afford to buy with a fixed-rate mortgage.

How many years do you expect to stay put?

Saving interest on most adjustables is usually a certainty in the first two or three years. An adjustable-rate mortgage starts at a lower interest rate than a fixed one. If rates rise, you can end up giving back the savings that you achieve in the early years of the mortgage.

If you aren't going to keep your mortgage for more than five to seven years, you'll end up paying more interest to carry a fixed-rate mortgage. A mortgage lender takes extra risk in committing to a fixed-interest rate for 15 to 30 years. Lenders often don't know any better than you about what may happen in the intervening years, so they charge you a premium in case interest rates move much higher in future years.

You may also consider a hybrid loan, which combines features of fixed- and adjustable-rate mortgages. For example, the initial rate may hold constant for several years and then adjust once a year or every six months thereafter. Such loans may make sense for you if you foresee a high probability of keeping your loan seven years or less but want some stability in your monthly payments. The longer the initial rate stays locked in, the higher the interest rate.

Choosing between a short- or long-term mortgage

Most mortgage lenders offer you the option of 15-year or 30-year mortgages. You can also have 20-year and 40-year options, but these are unusual. These choices raise an important question: Should you opt for a short- or long-term mortgage?

To afford the monthly payments, many first-time property buyers need to spread their mortgage loan payments over a longer period of time, and a 30-year mortgage is the way to do it. Thirty-year mortgages also attract investment property buyers who can't handle negative cash flow (see Chapter 12).

A 15-year mortgage has higher monthly payments because you pay it off quicker. At a fixed-rate mortgage interest rate of 7 percent, for example, a 15-year mortgage comes with payments that are about 35 percent higher than those for a 30-year mortgage.

Locking yourself into higher monthly payments with a 15-year mortgage may put you at risk. If your finances worsen or your property declines in value, odds are you'll have trouble qualifying for a refinance. You *may* be able to refinance your way out of the predicament, but you can't count on it.

Don't consider a 15-year mortgage unless you can afford the higher payments that come with it. Even if you can afford these higher payments, taking the 15-year option isn't necessarily better. You may find better uses for the money instead of making extra payments.

Consider other productive uses you may have for the extra money that you're considering throwing into the mortgage payments. If you can earn a higher rate of return investing your extra cash versus paying the interest on your mortgage, you may come out ahead investing your money instead of paying down your mortgage faster. For example, you can contribute the "extra" money to a retirement account such as a 401(k), SEP-IRA or Keogh (see Chapter 3), all of which are tax-deductible.

Suppose that you have an extra $400 per month. If you put that $400 into a retirement account, you get to subtract that $400 from the income on which you pay taxes. If you pay a moderate 35 percent in federal and state income taxes, you shave $140 per month (that's $400 multiplied by 35 percent) off your tax bill. By contrast, if you add $400 to your mortgage payment to pay off your mortgage faster, you get no tax benefits.

If you have children who will someday go off to college, you have an even greater reason to fund your retirement accounts instead of paying down your mortgage faster. Under the current rules that determine financial aid for college expenses, money in your retirement accounts is not counted as an asset.

Many schools still count the equity in your home (the difference between its market value and your loan balance) as an asset. When you pay down your mortgage balance faster, you build more equity in your home. On paper, you appear wealthier to the financial aid folks than when you save the money in a retirement account. In other words, your reward for paying down your mortgage balance is likely less financial aid!

If you choose a 30-year mortgage, you maintain the flexibility to pay it off faster if you want (except in those rare cases where there is a prepayment penalty; see the next paragraph for more details). If you choose to make larger-than-necessary payments, you can create your own 15-year mortgage.

However, you can fall back to making only the payments required on your 30-year schedule when the need arises.

One final word of advice related to this topic: Avoid loans with prepayment penalties. You pay this charge, usually 2 to 3 percent of the loan amount, when you pay off your loan before you're supposed to. Normally, prepayment penalties don't apply if you pay off a loan because you sell the property, but when you refinance a loan with prepayment penalties, you have to pay the penalty.

Getting a great fixed-rate mortgage

The interest rate on a fixed-rate loan is the rate that you pay month in and month out, year in and year out, for borrowing the money. You may think that comparing one fixed-rate loan to another then, is quite simple. As with your golf score and the number of times that your boss catches you showing up late for work, a lower number (interest rate) is better, right?

Unfortunately, banks generally charge an up-front chunk of interest, known as *points,* in addition to the ongoing interest over the life of the loan. Points are actually percentages: One point is equal to 1 percent of the loan amount. So when a lender tells you a quoted loan has 1.5 points, you pay 1.5 percent of the amount you borrow as points. On a $100,000 loan, for example, 1.5 points cost you $1,500. The interest rate on a fixed-rate loan must always be quoted with the points on the loan.

You may want to take a higher interest rate on your mortgage if you don't have enough cash to pay for a lot of points, which you pay up front when you close the loan. On the other hand, if you're willing and able to pay more points, you can lower your interest rate. You may want to pay more points because the interest rate on your loan determines your payments over a long period of time — 15 to 30 years.

Suppose one lender quotes you a rate of 6.75 percent on a 30-year fixed-rate loan and charges one point (1 percent). Another lender, which quotes 7 percent for 30 years, doesn't charge any points. Which is better? The answer depends on how long you plan to keep the loan.

The 6.75-percent loan is 0.25 percent less than the 7-percent loan. But, because you have to pay 1 percent (one point) up front on the 6.75-percent loan, it takes you about four years to earn back the savings to cover the cost of that point. So if you expect to keep the loan more than four years, go with the 6.75 percent option. If you plan to keep the loan less than four years, go with the 7 percent option.

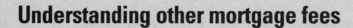

Understanding other mortgage fees

In addition to points and the ongoing interest rate, lenders tack on all sorts of other up-front charges in processing your loan. Get an itemization of these other fees and charges in writing from all lenders that you're seriously considering. You need to know the total of all lender fees so that you can accurately compare different lenders' loans and determine how much closing on your loan will cost you.

Other mortgage fees can pile up in a hurry. Here are the common ones that you may see:

✔ **Application and processing fees.** Most lenders charge a couple hundred dollars to work with you to complete your paperwork and funnel it through their loan evaluation process. Should your loan be rejected, or if it's approved and you decide not to take it, the lender needs to cover its costs. Some lenders return this fee to you upon closing with their loan.

✔ **Credit report.** Most lenders charge you for the cost of obtaining your credit report, which tells the lender whether you've repaid other loans on time. Your credit report should cost about $50.

✔ **Appraisal.** The property for which you borrow money needs to be valued. If you default on your mortgage, a lender doesn't want to get stuck with a property that's worth less than you owe. The cost for appraisal typically ranges from several hundred dollars for most residential properties to as much as $1,000 or more for larger investment properties.

Some lenders offer loans without points or other lender charges. Remember: If they don't charge points or other fees, they charge a higher interest rate on your loan to make up the difference. Such loans may make sense for you when you lack the cash to close a loan or when you plan to hold onto the loan for just a few years.

To minimize your chances of throwing money away on a loan that you may not qualify for, ask the lender if there is any reason he or she may not approve you. Be sure to disclose any problems on your credit report or any problems with the property that you're aware of. Don't expect the lender to run through a list of qualities on why it doesn't like taking risks. Lenders may not take the time to ask about these sorts of things in their haste to get you to complete their loan applications.

To make it easier to perform an apples-to-apples comparison of mortgages from different lenders, get interest rate quotes at the same point level. For example, ask each lender for the interest rate on a loan for which you pay one point.

Never, ever forget that if a loan has no points, it's sure to have a higher interest rate. That's not to say that no-point loans are better or worse than comparable loans from other lenders, but don't get sucked into a loan because of a no-points sales pitch. Many lenders who spend big bucks on advertising these types of loans rarely have the best mortgage terms.

All things being equal, no-point loans make more sense for refinances because points aren't immediately tax-deductible as they are on purchases (you can deduct the points that you pay on a refinance *only* over the life of the mortgage). On a mortgage for a property that you're purchasing, a no-point loan may help if you are cash poor at closing.

Consider a no-point loan if you can't afford more out-of-pocket expenditures now or if you think that you'll only keep the loan a few years. Make sure to shop around and compare different lenders' no-point loans.

Finding a great adjustable-rate mortgage

Selecting an adjustable-rate mortgage (ARM) has a lot in common with selecting a home to buy. You need to make trade-offs and compromises. Adjustables come with many more features and options — *caps, indexes, margins,* and *adjustment periods* — that aren't issues with fixed-rate loans.

Start rate

Just as the name implies, this interest rate is the one that your mortgage begins with. Don't judge a loan by this rate alone. You won't pay this attractively low rate for long. With ARMs, interest rates generally rise as soon as the terms of the mortgage allow.

Think of the start rate as a teaser rate — the initial rate on your loan is set artificially low to entice you. In other words, even if the market level of interest rates doesn't change, your adjustable is destined to increase. An increase of one or two percentage points is common.

The formula for determining the future interest rates on an adjustable-rate mortgage and rate caps are far more important in determining what a mortgage is going to cost you in the long run.

Future interest rate

The first thing that you need to ask a mortgage lender or broker about an adjustable is the formula for determining the future interest rate on your loan. You need to know exactly how a lender figures how your interest rate changes over the life of the loan. All adjustables are based on the following formula, which specifies how the interest rate is set on your loan in the future:

Index + Margin = Interest Rate

The *index* measures the overall level of interest rates that the lender chooses to calculate the specific interest rate for your loan. Indexes are generally (but not always) widely quoted in the financial press. For example, suppose that the current index value for the six-month Treasury bill index is 5 percent. The *margin* is the amount added to the index to determine the interest rate that you pay on your mortgage. Most loans maintain margins of around 2.5 percent. Thus, the rate of a mortgage, driven by the following formula

Six-month treasury bill rate + 2.5 percent

is set at 5 + 2.5 = 7.5 percent. This figure is known as the *fully indexed rate*. If this loan starts out at just 5 percent, you know that if the index (six-month Treasuries) stays at the same level, your loan can increase to 7.5 percent.

Compare the fully indexed rate to the current rate for fixed-rate loans. You may be surprised to learn that the fixed-rate loan is at about the same interest rate or even a hair lower. This insight may cause you to reconsider your choice of an adjustable-rate loan, which can of course, rise to an even higher rate in the future.

Common indexes for adjustable-rate mortgages

The different indexes vary mainly in how rapidly they respond to changes in interest rates. *Treasury bills (T-bills)* are IOUs (bonds) that the U.S. government issues. Most adjustables are tied to the interest rate on 6-month or 12-month T-bills.

Certificates of deposit (CDs) are interest-bearing bank investments that lock you in for a specific period of time. ARMs are usually tied to the average interest rate that banks are paying on six-month CDs. Like T-bills, CDs tend to respond quickly to changes in the market's level of interest rates.

The *11th district cost of funds (cost of funds)* index is among the slower-moving indexes. Adjustable-rate mortgages tied to 11th district cost of funds (also known as COFI) tend to start out at a higher interest rate. A slower-moving index has the advantage of moving up less quickly when rates are on the rise. On the other hand, you have to be patient to benefit from falling interest rates.

If you select an adjustable-rate mortgage that's tied to one of the faster-moving indexes, you take on more of a risk that the next adjustment may reflect interest rate increases. Because you take on more of the risk that interest rates may increase, lenders cut you breaks in other ways, such as through lower caps or points.

Should you want the security of an ARM tied to a slower-moving index, you'll pay for that security in one form or another, such as a higher start rate, caps, margin, or points. You may also pay in other, less-obvious ways. A slower-moving index, such as the 11th district cost of funds index (COFI), lags behind general changes in market interest rates, so it continues to rise after interest rates peak and goes down more slowly after rates have turned tail.

Trying to predict interest rates is a dangerous game. When you choose a mortgage, keeping sight of your own financial situation is far more important.

Adjustments

After the initial interest rate expires, the interest rate on an ARM fluctuates based on the loan formula. Most adjustables adjust every 6 or 12 months, but some may adjust as frequently as monthly. In advance of each adjustment, the lender sends you a notice telling you your new rate. Be sure to check these adjustments because lenders sometimes make mistakes.

All things being equal, the less frequently your loan adjusts, the less financial uncertainty you have in your life. However, less-frequent adjustments usually mean that your loan starts at a higher interest rate.

Almost all adjustables come with a rate cap, which limits the maximum rate change (up or down) that each adjustment allows. This limit is usually referred to as the *adjustment cap.* On most loans that adjust every six months, the adjustment cap is 1 percent. In other words, the interest rate that the loan charges can move up or down no more than one percentage point in a given adjustment period.

Loans that adjust more than once per year usually limit the maximum rate change that's allowed over the entire year as well. On the vast majority of such loans, 2 percent is the annual rate cap. Likewise, almost all adjustables come with lifetime caps. These caps limit the highest rate allowed over the entire life of the loan. It's common for adjustable loans to have lifetime caps of 5 to 6 percent higher than the initial start rate.

Never take an ARM that lacks rate caps! Doing so is worse than giving a credit card with an unlimited line of credit to your 16-year-old for the weekend — at least you get the credit card back on Monday!

When you want to take an adjustable-rate mortgage, you must identify the maximum payment that you can handle. If you can't handle the payment that comes with a 10 or 11 percent interest rate, for example, then don't look at ARMs that may go that high.

Avoid negative amortization ARMs

As you make mortgage payments over time, the loan balance you still owe is gradually reduced or amortized. *Negative amortization* — increasing your loan balance — is the reverse of this process.

Some ARMs allow negative amortization. How can your outstanding loan balance grow when you continue to make mortgage payments? This phenomena occurs when your mortgage payment is less than it really should be.

Some loans cap the increase of your monthly payment but don't cap the interest rate. Thus, the size of your mortgage payment may not reflect all the interest that you owe on your loan. So, rather than paying the interest that you owe and paying off some of your loan balance (or *principal*) every month, you end up paying off some, but not all, of the interest that you owe. Thus, lenders add the extra unpaid interest that you still owe to your outstanding debt.

Negative amortization resembles paying only the minimum payment that your credit card bill requires. You continue to rack up finance charges (in this case, greater interest) on the balance as long as you only make the artificially low payment. Taking a loan with negative amortization defeats the whole purpose of borrowing an amount that fits your overall financial goals.

My advice — avoid adjustables with negative amortization. The only way to know whether a loan includes negative amortization is to explicitly ask. Most lenders and mortgage brokers aren't forthcoming about telling you. You find negative amortization more frequently on loans that lenders consider risky. If you have trouble finding lenders that will deal with your financial situation, make sure that you're especially careful.

Finding the best lenders

You can easily save thousands of dollars in interest charges and other fees if you shop around for a mortgage deal. It doesn't matter whether you do so on your own or hire someone to help you, but you should shop because much money is at stake!

Shopping yourself

Many mortgage lenders compete for your business. Although having a large number of lenders to choose from is good for keeping interest rates lower, it also makes shopping a chore.

Real estate agents can refer you to lenders with whom they've done business. Those lenders don't necessarily offer the most competitive rates — the agent simply may have done business with them in the past or received client referrals from them.

Look in the real estate section of one of the larger Sunday newspapers in your area for charts of selected lender interest rates. Just as with Internet sites that advertise lender rates, these tables are by no means comprehensive or reflective of the best rates available. In fact, many of these rates are sent to newspapers for free by firms that distribute mortgage information to mortgage brokers. Use them as a starting point and call the lenders that list the best rates.

HSH Associates (800-873-2837; http://www.hsh.com) publishes mortgage information for most metropolitan areas. For $20, you can receive a list of dozens of lenders' rate quotes, but you need to be a real data junkie to wade through all the numbers on the multi-page report of abbreviations in small print.

Mortgage brokers

Mortgage brokers are of greatest value to those who don't bother shopping around for a good deal or who most lenders may shun. If you're too busy or disinterested to dig for a good deal on a mortgage, a good mortgage broker can probably save you money.

A competent mortgage broker can be a big help in getting you a good loan and closing the deal. A good mortgage broker also keeps abreast of the many different mortgages that the marketplace offers. He or she can shop among lots of lenders to get you the best deal available.

An organized and detail-oriented mortgage broker can also help you through the process of completing all those tedious documents that lenders require. Mortgage brokers can help polish your loan package so that the information that you present is favorable yet truthful. The best brokers can also help educate you about various loan options and the pros and cons of available features.

Brokers can also help you if you anticipate that lenders may be skittish about offering you a loan. Problems on your credit report make lenders uncomfortable. If you want to borrow a large amount (90 percent or more) of the value of a property, many lenders aren't interested. Certain types of properties, such as co-ops and tenancies-in-common, give many lenders cold feet because these buildings tend to give them more problems.

Be careful when you choose a mortgage broker, because some brokers are lazy and don't shop the market for the best current rates. Even worse, some brokers may direct their business to specific lenders so they can take a bigger cut or commission.

A mortgage broker typically gets paid a percentage, usually 0.5 to 1 percent, of the loan amount. This commission is completely negotiable, especially on larger loans that are more lucrative.

You need to ask what the commission is on loans that a broker pitches. Some brokers may be indignant that you ask — that's their problem. You have every right to ask — it's your money.

Even if you plan to shop on your own, talking to a mortgage broker may be worthwhile. At the very least, you can compare what you find with what brokers say they can get for you. Again, be careful. Some brokers tell you what you want to hear — that is, that they can beat your best find — and then aren't able to deliver when the time comes.

If your loan broker quotes you a really good deal, make sure you ask who the lender is. (Most brokers refuse to reveal this information until you pay the necessary fee to cover the appraisal and credit report.) You can check with the actual lender to verify the interest rate and points that the broker quotes you and make sure that you're eligible for the loan.

Dealing with loan problems

Even if you have perfect or near-perfect credit, you may encounter financing problems with some properties. And of course, not all real estate buyers have a perfect credit history, tons of available cash, and no debt. If you're one of those borrowers who ends up jumping through more hoops than others to get a loan, don't give up hope. Few borrowers are perfect from a lender's perspective, and many problems aren't that difficult to fix.

The best defense against loan rejection is avoiding it in the first place. You can sometimes disclose to your lender anything that may cause a problem before you apply for the loan to head off potential rejection. For example, if you already know that your credit report indicates some late payments from when you were out of the country for several weeks five years ago, write a letter that explains this situation.

Lack of down payment money

Most people, especially when they make their first real-estate purchase, are strapped for cash. In order to qualify for the most attractive financing, lenders typically require that your down payment be at least 20 percent of the property's purchase price. The best investment property loans sometimes require 25 to 30 percent down for the best terms. In addition, you need reserve money to pay for other closing costs such as title insurance and loan fees.

If you don't have 20-plus percent of the purchase price available, don't panic and don't get depressed — you can still own real estate. Some lenders may offer you a mortgage even though you may be able to put down only 5 to 10 percent of the purchase price. These lenders will likely require you to purchase private mortgage insurance (PMI) for your loan. This insurance generally costs a few hundred dollars per year and protects the lender if you default on your loan. (When you do have at least 20 percent equity in the property, you can generally eliminate the PMI.)

Another way to raise the level of your down payment funds is to dip into your retirement savings. Some employers allow you to borrow against your retirement account balance, under the condition that you repay the loan within a set number of years. Subject to eligibility requirements, first-time homebuyers can make penalty-free withdrawals of up to $10,000 from IRA accounts. (*Note:* You still must pay regular income tax on the withdrawal.)

If you don't want the cost and strain of extra fees and bad mortgage terms, you can also postpone your purchase. Go on a financial austerity program and boost your savings rate. You may also consider lower-priced properties. Smaller properties and ones that need some work can help keep down the purchase price and the required down payment.

If lower-priced properties don't meet your needs, you may be able to find a partner to have your cake and eat it too. Make sure that you write up a legal contract to specify what happens if a partner wants out. Family members sometimes make good partners. Your parents, grandparents, and maybe even your siblings may have some extra cash they'd like to loan, invest, or even give to you as a gift!

Finally, some property owners or developers may finance your purchase with as little as 5 to 10 percent down. However, you can't be as picky about such seller-financed properties because a limited supply is available and many that are available need work or haven't yet sold for other reasons.

Credit history blemishes

Late payments, missed payments, or debts that you never bothered to pay can tarnish your credit report and squelch a lender's desire to make you a mortgage loan. If you are turned down for a loan because of your less-than-stellar credit history, request (at no charge to you) a copy of your credit report from the lender that turned down your loan.

If problems are accurately documented on your credit report, try to explain them to your lender. If the lender is unsympathetic, try calling other lenders. Tell them your credit problems up front and see whether you can find one willing to offer you a loan. Mortgage brokers may also be able to help you shop for lenders in these cases.

Sometimes you may feel that you're not in control when you apply for a loan. In reality, you can fix a number of credit problems yourself. And you can often explain those that you can't fix. Remember that some lenders are more lenient and flexible than others. Just because one mortgage lender rejects your loan application doesn't mean that all the others will as well.

As for erroneous information listed on your credit report, get on the phone to the credit bureaus and start squawking. If specific creditors are the culprits, call them too. Keep notes from your conversations and make sure that you put your case in writing and add your comments to your credit report. If the customer service representatives you talk with are no help, send a letter to the president of each company. Let the head honcho know that his or her organization caused you problems in obtaining credit.

Another common credit problem is having too much consumer debt at the time you apply for a mortgage. The more credit card, auto loan, and other consumer debt you rack up, the less mortgage you qualify for. If you're turned down for the mortgage, consider it a wake-up call to get rid of this high-cost debt. Hang onto the dream of buying real estate and plug away at paying off your debts before you make another foray into real estate.

Low appraisals

Even if you have sufficient income, a clean credit report, and an adequate down payment, the lender may turn down your loan if the appraisal of the property that you want to buy comes in too low. It's unusual for a property not to appraise for what a buyer agrees to pay — odds are the real market value of the property is less than you agreed to pay.

Assuming that you still like the property, renegotiate a lower price with the seller using the low appraisal. If the appraisal is too low with a property that you already own and are refinancing, you obviously need to follow a different path. If you have the cash available, you can simply put more money down to get the loan balance to a level for which you qualify. If you don't have the cash, you may need to forgo the refinance until you save more money or until the property value rises.

In rare cases, lenders sometimes lowball an appraisal on refinances to sabotage a loan. A lender may do so, for example, if your current mortgage is under better terms (from their point of view). If you suspect that the lender is sabotaging your appraisal, make sure to ask for a copy of your appraisal, which you are entitled to. If you have comparable sale prices of homes from your area that support your case, go back to the lender and see what he or she has to say. If you're still not satisfied, complain to the state regulator of mortgage lenders. However, applying for a new mortgage through another lender may be less of a hassle.

Not enough income

If you're self-employed or have changed jobs, your income may not resemble your past income, or more important, your income may not be what a mortgage lender likes to see in respect to the amount that you want to borrow. A simple (but often not possible) way around this problem is to make a larger down payment. For example, if you put down 30 percent or more when you purchase a primary residence, you may be able to get a no-income verification loan. If you can make that large a down payment, lenders probably don't care what your income is — they'll simply repossess and then sell your property if you default on the loan.

If you can't make a large down payment, another option is to get a cosigner for the loan — your relatives may be willing. As long as they aren't overextended themselves, they may be able to help you qualify for a larger loan than you can get on your own. As with partnerships, make sure that you put your agreement in writing so that no misunderstandings occur.

Refinancing

When you buy a property, you take out a mortgage based on your circumstances and available loan options at that time. But, things change. Maybe interest rates have dropped or you have access to better loan options now than when you first purchased. Or, perhaps you want to tap into some of your real estate equity for other investments.

If interest rates drop and you're able to refinance, you can lock in interest rate savings. But a lower interest rate since you took out your original mortgage isn't reason enough to refinance your mortgage. Remember that when you refinance a mortgage, you have to spend money and time to save money. So you need to crunch a few numbers to determine whether refinancing makes sense for you.

Calculate how many months it will take you to recoup the costs of refinancing, such as appraisal costs, loan fees and points, title insurance, and so on. For example, if the refinance costs you $2,000 to complete and reduces your monthly payment by $100, it may appear that you can make the cost of the refinance back in 20 months. However, because you lose some tax write-offs if you reduce your mortgage interest rate and payment, you can't simply look at the reduced amount of your monthly payment.

If you want a better estimate but don't want to spend hours crunching numbers, take your tax rate as specified in Chapter 3 (for example, 28 percent) and reduce your monthly payment savings on the refinance by this amount. That means, continuing with the example in the preceding paragraph, that if your monthly payment drops by $100, you're actually only saving around $72 a month after you factor in the lost tax benefits. So it takes 28 months ($2,000 divided by $72), not 20 months, to recoup the refinance costs.

If you can recover the costs of the refinance within a few years or less and you don't plan to move in that time frame then refinance. Should it take longer to recoup the refinance costs, refinancing may still make sense if you anticipate keeping the property and mortgage that long. If you estimate it taking more than five to seven years to break even, refinancing is probably too risky to justify the costs and hassles.

Refinancing a piece of real estate that you own to pull out cash for some other purpose can make good financial sense because under most circumstances, mortgage interest is tax-deductible. Perhaps you want to purchase another piece of real estate, start or purchase a business, or get rid of some high-cost consumer debt on credit cards or an auto loan. The interest on consumer debt is not tax-deductible and is usually at a much higher interest rate than what mortgage loans charge you.

When to consider a home equity loan

Home equity loans, also known as second mortgages, allow you to borrow against the equity in your home in addition to the mortgage that you already have (a first mortgage).

A home equity loan may benefit you if you need more money for just a few years, or if your first mortgage is at such a low interest rate that refinancing it to get more cash would be too costly. Otherwise, I advise you to avoid home equity loans.

If you need a larger mortgage, why not refinance the first one and wrap it all together? Home equity loans have higher interest rates than comparable first mortgages. They are riskier from a lender's perspective because the first mortgage lender gets first claim against your property if you file bankruptcy or you default on the mortgage.

Interest on home mortgage loans of up to $1 million (first or second residences) is tax deductible for loans taken out after October 13, 1987. (Loans taken before that date have no monetary limit.) Interest deduction on home equity loans is limited to the first $100,000 of such debt.

Be careful that you don't borrow more than you need to accomplish your financial goals. For example, just because you can borrow more against the equity in your real estate doesn't mean that you should do so to buy an expensive new car or take your dream vacation.

Working with Real Estate Agents

When you purchase real estate, if you're like most people, you enlist the services of a real estate agent. A good agent can help screen property so you don't spend all your free time looking at potential properties to buy, negotiating a deal, helping coordinate inspections, and managing other preclosing items.

Agent conflicts of interest

But all agents, good, mediocre, and awful, are subject to a conflict of interest because of the way they're compensated — on commission. I must say that I respect real estate agents for calling themselves what they are. Real estate agents don't hide behind an obscure job title, such as "shelter consultant." (Many financial "planners," "advisors," or "consultants," for example, actually work on commission and sell investments and life insurance and therefore, are really stockbrokers and insurance brokers, not planners or advisors.)

Real estate agents aren't in the business of providing objective financial counsel either. They don't tell you to spend less money on a home because you aren't saving enough for retirement. They also won't tell you to rent because of your current financial circumstances and the state of the real estate market. Just as car dealers make their living selling cars, real estate agents make their living selling real estate. Never forget this fact as a buyer. The pursuit of a larger commission may encourage an agent to get you to do things that aren't in your best interests, such as the following:

✔ **Buy, and buy sooner rather than later.** If you don't buy, your agent doesn't get paid for all the hours he or she spends working with you. The worst agents fib and use tricks to motivate you to buy. They may say that other offers are coming in on a property that interests you, or they may show you a bunch of dumps and then one good listing because they think the bad listings will motivate you to buy the one good listing.

✔ **Spend more than you should.** Because real estate agents get a percentage of the sales price of a property, they have a built-in incentive to encourage you to spend more on a property than what fits comfortably with your other financial objectives and goals. An agent doesn't have to consider or care about your other financial needs.

✔ **Buy their company's listings.** Agents also have a built-in incentive (higher commission) to sell their own listings.

✔ **Buy in their territory.** Real estate agents typically work a specific territory. As a result, they usually can't objectively tell you the pros and cons of the surrounding region.

✔ **Use people that scratch their backs.** Some agents refer you to lenders, inspectors, and title insurance companies that have referred customers to them. Some agents also solicit and receive referral fees (or bribes) from mortgage lenders, inspectors, and contractors to whom they refer business.

How to find a good agent

A mediocre, incompetent, or greedy agent can be a real danger to your finances. Whether you're hiring an agent to work with you as a buyer or seller, you want someone who is competent and with whom you can get along. Working with an agent costs you a lot of money, so make sure that you get your money's worth.

Interview several agents. Check references. Ask agents for the names and phone numbers of at least three clients with whom they've worked with in the past six months in the geographical area in which you're looking. By narrowing the period during which they worked with references to six months, you maximize the chances of speaking with clients other than the agent's all-time favorite clients.

Look for these traits in any agent that you work with (ask the agent's references), whether as a buyer or seller:

- ✔ **Full-time employment.** Some agents work in real estate as a second or even third job. Information in this field changes constantly — keeping track of it is hard enough on a full-time basis. It's hard to imagine a good agent being able to stay on top of the market and moonlight elsewhere.

- ✔ **Experience.** Hiring someone with experience doesn't necessarily mean looking for an agent who's been around for decades. Many of the best agents come into the field from other occupations, such as business and teaching. Agents can acquire some sales, marketing, negotiation, and communication skills in other fields, but experience in real estate does count.

- ✔ **Honesty and integrity.** You need to trust your agent with a lot of information. If the agent doesn't level with you about what a neighborhood or particular property is really like, you suffer the consequences.

- ✔ **Interpersonal skills.** An agent must get along not only with you but also with a whole host of other people who are involved in a typical real estate deal: other agents, property sellers, inspectors, mortgage lenders, and so on. An agent needs to know how to put your interests first without upsetting others.

- ✔ **Negotiation skills.** Putting a real estate deal together involves negotiation. Is your agent going to exhaust all avenues to get you the best deal possible? Most people don't like the sometimes aggravating process of negotiation, so they hire someone else to do it for them. Be sure to ask the agent's former client references how the agent negotiated for them.

- ✔ **High quality standards.** Sloppy work can lead to big legal or logistical problems down the road. If an agent neglects to recommend an inspection, for example, you may get stuck with undiscovered problems after the deal is done.

Some agents who pitch themselves as buyer's brokers claim that they work for your interests. Agents who represent you as buyer's brokers still get paid only when you buy. And agents still get paid a commission that's a percentage of the purchase price. So they still have an incentive to sell you a piece of real estate that's more expensive because their commission increases.

Agents sometimes market themselves as *top producers,* which means that they sell a relatively larger volume of real estate. This title doesn't count for much for you, the buyer. In fact, you may use this information as a red flag for an agent who focuses on completing as many deals as possible.

When you buy a home, you need an agent who is patient. The last thing you need or want is an agent who tries to push you into making a deal. You need an agent who allows you the necessary time to educate yourself and helps you make the decision that's best for you.

Buying without a real estate agent

You can purchase property without an agent if you're willing to do some additional legwork. You need to do the things that a good real estate agent does, such as searching for properties, scheduling appointments to see them, negotiating the deal, determining fair market value, and coordinating inspections.

If you don't work with an agent, have an attorney review the various contracts, unless you're a legal expert. Having someone else not vested in the transaction look out for your interests helps your situation. Real estate agents generally

aren't legal experts, so getting legal advice from an attorney is generally better. (In some states, you need to hire an attorney in addition to the real estate agent.)

One possible drawback to working without an agent is that you have to perform the negotiations yourself. If you're a good negotiator, working without an agent can work to your advantage, but if you get too caught up emotionally in the situation, negotiating for yourself can backfire.

You also need an agent who is knowledgeable about the local market and community. If you want to buy a home in an area in which you don't currently live, an informed agent can have a big impact on your decision.

As a buyer, especially a first-time buyer or someone with credit problems, finding an agent with financing knowledge is a plus. Such an agent may be able to refer you to lenders that can handle your type of situation, which can save you a lot of legwork.

Closing the Deal

After you locate a property that you want to buy and understand your financing options, the real fun begins. Now you have to put the deal together. The following sections discuss key things to keep in mind.

Negotiating 101

When you work with an agent, the agent usually carries the burden of the negotiation process. Even if you delegate responsibility for negotiating to your agent, you still need to have a plan and strategy in mind. Otherwise, you may overpay for real estate.

Learn about the property and the owner before you make your offer. How long has the property been on the market? What are its flaws? Why is the owner selling? The more you understand about the property you want to buy and the seller's motivations, the better your ability is to draft an offer that meets everyone's needs. Some listing agents love to talk and will tell you the life history of the seller. Either you or your agent may be able to get them to reveal helpful information about the seller.

Also, bring facts to the bargaining table. Get comparable sales data to support your price. Too often, homebuyers and their agents pick a number out of the air when they make an offer. If you were the seller, would you be persuaded to lower your asking price? Pointing to recent and comparable home sales to justify your offer price strengthens your case.

Remember that price is only one of several negotiable items. Sometimes sellers fixate on selling their homes for a certain amount. Perhaps they want to get at least what they paid for it themselves several years ago. You may get a seller to pay for certain repairs or improvements or to offer you an attractive loan without all the extra fees that a bank charges. Also, be aware that the time that you need to close on your purchase is a bargaining chip. Some sellers may need cash soon and may concede other points if you can close quickly. Likewise, the real estate agent's commission is negotiable too.

Finally, try as best you can to leave your emotions out of any property purchase. This is easier said than done and hardest to do when you purchase a home in which you'll live. Try, as best you can, not to fall in love with a property. Keep searching for other properties even when you make an offer because you may be negotiating with an unmotivated seller.

Inspections

When you buy a property, you're probably making one of the biggest financial purchases and commitments of your life. Unless you've built homes and other properties and performed contracting work yourself, you probably have no idea what you're getting yourself into when it comes to furnaces and termites.

Spend the money and time to hire inspectors and other experts to evaluate the major systems and potential problem areas of the home. Because you can't be certain of the seller's commitment, I recommend that you do the inspections *after* you've successfully negotiated and signed sales contract. Although you won't have the feedback from the inspections to help with this round of negotiating, you can always go back to the seller with the new information. Make your purchase offer contingent on a satisfactory inspection.

Areas that you want to hire people to help you inspect include:

- ✔ Overall condition of the property. For example, is the paint peeling, are the floors level, are appliances present and working well, and so on?
- ✔ Electrical, heating and air conditioning, and plumbing systems
- ✔ Foundation

> ✔ Roof
>
> ✔ Pest control and dry rot
>
> ✔ Seismic/slide/flood risk

(With multi-unit rental property, be sure to read Chapter 12 for other specifics that you need to check out, such as parking.)

Inspection fees often pay for themselves. If you uncover problems that you weren't aware of when you negotiated the original purchase price, the inspection reports give you the information you need to go back and ask the property seller to fix the problems or reduce the property's purchase price.

Never accept a seller's inspection report as your only source of information. When a seller hires an inspector, he or she may hire someone who isn't as diligent and critical of the property. Review the seller's inspection reports if available, but get your own as well. Also, beware of inspectors who are popular with real estate agents. They may be popular because they are soft touches and don't bother to document all the property's problems.

As with other professionals whose services you retain, interview a few different inspection companies. Ask which systems they inspect and how detailed a report they will prepare for you. Consider asking the company that you're thinking of hiring for customer references. Ask for names and phone numbers of three people who used the company's services within the past six months. Also, request from the inspection company a sample of one of its reports.

The day before you close on the purchase of your home, take a brief walk-through of the property to make sure that everything is still in the condition it was before and that all the fixtures, appliances, curtains, and other items the contract lists are still there. Sometimes, sellers don't recall or ignore these things, and consequently don't leave what they agreed to in the sales contract.

Title insurance and escrow fees

Mortgage lenders require title insurance to protect against someone else claiming legal title to your property. This can happen, for example, when a husband and wife split up, and the one who remains in the home decides to sell and take off with the money. If the title lists both spouses as owners, the spouse who sells the property (possibly by forging the other's signature) has no legal right to do so. The other spouse can come back and reclaim rights to the home even after it has been sold. In this event, both you and the lender can get stuck holding the bag. (If you're in the enviable position of paying cash for a property, buying title insurance is still wise even though a mortgage lender won't prod you to do so. You need to protect your investment.)

Title insurance and escrow fees may vary from company to company. (Escrow charges pay for neutral third-party services to ensure that the instructions of the purchase contract or refinance are fulfilled and that everyone gets paid.) Don't simply use the company that your real estate agent or mortgage lender suggests — shop around. When you call around for title insurance and escrow fee quotes, make sure that you understand all the fees. Many companies tack on all sorts of charges for things such as courier fees and express mail. If you find a company with lower prices and want to use it, consider asking for an itemization in writing so that you don't have any surprises.

An insurance company's ability to pay claims is always important. Most state insurance departments monitor and regulate title insurance companies. Title insurers rarely fail, and most state departments of insurance do a good job shutting down financially unstable ones. Check with your state's department if you're concerned. You can also ask the insurer for copies of its ratings from insurance-rating agencies.

Selling Real Estate

You should buy and hold real estate for the long term. If you do your homework and buy in a good area and work hard to find a fairly priced or underpriced property, why sell it in a few years and incur all the selling costs, time, and hassle to locate and negotiate another property to purchase?

Some real estate investors like to buy properties in need of improvement, fix them up, and then sell them and move on to another. Unless you're a contractor and have a real eye for this type of work, don't expect to make a windfall. In fact, it's more likely that you'll erode your profit through the myriad costs of frequent buying and selling. In the long run, the vast majority of your profits come from the appreciation of the overall real estate market in the communities that you own property in, rather than from improving the value of your properties so you can get more out of them than the cost of the improvements that you make to them.

Use the reasons that you bought in an area as a guide if you think you want to sell. Use the criteria that I discuss in Chapter 12 as a guideline. For example, if the schools in the community are deteriorating and the planning department is allowing development that will hurt the value of your property and the rents that you can charge, you may have cause to sell. Unless you see significant problems like these in the future, holding good properties over many years is a great way to build your profits and minimize transaction costs.

Negotiating real estate agents' contracts

Most people use an agent to sell real estate. As I discuss in "How to find a good agent," earlier in this chapter, selling and buying a home demands agents with different strengths. When you sell a property, you want an agent who can get the job done efficiently and for as high a sales price as possible.

As a seller, seek agents who have marketing and sales expertise and who are willing to put in the time and money necessary to sell your house. Don't be impressed by an agent just because he or she works for a large company. What matters more is what the agent can do to market your property.

When you list your house for sale, the contract that you sign with the listing agent includes specification of the commission that you pay the agent if he or she succeeds in selling your house. In most areas of the country, agents usually ask for a 6 percent commission. In an area that maintains lower-cost housing, agents may ask for 7 percent.

Regardless of the commission an agent says is "typical," "standard," or "what my manager requires," always remember that you can negotiate commissions. Because the commission is a percentage, you have much greater ability to get a lower commission on a higher-priced property. If an agent makes 6 percent selling both a $200,000 house and a $100,000 house, the agent makes twice as much on the $200,000 house. Yet selling the higher-priced property does not take twice as much work. (And selling a $400,000 house certainly doesn't take four times the effort of selling a $100,000 house.)

If you live in an area with higher-priced homes, you may be able to negotiate a 5 percent commission. For expensive properties, a 4 percent commission is reasonable. You may find, however, that your ability to negotiate a lower commission is greatest when an offer is on the table. Because of the cooperation of agents that work together through the multiple listing service (MLS), if you list your home for sale at a lower commission than most other properties, some agents won't show it to prospective buyers. This fact is why you're better off having your listing agent cut his take rather than cutting the commission that you pay to a real estate agent who brings a buyer for your property to you.

In terms of the length of the listing agreement, three months is reasonable. If you give an agent too long to list your property (6 to 12 months), the agent may simply toss your listing into the multiple listing book and not expend much effort to get your property sold. Practically speaking, you can fire your agent whenever you want, regardless of the length of the listing agreement, but a shorter listing may motivate your agent more.

Selling without a real estate agent

The temptation to sell real estate without an agent is usually to save the commission that an agent deducts from your home's sale price. If you have the time, energy, and marketing experience, you can sell your home and possibly save some money.

The major problem with attempting to sell your home on your own is that you can't list it in the MLS, which, in most areas, only real estate agents can access. If you're not listed in the MLS, many potential buyers never know that your home is for sale. Agents who work with buyers don't generally look for or show their clients homes that are for sale by owner or listed with discount brokers.

Besides saving you time, a good agent can help ensure that you're not sued for failing to disclose known defects of your property. If you decide to sell your home yourself, make sure that you have access to a legal advisor who can review the contracts. Take the time to educate yourself about the many facets of selling property for top dollar — read *House Selling For Dummies,* which I co-wrote with Ray Brown, from IDG Books Worldwide, Inc.

Part IV
Small Business

The 5th Wave   By Rich Tennant

"Einstein over there miscalculated our start-up costs, and we ran out of money before we could afford to open a 24-hour store."

In this part . . .

Although the businesses may be small, the potential for earning profits and finding a fulfilling career isn't. Here, I explain such things as how to develop a business plan, identify marketable products or services, find customers, and wallop the competition! If starting your own shop seems either too overwhelming or too uninspiring, you also find out how to buy an existing business.

Chapter 14

Launching Your Own Business

· ·

In This Chapter

▶ What is takes to be a successful entrepreneur

▶ Alternatives to starting your own company

▶ Small-business investment options

▶ Planning for success

· ·

*A*t the corner of Telegraph and Durant Avenues in Berkeley, California, Alex Popov sold shoes as fast as he could. He wasn't particularly interested in shoes, yet he spent 12 months finding this costly retail location a stone's throw away from the teeming University of California at Berkeley campus.

Selling the 5,000 pairs of shoes that came with the location and securing the lease were just two of the many obstacles on Popov's road to pursuing his dream — starting and building his own business. The business that he ultimately opened was Smart Alec's Intelligent Fast Food, a restaurant that sells healthy, gourmet fast food. "I wanted a business that could grow, but I also wanted psychic income — I want to raise people's awareness about health and nutrition."

But by the time the business opened, few people saw or appreciated all the little and big steps Popov had taken to achieve his dream. While previously working as a sales engineer, Popov started seriously contemplating an entrepreneurial path. "The desire to start my own business came before the idea," Popov says. "I eventually saw that even with a college education, I didn't know what made for good nutrition and the connection between diet and health." Popov soon learned — he spent hundreds of hours researching the harmful health effects of the standard American diet.

Like many entrepreneurs, Popov transitioned gradually into running his own business. After six months of research, which came after regular work hours, he quit his job as an engineer and started an export business. Even though the export business had nothing to do with what he ultimately desired to do — open a healthy fast-food restaurant — it did pay the bills. More important, unlike his job as an engineer, his new job wasn't full time, so Popov had more time to develop his restaurant business ideas. And, even once he secured his desired location for the restaurant, he took on the task of selling all those shoes at the location.

Do You Have the Right Stuff?

Many people dream about running their own company. Tales of entrepreneurs becoming multimillionaires focus attention on the financial rewards without revealing the business and personal challenges and costs associated with being in charge.

Consider all the activities that your company has to do well in order to survive and succeed in the competitive business world. Your company must develop products and services that the marketplace purchases. You also have to price your offerings properly and promote them. What good are your products and services if others don't know about them? After you've been successful in developing offerings that meet a need, new worries begin: competitors. Your success will likely spur imitators.

Even though you may never desire a career in accounting, you'll be confronted with tracking revenue and expenses, making tax payments, and perhaps handling a payroll. You may find yourself poring over lease contracts and evaluating office space. You also need to read trade and professional journals to keep current with changes in your field. Although you may never want to be a human resource manager, you need to know the right ways to hire, train, and retain good employees. You may soon become an expert on insurance and other employee benefits.

Business owners also face personal and emotional challenges, which rarely get airtime among all the glory of the rags-to-riches tales of multimillionaire entrepreneurs. Major health problems, divorces, fights and lawsuits among family members who are in business together, the loss of friends, and even suicides have been attributed to the passions of business owners who are consumed with winning or become overwhelmed by their failures.

Had enough already? I'm not trying to *scare* you, but I do want you to be *realistic* about starting your own business. Maybe you do have the right stuff to run your own company, but most people don't.

Myths of being an entrepreneur

Many myths persist about what it takes to be an entrepreneur, partly because those who aren't entrepreneurs tend to hang out with others who aren't. The mass media's popularization of "successful" entrepreneurs such as Bill Gates, Ted Turner, and Oprah Winfrey leads to numerous misperceptions and misconceptions.

One myth is that you must be well-connected or know "important" people to succeed as an entrepreneur. However, I think that being a decent human being is far more important. Enough rude, inconsiderate, and self-centered people are in the business world (and, yes, some of them do succeed in spite of their character flaws), and if you're not that way, you'll be able to meet people who can help you in one way or another. But remember that looking in the mirror shows you your best and most trusted resource.

Another myth is that you need to be really smart and have an M.B.A. or some other fancy degree. Many successful entrepreneurs — Bill Gates and Steve Jobs, for example — don't even have college degrees, for goodness sakes. Perusing *Forbes* magazine's list of the 200 most financially successful small companies shows that about 20 percent of the CEOs didn't earn a college degree and more than 60 percent don't have advanced degrees! These statistics are even more amazing when you consider that a relatively large number of entrepreneurs with humble backgrounds leave or are forced out of the successful enterprises they started.

I'm not saying that a good education isn't worthwhile in general and that it can't help you succeed in your own business. (For example, Ivy Leaguers run about 5 percent of the 200 best small businesses, yet Ivy League college grads make up less than 1 percent of all graduates.) But a formal education isn't necessary.

As for intelligence, which is admittedly a difficult thing to measure, the majority of entrepreneurs have IQs under 120, and a surprising percentage have IQs under the average of 100 — more entrepreneurs, in fact, have IQs under 100 than have IQs greater than 130!

Another commonly held belief is that you must be a gregarious, big-egoed extrovert to succeed as an entrepreneur. Although some studies show that more entrepreneurs are extroverted, many entrepreneurs are not.

A final myth to dispel is the notion that starting your own business is risky. Some people focus on the potential for failure. Consider the worst-case scenario — if your venture doesn't work out, you can always go back to a job similar to the one you left behind. Also, recognize that risk is a matter of perception, and as with investments, people completely overlook some risks.

What about the risk to your happiness and career if you stay in a boring, claw-your-way-up-the-corporate-ladder kind of job? You always risk a layoff when you work for a company. An even greater risk is that you'll wake up in your 50s and 60s and think that it's too late to do something on your own and wish you had tried to sooner.

An entrepreneurial quiz

The keys to success and enjoyment as an entrepreneur vary as much as the businesses do. But if you can answer yes to most of the following questions, you probably have the qualities and perspective needed to succeed as a small-business owner.

Don't be deterred by those questions that you can't answer in the affirmative. A perfect entrepreneur doesn't exist. Part of succeeding in business is knowing what you can't do as well as what you can do and finding creative ways (or people) to help you.

1. Are you a self-starter? Do you like challenges? Are you persistent? Are you willing to do research to solve problems?

Running your own business is not glamorous most of the time, especially in the early years. You have lots of details to mind and things to do. Success in business is the result of doing lots of little things well. If you're accustomed to working for larger organizations where much of the day is spent in meetings, on office politics and gossip, and with little accountability, you probably won't enjoy or succeed at running your own business.

2. Do you value independence and self-control?

Particularly in the early days of your business, you need to enjoy working on your own. If you're a people person, however, many businesses offer lots of contact. But you must recognize the difference between socializing with coworkers and networking with business contacts and customers. When you leave a company environment and work on your own, you give up a lot of socializing. Of course, if you work in an unpleasant environment or with people you don't really enjoy socializing with, venturing out on your own may be a plus.

3. Can you develop a commitment to an idea, product, or principle?

Most entrepreneurs work 50 hours per week, 50 or so weeks a year — that's about 2,500 hours per year. If your product, service, or cause that you're pursuing doesn't excite you, and you can't motivate others to work hard for you, it's going to be a long year!

One of the worst reasons to start your own business is for the pursuit of great financial riches. Don't get me wrong — if you're good at what you do and you know how to market your services or products, you may make more money working for yourself. But for most people, money isn't enough of a motivation, and many people make the same or less money on their own than they did working for a company.

4. Are you willing to make financial sacrifices and live a reduced lifestyle before and during your early entrepreneurial years?

"Live like a student, before and during the start-up of your small business" was the advice that my best business school professor, James Collins, gave me before I started my business. With most businesses, you expend money during the start-up years and likely have a reduced income compared to the income you receive while working for a company.

In order to make your entrepreneurial dream a reality, you need to live well within your means both before and after you start your business. But if running your own business really makes you happy, sacrificing expensive vacations, overpriced luxury cars, the latest designer clothing, and $3 lattes at the corner cafe shouldn't be too painful.

5. Do you recognize that, when you run your own business, you must still report to bosses?

Besides the allure of huge profits, the other reason some people mistakenly go into business for themselves is that they are tired of working for other people. Obnoxious, evil bosses can make anyone want to become an entrepreneur. I understand — I've been there. When I worked at a consulting firm, I had a boss — I'll call him Goofus — whom I positively detested. Although the team that I led had many weeks to prepare client presentations, Goofus didn't really focus on our material until a couple of days before the presentation. He then made massive changes, causing the entire team, as well as the production department that produced the presentation, to work 16-hour days and into the wee hours of the morning. Goofus also made himself inaccessible for input and advice and ignored voice mails until he got into crisis mode. He never apologized for his behavior and couldn't have cared less about people's personal lives. Because of people like Goofus, employees who wanted some semblance of control in their professional and personal lives left the consulting business.

When you run your own business, you have customers and other bosses just like Goofus who are miserable to deal with. If you have enough customers, you can simply decide not to do business with such jerks. Fortunately, the worst customers usually can't make your life anywhere near as miserable as bosses like Goofus.

Don't start a business for tax write-offs

"Start a small business for fun, profit, and huge tax deductions," a financial advice book declares, adding that "the tax benefits alone are worth starting a small business." A seminar company offers a course entitled "How to Have Zero Taxes Deducted from Your Paycheck." This tax seminar tells you how to solve your tax problems: "If you have a sideline business, or would like to start one, you're eligible to have little or no taxes taken from your pay."

All this sounds too good to be true — and of course it is. Not only are the strategies sure to lead to IRS audit purgatory, but such books and seminars may seduce you to pony up $100 or more for audiotapes or notebooks of "inside information."

Unfortunately, many self-proclaimed self-help gurus state that you can slash your taxes simply by finding a product or service that you can sell on the side of your regular employment. The problem they argue, is that as a regular wage-earner who receives a paycheck from an employer, you can't write off many of your other (personal) expenses. Open a sideline business, they say, and you can deduct your personal expenses as business expenses.

The pitch is enticing, but the reality is something quite different. You have to spend money to get tax deductions, and the spending must be for legitimate purposes of your business in its efforts to generate income. If you think that taking tax deductions for your hobby is worth the risk because you won't get caught unless

you're audited, the odds are stacked against you. The IRS audits an extraordinarily large portion of small businesses that show regular losses.

The bottom line is that you need to operate a real business for the purpose of generating income and profits, not tax deductions. The IRS considers an activity a hobby (and not a business) if it shows a loss for three or more of the preceding five tax years. (For example, the IRS considers horse racing and breeding a hobby if it shows a loss for five or more of the preceding seven tax years.) Some years, a certain number of businesses lose money, but a real business can't afford to do so year after year and remain in operation. Even if your sideline business passes this hobby test, as well as other IRS requirements, deducting any expenses that aren't directly applicable to your business is illegal.

If these hobby loss rules indicate that you're engaging in a hobby but you still want to claim your losses, you must convince the IRS that you are seriously trying to make a profit and run a legitimate business. The IRS will want to see that you are actively marketing your services, building your skills, and accounting for income and expenses. The IRS also wants to see that you don't derive too much pleasure from an activity. If you do, the IRS says that what you're doing is a hobby and not a business. Business isn't supposed to give you too much enjoyment!

6. Can you withstand rejection, naysayers, and negative feedback?

"I thought every *no* that I got when trying to raise my funding brought me one step closer to a yes," says Alex Popov, the entrepreneur I introduce earlier in this chapter. Unless you come from an entrepreneurial family, don't expect

Wet blankets through history

"This 'telephone' has too many shortcomings to be seriously considered as a means of communication. The device is inherently of no value to us," — Western Union internal memo in response to Alexander Graham Bell's telephone, 1876.

"The concept is interesting and well formed, but in order to earn better than a C, the idea must be feasible." — A Yale University management professor in response to Fred Smith's paper proposing reliable overnight delivery service. Smith went on to found Federal Express Corporation.

"We don't tell you how to coach, so don't tell us how to make shoes." — A large sporting shoe manufacturer to Bill Bowerman, inventor of the waffle shoe and cofounder of NIKE, Inc.

"So we went to Atari and said, 'Hey, we've got this amazing thing, even built with some of your parts, and what do you think about funding us? Or we'll give it to you. We just want to do it. Pay our salary, we'll come work for you.' And they said, 'No.' So then we went to Hewlett-Packard, and they said, 'Hey, we don't need you. You haven't got through college yet.'" — Steve Jobs, speaking about attempts to get Atari and Hewlett-Packard interested in his and Steve Wozniak's personal computer. Jobs and Wozniak founded Apple Computer.

"'You should franchise them,' I told them. 'I'll be your guinea pig.' Well, they just went straight up in the air! They couldn't see the philosophy. . . . When they turned us down, that left Bud and me

to swim on our own." — Sam Walton, describing his efforts to get the Ben Franklin chain interested in his discount retailing concept in 1962. Walton went on to found Wal-Mart.

"We don't like their sound, and guitar music is on the way out." — Decca Recording Company in rejecting The Beatles, 1962.

In 1884, John Henry Patterson was ridiculed by his business friends for paying $6,500 for the rights to the cash register — a product with "limited" or no potential. Patterson went on to found National Cash Register (NCR) Corporation.

"What's all this computer nonsense you're trying to bring into medicine? I've got no confidence at all in computers and I want nothing whatsoever to do with them." — a medical professor in England to Dr. John Alfred Powell, about the CT scanner.

"That is good sport. But for the military, the airplane is useless." — Ferdinand Foch, Commander in Chief, Allied Forces on the Western Front, World War I.

"The television will never achieve popularity; it takes place in a semi-darkened room and demands continuous attention." — Harvard Professor Chester L. Dawes, 1940.

Reprinted with permission from _Beyond Entrepreneurship, Turning Your Business into an Enduring Great Company_, James C. Collins and William C. Lazier, Prentice Hall.

your parents to endorse your "risky, crazy" behavior. Most of the time, parents simply think that working for a giant company makes you safer and more secure (which, of course, is a myth, because corporations can lay you off in a snap). It's also easier for them to say to their friends and neighbors that you're a big manager at a well-known corporation rather than explaining that you're working on some kooky business idea out of a spare bedroom.

Even other entrepreneurs can ridicule your good ideas. Two of my entrepreneurial friends were critical of each other's idea, yet both have succeeded!

7. Are you able to identify your shortcomings and hire or align yourself with people and organizations that complement your skills and expertise?

To be a successful entrepreneur, you need to be a bit of a jack-of-all-trades: marketer, accountant, customer service representative, administrative assistant, and so on. Unless you get lots of investor capital, which is rare for a true start-up, you can't afford to hire help in the early months, and perhaps even years, of your business.

Partnering with or buying certain services or products rather than trying to do everything yourself may make sense for you. And over time, if your business grows and succeeds, you should be able to afford to hire more help. If you can be honest with yourself and surround and partner yourself with people whose skills and expertise complement yours, you'll have a winning team!

8. Do you deal well with ambiguity? Do you believe in yourself?

When you're on your own, determining when and if you're on the right track is difficult. Some days, things don't go well. If you are the company, bad days are much harder to take. Therefore, being confident, optimistic, and able to work around obstacles are necessary skills.

9. Do you understand why you started the business or organization and how you personally define "success"?

Many business entrepreneurs define success by such measures as sales revenue, profits, number of branch offices and employees, and so on. These are fine measures, but other organizations, particularly non-profits, have other measures. For example, the Washington D.C.-based non-partisan Violence Policy Center (VPC) seeks "...to fight firearms violence through research, education, and advocacy." The following is a passage from VPC's materials illustrating how the organization produces research for the purpose of public policy advances:

> "The VPC study *Joe Camel with Feathers: How the NRA with Gun and Tobacco Industry Dollars Uses its Eddie Eagle Program to Market Guns to Kids* revealed how the National Rifle Association is following a trail blazed by the tobacco industry — from youth 'educational' programs that are in fact marketing tools to appealing cartoon characters that put a friendly face on a hazardous product — in its efforts to market guns to children and youth."

In order to accomplish such goals as affecting public policy and public opinion about an issue like gun violence, money is necessary, but such a cause-focused organization has a very different "bottom line" than a for-profit organization.

10. Can you accept lack of success in the early years of building your business?

A few, rare businesses are instant hits, but most businesses take time — years, perhaps even decades — to build momentum. Some successful corporate people suffer from anxiety when they go out on their own and encounter the inevitable struggles and lack of tangible success as they build their company.

Alternatives to Starting Your Own Company

Sometimes, entrepreneurial advocates imply that running your own business or starting your own non-profit is the greatest thing in the world and that everyone would be happy owning their own business if they just set their mind to it. The reality is that some people won't be happy as entrepreneurs. If you didn't score highly on my ten-question entrepreneur quiz in the last section, don't despair. You can probably be happier and more successful doing something other than starting your own business.

Some people are happier working for a company, either for-profit or non-profit. Others do well buying an existing small business instead of trying to start one from scratch. Consider the following options.

Being an entrepreneur inside a company

A happy medium is available for people who want the challenge of running their own show without giving up the comforts and security that come with a company environment — for example, you can manage an entrepreneurial venture at a company. That's what John Kilcullen, president and chief executive officer of IDG Books Worldwide (this book's publisher), did when he helped launch the book publishing division of IDG in 1990.

Kilcullen had publishing industry experience and wanted to take on the responsibility of growing a successful publishing company. But he also knew that being a player in the book-publishing industry takes a lot of money and resources. Because he was a member of the founding team of the new IDG Books division, Kilcullen had the best of both worlds.

Kilcullen always had a passion to start his own business but found that most traditional publishers weren't interested in giving autonomy and money to a division and letting it run with the ball. "I wanted the ability to build a business on my own instincts . . . the appeal of IDG was that it was decentralized. IDG was willing to invest and provide the freedom to spend as we saw fit."

If you're able to secure an entrepreneurial position inside a larger company, in addition to significant managerial and operational responsibility, you can also negotiate your share of the financial success that you helped create. The parent company's senior management wants you to have the incentive that comes from sharing in the financial success of your endeavors. Bonuses, stock options, and the like are often tied to the performance of a division.

Investing in your career

Some people are happy or content as employees. Companies need and want lots of good employees, so you can find a job if you have skills, a work ethic, and the ability to get along with others.

You can improve your income-earning ability and invest in your career a variety of different ways:

- ✔ **Work.** Be willing to work extra hours and take on more responsibility. Don't bite off more than you can chew — otherwise your supervisors won't have faith that they can count on you to deliver. Those who take extra initiative and then deliver really stand out in a company where many people working on a salary have a time-clock, 9-to-5 mentality.

- ✔ **Read.** One of the reasons that you don't need a Ph.D., master's degree, or even an undergraduate college degree to succeed in business is that you can learn a lot on your own. You can learn by doing, but you can also learn a lot by reading. A good bookstore has no entrance requirements, such as an elevated high school grade point average or high SAT scores — you only have to walk through the doors. A good book isn't free, but it costs a heck of lot less than taking more college or graduate courses!

- ✔ **Study.** If you haven't completed your college or graduate degree and the industry you're in values those who have, investing the time and money to finish your education may benefit you. Speak with others who have taken that path and see what they have to say.

Small-Business Investment Options

Only your imagination limits the ways that you can make money with small businesses. Choosing the option that best meets your needs is not unlike choosing other investments, such as in real estate or in the securities markets. Following are the major ways you can invest in small business and information on what's attractive and not about each option.

Starting your own business

Of all your small-business options, starting your own business involves the greatest amount of work. Although you can perform this work on a part-time basis in the beginning, most people end up working in their business full time — it's your new job, career, or whatever you want to call it.

For most of my working years, I've run my own business and, overall, I really like it. However, that's not to say that running my own business doesn't have its drawbacks and down moments. In my experience counseling small-business owners, I've seen many people of varied backgrounds, interests, and skills achieve success and happiness running their own businesses.

Most people perceive starting their own business as the riskiest of all small-business investment options. But if you get into a business that utilizes your skills and expertise, the risk isn't nearly as great as you may think. Suppose that you teach and make $30,000 per year working for a school district, and you want to set up your own tutoring service, making a comparable amount of money. If you find through your research that others who perform these services charge $30 per hour, you need to actually tutor about 20 or so hours per week, assuming that you work 50 weeks per year. Because you can run this business from your home (which can possibly generate small tax breaks) without purchasing new equipment, your expenses should be minimal.

Instead of leaving your job cold turkey and trying to build your business from scratch, you can start moonlighting as a tutor. Over a couple of years, if you can average ten hours per week, you're halfway to your goal. If you leave your job and focus all your energies on your tutoring business, getting to 20 hours per week of billable work shouldn't be a problem. Still think starting a business is risky?

Many businesses can be started with low start-up costs, by leveraging your existing skills and expertise. If you have the time to devote to building "sweat equity," you can build a valuable company and job. As long as you check out the competition and offer a valued service at a reasonable cost, the principal risk with your business is that you won't do a good job marketing what you have to offer. If you can market your skills, you should succeed.

Buying an existing business

If you don't have a specific idea for a business that you want to start but you have business-management skills and an ability to improve existing businesses, you may consider buying an established business. Although you don't have to go through the riskier start-up period if you take this route, you'll likely need more capital to buy a going enterprise.

You also need to be able to deal with stickier personnel and management issues. The history of the organization and the way things work predates your ownership of the business. If you don't like making hard decisions, firing people who don't fit with your plans, and coercing people into changing the way they did things before you arrived on the scene, buying an existing business likely isn't for you. Also realize that some of the good employees may be loyal to the old owner and may split when you arrive.

Some people perceive that buying an existing business is safer than starting a new one, but buying someone else's business can actually be riskier. You'll have to shell out far more money up front, in the form of a down payment, to buy a business. If you don't have the ability to run the business and it does poorly, you may lose much more financially. Another risk is that the business is for sale for a reason — it's not very profitable, it's in decline, or it's generally a pain in the posterior to operate.

Good businesses that are for sale don't come cheaply. If the business is a success, the current owner has removed the start-up risk from the business, so the price of the business should include a premium to reflect this lack of risk. If you have the capital to buy an established business and you have the skills to run it, consider going this route. Chapter 16 goes into detail about how to buy a good business.

Investing in someone else's business

If you like the idea of profiting from successful small businesses but don't want the day-to-day headaches of being responsible for managing the enterprise, you may want to invest in someone else's small business. Although this route may seem easier, fewer people are actually cut out to be investors in other people's businesses.

Businesses often want your money for the wrong reasons

Although some people are extra careful when they invest other people's money, you need to know that many small-business owners seek investors' money for the wrong reasons. Some business owners are impatient and perhaps don't understand the feasibility of making do with a small amount of capital (a process called bootstrapping, which I discuss in the next chapter).

Other businesses need money because they're in financial trouble. One small furniture retailer in my area conducted a stock offering to raise money. On the surface, everything seemed fine, and the company made it onto the Inc. 500 list of fast-growing small companies. But it turns out that the company wanted to issue stock because it expanded too quickly and didn't sell enough merchandise to cover its high overhead. The company ended up in bankruptcy.

Another problem with small businesses that seek investors is that many small-business owners may take more risk and do less up-front planning and homework with other people's money. Many well-intentioned people fail at their businesses. An M.B.A. whom I know from a top business school — I'll call him Jacob — convinced an investor to put up about $300,000 to purchase a small manufacturing company. Jacob put a small amount of his own money into the business and immediately blew about $100,000 on a fancy-schmancy computer scheduling and order-entry system.

Likewise, Jacob wasn't interested much in sales, (a job that the previous owner managed), so he hired a sales manager. The sales manager he hired was a disaster — many of the front-line salespeople fled to competitors, taking key customers with them. By the time Jacob came to his senses, it was too late — the disaster had unfolded. He tried to cut costs, but this hurt the quality and timeliness of the company's products. The business dissolved, and the investor lost everything.

Investing for the right reasons

Consider investing in someone else's business if you meet the following criteria:

- ✔ You have sufficient assets so that what you are investing in small privately held companies is a small portion (20 percent or less) of your total financial assets.

- ✔ You can afford to lose what you invest. Unlike investing in a diversified stock mutual fund (Chapter 9), you may lose all your investment when you invest in a small, privately held company.

- ✔ You're astute at evaluating corporate financial statements and business strategies. Investing in a small privately held company has much in common with investing in a publicly traded firm. The difference is that private firms aren't required to produce comprehensive, audited financial statements that adhere to certain accounting principles the way that public companies are. Thus, you have a greater risk of not receiving sufficient or accurate information when you evaluate a small private firm.

Putting money into your own business (or someone else's) can be a high-risk — but potentially high return — investment. The best options to pick are those that you understand well. If you hear about a great business idea or company from someone you know and trust, do your research and make your best judgment. That company or idea may well be a terrific investment.

Before you invest in a project, ask to see a copy of the business plan and compare it with the business plan model that I suggest later in this chapter. Thoroughly check out the people running the business. Talk to others who don't have a stake in the investment and learn from their comments and concerns. But, don't forget that many a wise person has rained on the parade of what turned out to be a terrific business idea.

Blueprinting a Business Plan

If you're psyched about starting your own business, the next step is to figure out what you want to do and how you're going to do it. You don't need a perfectly detailed plan that spells out all the minutiae. Making such an involved plan is a waste of your time because things change and evolve over time.

However, you do need a general plan that helps you define what you think you want to do and the tasks that you need to perform to accomplish your goal. The business plan should be a working document or blueprint for the early days, months, and years of your business.

The amount of detail that your plan needs depends upon your goals and the specifics of your business. A simple, more short-term focused plan (ten pages or so) is fine if you don't aspire to build an empire. However, if your goal is to grow, hire employees, and open multiple locations, then your plan needs to be longer (20 to 50 pages) to cover longer-term issues. If you want outside investor money, a longer business plan is a necessity.

As you put together your plan and evaluate your opportunities, open your ears and eyes. Expect to do research and to speak with other entrepreneurs and people in the industry. Many people will spend time talking with you as long as they realize that you don't want to compete with them.

Identifying your business concept

What do you want your business to do? What product or service do you want to offer? Maybe your business goal is to perform tax-preparation services for small-business owners. Or, perhaps you want to start a consulting firm, open a restaurant that sells healthy fast food, run a gardening service, or manufacture toys.

Alan Tripp started a company called Score Advantage Learning Centers. He describes his concept like this: "Score is a storefront center for computer-assisted learning, where kids use computers to improve their reading, writing, math, and science skills."

Your concept doesn't need to be unique to survive in the business world. Tons of self-employed consultants, plumbers, tax preparers, and restaurant owners are out there. The existence of many other people who already do what you want to do validates the potential for your small-business ideas. I know many wage slaves who say they would love to run their own business if they could only come up with "the idea." Most of these people still dream about their small-business plans as they draw their Social Security checks. Being committed to the idea of running your own business is more important than developing the next great product or service. In the beginning, the business opportunities that you pursue can be quite general to your field of expertise or interest. What you eventually do over time will evolve.

I'm not saying that a new innovative idea doesn't have any merit. An innovative idea gives you the chance to hit a big home run, and the first person to successfully develop a new idea can achieve big success.

Even if you aspire to build the next billion-dollar company, you can put a twist on older concepts. Suppose that you're a veterinarian but you don't want a traditional office where people must bring their cats and dogs for treatment. You believe that because many people are starved for free time, they want a vet who makes house calls. Thus, you open your Vet on Wheels business. You may also want to franchise the business and open locations around the country. However, you also can succeed by doing what thousands of other vets are now doing and have done over the years with a traditional office.

Outlining your objectives

The reasons for starting and running your own small business are as varied as the entrepreneurs behind their companies. Before you start your firm, it's useful to think about what you're seeking to achieve. Your objectives need not be cast in concrete and will surely change over time. If you like, you can write a short and motivating mission statement.

When you ask an M.B.A., especially one from a big-name school, to think about objectives, he or she usually says something like, "My goal is to run a $20 million company in seven years." Financial objectives are fine, but don't make your objectives strictly financial, unless money is the only reason that you want to run your own business.

Introductory economics courses teach students that the objective of every for-profit firm is to maximize profits. As with many things taught in economics courses, this theory has one problem — it doesn't hold up in reality. Most small-business owners I know don't manage their businesses maniacally in the pursuit of maximum profits. The following list gives you some other possible objectives to consider:

- ✔ **Working with people you like and respect.** Some customers may buy your products and services, and some employees and suppliers may offer you their services for a good price, but what if you can't stand working with them? If you have sufficient business or just have your own standards, you can choose whom you do business with.

- ✔ **Educating others.** Maybe part of your business goal is to educate the public about something that you're an expert in. Alex Popov, the entrepreneur I discuss earlier in this chapter, saw education as an important part of his company's purpose.

> ✔ **Improving an industry/setting a higher standard.** Perhaps part of your goal in starting your business is to show how your industry can better serve its customers. John Bogle, who founded the Vanguard Group of mutual funds, is a good example of someone who wanted to improve an industry. When he started Vanguard three decades ago, Bogle structured the company so that the shareholders (customers) of the company's individual mutual funds would own the company. Because he relinquished ownership of his company, Bogle gave up the opportunity to build a personal net worth that would easily be worth several billion dollars today. But Bogle wanted to build a mutual fund company that kept operating costs to a minimum and returned profits to the customers in the form of lower operating fees, which are deducted from a mutual fund's returns. He's also been outspoken about how owners of many mutual fund companies operate their funds out of self-interest rather than keeping their customers in mind.

Of course, you can't accomplish these objectives without profits, and doing these things isn't inconsistent with generating greater profits. But if your objectives are more than financial or your financial objectives are not your number-one concern, don't worry — that's usually a good sign.

Analyzing the marketplace

The single, most important area to understand is the marketplace that your business competes in. To be successful, your business must not only produce a good product or service, but it must also reach and convince customers to buy your product. You should also discern what the competition has to offer, as well as its strengths and vulnerabilities. In most industries, you also need to understand government regulations that affect the type of business that you're considering.

Meeting customer needs

If the market analysis is the most important part of the business plan, then understanding your customers is the most important part of your market analysis. If you don't understand your desired customers and their needs, don't expect to have a successful business.

If you're in a business that sells to consumers, consider your customer's gender, age, income, geographic location, marital status, number of children, education, living situation (rent or own), and the reasons he or she wants your product or service. Who are your prospective customers? Where do they live, what do they care about? If you sell to businesses, you need to understand similar issues. What types of businesses may buy your product or services? Why?

Research model companies

If your business provides products or services similar to those that other companies offer, identify two or three of your competitors that do a good job or seem most similar. Which of these companies' practices do you want to emulate? In what areas can you improve upon or differentiate your offerings?

Even if you have an innovative and apparently unique concept, examine companies in related and even dissimilar fields to identify those that you want to emulate. Identify traits and characteristics from several so you can build them into the composite of your own firm.

For the model companies that you examine, find information about the following:

✔ Why they chose their location

✔ How they promote their services and products

✔ How they provide or manufacture their products and services

✔ What types of customers they attract

✔ What their revenues, expenses, and profitability are

✔ How they've expanded their locations over time (if this is your goal)

The best way to get to know your potential customers is to get out and talk to them. In-person interviews or a paper-based survey both have their benefits. Although more time-consuming, live interviews provide the most accurate and useful information. These interviews allow you to go with the flow of the conversation, improvise questions, and probe more interesting areas. Although you can mail or fax paper-based surveys to many people with a minimal investment of your time, the response rate is usually quite low and the answers are usually not as illuminating. Offer a product or service sample, or some other promotional item to those who help you with your research. Doing so attracts people who are interested in your product or service, which helps you define your target customers.

Also, try to get a sense of what customers pay and will pay for the products or services that you offer. Analyzing the competition's offerings helps, too. Some products or services also require follow-up or additional servicing. Understand what customers need and what they will pay for your services.

If you want to raise money from investors, include some estimates as to the size of the market for your product or services. Of course such numbers are ballpark estimates, but sizing the market for your product helps you estimate profitability, the share of the market needed to be profitable, and so on.

Besting the competition

Examining competitor strategies is a must for any business owner. Otherwise, you go on blind faith that what you offer stacks up well versus the other alternatives in the industry. Always examine the products, services, benefits, and prices that competitors offer.

You first need to decide if you have a realistic chance of winning the consumer choice battle. I think you'll agree that going into the same discount warehouse retailing business and competing head-to-head with Wal-Mart, Costco, or Home Depot is crazy — you'll likely lose.

You next want to discover your competitors' weaknesses so you can exploit them. Rather than trying to beat Costco and Wal-Mart on their terms, maybe you've identified a need for a neighborhood pet supply store that offers a much broader and specialized range of pet supplies than the big-selling brands of dog and cat food that Costco and Wal-Mart sell. Providing knowledgeable customer sales representatives to answer customer questions and make product suggestions can also give you a competitive edge.

Thus, you may be able to surpass Costco and Wal-Mart on three counts: convenience of location for people in your neighborhood, breadth of product offerings, and customer assistance. Offering only economy sizes of the best-selling brands of pet food to compete with Costco and Wal-Mart would be foolish. Your prices may have to be higher because you can't negotiate the volume discount purchases that they can. You may also have greater overhead (not in absolute dollars but as a percentage of your revenue) running a small business.

However, that's not to say that your neighborhood pet supply store can't offer some best-selling pet food. As I'm sure you know, some convenience store customers pay top dollar for smaller bags of supplies that they can purchase close to home.

If you want to open a neighborhood pet supply store, evaluate a number of different locales to see where other similar stores are located. Visit those stores and observe their strengths and weaknesses. If you're discreet, you may be able to interview some customers outside the stores to see what they like and don't like about the competition.

Don't make the mistake of thinking that even if you have a completely innovative product or service that no other business currently offers, you don't have competitors. All businesses have competitors. For example, suppose you start a business that sells a particular type of classified advertising space on a World Wide Web site. If you're the first to offer this service, you may think that you don't have competitors, but of course you do. Although not online, many newspapers and magazines offer classified ads. A competitor is an alternative company that a customer can use to meet a similar need. Remember, customers *don't* think, "I want to place this ad on the Internet." They *do* think, "What are the costs and benefits of the different places where I can place this ad?"

Complying with regulations

Most businesses are subject to some sort of regulation. If you want to start a retail business, for example, few communities permit you to run it out of your home. If you lease or purchase a private location, the zoning laws in that location may restrict you. Therefore, you need to check what you can and cannot sell at that location. Check with the zoning department of your city or town — don't follow the word of a real estate broker or property owner who says, "No problem!" because he or she wants to sell the property.

If you were going to start a veterinary practice, you would quickly discover that special zoning is required to use a piece of real estate for a vet's office. Convincing a local zoning board to allow a new location to get such special zoning is quite difficult, if not impossible, in some areas.

With some businesses, other licenses and filings with local, state, or even the federal government are required. For example, financial advisors who provide investment advice must register with the U.S. Securities and Exchange Commission as well as with a state agency (in most states) where advisors are monitored.

If you enter an industry that you're relatively new to, ask questions and open your ears to start learning more about the location and function of your business. Speak to people who are currently in the field and your local Chamber of Commerce to see what, if any, licenses or filings you must complete. Also, check out your local bookstore. If running a veterinary practice interests you, read books on the subject. Also, check the newsstand and local library for trade magazines that may deal with your questions. Libraries have books and online services that can help you locate specific articles on topics that interest you.

Delivering your service or product

Every business has a product or service to sell. How are you going to provide this product or service? Suppose you want to start a business that delivers groceries and runs errands for busy people or older and disabled people who can't easily perform daily tasks for themselves.

Delineate the steps that you will take to provide the service. When potential customers call you to inquire about your business, what kinds of information do you want to record about their situation? Create a pricing sheet and other marketing literature (discussed later in this chapter) that you can mail curious customers.

After someone calls and says, "I want to hire you!" you need to collect more details. Try drawing up an information sheet that prompts you for the information that you need (for example, address, promised delivery time, desired items, and so on).

If you want to be a tax preparer, you need forms or a filing system to give to your customers to help them organize the information that they give to you. The point of these examples is to map out in advance a system that you can work with. Your system may evolve over time — you can be guaranteed of that — but a tentative game plan has great value.

If you want to manufacture a product, you definitely need to map out the process that you're going to use. Otherwise, you have no idea how much time the manufacturing process may take or what the process may cost.

As your business grows and you hire employees to provide services or create your products, the more you codify what you do, the better your employees can replicate your good work.

Marketing your service or product

After you get more in-depth information about your company's services or products, you need to find more specific information about the following:

- ✔ **How much will you charge for your services and products?** Look at what competing products and services cost. Also, estimating your costs helps you figure out what you need to charge to cover your costs and make a reasonable profit.

- ✔ **How will you promote and advertise?** Having a great product or service is not enough if you keep it a secret — you gotta get the word out. It's doubtful that you have the budget or want to reach the same region that television and radio reach.

Start marketing your product to people you know. Develop a punchy, informational one-page letter that announces your company's inception and the products or services it offers, and mail it to your contacts. Include an envelope with a reply form that allows recipients to provide the addresses of others who may be interested in what you have to offer. Send these folks a mailing as well, referencing who passed their name along to you.

Finding and retaining customers is vital to any business that wants to grow and keep its costs in line. One simple, inexpensive way to stay in touch with customers you've dealt with or others who have made inquiries and expressed interest in your company's offerings is via a mailing list. Once a quarter, once a year, or whatever makes sense for your business, send out a simple, professional-looking postcard or newsletter announcing new information about your business and what customer needs you can fulfill. Such mailings also allow you to remind people that you're still in business and that you provide a wonderful product or service. Computer software gives you a fast, efficient way to keep a customer mailing list up to date and to print mailing labels.

✔ **How will you position your product and services versus the competition?** Remember the local pet supply store example that I mention earlier in this chapter? It positions itself as a convenient store equipped with a broad selection and knowledgeable customer assistance. Books similarly position themselves in the book marketplace. I hope, in your mind, that my financial books are down-to-earth, practical, answer-oriented, and educational.

✔ **Where will you sell your product or service?** Business consultants label this decision the *distribution channel question.* For example, if you're going to go into the hula-hoop manufacturing business, you may consider selling via mail order and Internet, through toy stores, or through discount warehouse stores. Selling through each of these different distribution channels requires unique marketing and advertising programs. If you market a product or service to companies, you need to find out who the key decision-makers are at the company and what it will convince them to buy your product or service.

Organizing and staffing your business

Many small businesses are one-person operations. So much the better for you — you have none of the headaches of hiring, payroll, and so on. You only have to worry about you — and that may be a handful in itself!

But if you desire to manage the work being done rather than doing all the work yourself, and if you hope to grow your business, you'll eventually want to hire people. (I explain the best way to fill your personnel needs in the next chapter.) If hiring is your goal, give some thought now to the skills and functional areas of expertise that future hires need. If you want to raise money, the employment section of your business plan is essential to show your investors that you're a long-term planner and thinker.

Maybe you'll want an administrative assistant, researcher, marketing person, or sales representative. What about a training specialist, finance person, or real estate person if your company expands to many sites? Consider the background that you desire in those you hire, and look at the types of people that similar companies select and hire. (See the model companies that I discuss earlier in this chapter.)

You should also consider what legal form of organization — for example, a sole proprietorship, partnership, S corporation, limited liability company, and so on — your business will adopt. I also address this topic in the next chapter.

Projecting finances

An idea often becomes a bad idea or a business failure if you neglect to consider or are unrealistic about the financial side of the business that you want to start. If you're a creative or people-person type who hates numbers, the financial side may be the part of the business plan that you most want to avoid. Don't — doing so can cost you perhaps tens of thousands of dollars in avoidable mistakes. Ignoring the financial side can even lead to the bankruptcy of a business founded with a good idea.

Before you launch your business, you should do enough research so that you can come up with some decent financial estimates to address these issues. Financial projections are mandatory, and knowledgeable investors will likely closely scrutinize them if you seek outside money. You also need to think through how and when investors can cash out.

Start-up and development costs

Spending money to get your business from the idea stage to an operating enterprise is inevitable. Before the revenue begins to flow in, you'll make expenditures to develop and market your products and services. Therefore, you need to understand what you must spend money on and the approximate timing of the needed purchases.

If you were going to build a house, you would develop a list of all the required costs. How much is the land, construction, carpeting, landscaping, and so on, going to cost? You can try to develop all these cost estimates yourself, or you can speak with local builders and have them help you. Likewise, with your business, you can hire a business consultant who knows something about your type of business. However, I think you're best served by doing the homework yourself — you learn a lot more, and it's far cheaper.

If you're going to work in an office setting, either at home or in outside space, you need furniture (such as a desk, chair, filing cabinets, and so on), a computer, printer, and other office supplies. Don't forget to factor in the costs of any licenses or government registrations that you may need.

If you run a retailing operation, you need to also estimate your initial inventory costs. Remember, selling your inventory takes time, especially when you first start up. And as a new business, suppliers won't give you months on end to pay for your initial inventory. Be realistic — otherwise the money that you tie up in inventory can send you to financial ruin.

Income statement

Preparing an estimated *income statement* that summarizes your expected revenue and expenses is a challenging and important part of your business plan. (I explain the elements of an income statement in Chapter 7.) Preparing an income statement is difficult because of all the estimates and assumptions that go into it. As you prepare your estimated income statement, you may discover that making a decent profit is tougher than you thought. This section of your business plan helps you make pricing decisions.

Consider the Vet on Wheels business idea that I discuss in the "Identifying your business concept" section, earlier in this chapter. What range of veterinary services can you provide if you make house calls? You can't perform all the services that you can in a larger office setting. What equipment do you need to perform the services? How much do you charge for the services? You need to estimate all these things to develop a worthwhile income statement. You should be able to answer these questions from the insights and information you pulled together regarding what customers want and what your competitors are offering.

With service businesses in which you or your employees sell your time, be realistic about how many hours you can bill. You may end up only being able to bill a third to half of your time given the other management activities that you need to perform.

Because building a customer base takes several years, try to prepare estimated income statements for the first three years. In the earlier years, you have more start-up costs. In later years, you reap more profits as your customer rolls expand. Doing income statements over several years is also essential if you're seeking investor money.

Balance sheet

An income statement measures the profitability of a business over a span of time, such as a year, but it tells you nothing of a business's resources and obligations. That's what a *balance sheet* does. Just as your personal balance sheet itemizes your personal assets (for example, investments) and liabilities (debts you owe), a business balance sheet details a company's assets and liabilities.

If you operate a cash business — you provide a service and are paid for that service, and you don't hold an inventory, for example — a balance sheet has limited use. An exception is if you're trying to get a bank loan for your service business.

A complete balance sheet isn't as important as tracking the available cash, which will be under pressure in the early years of a business because expenses can continue to exceed revenue for quite some time.

A complete balance sheet is useful for a business that owns significant equipment, furniture, inventory, and so on. The asset side of the balance sheet provides insight into the financial staying power of the company. For example, how much cash does your business have on hand to meet expected short-term bills? Conversely, the liability side of the ledger indicates the obligations, bills, and debts the company has coming due in the short and long term.

See Chapter 7 for more information on all the elements of a balance sheet.

Writing an executive summary

An *executive summary* is a two- to three-page summary of your entire business plan that you can share with interested investors who may not want to wade through a 40- to 50-page plan. The executive summary whets the prospective investor's appetite by touching on the highlights of your entire plan. Because this summary should go in the front of your plan document, you may find it odd that I list this element last. My reasoning? You're not going to be able to write an intelligent summary of your plan until you flesh out the body of your business plan.

Chapter 15

Running Your Small Business

After you research and evaluate the needs of your business, at some point you need to decide whether to actually start your business. In reference to his business plan, Alex Popov (I introduce Alex in Chapter 14), founder of Smart Alec's, a healthy fast-food restaurant, says, ". . . something just clicked one day, and I said to myself, 'Yes, this is a business that is viable and appropriate now.'"

Most entrepreneurs experience this sudden realization, including me — I've experienced it with every business that I've ever started. If you really want to, you can conduct and analyze market research and crunch numbers until the cows come home. Even if you're a linear, logical, analytic, quantitative kind of person, you need to make a gut-level decision in the final analysis: Do you want to jump in the water and start swimming, or do you want to stay on the sidelines and remain a spectator? In my opinion, watching isn't nearly as fun as doing. If you feel ready but have some trepidation, you're normal — just go for it!

Business Start-Up: Your Preflight Check List

When you decide to start your own business, you also need to ponder and make some decisions about a number of important issues. Just like a pilot before he or she launches an airplane into flight, you need to make sure that all systems are in order and ready to do the job. If your fuel tanks aren't adequately filled, your engines clean and in working order, and your wing flaps in the proper position, you may never get your business off the ground.

Preparing to leave your job

The top reasons that wannabe entrepreneurs remain wannabe entrepreneurs are the psychological and financial aspects. You may never discover that you have the talent to run your own business, and perhaps a good idea to boot, unless you prepare yourself fiscally and emotionally to leave your job. Money and mind issues cause many aspiring entrepreneurs to remain their employers' indentured servants and cause those who do break free to soon return to their bondage.

The money side of this self-exploration is easier to deal with than your mind, so I'll start with that. A net reduction in the income that you bring home from your work — at least in the early years of your business — is a foregone conclusion for the vast majority of small-business opportunities that you may pursue. Accept this fact and plan accordingly.

Do all that you can to reduce your expenses and lifestyle to a level that fits the entrepreneurial life that you want to lead. You must examine your monthly spending patterns now to make your budget lean, mean, and entrepreneurially friendly. Determine what you spend each month on your rent (or mortgage), groceries, eating out, telephone calls, insurance, and so on. Unless you're one of those organized computer geeks who everyone loves to hate, who keeps all this data detailed in a software package, you need to whip out your checkbook register, ATM receipts, credit card statement, and anything else that documents your spending habits. Don't forget to estimate your cash purchases that don't leave a trail, like when you eat lunch out or drop a $20 bill on gas and a Ring Ding.

Don't tell me that everything you spend your money on is a necessity and that you can't cut anywhere. Question every expenditure! If you don't, working as an employee will be a necessity, and you'll never be able to pursue your entrepreneurial dream.

Beyond the bare essentials of food, shelter, health care, and clothing, most of what we spend money on is discretionary — that is, you spend money on luxuries. Even the amount that you spend on the necessities, such as food and shelter, is part necessity and a fair amount of luxury and waste. If you need a helping hand and an analyst's eye in preparing and developing strategies for reducing your spending, pick up a copy of my first book, *Personal Finance For Dummies* (IDG Books Worldwide, Inc.).

Reduce your expenses to the level that they were when you lived at home or when you were a college student — remember those enjoyable days. Spending more doesn't make you happy; you'll be miserable over the years if your excess spending makes you feel chained to a job you don't like. Life is too short to spend most of it working at a full-time job that makes you unhappy.

If reducing your spending is the most important financial move you can take before and during the period that you start your business, the second-best thing you can do is to spend some time figuring how you'll manage the income side of your personal finances. The following list gives you some good strategies to ensure that you'll earn enough income to live on:

- ✔ **Transition gradually.** One way to pursue your entrepreneurial dreams (and not starve while doing so) is to continue working part time in a regular job while you work part time at your own business. If you have a job that allows you to work part time, seize the opportunity. Some employers may even allow you to maintain your benefits.

  In addition to ensuring a steady source of income, splitting your time allows you to adjust to a completely new way of making a living. Some people have a hard time adjusting to their new lifestyle if they quit their job cold turkey and confront themselves with working full time as an entrepreneur.

  Another option you can consider is to completely leave your job but line up a chunk of work that provides a decent income for at least some of your weekly work hours. Consulting for your old employer is a time-tested first "entrepreneurial" option with low risk.

- ✔ **Get/stay married.** Actually, as long as you're attached to someone who maintains a regular job and you manage your spending so you can live on that person's income alone, you're golden! Just make sure that you talk things through with the love of your life to minimize misunderstandings and resentments. Maybe someday you can return the favor — that's what my wife and I did. She was working in education (no big bucks there!) when I started an entrepreneurial venture after business school. We lived a spartan lifestyle and made do just fine on her income. Several years later, when things were going swimmingly for me, she left her job to work on her own business.

Valuing and replacing your benefits

Part of the money dilemmas that you may encounter deal with the benefits that your employer provides. For many people, walking away from these benefits is both financially and psychologically challenging. Benefits are valuable, but you may be surprised how quickly you can replicate them in your own business.

Health insurance

Some prospective entrepreneurs fret over finding new health insurance. Unless you have a significant existing medical problem (known in the insurance business as a *pre-existing condition*), getting health insurance as an individual is not difficult.

The first option to explore is whether your existing coverage through your employer's group plan can be converted into individual coverage. If it can be, great, just don't act on this option until you've explored other health plans on your own, which may offer similar benefits at lower cost. Also, get proposals for individual coverage from Blue Cross/Blue Shield, Kaiser, and other major health plans in your area. Take a high deductible, if available, to keep costs down.

Government regulations called *COBRA* require an employer with 20 or more employees to continue your health insurance coverage (at your own expense) for up to 18 months after you terminate employment. Moreover, if you have or develop a health problem while covered under COBRA, the law enables you to purchase an individual policy at the same price that a healthy individual can. These laws create a nice buffer zone for the budding entrepreneur, but don't get lazy and wait until the last minute of the 18th month to start shopping for your individual plan — COBRA plans can be costly. Shopping around and locking in an individual plan as soon as possible can save you money and prevent headaches.

Long-term disability insurance

Equally, if not more important than health insurance, is long-term disability insurance. For most people, their greatest asset is their ability to earn money. If you suffer a disability and can't work, how would you manage financially? Long-term disability insurance protects your income in the event of a disability.

Before you leave your job, secure an individual long-term disability policy. After you leave your job and are no longer earning steady income, you can't qualify for a policy. Most insurers want to see at least six months of self-employment income before they will write you a policy. If you become disabled during this time, you're uninsured and out of luck — that's a great risk to take!

Check with any professional associations that you belong to or could join to see if they offer long-term disability plans. As with many employer-based programs, association plans are sometimes less expensive because of the group's purchasing power.

Life insurance

If you have dependents who count on your income, you need life insurance. And, unlike disability insurance, in the vast majority of cases, you can purchase a life insurance policy at a lower cost than you can purchase additional coverage through your employer.

Retirement plans

If your employer offers retirement savings programs, such as a 401(k) plan or a pension plan, don't despair about not having these in the future. (Of course, what you've already earned and accumulated while employed is yours.) One of the best benefits of self-employment are retirement savings plans — SEP-IRAs (Simplified Employee Pension Individual Retirement Accounts) and Keoghs — that allow you to sock away a hefty chunk of your earnings on a tax-deductible basis.

Retirement plans are a terrific way for you and your employees to tax-shelter a healthy portion of earnings. If you don't have employees, regularly contributing to one of these plans is usually a no-brainer. With employees, the decision is a bit more complicated but often still a great idea. Small businesses with a number of employees can also consider 401(k) plans. I explain retirement plans in Chapter 3.

Other benefits

Yes, employers offer other benefits that you may value. For example, you *seem* to get paid holidays and vacations. In reality though, your employer simply pays you for working the other 47 weeks or so out of the year and spreads your salary over 52 weeks. You can do the same by building the cost of this paid time off into your product and service pricing.

Another "benefit" of working for an employer is that the employer pays for half (7.65 percent) of your Social Security and Medicare taxes. Although you must pay the entire tax (15.3 percent) when you're self-employed, the IRS allows you to take half of this amount as a tax deduction on your Form 1040, so that tax isn't as painful as you think. As with vacations and holidays, you can build the cost of this tax into your product and service pricing. Just think: Your employer could pay you a higher salary if it wasn't paying half of these taxes as a benefit.

Some employers offer other insurance plans, such as dental or vision care plans. Ultimately, these plans cover small out-of-pocket expenditures that aren't worth insuring for. Don't waste your money purchasing such policies, especially when you're self-employed.

Financing Your Business

When you create your business plan (which I explain how to do in Chapter 14), you should estimate your start-up and development costs. You can start many worthwhile small businesses with little capital. The following sections explain methods for financing your business.

Bootstrapping

Making do with a small amount of capital and spending it as you can afford to is known as *bootstrapping*. Bootstrapping is just a fancy way of saying that a business lives within its means. This forces a business to be resourceful and less wasteful. Bootstrapping is also a great training mechanism for producing cost-effective products and services. It offers you the advantage of getting into business in the first place with little capital.

Millions of successful small companies were bootstrapped at one time or another. Like small redwood saplings that grow into towering trees, small companies that had to bootstrap in the past can eventually grow into hundred million and even multibillion-dollar companies. For example, Ross Perot started EDS with a mere $1,000, and Hewlett-Packard's founders started the company out of a garage in Palo Alto, California. Motorola, Sony, and Disney were all bootstrapped, too.

Whether you want to maintain a small shop that employs just yourself, hire a few employees, or dream about building the next Wal-Mart, you need capital. However, misconceptions abound about how much money a company needs to achieve its goals and sources of funding.

"There's an illusion that most companies need tons of money to get established and grow," says James Collins, former lecturer at the Stanford Graduate School of Business and coauthor of the best seller, *Built to Last*. "The Silicon Valley success stories of companies that raise gobs of venture capital and grow 4,000 percent are very rare. They are statistically insignificant but catch all sorts of attention," he adds.

Studies show that the vast majority of small businesses obtain their initial capital from personal savings and family and friends rather than outside sources such as banks and venture capital firms. A Harvard Business School study of 100 of the Inc. 500 (500 large, fast-growing private companies) found that more than 80 percent of the successful companies were started with funds from the founder's personal savings. The median start-up capital was a modest $10,000, and these are successful, fast-growing companies! Slower-growing companies tend to require even less capital.

Even among high-technology firms, which tend to be more capital intensive, 79 percent are initially funded through the founder's personal savings and family and friends, according to a study by Edward B. Roberts, author of *Entrepreneurs in High Technology* (Oxford Press).

With the initial infusion of capital, many small businesses can propel themselves for years after they develop a service or product that brings in more cash flow. Jim Gentes, the founder of Giro, the bike helmet manufacturer, raised just $35,000 from personal savings and loans from family and friends to make and distribute his first product and then used the cash flow for future products.

Eventually, a successful, growing company may want outside financing to expand even faster. Raising money from outside investors or lenders is much easier after you demonstrate that you know what you're doing and that a market exists for your product or service.

As I explain earlier in the chapter, aspiring entrepreneurs must examine their personal finances for opportunities to reduce their own spending. If you want to start a company, the best time for you to examine your finances is years before you want to hit the entrepreneurial path. As with other financial goals, advance preparation can go a long way toward achieving the goal of starting a business. The best funding source and easiest investor to please is you.

Alan Tripp, founder and CEO of Score Advantage Learning Centers, a chain of storefront interactive learning centers, planned for seven years before he took the entrepreneurial plunge. He funded his first retail center fully from personal savings. He and his wife lived frugally to save the necessary money — they were caretakers for two years in order to save more money. Tripp's first center, opened in 1992, proved the success of his business concept: retail learning centers where kids can use computers to improve their reading, math, and science skills. With a business plan crafted over time and hard numbers to demonstrate the financial viability of his operation, Tripp then successfully raised funds from investors to open his next four centers.

Some small-business founders put the cart before the horse and don't plan and save for starting their business the way that Tripp did. And in many cases, small-business owners want capital but don't have a clear plan or need for it.

Borrowing from banks

If you're starting a new business or have been in business for just a few years, borrowing, particularly from banks, may be difficult. Borrowing money is easier when you don't really need to do so. No one knows this fact better than small-business owners.

Small-business owners who successfully obtain bank loans do their home-work. To borrow money from a bank, you generally need a business plan, three years of financial statements and tax returns for the business and its owner, as well as projections for the business. Be sure to hunt around for banks that are committed to and understand the small-business marketplace.

The Small Business Administration (SBA) guarantees some small-business loans that banks originate. Many of these loans would not otherwise be made by banks because of the business's lack of collateral and risk. In addition to guaranteeing loans for existing businesses, about 20 percent of SBA-backed loans go to start-up businesses, which must have founders who put up at least a third of the funds needed and demonstrate a thorough understanding of the business, ideally through prior related industry experience.

The SBA offers a number of workshops and counseling services for small business owners. Its SCORE (Service Corps of Retired Executives) consulting services provide free advice and critiques of business plans, as well as advice on raising money for your business. The SBA charges a nominal fee for seminars. To get more information on SBA's services and how to contact a local office, call 800-827-5722.

In addition to SBA-backed loans that you can apply for at banks, credit unions are often more willing to make personal loans to individuals. Borrowing against the equity in your home or other real estate is also advantageous because real estate loans generally entail lower and tax-deductible interest.

You can use retirement savings plans as another potential source of capital. These loans allow you to borrow against your investment balance and are usually available at competitive rates. Just make sure that you don't take on too much debt and jeopardize your retirement savings.

If you've got the itch to get your business going and can't wait to save the necessary money and lack other ways to borrow, the plastic in your wallet may be your ticket to operation. You can acquire many credit cards at interest rates of 10 percent or less. Because credit cards are unsecured loans, if your business fails and you can't pay back your debt, your home equity and assets in retirement accounts aren't at risk.

No matter what type of business you have in mind and how much money you think you need to make your dream come true, be patient. Start small enough that you don't need outside capital (unless you're in an unusual situation where your window of opportunity is now, and it will close if you don't get funding soon). Starting your business without outside capital instills the discipline required for building a business piece by piece over time. The longer you can wait to get a loan or equity investment, the better the loan terms because the risk is lower for the lender or investor.

Borrowing from family and friends

Because they know you and hopefully like and trust you, your family and friends may seem like a good source of investment money for your small business. They also have the added advantage of offering you better terms than a banker, wealthy investor, or a venture capitalist.

Before you solicit and accept money from those you love, consider the pitfalls. First, defaulting on a loan made by a large, anonymous lender if your business hits the skids is one thing, but defaulting on a loan from your dear relatives can make future Thanksgiving meals mighty uncomfortable!

Second, most entrepreneurs receive surprisingly little encouragement from people that they're close to. Most parents, for example, think you've snapped a few of your cerebral synapses if you announce your intention to quit your job with lofty job title, decent pay, and benefits. The lack of emotional support can discourage you far more than the lack of financial support.

From entrepreneurs I've observed, family investments in a small business work best under the following conditions:

- ✔ You prepare and sign a letter of agreement that spells out the terms of the investment or loan, as if you're doing business with a banker or some other investor you know for business purposes only. As time goes on, people have selective recall. Putting things in writing reminds everyone what you agreed to.

- ✔ You make a safe loan. Borrowing from family works best in cases where you're quite certain that you can repay the loan.

- ✔ You can start your business with an equity investment. With an equity investment, a person is willing and able to lose all the money invested but hopes to hit a home run while helping you with your dream.

Courting investors and selling equity

Beyond family members and friends, private individuals with sufficient money — also known as wealthy individuals — are your next best source of capital if you want an equity investor (and not a loan from a lender). Before you approach wealthy people, you must have a good business plan, which I explain how to prepare in Chapter 14.

Although you want such people to care about your business, it's best if their investment in your business is no more than 5 to 10 percent of their total investment portfolio. No one wants to lose money, but doing so is less painful if you diversify well. A $10,000 loan from a millionaire is 1 percent of his portfolio.

Finding people who may be interested in investing isn't difficult, but you need to be persistent and creative. Accountants and attorneys you know may have contacts. Networking with successful entrepreneurs in similar fields may produce an investor or two. Also, consider customers or suppliers of your business who like your business and believe in its potential.

Finding your way to wealthy individuals who don't know you may prove fruitful as well. Alex Popov, whom I introduce in Chapter 14 and earlier in this chapter, sent hundreds of letters to people who lived in upscale neighborhoods. The letter, a one-page summary of Alex's investment opportunity, got an astounding 5 percent response for interest in receiving a business plan. Ultimately through this search method, Popov found one wealthy investor who funded his entire deal.

Determining how much of the business you're selling for the amount invested is not easy. Basically, the equity percentage should hinge upon what the whole business is worth (see Chapter 16 to find out how to value a business). If your whole business is worth $500,000 and you're seeking $100,000 from investors, that $100,000 should buy 20 percent of the business.

New businesses are the hardest to value — yet another reason you're best off trying to raise money after you demonstrate some success. The further along you are, the lower the risk to an investor and the lower the cost to you (in terms of how much equity you must give up) to raise money.

Deciding Whether to Incorporate

Most businesses operate as *sole proprietorships*. The term sole proprietorship doesn't mean that only one person owns the business, but rather that for legal and tax purposes, your business is not a corporation. If you run a sole proprietorship, you report your business income and costs on your tax return on Schedule C (Profit or Loss From Business), which you attach to your personal income tax return, Form 1040.

Incorporating, which establishes a distinct legal entity under which you do business, takes time and costs money. Therefore, incorporation must offer some benefits. A major reason to consider incorporation is liability protection. Incorporation effectively separates your business from your personal finances, which protects your personal assets from lawsuits that may arise from your business.

Before you incorporate, ask yourself (and perhaps others in your line of business or advisors — legal, tax, and so on — who work with businesses like yours) what can or may cause someone to sue you. Then see if you can purchase insurance to protect against these potential liabilities. Insurance is superior to incorporation because it pays claims, and people can still sue you, even if you're incorporated. If you incorporate and someone successfully sues you, your company must cough up the money for the claim, and doing so may sink your business. Only insurance can cover such financially destructive claims.

People can also sue you if they slip and break a bone or two while on your property. To cover these types of claims, you can purchase a property or premises liability policy from an insurer.

Accountants, doctors, and a number of other professionals can buy liability insurance. A good place to start searching for liability insurance is through the associations that exist for your profession. Even if you're not a current member, check out the associations anyway — you may be able to access the insurance without membership, or you can join the association long enough to sign up. (Associations also sometimes offer competitive rates on disability insurance.)

Because corporations are legal entities distinct from their owners, they offer other features that a proprietorship or partnership doesn't. For example, corporations can have shareholders who own a piece or percentage of the company. These shares can be sold or transferred to other owners, subject to any restrictions in the shareholder's agreement. Corporations also offer *continuity of life,* which simply means that they can continue to exist despite an owner's death or the owner's transfer of his or her stock in the company.

Don't waste your money incorporating if you simply want to maintain a corporate-sounding name. If you operate as a sole proprietor, you can choose to operate under a different business name ("doing business as," or d.b.a.) without the cost and hassles of incorporating.

Tax-deductible insurance and other benefits

A variety of insurance and related benefits are tax-deductible to corporations for all employees. These benefits include the full cost of health and disability insurance as well as up to $50,000 in term life insurance per employee.

In addition to insurance, companies that incorporate can also have dependent-care plans where up to $5,000 per employee may be put away on a tax-deductible basis for child care and/or care for elderly parents. Corporations can also offer cafeteria or flexible spending plans that allow employees to pick and choose which benefits they spend their benefit dollars on.

If your business isn't incorporated, you and the other business owner(s) cannot deduct the cost of the preceding insurance plans for yourselves. However, you can deduct these costs for your employees as well as a portion of your health insurance costs for yourself and covered family members.

Corporate taxes

Aside from the tax treatment of insurance and other benefits, another difference between operating as a sole proprietor and as a corporation is that the government taxes a corporation's profits differently than those realized in a sole proprietorship. Which is better for your business depends on your situation.

Suppose that your business performs well and makes lots of money. If your business isn't incorporated, the government taxes all profits from your business on your personal tax return in the year that your company earns those profits. If you intend to use these profits to reinvest in your business and expand, incorporating can potentially save you some tax dollars. If you incorporate your business (as a regular or so-called C corporation), the first $75,000 of profits in the business are generally taxed at a lower rate in the corporation than on your personal tax return if you operated as a sole proprietorship. One exception to this rule is personal service corporations, such as accounting, legal, and medical firms, which pay a higher rate up to $335,000 in profits.

Resist the short-term temptation to incorporate just so you can have money left in the corporation taxed at a lower rate. If you want to pay yourself the profits in the future, you can end up paying more taxes. Why? Because you first pay taxes at the corporate tax rate in the year that your company earns the money, and then you pay taxes again on your personal income tax return when the corporation pays you.

S corporations and limited liability companies: The best of both worlds?

Wouldn't it be nice to get the liability protection and other benefits that come with incorporating without the tax complications and hassles that come with incorporation? Well, S corporations or limited liability companies may be for you.

Subchapter S corporations provide the liability protection that comes with incorporation. Likewise, the business profit or loss passes through to the owner's personal tax return, so if the business shows a loss in some years, the owner may claim those losses in the current year of the loss on his or her personal tax return. If you plan to take all the profits out of the company (instead of reinvesting the profits in the company), an S corporation may make sense for you.

The IRS allows most small businesses to operate as S corporations, but not all. In order to be an S corporation, a company must be a U.S. company, have just one class of stock, and have no more than 35 shareholders, who are all U.S. residents or citizens and who are not partnerships, corporations, or (with certain exceptions) trusts.

Limited liability companies (LLCs) offer business owners benefits similar to those of S corporations but are even better in some cases. Like an S corporation, an LLC offers liability protection for the owners. LLCs also pass the business's profits and losses through to the owner's personal income tax returns.

But limited liability companies have fewer restrictions regarding shareholders. For example, LLCs have no limits on the number of shareholders, and the shareholders in an LLC can be foreigners, corporations, and partnerships.

Compared with S corporations, the only additional restriction LLCs carry is that sole proprietors and professionals cannot always form an LLC (although they can in some states). Most state laws require you to have at least two partners and not be a professional firm.

Another reason not to incorporate, especially in the early months of a business, is that you cannot immediately claim the losses for an incorporated business on your personal tax return. Because most businesses produce little revenue in their early years and have all sorts of start-up expenditures, losses are common.

Making the decision

If you're totally confused about whether to incorporate because your business is undergoing major financial changes, it's worth getting competent professional help. The hard part is knowing where to turn because finding one advisor who can put all the pieces of the puzzle (financial, legal, and taxes) together is challenging. Also be aware that you may get wrong or biased advice.

Attorneys who specialize in advising small businesses can help explain the legal issues. Tax advisors who perform a lot of work with business owners can help explain the tax considerations. Although most attorneys and tax advisors don't understand the business side of business, try to find one that does, or you may also need a business advisor.

If you've weighed the factors and you still can't decide, my advice is to keep your business simple — don't incorporate. Why? Because, once you incorporate, it takes time and money to unincorporate. Start your business off as a sole proprietorship and then take it from there. Wait until the benefits of incorporating your business clearly outweigh the costs and drawbacks of incorporating.

Finding and Keeping Customers

When you write a plan for your business (see Chapter 14), you need to think about your business's customers. Just as the sun is the center of our solar system, everything in your business revolves around your customers. If you take care of your customers, they'll take care of you and your business for many years.

The first thing I recommend doing is putting together a mailing list of people you know who may be interested in what you're offering. Draft and mail an upbeat, one-page letter that provides an overview of what your business offers. As you have new news — successes to report, new products and services, and so on — do another mailing. Your letter doesn't need to be a color, multi-page newsletter-type thing, although you can do those if your budget and desire allow. Short letters get read more than something that looks like another glossy, advertorial, multi-page newsletter. Most people are busy and don't care about your business enough to read something lengthy.

In addition to mailings, other successful ways to get the word out and attract customers are limited only to your imagination and resourcefulness. Consider the following ideas:

✔ If your business idea is indeed innovative or somehow different, or if you have grand expansion plans, add some local media people to your mailing list and send them the one-page updates on your business, too. Newspaper, radio, and even television business reporters are always looking for story ideas. Just remember to make your press releases informational and not an advertisement.

✔ If your business seeks customers in a specific geographic area, blanket the area with your one-page letter by going door to door. You can include a coupon that offers your products or services at a reduced cost (perhaps at your cost) to get people to try it. Make sure that people know that this is a special opening-for-business bargain.

After you attract customers, don't treat them as if business is a one-night stand. Treat your customers as you would like to be treated by a business. If customers like your products and services, they not only come back to buy more when the need arises, but they also tell others. Satisfied customers are every business's best, cost-effective marketers.

Although good customer service is just good common sense, I never cease to be amazed by how many businesses have mediocre or poor customer service. One of the reasons for poor service is that, as your business grows, your employees are on the customer service front lines. If you don't hire good people and give them the proper incentives to service customers, many of them won't do it. If most people are on a salary, the day-to-day servicing of customers may be just an annoyance for them. One way to make your employees care about customer service is to base part of their pay on the satisfaction of the customers they work with. Tie bonuses and increases at review time to this issue. You can easily measure customer satisfaction with a simple survey form.

Think about your own experiences with poor customer service. For example, not having a green thumb, I hired a gardening company to install a garden. The company did a decent job in the early days of the project and expressed interest in providing ongoing maintenance. Within days of the garden installation, some problems (minor from my perspective) surfaced. A large jasmine vine that had survived for more than a year started to die. One worker thought that the vine could be dying because some roots were inadvertently cut during installation, but no one ever came out to look at the vine or suggest what to do. A number of plants were poorly placed and quickly encroached onto the lawn. Again and again I asked someone to come out and take a look, but no one did.

Unfortunately, I figured out that because I had already paid for the job, the company wasn't interested in addressing the problems. Even though the company's workers did a good job with the project overall, the lack of follow-up left a bad taste in my mouth and caused me to not recommend the company.

Treating the customer right starts the moment that the selling process begins. Honesty is an often underused business tool. More than a few salespeople mislead and lie in order to close a sale. Many customers discover after their purchase that they've been deceived, and they get angry. Not only has the unethical business likely lost future business from this customer, but it will surely — and justifiably — lose referrals.

If your business didn't perform well for a customer, apologize and bend over backward to make the customer happy. Offer a discount on the problem purchase or, if possible, a refund on product purchases. Also, make sure that you have a clear return-and-refund policy. Bend that policy if doing so helps you satisfy an unhappy customer or rids you of a difficult customer.

Setting Up Shop

No matter what type of business you have in mind, you'll need space to work from, whether it's your bedroom, a spare room in your home, or a small factory. You're also going to need to outfit that space with tools of your trade. This section explains how to tackle these tasks.

Finding business space and negotiating a lease

You may be in the market for office or retail space unless you can run your business from your home. Finding good space and buying or leasing it takes tons of time if you do it right.

In the early months and years of your business, buying an office or a retail building generally doesn't make sense. The down payment consumes important capital, and you may end up spending lots of time and money on a real estate transaction for a location that may not interest you in the long term. Buying this type of real estate rarely makes sense unless you plan to stay put for five or more years.

Leasing a space for your business is far more likely. Renting office space is simpler than renting retail space because a building owner worries less about your business and its financial health. Your business needs more credibility to rent retail because your retail business affects the nature of the strip mall or shopping center where you lease. Owners of such properties don't want quick failures, or someone who does a poor job of running his business.

Because renting retail is harder, if you and your business don't have a track record with renting space, getting references is useful. If you seek well-located retail space, you must compete with national chains like Starbucks, so you'd better have an A+ credit rating and track record. Consider subletting — circulate flyers to businesses that might have some extra space in the area where you want to place your business. Also prepare financial statements that show your creditworthiness (personally and in business). Most property owners want a personal guarantee that your business will succeed — try to avoid giving a personal guarantee because doing so is hard.

Brokers list most spaces for lease. Working with a broker can be useful, but the same conflicts exist as with residential brokers (see Chapter 11). You also need to examine spaces for lease without a broker, where you deal with the landlord directly. Such landlords may give you a better deal, and they don't worry about recouping a brokerage commission.

The biggest headaches with leasing space are understanding and negotiating the lease contract. Odds are good that the lessor presents you with a standard, preprinted lease contract that he or she says is fair (it's also the same lease that everyone else signs). Don't sign it! This contract is the lessor's first offer — have an expert review it and help you modify it. Find yourself an attorney who regularly deals with such contracts.

Office leases are simple — they can be full service, which includes janitorial benefits. Retail leases, however, are _triple-net,_ which means that you as the tenant pay for maintenance (for example, resurfacing the parking lot, cleaning, and gardening), utilities, and property taxes. You're correct to worry about a triple-net retail lease because you can't control many of these expenses. If the property is sold, property taxes can also jump. Your lease contract needs to include a cap for the triple-net costs at a specified limit per square foot. Also compare your site's costs to other sites to evaluate the deal that the lessor offers you.

Try to exclude from the lease contract removal costs for any toxic waste you may discover during your occupation. Also exclude increased property taxes that the sale of the property may cause. If feasible, get your landlord to pay for remodeling — it's cheaper for the landlord to do it and less hassle for you. With retail leases, get an option for renewal — this is critical in retail, where location is important. The option should specify the cost — for example, something like 5 percent below market, as determined by arbitration. Also get an option that the lease can be transferred to a new owner if you sell the business.

If you really think that you want to purchase rather than lease because you can see yourself staying in the same place for at least five years, read Chapter 12.

Equipping your business space

You can easily go overboard spending money when it comes to leasing or buying office space and outfitting that space. The most common reason that small-business owners spend more than they should is to attempt to project a professional, upscale image.

You can have an office or retail location that works for you and your customers without spending a fortune if you observe some simple rules:

> ✔ **Buy — don't lease or finance — equipment.** Unless you're running a manufacturing outfit where the cost of equipment is prohibitive to buy outright, try to avoid borrowing and leasing. If you can't buy office furniture, computers, cash registers, and so on with cash, then you probably can't afford them! Buying such things on credit or leasing them — leasing is invariably the most expensive way to go — encourages you to spend beyond your means.

Should you work from home?

You may be able to run a relatively simple small business from your home. If you have the choice of running your business out of your home versus securing outside office space, consider the following issues:

- **Cost control.** As I discuss earlier in the chapter, bootstrapping your business can make a lot of financial and business sense. If you have space in your home that you can use, then you've found yourself a rent-free business space. (If you consider buying a larger home to have more space, then you can't really say that your home office is rent free.)

- **Business issues.** What are the needs of your business and customers? If you don't require fancy office space to impress others or to meet with clients, work at home. If you operate a retail business that requires lots of customers coming to you, getting outside space is probably the best (and legally correct) choice. Check with the governing authorities of your town or city to learn what regulations exist for home-based businesses.

- **Discipline.** At home, do you have the discipline to work the number of hours that you need and want, or will the kitchen goodies tempt you to make half a dozen snack trips and turn on the television for late-breaking news? The sometimes amorphous challenge of figuring out how to grow the business may cause you to focus your energies elsewhere.

- **Family matters.** Last, but not least, your home life should factor into where you decide to work. If you're single and living alone, home life is less of an issue. One advantage to working at home when you're a parent is that you can be a more involved parent. If nothing else, you can spend the one to two hours per day that many people spend commuting with your kids! Just make sure that you try to set aside work hours, during which time your office is off-limits.

Ask other family members how they feel about you working at home. Be specific about what you plan to do, where, when, and how. Will clients come over? What time of day and where in the home will you meet with them? You may not think it's an imposition, but your spouse may. Home business problems come between many couples.

Consider buying used equipment, especially furniture, which takes longer to become obsolete. The more other businesses use a piece of equipment, the more beneficial it is for you to purchase rather than lease: Many other businesses using the equipment should make it easier for you to unload it if you want to sell it down the road. Leasing may make more sense with oddball-type equipment that is more of a hassle and costly for you to unload after a short usage period.

- **Don't get carried away with technological and marketing gadgets.** I know it's hard to imagine, but the business world worked just fine (and in some respects better) before faxes, e-mail, and the growth of the World Wide Web. Many small-business owners I speak with spend all sorts of money on such things because they feel the need to be "competitive" and "current." Think of a Web site as buying an expensive online Yellow Pages ad, because that's what it basically is. As for e-mail and faxes, the mail works just fine. So does picking up the phone or meeting in person — and these are much more personal ways of doing business.

Voice mail is one device that many small-business owners find worth spending money on. Voice mail sounds more professional than an answering machine and can handle simultaneous calls with ease. Best of all, voice mail can save you money on administrative help.

Bootstrap-equipping your office makes sense within certain limits (see "Bootstrapping," earlier in this chapter). If customers come to you, of course, you don't want a ratty-looking store or office. But on the other hand, you don't have to purchase the Rolls Royce equivalent of everything that you need for your office. For example, I didn't buy my fax machine until several years after I started my business, and I wish I had waited even longer because its presence encourages people I work with to procrastinate sending me things!

Small-Business Accounting

One of the less glamorous aspects of running your own business is dealing with accounting. Unlike when you work for an employer, you must track your business's income, expenses, and taxes (for you *and* your employees). Although you may be able to afford to hire others to help with these dreary tasks, you must know the inner workings of your business to keep control of your business, to stay out of trouble with the tax authorities, and to minimize your taxes. The following sections show you how to handle the accounting aspect of your business.

Tax recordkeeping and payments

With revenue hopefully flowing into your business, and expenses surely heading out, you must keep records to help satisfy your tax obligations and to keep a handle on the financial status and success of your business. You can't accurately complete the necessary tax forms for your business if you don't properly track your income and expenses. And, if the IRS audits you — the probability of being audited as a small-business owner is about four times higher than when you're an employee at a company — you'll need to prove some or even all of your expenses and income.

In order to keep your sanity, and keep the IRS at bay, make sure that you do the following:

✔ **Pay your taxes each quarter and on time.** When you're self-employed, you're responsible for the accurate and timely filing of all taxes that you owe on your income on a quarterly basis. You must pay taxes by the 15th of January, April, June, and September (unless the 15th falls on the weekend, in which case the payment is due the Monday that follows the 15th). To pay correctly, call the IRS at 800-TAX-FORM and ask for Form 1040-ES (Estimated Tax for Individuals). This form comes complete with an easy-to-use estimated tax worksheet and four payment coupons that you send in with your quarterly tax payments. Mark the due dates for your quarterly taxes on your calendar so that you don't forget!

If you have employees, you also need to withhold taxes from each paycheck they receive. You must then use the money that you deduct from their paychecks to make timely payments to the IRS and to the appropriate state authorities. In addition to federal and state income tax, you also need to withhold and send in Social Security and any other state- or locally-mandated payroll taxes. Pay these taxes immediately and *never* use the money to fund your business needs. I recommend using a payroll service to ensure that your payments are made on time and correctly to all the different places that these tax filings need to go.

✔ **Keep your business accounts separate from your personal accounts.** The IRS knows that small-business owners, as a group, cheat more on their tax returns than do company employees. One way that dishonest entrepreneurs cheat is hiding business income and inflating business expenses. Thus, the IRS looks with a jaundiced eye at business owners who use and commingle funds in personal checking and credit card accounts for business transactions.

Although you may find opening and maintaining separate business accounts troublesome, do so. And remember to only pay for legitimate business expenses through your business account. You'll be thankful come tax preparation time to have separate records. Having separate records can also make the IRS easier to deal with if and when you're audited.

✔ **Keep good records of your business income and expenses.** You can use file folders, software, or a shoebox to collect your business income and expenses, but just do it! When you need to file your annual return, you want to be able to find the documentation that allows you to figure your business income and expenses. For most people, the file folder system works best. If your business is small, one folder for income and one for your expenses will do. Computer software can help you with this drudgery as well. Because you must go through the hassle of entering the data, software is more useful with larger small businesses and in those businesses that process lots of checks or expenses.

> Charging expenses on a credit card or writing a check can make the documentation for most businesses easier. These methods of payment leave a paper trail that simplifies the task of tallying up your expenses come tax time and makes the IRS auditor less grumpy in the event that he or she audits you. (Just make sure that you don't overspend, as many people do with credit cards!)

In addition to keeping good records, you also need to decide on what basis, cash or accrual, you want your company to keep its books. Most small-business owners use the cash method, which simply means that for tax purposes, you recognize or report income in the year it's received and expenses in the year they're paid. Sole proprietorships, partnerships, and S and personal service corporations generally can use the cash method. C corporations and partnerships that have C corporations as partners may not use the cash accounting method.

The advantage of operating on a cash basis is that you can control the amount of your business income and expenses that your business reports for tax purposes year to year. Doing so can lower your tax bill. Suppose that, looking ahead to the next tax year, you have good reason to believe that your business will make more money, and thus push you into a higher tax bracket. You can likely reduce your tax bill if you pay more of your expenses in the next year. For example, instead of buying a new computer late this year, wait until early next year. (*Note:* The IRS recognizes credit card expenses by the date when you make the charges, not when you pay the bill.) Likewise, you can somewhat control when your customers pay you. If you expect to make less money next year, simply don't invoice customers in December of this year. Wait until January so that you receive the income from those sales next year.

How to (legally) pay lower taxes

Every small business must spend money, and spending money in your business holds the allure of lowering your tax bill. But don't spend money on your business just for the sake of generating tax deductions. Spend your money to make the most of the tax breaks that you can legally take. The following are some examples of legal tax breaks:

✔ **Take it all off now or spread it around for later.** As a small-business owner, you can deduct up to $19,000 (for tax year 1999) per year for equipment purchases (for example, espresso machines, computers, desks, chairs) for use in your business. By deducting via a section 179 deduction, you can immediately deduct the entire amount that you spent on equipment for your business. Normally, equipment for your business is *depreciated* over a number of years. With depreciation, you claim a tax deduction yearly for a portion of the total purchase price of the equipment. For example, if you drop two grand on a new computer, you can take a $400 deduction annually for this computer's depreciation (if you elect straight-line depreciation). If you elect the special 179 deduction, you can claim the entire $2,000 outlay at once (as long as you haven't exceeded the $19,000 annual cap).

Taking all the deduction in one year using the section 179-deduction method is enticing, but you may pay more taxes in the long run that way. Consider that in the early years of most businesses, profits are low. When your business is in a low tax bracket, the value of your deductions is low. If your business grows, you may come out ahead if you depreciate your early year big ticket expenses, thereby postponing to higher tax bracket years some of the deductions that you can take off.

✔ **Make the most of your auto deductions.** If you use your car for business, you can claim a deduction, but don't waste a lot of money on a car thinking that the IRS helps pay for all of it — because it doesn't. The IRS limits how large an annual auto expense you can claim for depreciation. The way the math works, you are effectively limited by these depreciation caps if you spend more than about $20,000 on a car. Another advantage of purchasing a more reasonably priced car: You won't be burdened with documenting your actual auto expenses and calculating depreciation. You can use the auto expense method of just claiming a flat 31 cents per mile (tax year 1999).

✔ **Deduct travel, meal, and entertainment expenses.** For the IRS to consider your expenses deductible, your travel must be for a bona fide business purpose. For example, if you live in Chicago and fly to Honolulu for a week, spend one day at a seminar for business purposes, and then the other six days snorkeling and getting skin cancer on Waikiki Beach, you can only deduct the expenses for the one day of your trip that you devoted to business. (An exception to this rule to get more of your trip written off does exist: If you extend a business trip to stay over a Saturday night to qualify for a lower airfare and you save money in total travel costs, you can claim the extra costs that you incurred to stay over through Sunday!)

Don't waste your money on meal and entertainment expenses. You can only deduct 50 percent of your business expenses; by all means, take that 50 percent deduction when you can legally do so, but don't spend frivolously on business trips and think that you can deduct everything. The IRS doesn't allow business deductions for club dues, such as for health, business, airport, or social clubs; or entertainment such as executive boxes at sports stadiums.

Keeping a Life and Perspective

David Packard, cofounder of Hewlett-Packard, said, "You are likely to die not of starvation for opportunities, but of indigestion of opportunities."

Most small businesses succeed in keeping their owners more than busy — in some cases, too busy. If you provide needed products or services at a fair price, customers will beat a path to your door. You'll grow and be busier than what you can personally handle. You may need to start hiring people. I know small-business owners who work themselves into a frenzy and put in 80 or more hours a week, yet don't make enough money to show for it.

If you enjoy your work so much so that it's not really work and you end up putting in long hours because you enjoy it, terrific! But success in your company can cause you to put less energy into other important aspects of your life that perhaps don't come as easily.

Although careers and business successes are important, don't place these successes higher than fourth on your overall priority list. You can't replace your health, family, and friends — but you can replace a job or a business.

Chapter 16

Buying a Business

· ·

In This Chapter

▶ The pros and cons of buying a small business

▶ The skills you need to be successful when buying a small business

▶ Selecting the right business for yourself

▶ Considering franchises and multilevel marketing companies

▶ Checking out and negotiating a successful purchase

· ·

*E*ach year, hundreds of thousands of small businesses change hands. This chapter is for those of you who want to run or invest in an existing small business but don't want to start the business yourself. And, of course, this chapter is for those of you who want to make good money and have fun along the way!

Advantages of Buying a Business

When you decide to purchase a home, you can choose between buying an existing one (that someone has more than likely lived in) or building one from scratch. Purchasing an already-built home makes the vast majority of people happy. Why? Because building a home requires a lot of work, takes a lot of time, and has a lot of potential for screw-ups.

I don't want to scare you off if you want to start a business. However, as with buying an existing home, buying someone else's business works better for some people than others. The following list reflects the main advantages of buying a business:

▶ **You avoid start-up hassles and headaches.** Starting a business from scratch requires dealing with a lot of stuff — just take a look at Chapters 14 and 15 for starters. Beyond formulating a plan, in the early years of starting a business you must deal with a variety of issues, such as developing a marketing plan, finding customers, locating space, hiring employees, and incorporating. Although you still need a game plan for a business that you buy and you need to fix any problems it has, if you buy a good business, part of what you buy is a more-finished entity.

Consider the learning curve for the type of business you're considering purchasing. Buying an existing business makes more sense if the business is complicated. For example, purchasing a business that manufactures musical instruments makes more sense than purchasing a plumbing business that requires plumbing know-how and a few tools to start up. Unless you've built musical instruments before and understand the intricacies of the production process, starting such a business from scratch is quite risky and perhaps foolhardy. (However, purchasing an existing plumbing business may still make sense if you don't want to build a stable of customers from scratch.)

✔ **You don't have to come up with an idea for a product or service.** Starting a business is hard if you lack an idea for a product or service to sell. If nothing new strikes your fancy, you have a good reason to buy an existing business.

✔ **You reduce risk.** After a business has an operating history and offers a product or service with a demonstrated market, some of the risk in the company is removed. Although investing in something that is proven is far from a sure thing, your risk may be significantly lower than the risk involved in a start-up. Looking at historic financial statements also helps you make more accurate financial forecasts than you could make with a start-up venture.

✔ **You enhance your ability to attract investor or lender money.** You should have less difficulty raising money from investors and lenders for your business than with a start-up. Attracting most investors to something that's more than an idea is easier. And for the amount that they invest, investors demand a smaller piece of an existing business than they would with an investment in an idea.

✔ **Buying into an existing business is your only ticket into some businesses.** You can only enter some businesses — such as bottlers or car dealerships — through your purchase of a business that already exists.

✔ **You can find businesses where you can add value.** Some entrepreneurs who start businesses don't see the potential for growth or don't want to grow their business — they may be burned out, content with their current profit, or simply ready to retire. Finding businesses where the potential exists to improve operating efficiency and to expand into new markets is not too hard. Relative to investing in stocks or real estate, finding small companies that are undervalued relative to the potential that they can offer is easier for a business-minded person.

Just because you think you see potential to improve a business, don't pay a high price based on your high expectations. You can be wrong — you may be looking at the business through rose-colored glasses. Even if you are correct about the potential, don't pay the current owner for the hard work and ingenuity that you will bring to the business if you purchase it. Offer a fair price based on the value of the business *now* — I explain how to figure this value later in the chapter.

Disadvantages of Buying a Business

Just as everyone doesn't enjoy running or cooking, some people don't enjoy the negatives that come with buying an existing business. If the following issues don't turn you off, you may want to consider purchasing an existing business:

- **You buy the baggage.** When you buy an existing business, the bad comes with the good. All businesses include their share of the bad. The business may employ problem employees, for example, or it may have a less-than-stellar reputation in the marketplace. Even if the employees are good, they and the culture of the company may not mesh with where you want to take the company in the future.

  Do you have the disposition and desire to motivate people to change or to fire them? Do you have the patience to work at improving the company's products and reputation? All these issues are barriers to running and adding value to a company. Some people enjoy and thrive on such challenges, while others toss and turn in their sleep with such pressures. Think back on your other work experiences for clues as to what challenges you've tackled and how you felt about them.

- **You need to do a lot of inspection.** If you think that buying a company is easier than starting one, think again. You must know what you're buying *before* you buy. So you need to do a thorough inspection, perform due diligence, kick the tires, or whatever you want to call it. For example, you need to rip apart financial statements to ascertain if the company is really as profitable as it appears and to determine its financial health.

  After you close the deal and the checks and/or money are transferred, you can't change your mind. Unless a seller commits fraud or lies (which is difficult and costly for a buyer to prove in a court of law), it's buyer beware about the quality of the business you're buying. In "Evaluating a Small Business," later in this chapter, I cover the homework that you need to do before you buy.

- **You need more capital.** Existing businesses have value, which is why you generally need more money to buy a business than to start one. If you're short of cash, starting a company generally is a lower-cost path.

  ✔ **Lower risk means lower returns.** If you purchase a good business and
  run it well, you can make decent money. In some cases, you can make a
  lot of money. But you generally have less upside and potential for hitting
  it really big than with a business you start. Those who have built the
  greatest wealth from small business are those who have started them
  rather than those who buy existing ones.

  ✔ **You don't get the satisfaction of creating a business.** Whether for your
  ego or your psyche, entrepreneurs who build their own businesses get a
  different experience than those who buy someone else's enterprise. You
  can make your mark on a business that you buy, but doing so takes a
  number of years. Even then, the business is never completely your own
  creation.

Prerequisites to Buying a Business

Not everyone is cut out to succeed with buying an existing business. Even if
you have sufficient funds to buy an existing business, you may be blind to a
whole host of problems and pitfalls, and you can end up losing your entire
investment. Later in this chapter, I introduce you to some small-business
buyers who did just that.

Conversely, some people with little money for buying a business succeed
wildly. You can purchase a good small business with little and, in rare cases,
no money down. So what then, are the traits common to people who successfully buy and operate an existing small business?

Business experience

First, you should have business experience and background. If you were an
economics or business major in college and you took accounting and other
quantitatively oriented courses, you're off to a good start.

Even better than academic, ivory-tower learning is work experience in the
type of business that you want to buy. If you want to run a restaurant, go
work in one. Consider the experience as paid on-the-job training for running a
business.

If you've worked on business-management issues with a variety of industries,
you also have a good background. However, the danger in having done only
consulting is that you're usually not on the front lines where most of the serious business operational issues arise.

If none of the previous examples apply to you, I won't say that you're doomed to fail if you buy a business, but I will say that the odds are against you.

If you don't have business experience, you will likely do far better in your first business venture after some remedial work. Get some hands-on experience, which is more valuable than any degree or credential that you can earn through course work. There's no substitute for real-life experience marketing to and interacting with customers, grappling with financial statements, dealing with competitive threats, and doing the business of business. However, I don't endorse not doing *any* academic course work. You may, in fact, be required to get a credential to be able to do the work that you want to do — such as an M.D., if you want to practice medicine. If you don't need a specific credential, taking selected courses and reading good business books (I recommend some in Chapter 19), can boost your knowledge.

Financial background

To purchase a business, as with real estate, you need to make a down payment on the purchase price. In most cases, you need to put down 25 to 30 percent. Bankers and business sellers who make loans to business buyers normally require such down payments in order to protect their loan. Small business buyers who make such a down payment are less likely to walk away from a loan obligation if the business gets into financial trouble.

If you lack significant capital for a down payment, try asking family or friends to invest. You can also set your sights on a less-expensive business or seek business owners willing to accept a small down payment. If you can find a business for sale where the owner wants less than 20 percent down, you may be on to something good. Be careful, though, because an owner who accepts such a small down payment may have a difficult time selling because of problems inherent in the business or because the business is overpriced.

You can purchase many existing small businesses with a loan from the selling owner. Also, check for loans with banks in your area that specialize in small business loans. (See Chapter 15 for other financing ideas.)

Finding a Good Business to Buy

Unless you're extraordinarily lucky, finding a good business to buy takes a great deal of time. If you spend time outside of your work hours, finding a business to buy can easily take you a year or two. Even if you have the money to afford the luxury of looking for a business full time and not working, finding, analyzing, negotiating, and closing on a business can still take you many months.

Above all else, it pays to be persistent, patient, and willing to spend some time on things that don't lead immediately to results. You must be willing to sort through some rubbish to find a keeper. If you require immediate gratification in terms of completing a deal, you can either make yourself miserable in your search or rush into a bad deal. The following sections give you the best techniques for identifying good businesses for sale that meet your needs.

Define what you want

You're going to end up spinning your wheels (and likely ending up with the wrong type of business for yourself) unless you set some boundaries for your business search. You don't need to be rigid or precisely define every detail of the business that you want to purchase, but the better you set some parameters, the sooner you can start laying the groundwork to purchase.

Each person has unique shopping criteria. The following list exemplifies some good ones to help narrow your field of search:

- ✔ **Size/purchase price.** Unless you're already wealthy, the money you have to invest in a business will constrain the size of business that you can afford. As a rough rule of thumb, figure that you can afford to pay a purchase price of about three times the amount of cash you have earmarked for the business. For example, if you have $50,000 in the till, you should look at buying a business for $150,000 or less. Because many business sellers overprice their businesses, you can probably look at businesses listed at a price above $150,000, perhaps as high as $200,000.

- ✔ **Location.** If you're already rooted and you don't want to move or have a long commute, the business's location further narrows the field. Although you may be willing to look at a broader territory, maybe even nationally if you're willing to relocate, evaluating businesses long distance is difficult and costly. Unless you want a highly specialized type of company, try to keep your business search local.

- ✔ **Industry.** Industry-specific expertise that you want to use in the business you buy can help whittle the pool of businesses down further. If you don't have industry-specific expertise, I highly recommend that you focus on some specific niches in industries that interest you or that you know something about. Focusing on an industry helps you conduct a more thorough search and turns up higher-quality companies. The industry knowledge that you accumulate in your search process can pay big dividends during your years of ownership in the business.

If you have a hard time brainstorming about specific industries, use this trick to jump-start your creativity — take a walk through the Yellow Pages! All the businesses known to exist in your area are listed alphabetically. Remember that a separate Yellow Page directory exists for businesses that sell mainly to consumers, while a "business-to-business"

Yellow Page directory lists businesses whose customers are primarily other businesses. Look at either or both, depending on the types of business that may interest you. You also may want to buy a business in a sector that is experiencing fast growth so that you too, can ride the wave. Check out *Inc.* magazine's annual Inc. 500 list of the fastest-growing smaller companies in America.

✔ **Opportunity to add value.** Some buyers want to purchase a business with untapped opportunities or problems that need fixing. As with real estate, however, many people are happier leaving the fixer-uppers to the contractors. Likewise, some businesses without major problems can offer significant untapped potential.

After you define your shopping criteria, you're ready to go to the marketplace of businesses for sale. I recommend that you type up your criteria on a single page so that you can hand it to others who may put you in touch with businesses for sale. Shopping for a small business is like a challenging Easter egg hunt: You never know what may turn up in the bushes. Use several of the following methods to shop for businesses that meet your needs.

Look at publications

If you're focused on specific industry sectors, you may be surprised to learn that there are all sorts of specialty newsletters and magazines. Just think of the fun you can have reading publications such as the *Alternative Energy Retailer, Specialty Foods Merchandising, Coal Mining Newsletter, Advanced Battery Technology,* or *Gas Turbine World!* Specialty publications get you into the thick of an industry and also contain ads for businesses for sale or business brokers who work in the industry.

A useful reference publication that you can find in public libraries with decent business sections is a two-volume set entitled *Small Business Sourcebook* (Gale). Organized alphabetically by industry, this reference contains listings of publications, trade associations, and other information sources.

Conducting literature searches of general interest business publications can help you identify articles on your industry of interest. The *Reader's Guide to Periodicals* and online computer searches can help you find the articles.

Network with advisors

Speak with accountants, attorneys, bankers, and business consultants who specialize in working with small businesses. These advisors are sometimes the first to learn of a small-business owner's desire to sell. Advisors may also suggest good businesses that aren't for sale, but whose owners may consider selling (see the next section).

Knock on some doors

If you own a home and someone came to your door and said he or she was interested in buying your home, you'd likely say that you're not interested in selling. If the interested buyer said that he or she really liked the type of property that you had and that she was willing to pay you a good price, the person may get a little more of your attention, but you'd still likely turn her away. If you, as the homeowner, were considering selling anyway, you might be all ears, especially if you can sell your house directly and save paying a broker's commission.

Some business owners who haven't listed their business for sale may still think about selling, so if you approach enough businesses that interest you, you may find some of these not-yet-on-the-market businesses with owners interested in selling.

Why would you want to go to this trouble and bother business owners? You can increase the possibility of finding your desired business, and you may get a good deal on such a business. You can negotiate with such a seller from the beneficial position of not having to compete with other potential buyers.

Instead of calling on the phone or literally knocking on the business's door, start your communications by mail. Sending a concise letter of introduction explaining what kind of business that you're looking for and what a wonderful person you are demonstrates that you're investing some time in this endeavor. Follow up with a call a week or so after you send the letter.

Work with business brokers

A decent number of small businesses for sale list their properties through business brokers. Just as a real estate agent makes a living selling real estate, a business broker makes a living selling businesses.

Business brokers generally sell smaller small businesses — those with less than $1 million in annual sales. These businesses tend to be family-owned or sole proprietorships, such as restaurants, dry cleaners, other retailers, and service firms. About half of such small businesses are sold through brokers.

One advantage of working with brokers to buy a business is that they can expose you to other businesses you may not have considered (a doughnut shop, for example). Brokers can also share their knowledge with you about some of your ideas — like the fact that you need to get up at 2 a.m. to make doughnuts. Still want to buy one?

Most business brokerage firms sell different types of businesses. Some firms, however, specialize in one industry or a few industries.

The pitfalls of working with brokers are numerous:

- **Commission.** Brokers are not your business advisors; they are salespeople. That fact doesn't make them corrupt or dishonest, but it does mean that their interests are not aligned with yours. Their incentive is to do a deal and do the deal soon — and, the more you pay for your business, the more they make. Business brokers typically get paid 10 to 12 percent of the sales price of the business. Technically, the seller pays this fee, but as with real estate deals done through brokers, the buyer actually pays. Remember, if a broker isn't involved, the seller can sell for a lower price and still clear more money, and the buyer is better off too.

- **Undesirable businesses.** Problem businesses are everywhere, but a fair number end up with brokers when the owners encounter trouble selling on their own.

- **Packaging.** This problem relates to the last two. Brokers help not-so-hot businesses look better than they really are. Doing so may involve lying, but more typically it involves stretching the truth, omitting negatives, and hyping potential. (Owners who sell their business themselves may do these things as well).

You (and your advisors) need to perform the due diligence on a business that you may buy (see Chapter 15). Never, ever trust or use the selling package that a broker prepares for a business as your sole source of information. Brokers, as well as sellers, can stretch the truth, lie, and commit fraud.

- **Access to limited inventory.** Unlike real estate brokers who can access all homes listed with brokers for sale in an area through a shared listing service, a business broker can only generally tell you about his office's listings. (Confidentiality is an issue because a shared listing service increases the number of people who can find out that a business is for sale and the particulars of the sale.)

If you want to work with a business broker, use more than one. Working with a larger business brokerage firm or one that specializes in listing the type of business that you're looking for can maximize the number of possible prospects that you see. Some areas, such as Florida, for example, have a state association of business brokers that share their listings. However, even in areas like Florida, some of the larger brokerages opt to not include themselves because they benefit less from sharing their information.

- **Few licensing requirements.** Unlike real estate agents in most states, the business brokerage field is little regulated. Approximately 20 states require real estate licenses of the business brokers who operate in their state. Some states allow those with securities brokerage licenses to operate as business brokers. The majority of states have no requirements — anyone can hang out a shingle and work as a business broker.

You can find business brokers in the Yellow Pages under "Business Brokers." Ads for businesses for sale may lead you to a broker as well. You can also ask tax, legal, and business consultants for names of good brokers they may know. If you find a broker you think you'd like to work with, check references from other buyers who have worked with the broker. Be sure that the broker works full time and has solid experience. Some business brokers dabble in it part time and make a living in other ways.

Ask the broker you're interested in for the names of several buyers of similar businesses that they've worked with over the past six months to narrow down the field so that they don't just refer you to the three best deals of their career. Also, check whether anyone has filed complaints against the brokerage with the local Better Business Bureau (although the BBB favors member companies more) and state regulatory departments (real estate, attorney general, department of corporations, and so on) that oversee business brokers.

Considering a Franchise or Multilevel Marketing Company

Among the types of businesses that you may buy are franchises and multi-level marketing companies. Both of these types of businesses for sale offer more of a prepackaged and defined system for running a business. While both types may be worth your exploration, significant pitfalls could trip you up, especially with multilevel marketing companies.

Pondering a franchise

Among the businesses that you can purchase are those that are clones of one another. Some companies expand their locations through selling replicas, or *franchises,* of their business. When you purchase a franchise, you buy the local rights to a specified geographic territory to sell the company's products or services under the company's name and to use the company's system of operation. In addition to an up-front franchisee fee, franchisers also typically charge an ongoing royalty.

As a consumer, you likely have done business with franchises. Franchising makes up a huge part of the business world. Companies that franchise — such as McDonald's, Pizza Hut, H&R Block, Midas Muffler, 7-11 stores, Gymboree, Century 21 Real Estate, Holiday Inn, Avis, Subway, and FootLocker — account for more than $1 trillion in sales annually. Purchasing a good franchise can be your ticket into the world of small-business ownership.

Franchise advantages

When you purchase a franchise, unlike buying other businesses, you don't buy an operating enterprise. Although the parent company should have a track record and multiple locations with customers, you start with no customers if you purchase a new franchise. (You can purchase existing franchises from owners who want to sell.) As the owner of a new franchise, you don't already have customers — just like starting a business, you must find them.

So why would you want to pay a good chunk of money to buy a business without customers? Actually, you should consider purchasing a good franchise for the same reasons that you would purchase other worthy, established businesses. A company that has been in business for a number of years and has successful franchisees proves the demand for the company's products and services, and that the company's system for providing those products and services works. The company has worked the bugs out and hopefully solved common problems. As a franchise owner, you benefit from and share in the experience that the parent company has gained over the years.

Franchises offer two additional advantages that most other freestanding businesses don't. A larger and successful franchise company should have brand-name recognition. In other words, some consumers recognize the company name and may be more inclined to purchase its products and services. Some consumers feel more comfortable getting a muffler job done at franchiser Midas Muffler rather than hunting around and calling Discount Muffler World or Manny's Muffler Bazaar from a Yellow Page listing. The comfort from dealing with Midas may stem from the influence of advertisements, recommendations of friends, or your own familiarity with Midas's services, perhaps in another part of the country.

Another advantage of owning a franchise is the centralized purchasing power that it offers. You would hope and expect that as a corporation made up of hundreds of locations, Midas buys mufflers at a low price — volume purchasing generally leads to bigger discounts. In addition to possibly saving franchisees money on supplies, the parent company can also take the hassle out of figuring out where and how to purchase supplies.

Franchise pitfalls

As with purchasing other small businesses, pitfalls abound in buying a franchise. Franchises are not for everyone. Some of the more common problems that you should be on guard for include the following:

- ✔ **You're not the franchise type.** When you buy a franchise, you buy into an established system. People who like structure and following established rules and systems more easily adapt to the franchise life. But if you're the creative sort who likes to experiment and change things, you may be an unhappy franchisee. Unlike starting your own business where you can get into the game without investing lots of your time and money, buying a business that you end up not enjoying can make for an expensive learning experience.

✔ **You must buy overpriced supplies.** Centralized, bulk purchasing through the corporate headquarters supposedly saves franchisees time and money on supplies and other expenditures. Some franchisers, however, take advantage of franchisees through large markups on proprietary items that franchisees must buy from the franchisers.

✔ **The franchise is unproven.** If the company's concept has not stood the test of time and other franchises, don't make yourself a guinea pig. Some franchisers show more interest in simply selling franchises to collect the up-front franchise money. Reputable franchisers want to help their franchisees succeed so that they can collect an ongoing royalty from the franchisees' sales.

✔ **The franchise is a pyramid scheme.** Unscrupulous, short-term focused business owners sometimes attempt to franchise their business and sell as many franchises as they can as quickly as possible. Some even allow their franchisees to sell franchises and share the loot with them. The business soon focuses on selling franchises rather than operating a business that sells a product or service well. In rare cases, franchisers engage in fraud and sell next to nothing, except the hopes of getting rich quick.

Evaluating a franchise

Make sure that you do plenty of homework before you agree to buy a franchise. The following list is my catalog of critical issues that you need to examine before buying a franchise that interests you.

1. **Request and read the Uniform Franchise Offering Circular (UFOC).**

   The Federal Trade Commission (FTC) requires all franchisers to issue this document at least ten days before a prospective franchise buyer writes a check or signs a document to purchase. If you think you're interested in a particular franchise, ask for this important document. Don't be put off by its size. Read the document cover to cover. The UFOC contains a treasure trove of valuable information, such as the names and addresses of the ten closest franchisees, as well as a list of franchises that the company terminated, didn't renew, or bought back. The document discloses pending or settled litigation and should indicate potential or actual troubles between franchisers and franchisees. The UFOC also gives you the employment background of the franchiser's senior management, your costs to purchase a franchise, as well as required inventory, leases, and other costs.

2. Determine whether the franchisers are looking for a partner or your wallet.

In your first interactions with the franchising company, observe the demeanor and approach of those you speak with. Although all such companies have enthusiastic salespeople, the best franchising companies want to check you out almost as much as you want to check them out. Smart franchisers don't want to sell a franchise to someone who is likely to crash and burn or tarnish the company's good reputation. Smart companies know that their interests are aligned with yours — they make more money from ongoing royalties if they sell franchises to capable franchisees who succeed.

Run as fast as you can in the opposite direction if the franchisers tell tales of great riches from just a small investment of your time and money. Some franchisers are more interested in selling franchises than in finding and helping the most-qualified franchisees succeed. Such franchisers may also attempt to pressure you into making a quick decision to buy, and be evasive about providing detailed information about their business. If they don't want to give you the UFOC, run extra fast.

3. Speak with franchisees.

Talk with franchisees currently part of the company, as well as those who quit or were terminated. Start with the lists of franchisees that the UFOC provides — not with references that the company provides. Ask the franchisees about their experiences, both good and bad, with the parent company. Those franchisees for whom things didn't work out generally tell you more about the warts of the system, but also try to identify whether some of these people were poor fits. Conversely, active franchisees may likely see their franchise experience through rose-colored glasses, if, for no other reason, than to reinforce their decision to buy a franchise. Observe the happiest and most successful franchisees and see if you share their business perspectives and traits.

4. Understand what you're buying.

Good franchises can cost you a reasonable chunk of change up front. On the low end, service businesses, which you can run from your home, sell for around a $25,000 up-front franchise fee; compare that to the several hundred thousand to a million dollars required for the brick-and-mortar locations of established franchisers, such as McDonald's. Additionally, ongoing franchise royalties run about 3 to 10 percent of gross revenue. The UFOC details all the up-front costs. What do you get for this up-front payment? Is the system and name brand really worth this fee? What kind of training will you receive?

5. Look at comparable franchises.

Few franchises are unique. Compare the cost of what a franchise offers you to the cost of purchasing franchises from different companies in the same business. For example, if you're considering purchasing a tax-preparation franchise from a newer company, compare the terms and offerings to H&R Block and Jackson Hewitt, two large, established, and successful tax preparation franchise firms.

6. **Consider the start-up alternative.**

If you look at the "best" franchises in a particular business and think, "Hey, I can do this as well or better and at less cost on my own," then consider starting your business from scratch. Make sure that you're realistic though, because starting a business involves many hidden costs — both out-of-pocket financial costs and time costs.

7. **Check with regulators.**

Generally, both the federal and state levels of government regulate franchises. The FTC regulates nationally, and the state level regulatory agency is usually called something like the Department of Corporations or the Attorney General's Office. Check with these regulators to see whether any complaints are on file. (As I mention at the start of this list, the UFOC should also detail pending litigation against the company by disgruntled franchisees.) You may also want to check with the Better Business Bureau in the city where the franchising company is headquartered to discover whether any information is on file (recognize, however, that if the company is a BBB member, the BBB is less demanding and too lenient about reporting problems).

8. **Run a credit report on the company.**

You can examine the franchiser's credit report to get another indicator of the kinds of business relationships that the franchiser maintains. Just as you have a personal credit report on file, business credit reports show how a company deals with payments and debts that it owes to suppliers and creditors.

9. **Review the franchise contract.**

If your digging makes you feel more, rather than less, comfortable with the franchise purchase, you now need to get down to the nitty-gritty of the contract. Franchise contracts are usually long and tedious. Read the contract completely to get a sense of what you're getting yourself into. Have an attorney who's experienced with franchising agreements review the contract as well. In addition to the financial terms, the contract should specify how the company handles disputes, what rights you have to sell the franchise in the future, and under what conditions the parent company may terminate the franchise. Make sure that you can live with and be happy with the non-financial parts of the contract.

10. **Negotiate.**

Different companies negotiate differently. Some companies offer their best deal up front and don't engage in haggling. Others don't put their best foot forward in the hopes that you may simply sign and accept the inferior terms and conditions. Some naive franchise buyers see the contract as cast in stone and don't negotiate. Remember that almost everything is negotiable.

Cover all ten issues when you evaluate any franchise. You may be most tempted to cut corners in reviewing a franchise from a long-established company. Don't. You may not be right for the specific franchise, or perhaps the "successful" company has been good at keeping problems under wraps.

In "Evaluating a Small Business," later in this chapter, I explain the homework you should complete prior to buying an existing business. Read that section as well, especially if you want to purchase an existing franchise from another franchisee.

Considering a multilevel marketing company

A twist, and in most cases a bad one, on the franchising idea is multilevel marketing (MLM) companies. Sometimes known as network companies, MLMs can be thought of as a poor person's franchise. I know dozens of people, from clients I've worked with to students I've taught in my courses, who have been sorely disappointed with the money and time they've spent on MLMs.

Some people are enthusiastic about MLMs. One book on the subject says,

> . . . like an elemental force of nature, network marketing has
> risen from the soil and roots of America's heartland, boldly
> promising wealth, freedom, and limitless horizons to those
> with the courage to seek them out.

One day I received a letter from a client of mine describing an MLM opportunity. "It is the best thing I've ever seen," gushed the letter, ". . . I have friends who are making $10,000, $25,000, $70,000, and $125,000 per month! $195 starter fee gets you literally a national distributorship."

The company, which I'll call "Superhype Telemarketing," sells long-distance phone service and claims to offer rates far lower than AT&T's, Sprint's, and MCI's. You pay for your starter kit, go through a short training seminar, and — voilà — you're in business for yourself. Work when you want, get a share of every dollar that your customers spend on long distance, and recruit others as representatives and make money off of the business that they bring in.

Quality multilevel marketing companies are the exception

A number of network companies have achieved success over the years. Amway, HerbaLife, and Mary Kay have stood the test of time and achieved significant size. Amway founders Richard De Vos and Jay Van Andel achieved multibillionaire status.

Not all multilevel companies are created equal, and few are worth a look. However, Mary Kay is an example of a successful network company with a 30-plus year history. Mary Kay has hundreds of thousands of sales representatives and does business worldwide. Although not shy about the decent money that its more successful salespeople make, Mary Kay doesn't hype the income potential. Local sales directors typically earn $50,000 to $100,000 per year, but this income comes after many years of hard work. Mary Kay rewards top sellers with gifts, such as the infamous pink Cadillac.

The ingredients for Mary Kay's success include competitive pricing, personal attention, and social interaction, which many stores don't or can't offer their customers. "We make shopping and life fun . . . we make people look and feel good," says Mary Gentry, one of Mary Kay's sales directors.

Mary Kay encourages prospective Mary Kay reps to try the products first and then host a group before they sign up and fork over the $100 to purchase a showcase of items to sell. To maximize sales, the company encourages Mary Kay representatives to keep a ready inventory because customers tend to buy more when products are immediately available. If reps want out of the business, they can sell their inventory back to the company at 90 cents on the dollar originally paid, a good sign that the company stands behind its product.

Quality multilevel marketing companies make sense for people who really believe in and want to sell a particular product or service and don't want to or can't tie up a lot of money buying a franchise or other business. Just remember to check out the MLM company, and that you won't get rich in a hurry, or probably ever.

For those weary of traditional jobs, the appeal of multilevel marketing is obvious. Work at home, part time with no employees, no experience necessary, and make big bucks. If your parents raised you right, however, you should be skeptical of deals like these. If you can make $10,000, $25,000, $70,000, and $125,000 per month, wouldn't everyone do it?

Superhype Telemarketing is one of many companies that use multilevel marketing. Representatives who work as independent contractors solicit customers as well as recruit new representatives, known in the industry as your "down line."

A big problem to watch out for is the business equivalent of the pyramid scheme — businesses that exist to sign up other people. A little bit of digging on my part revealed the following about Superhype Telemarketing: Its marketing director advocates that you ". . . sell directly to those that you have direct influence over. The system works great because you don't need to resell month after month. It's an opportunity for anybody — it's up to them how much work they want to put into it."

Any MLM examination should start with the company's product or service. In Superhype Telemarketing's case, hundreds of companies offer telephone service, so the service is hardly unique. Superhype Telemarketing claims to provide cheaper services than AT&T, Sprint, and MCI, as well as local toll-call providers. Some of the company's marketing materials claim savings of as much as 50 percent to 75 percent. The reality: Comparing Superhype Telemarketing's cost to AT&T, which certainly isn't the cheapest service, shows little difference. If you make more than $10 in long-distance calls per month, Superhype Telemarketing is about 7 percent cheaper. If you place more than $50 per month in calls, AT&T rates drop to the same level as Superhype's.

A call to the Better Business Bureau in the city where Superhype Telemarketing is headquartered revealed that the company has been the subject of dozens of filed complaints of unauthorized switching of consumers' long-distance phone service by Superhype sales representatives and misrepresentation of savings.

So what about the big money — can you make tens of thousands to a hundred thousand dollars per month or more working for Superhype? For starters, you must pay to become a Superhype representative. The fee of $195 gets you a kit that provides advice, 12 months of a corporate newsletter, and a small amount of training. If you want to get paid a $40 fee for training others who sign up with the company, you pay $395 to become a trainer and have the ability to train others.

Superhype Telemarketing put me in touch with one of its most successful salespeople: Big Al. Big Al told me that he had been a representative with the company since 1990. "I used to be in real estate and got tired of the headaches of dealing with tenants. . . the idea of earning residual payments for everyone signed up to use a phone service appealed to me," Big Al said. Working part time in 1991, he said without my asking, he made $17,000 in his first year and then, working full time, he earned $60,000 in 1992, $670,000 in 1993, and $1.4 million in 1994.

Being a skeptic, I asked Big Al for proof. He said he'd be happy to fax me a copy of a big check that he was presented with in 1993. What he sent were marketing materials that showed photos of "top leaders" being presented with oversized checks, similar to the props that companies use for public relations opportunities when they make a big contribution to charity. Big Al's check (which was supposedly for one month in 1993) was for $57,000.

Not satisfied with this copy as proof, I asked Big Al for his monthly sales report from Superhype, which I know the company provides to all its representatives. He said he didn't have this information because his tax preparer was working on his return. When I pointed out that the month in question was in 1993, not 1994, he said that all his financial statements were in storage and because he was soon heading out of town for ten days, he wouldn't have a chance to retrieve them until he got back. I then suggested that his tax preparer send me his proof of income for 1994 or some other sort of proof. I'm still waiting.

As for the company's other top producers, the company never provided proof of the hyped income claims. All this hype reminds me of the movie *Quiz Show* (I recommend that you see it if you haven't yet), an eye-opening account of how television quiz shows in the 1950s were rigged to dupe the public.

Big Al, who is also one of the company's most successful recruiters, also claims that the company is contractually obligated to pay residuals and can't cut sales reps out of the picture financially after they sign up others. However, according to Superhype's marketing director, "There is no guarantee of future payments. The company has the ability to change its program at any time." So if Superhype's management or a future buyer of the company decides to cut commissions, reps will be left holding an empty bag.

Also cause for pause: Superhype's marketing packages contain a feature article (which is from a supposed business periodical) that praises the company. Buried in the fine print on the back page of the reprint of the "article," which is sandwiched around a two full-page ad for the company, is the following: "Information contained in feature articles is provided by the company." Turns out that when a company like Superhype buys the space for the ad, the "story" comes with it as well! The sticker price for the ad exceeds $10,000. Rather than an independent appraisal of the company, this article is basically an ad that Superhype bought.

The bottom line on any network marketing "opportunity" is to remember that it's a job. No company is going to pay you a lot of money for little work. As with any other small-business venture, if you hope to earn a decent income, multilevel marketing opportunities require at least three to five years of low income to build up your business. Most people who buy into networks such as Superhype make little money, and many quit and move on. According to a Superhype company document, more than 60 percent of its representatives make less than $100 per month and fewer than 5 percent make more than $1,000 monthly, but you'd never know this information from its advertising or sales hype.

Work-from-home "opportunities"

"We made $18,269.56 in just 2½ weeks! Remarkable, home-based business! We do over 90 percent of the work for you! Free info: 800-555-8975."

"Earn $4,000 per month on the new instant information superhighway."

"You can be earning $4,000 to $10,000 each month in less than 30 days! We'll even help you hire agents to do the work for you . . . FREE!"

"Work from home. Company needs help. Earn $500-$900 per week. Anyone can do this — will train. Full time or part time. Call 555-8974. Only for the serious — please!"

You can find lots of ad copy like this, especially in magazines that small-business owners and wannabe small-business owners read. In most cases, these ads come from grossly overhyped multilevel marketing companies. In other ads, no legitimate company exists but a person (or two or three) who simply tries to sell you some "information" that explains the business opportunity. This information may cost several hundred dollars or more. Such packages end up being worthless marketing propaganda and rarely provide useful information that you couldn't find at a far lower cost or no cost at all.

Never buy into anything like these ads that companies (or people) pitch to you through the mail or over the phone.

Also, think twice before you sign up relatives, friends, and coworkers — often the first people network marketers encourage you to sell to. A danger in doing business with those people whom you have influence over is that you put your reputation and integrity on the line. You could be putting your friendships and family relations on the line as well.

Do your homework and remember that due diligence requires digging for facts and talking to people who don't have a bias or reason to sell to you (see Chapter 14). Do the same homework that I recommended for franchises in the "Evaluating a franchise" section, earlier in this chapter. Be skeptical of multilevel marketing systems, unless the company has a long track record and many people who are happy. Assume that an MLM company is not worth pursuing until your immense due diligence proves otherwise.

Evaluating a Small Business

If you put in many hours, you may eventually come across a business that interests and intrigues you so much that you consider purchasing it. As with purchasing a piece of real estate, major hurdles stand between you and ownership of the business. You need to inspect what you want to buy, negotiate a deal, and finalize a contract — done correctly, these processes take a lot of time.

Due diligence — check this out

The American legal system presumes a person is innocent until a jury proves that person is guilty beyond a reasonable doubt. When you purchase a business, however, you must assume that the selling business owner is guilty of making the business appear better than what it is (and possibly lying) until you prove otherwise.

I don't want to sound cynical, but a business owner can use more than a few tricks to make a business look more profitable, financially healthier, and more desirable than it really is. You cannot decide how much inspection or due diligence to conduct on a business based on your gut-level feeling.

Because you can't guess what hidden surprises exist in a business, you must dig for them. Until you prove to yourself beyond a reasonable doubt that these surprises don't exist, don't go through with a business purchase.

When you find a business that you think you want to purchase, you absolutely, positively must do your homework before you buy. However, just as with purchasing a home, you don't want to expend buckets of money and time on detailed inspections until you can reach an agreement with the seller. What if you deal with a seller who is unrealistic about what the business is worth? You need to perform the most serious, time-consuming, and costly due diligence after you have an accepted offer to purchase a business. Make such inspections a contingency in your purchase contract (see "Contingencies," later in the chapter).

Ultimately, if you're going to buy a business, you need to follow a plan similar to, but likely shorter than, the one I present in Chapter 14. Addressing such issues in a plan goes a long way toward helping you perform your due diligence.

Following are some additional questions that you need to answer about a business you're contemplating purchasing (address as many of the easier questions as possible before you make your offer):

✔ **Why is the owner selling?** Ask the owner or the owner's advisors why the owner wants to sell and why now. The answer may shed insight on the owner's motivations and need to sell. Some owners want to bail when they see things getting worse.

✔ **What is the value of the assets that you want to buy?** This value includes not only equipment, but also "soft" assets, such as the firm's name and reputation with customers and suppliers, customer lists, patents, and so on. Interview key employees, customers, suppliers, advisors, and competitors. Ask key customers and key employees if they would still be loyal to the business if you took it over.

✔ **What do the financial statements reveal?** Search for the same things that you would look for in a company whose stock you're considering purchasing (see Chapter 7 for how to read financial statements and what to look for). Don't take the financial statements at face value simply because they are audited. The accountant who did the audit may be incompetent or chummy with the seller. One way to check for shenanigans is to ask for a copy of the business's tax returns from the seller. Owners are more likely to try to minimize reported revenue and maximize expenses on their tax return to keep from paying more tax. After you have an accepted purchase offer, ask a tax advisor experienced in such matters to do an audit.

✔ **If the company leases its space, what does the lease contract say?** A soon-to-expire lease at a low rate can ruin a business's profit margins. With a retail location, the ability to maintain a good location is also vital. Check comparables — that is, what other similar locations lease for — to see if the current lease rate is fair, and talk to the building owner to discover his plans for the building. Ask for and review (with the help of a legal advisor) the current owner's lease contract.

✔ **What liabilities, including those that may be hidden "off" the balance sheet, are you buying with a business?** Limit liabilities, such as environmental contaminations, through a contract. Conduct legal searches for liens, litigation, and tax problems.

✔ **What does a background check turn up on the owners and key employees?** Do they have good business experience, or do they have criminal records and a trail of unpaid debts?

Negotiating a good deal

After you find what you think is a good business and do some homework, you're ready to make an offer. Negotiating takes time and patience. Unless you're legally savvy, find an attorney who focuses his or her practice on small-business dealings. Have an attorney review and work with your contract. Also consider obtaining input from a qualified tax person.

Good advisors can help you inspect what you're buying and look for red flags in the company's financial statements. Advisors can also help structure the purchase to protect what you're buying and to gain maximum tax benefits. If you work with a business broker, make sure that you use an attorney and accountant as well.

To get a good deal, a number of things need to fall into place.

Valuing a business

How can you buy a business if you don't know its worth? The price that a business is listed for is often in excess of — and sometimes grossly so — the business's true worth.

Look at what similar businesses have sold for as a starting point for valuing a business that you want to buy. A smart home buyer or real estate investor looks at comparable properties when he's ready to make an offer on a property.

The challenging part is finding the specific sales price and other information on businesses that have sold. Small businesses are privately held, and the terms of sales aren't a matter of public record. Following are some good sources:

✔ **Business brokers.** If you're already working with a business broker or looking at businesses listed with a business broker, the broker should be able to provide a comparable market analysis of similar businesses that the broker's office has sold. Use this analysis as a starting point. Remember that the more you pay for a business, the more money brokers make. Brokers also generally have access to sales data for only the small number of similar businesses that their office has sold.

✔ **Businesses that you've looked at that have sold.** If your search lasts months or perhaps years, keep track of similar businesses that you've considered that eventually sell. These sales are extra valuable comparables because you may have been able to see the business and obtain more details about the company's financial position.

✔ **Advisors.** Attorneys, tax advisors, and business consultants you work with can help provide you with comparables. If an advisor doesn't have memories of or experience with similar deals, find another advisor. You need advisors who can bring applicable experience to the negotiating table.

✔ **Business appraisers.** If you really want to buy a business and your initial investigation suggests that the seller is committed to and serious about selling, consider hiring a business appraiser. The Institute of Business Appraisers (561-732-3202) can provide you with a list of association members in your area. Also check the business-to-business Yellow Pages in your area under "Appraisers — Business."

✔ **Research firms and publications.** A small number of companies publish comparable sales information or perform searches for a fee:

• **Bizcomps** is an annual publication that provides sales price, revenue, and other financial details for businesses sold. This compendium of sales information is available for different major regions of the U.S. (Western, Central, and Eastern editions). A national edition provides sales information for larger manufacturing, wholesale, and service businesses. Call 619-457-0366 for a sample of this publication. Each directory sells for $108.

- **Financial Research Associates (FRA)** provides balance sheet and income statement comparisons for small companies through its annual *Financial Studies of the Small Business* directory. Call 941-299-3969 to receive a background package on this directory, which sells for $104.

- **Read trade publications.** As I recommend earlier in the chapter, trade publications can help you find information about a particular industry and how to value companies within the industry. Many publications can, for a small fee, send you past articles on the topic.

When you look at comparables, figure the multiple of earnings that these businesses sold for. In Chapter 5, I discuss how the price-earnings ratio works for evaluating the value of larger, publicly traded companies. Because they are less well-established and riskier from an investment standpoint, small, privately held businesses sell for a lower multiple of earnings than comparable, but larger, companies.

Some advisors and business brokers advocate using a multiple of revenue to determine the value of a business. Revenue is a poor proxy for profitability: Two businesses in the same field can have identical revenue yet quite different profitability because of how well they are run, the pricing of their products and services, and the types of customers they attract.

In addition to looking at the sales price of other businesses relative to earnings, you can also consider the value of a company's assets. The so-called *book value* of a company's assets is what the assets are worth per the company's balance sheet. Check these figures to ensure that their asset values are correct. Another, more conservative way to value such assets is to consider the liquidation/replacement cost (see Chapter 7).

Contingencies

When you purchase a home, you make your offer contingent upon satisfactory inspections, mortgage loan approval, and the property seller legally holding title to the home. When you make a purchase offer for a business, you should make your offer contingent upon a number of similar issues:

- ✔ **Due diligence.** Make your purchase offer contingent upon a thorough review of the company's financial statements and interviews of key employees, customers, suppliers, and so on. Also, make sure that you can employ whomever you want to help with these evaluations. You may also want to defer paying a portion of the purchase price for 6 to 12 months to make sure that everything is as the owner/seller claims.

INVESTIGATE

Questioning profits

Don't blindly take the profit from the bottom line of a business's financial statement as the gospel. As part of your due diligence, ask a tax advisor to perform an audit after you negotiate a deal.

Even if the financial statements of a business are accurate, you (and your tax advisor) must still look for more-subtle problems that can make the profits of the business appear better or worse than they truly are. The issues that I explain to look for in Chapter 7 when you analyze the financial statements of public companies that issue stock apply to evaluating the financial statements of small companies.

If necessary, factor out one-time events from the profit analysis. For example, if the business last year received an unusually large order that is unlikely to be repeated and hasn't been the norm in the past, subtract this amount from the profitability analysis. Also, examine the owner's salary to see whether it's high or low for the field. Owners can reduce their draw to a minimum or pay family members less than fair market salaries to pump up the profitability of their company in the years before they sell.

Also consider whether the rent or mortgage expense may change when you buy the business. Consider what will happen to profits when you factor in your expected rent or mortgage costs.

- ✔ **Financing.** Unless you make an all-cash offer, make finding financing at an acceptable interest rate another condition of your purchase offer (specify acceptable loan terms, including the maximum interest rate at which you will go ahead with the purchase). By the time you make an offer, you should know whether the seller will loan you money for the purchase. Be sure to check with your area's banks that specialize in small-business loans (some of which the Small Business Administration backs) and compare their terms to a loan that the seller offers.

- ✔ **Limited liability.** Make sure that the seller is liable for environmental cleanup and undisclosed existing liabilities (debts).

- ✔ **Non-compete.** You don't want to buy the business and then have the former owner set up an identical business down the road. Insist that the owner places a non-compete clause in your purchase offer, which specifies that for, say, two years the seller can't establish a similar business. Also consider asking the owner to consult with you for 6 to 12 months to make sure that you tap all of his or her valuable experience, as well as to transition relationships with key customers, employees, and suppliers. Consider making the total purchase price dependent on the future success of the company.

Allocation of the purchase price

Unlike when you purchase a home and offer, for example, $200,000 for the home, when you offer $200,000 for a business you need to break down, or allocate, the purchase price among the assets of the business and other categories. The way that you structure your purchase can save you tens of thousands of dollars in taxes.

As a buyer, you're generally better off allocating as much of the purchase price to the assets of the business. Why? Because such assets can generally be depreciated (written off for tax purposes) faster than, say, land, which is not depreciable, or goodwill, which is depreciated over 15 years. For tax reasons, the seller's interests will likely oppose yours. You must report the purchase of the business and allocation of the purchase price among business assets on IRS Form 8594. Make sure that you report this information, because if you don't, you can pay a penalty of up to 10 percent of the amount that you don't report.

Final steps

With the help of an attorney, you should take these additional steps prior to closing the purchase of the business:

- ✔ Notify creditors of the transfer of ownership. In counties where the company does business, a transfer of ownership notice should be published in a general circulation newspaper. If you omit this step, unsecured creditors can come after your business if the previous owner has outstanding debts.

- ✔ Check to make sure no liens are filed against assets of the business and, if you're buying real estate, that the property title is clear.

- ✔ Get the seller to provide proof certifying that federal and state employment, sales, and use taxes are all paid up.

Part V

Investing Resources

In this part . . .

*E*verywhere you turn these days, you're bombarded
with investing tidbits, soundbites, trivia, advice, and
opinions. In this important part, I help you to evaluate the
reliability of a given source. Whether you're reading a
magazine or newspaper article or book, perusing an
Internet site or using software, or watching television or
listening to the radio, you need to know how to evaluate
what's worth considering and what to ignore.

Chapter 17

Choosing Investing Resources Wisely

"*F*inding the occasional straw of truth awash in an ocean of confusion and bamboozle requires intelligence, vigilance, dedication and courage. But, if we don't practice these tough habits of thought, we cannot hope to solve the truly serious problems that face us — and we risk becoming a nation of suckers, up for grabs by the next charlatan who comes along."

— The late Carl Sagan in "The Fine Art of Baloney Detection"

In the past, finding financial information was pretty cut and dried. You could subscribe to publications such as *Kiplinger's* magazine for general money issues and a local, big city newspaper for daily stock prices. The hard-core, upscale investor had the *Wall Street Journal* delivered daily.

Times have changed, though. Today's investor faces information overload. Radio, television, magazines, newspapers, books, the Internet, family, friends, neighbors, and cabdrivers. . . . Everywhere you turn these days, someone is offering investing opinions, tips, and advice. You can't pick up a newspaper or magazine or go channel surfing on cable or radio without bumping into articles, stories, segments, and entire programs devoted to investment issues.

You don't (directly) pay for most of this information, and unfortunately, you usually get your money's worth! Much of the financial advice out there is biased and wrong.

Sure, scores of "free" investing sites — most of which are run by investment companies or someone else with something to sell — are on the Internet. Why don't these sites charge you a fee? Gullible people think they're getting a free lunch, but what these sites give away is nothing but subtle and not-so-subtle advertising for whatever products and services they sell. If these sites charged people for frequenting their sites, few would visit. So why bother sifting through such rubbish? Chosen wisely, the best investing resources can further your investment education and knowledge and enable you to make better decisions. Because investment information and advice is so widespread, I devote this entire part of this book to helping you separate the good from the mediocre and awful. Although I name the best investment resources that I'm familiar with, I also explain how you can discern for yourself what's good from what's not. Because the world of investment resources is already large and continues to grow, knowing how to sift is just as important as hearing what the best resources are today.

Why the Overload?

Why are everybody and his brother in the media and publishing world putting out investing information? Has money become that much more complicated over the years? Are there simply more media and publishing executives who want to help us? The following sections explain some of the reasons why investing has become such a hot topic.

Economic change breeds uncertainty

Many factors have caused the explosion in financial information and advice that the media and publishers offer. Some are obvious: Global competition and rapid changes in technology are causing most industries to undergo dramatic changes in much shorter periods of time.

Although jobs are plentiful for many with particular training and skills, fear of job loss and financial instability run high. Economic change and widespread cynicism about the ability of Social Security to provide a reasonable retirement income to baby boomers has also caused many to seek investment guidance.

Financial planning is far from a "profession"

Ironically, the failure of the "financial planning" industry to meet the needs of those looking for help is one of the reasons why so many consumers seek investment advice elsewhere. "The high attraction to books and computer programs is because consumers are worried about planners' agendas," says Barbara Roper, director of investor protection at the non-profit Consumer Federation of America.

Roper was the author of the CFA's report, *Financial Planning Abuses, A Growing Problem,* which documented that 85 percent of financial planners earn some or all of their income from commissions from products they sell. The small number of fee-based advisors primarily manage money for the affluent. "Financial planning for middle-income consumers still tends to be extremely sales-driven, which creates a substantial conflict of interest," says Roper.

And fee-based planners who also manage money have their own conflicts of interest. These planners have a bias against recommending strategies, such as paying off a mortgage or investing in real estate or a small business, that take money away from them to manage.

Investment choices are increasing

The difficulty in finding objective financial help is all the more frustrating as individuals face increasingly complex choices. More employees are forced to take responsibility for saving money for their retirement *and* deciding how to invest that money. In the past, more employers offered pension plans. In these plans, the employer set aside money on behalf of employees and retained a pension manager that decided how to invest it. All the employees had to do was learn the level of benefits that they had earned and when they could begin drawing a monthly check.

With today's retirement plans, such as 401(k)s, employees need to educate themselves about how much money they need to save and how to invest it. In addition to learning retirement planning and investment allocation, individuals face a dizzying number of financial products, such as the thousands of mutual funds that are on the market.

Our society is obsessed with money

Our culture worships money. The pages of tabloid papers and magazines are filled with highly paid movie and sports celebrities and wealthy corporate executives. We don't care if someone has ditched his children or stepped on people to get to the top — sadly, we often hold the rich and famous in too high esteem.

Other warning signs abound for a society that cares more about money than people and human relationships. Some view hiring someone else to raise their children as a luxury of wealth. Others spend tens of thousands of dollars on fancy, financed cars that require years of work to pay off. We don't spend enough time with our children and then are puzzled why the teen suicide rate has tripled in the past two generations and why violence in schools and elsewhere is on the rise.

Communications options are expanding

Over the past generation, cable television has mushroomed the number of television channels. The explosion of the Internet has introduced a whole new medium.

Flip through your cable channels at any hour of the day and you see infomercials that promise to make you a real estate tycoon or stock market day-trader in your spare time. Now, at a relatively low cost, anybody can publish a Web page.

The accessibility of these communications mediums now lets just about anyone with an animated personality and a few bucks appear to be an expert. Rather than being driven by the quality of the content, these newer communications options are primarily structured around selling advertising.

Quality: Inversely Related to Advertising

Just because more sources offer investing advice doesn't mean that you should read, listen to, or watch much of it. I'll be the first to admit that it's a generalization; however, the first rule for maximizing your chances of finding the best investing information and advice is to recognize that there are no free lunches. Too many people get sucked into supposedly free resources. Click on your television, radio, or the Internet and you come across mountains of "free" stuff. In addition to more violence and sex than the world needs or wants, you'll find lots to do with the world of investing.

Of course, someone is paying for all this and it's all there for some reason. In the vast majority of cases, advertising is footing the bill. And therein generally lies a huge problem.

Imagine for a moment that, rather than paying for this book, you could obtain it for free by simply visiting your favorite bookstore and legally walking out with a copy. Further suppose that this book was totally financed by advertising. Instead of being 450 pages, it would be 900 pages with half the pages devoted to ads. Although the book would be heftier, it would be free.

If you think that's a worthwhile tradeoff because you'd still get to read the same useful advice written by yours truly, you'd be mistaken — I wouldn't write such a book.

As I discuss in the next chapter, some authors choose to write books that are the equivalent of an infomercial for something else — such as high-priced seminars — that the "author" really wants to sell. Such writers aren't interested in educating and helping you as much as they are seeking to sell you something. So, for example, an author might write about how complicated the investing markets are and what indicators he follows to time investments. However, at the end of such a book, the author might say that investing is simply too complicated to do on your own and that you really need a personal investment manager — which, to no great surprise, the author happens to be.

In the following sections, I explain how advertising often compromises the quality of investment advice.

Understanding how advertising affects content

I won't say that you can't find some useful investment resources in mediums with lots of advertising. You can find some good investing programs on radio and television and some helpful investing sites on the Internet. However, these resources are the exception to the rule that where there's lot of advertising, there's little valuable information and advice. Likewise, just because magazines and newspapers have quite a bit of advertising doesn't mean that some of their columnists and articles aren't worthy of your time.

However, and this is a big however, advertising causes more than a few problems with all the media outlets and other publications that profit from it:

✔ **Influencing content.** Although many organizations such as newspaper and magazine publishers and radio and television stations that accept ads say their ad departments are separate from their editorial departments, the truth is that in most of these organizations, advertisers wield influence over the content. At a minimum, the editorial environment must be perceived as conducive to the sale of the advertiser's product. The stock market cable television channels, for example, carry many ads from brokers catering to investors who pick and trade their own stocks. Furthermore, such stations carry ads from firms that purport to teach you how to make big bucks day-trading (see Chapter 6). Not surprisingly, such stations offer many "news" segments on their shows that cater to stock traders and condone and endorse foolish strategies such as day trading rather than condemning them. Rather than asking themselves what is in the best interests of their viewers, listeners, and readers, executives at too many media and publishing firms instead ask what will attract attention and advertisers.

✔ **Corrupting content.** In too many organizations, advertisers can have an even more direct and adulterating influence on editorial content. Specifically, some media organizations and publishers simply won't say something negative about a major advertiser or will highlight and praise investment companies that are big advertisers. I've had more than a few publications attempt to edit out critical comments that I've made about companies with lousy products that turned out to be advertisers in their publications. Some editors simply say that they don't want to bite the hand that feeds them. Others are less candid about why they remove such criticism. The bottom line is still the same: Advertisers' influence squashes freedom of speech and, more importantly, prevents readers, viewers, and listeners from getting the truth and best advice. (By the way, I don't write for organizations that edit my work in such a fashion.)

✔ **Low-quality content.** Because of the previously mentioned reasons and an overall lack of concern for the value of information and advice, some investing resources cut corners on the quality of their content. Because consumers often pay nothing or next to nothing for many investment resources, the media have an incentive to sell advertising space and not to hire high-quality writers who can offer sound advice to readers.

Recognizing quality resources

With the tremendous increase in the coverage of investing and other personal money issues, more and more journalists are writing about increasingly technical issues — often in areas in which they have no expertise. Some of these writers provide good information and advice. Unfortunately, some of these so-called experts dish out bad advice. In fields such as medicine or the law, you wouldn't be so willing to take advice from non-experts. Why should you care any less about your money?

In my personal financial-management course, I would point out poor and conflict-ridden advice from various sources. My students rightfully ask, "How can we know what's good and whom we can trust?"

Although I can suggest resources that I hold in high regard (and do so throughout this book, especially in Chapters 18, 19, and 20), I recognize that you may encounter many different investment resources and you need to understand how to tell the best from the rest. The answer to my students' queries about how to discern quality, dear reader, rests in educating thyself. The more knowledgeable you are about sound and flawed investment strategies, the better able you will be to tell good from not-so-good investment resources.

Whenever I encounter a financial magazine, newspaper, Internet site, or other resource for the first time, I investigate it. The following sections suggest some questions you should ask before you take investment advice.

How do they make their money?

All things being equal, you have a greater chance of finding quality content when subscriber fees account for the bulk of a company's revenue and advertising accounts for little or none of the revenue. This generalization, of course, is just that — a generalization. There are, however, exceptions.

Some publications that derive a reasonable portion of their revenues from advertising have some good columns and content. Conversely, some relatively ad-free sources aren't very good.

What's their philosophy?

Readers of my books can clearly understand my philosophies about investing. I advocate buying and holding, not trading and gambling. I explain how to build wealth through proven vehicles, including stocks, real estate, and small-business ownership. My guiding beliefs are clearly detailed on the Cheat Sheet in the front of this book.

Unfortunately, many publications and programs don't make it as easy for you to see or hear their operating beliefs. You may have to do some homework. For example, with a radio program, you probably have to listen to at least portions of several shows to get a sense of the host's investment philosophies. Warning signs include publications and programs that make investing sound overly complicated and that imply or say that you won't succeed or do as well if you don't hire a financial advisor or follow your investments like a hawk.

Just about everywhere you turn these days — radio, television, and the Internet — you can get up-to-the-minute updates on financial markets around the globe. Although most investors have a natural curiosity about how their investments are doing, from my experience, the constant barrage of updates causes a loss of focus on the big picture.

In many cases, publishing and media companies report what I call the "noise" rather than the news of the day. Some companies are far worse about doing so than others.

Over the next week, take a close look at how you spend your time keeping up with financial news and other information. Do the programs and publications that you most heavily use really help you better understand and map out sound investment strategies, or do they end up confusing, overwhelming, and paralyzing you with bits and pieces of contradictory and often hyped noise? I'm not saying that you should tune these resources out completely, but I am saying that you should devote less time to the noise of the day and more time to self-education. How can you do that? Read a few good books (a topic that I discuss in detail in Chapter 19).

What are their qualifications?

Examine the backgrounds, including professional work experience and education credentials, of a resource's writers, hosts, and/or anchors. If such information isn't given or easily found, that's usually a red flag. People with something to hide, or a lack of something significantly redeeming to say about themselves, usually don't promote their backgrounds.

Of course, just because someone seems to have a relatively impressive background doesn't mean that she has your best interests in mind or has honestly presented her qualifications. For example, in a December 28, 1998 article in *Forbes* magazine, journalist William P. Barrett presented a sobering review of financial author Suze Orman's (*9 Steps to Financial Freedom*) stated credentials and qualifications:

> "Orman's bio in *9 Steps* says she 'heads her own financial planning firm,' Suze Orman Financial Group of Emeryville, Calif. But neither she nor the firm has done any paid financial planning work in years. Besides books and other royalties, Orman's earned income has come mainly from selling insurance — which gets much more attention in her book than do stocks or bonds...The jacket of her video says she has '18 years of experience at major Wall Street institutions.' In fact, she has 7. The 'nearly 1,000 new clients each year' touted on her publisher's Web site are simply fans making inquiries by mail."

When the *Forbes* piece came out, Orman's publicist tried to discredit it and made it sound as if the magazine had falsely criticized Orman. *The San Francisco Chronicle,* which is the nearest major newspaper to Orman's hometown, picked up on the *Forbes* piece and ran a story of its own (written by Mark Veverka in his "Street Smarts" column), which substantiated the *Forbes* column. Veverka went through the *Forbes* piece point by point and gave Orman's company and the public relations firm numerous opportunities to provide information contrary to the piece. Neither organization did. Here's some of what Veverka recounts from dealing with Orman's firm and publicist:

> "If you want your side told, you have to return reporters' telephone calls. But alas, no callback. On Wednesday, December 6, Orman's publicist said a written response to the *Forbes* piece and the Street Smarts column would be sent by facsimile to *The Chronicle* that day. However, no fax was ever sent. They blew me off. Twice. In what was becoming an extraordinary effort to be fair, I placed more telephone calls over several days to Orman Financial and the publicist, asking for either an interview with Orman or an official response. If Orman didn't fudge about her years on Wall Street or didn't let her commodity-trading adviser license lapse, surely we could straighten all of this out, right? Still, no answer. Nada. On December 17, I called yet again. Finally, literally on deadline, a woman

who identified herself as Orman's 'consultant' called me to talk 'off the record' about the column. What she ended up doing was bashing the *Forbes* piece and my column but not for publication. More importantly, she offered no official retort to allegations made by veteran *Forbes* writer William Barrett. I have to say, it was an incredibly unprofessional attempt at spinning. And I've been spun by the worst of them."

So what's the lesson to be learned from this story? You can't accept stated credentials and qualifications at face value for the simple reason that some people lie. You can't sniff out a liar by the way he looks or by his gender or age. You can, however, increase your chances of being tipped off by being skeptical. In fact, *Forbes* journalist Barrett started his investigation of Orman by the sheer outrageousness of the number of new clients that Orman claimed to be getting each year. As I explain in Chapter 19, you can see a number of hucksters in the print publishing field for what they are simply by using common sense in reviewing some of their outrageous claims.

Chapter 18

Periodicals, Radio, and Television

● ●

In This Chapter

▶ Financial magazines and newspapers

▶ Investment newsletters

▶ Radio and television programs

● ●

*A*ll the news that's fit to print, air, or view — newspapers, magazines, newsletters, and radio and television programs all try to provide investing information and advice to the public. In this chapter, I explain what to look for — and what to look out for — when you tune into these media sources in the hopes of learning how to invest like the best.

The Magazine and Newspaper World

I've written many investing articles for various magazines and newspapers. Some of the experiences have been enjoyable, others okay, and some miserable. The best publications and editors I've written for take seriously their responsibility to provide qualify information and advice to their readers. The worst and mediocre allow too many obstacles to get in the way. In this section, I alert you to the main problems with investment articles in magazines and newspapers and help you choose the best publications for your investing needs.

Pitfalls with investment advice in magazines and newspapers

Visit a newsstand, and you find many investing publications as well as general-interest publications with investing columns. Here are the main drawbacks you will often find in such periodicals.

Oversimplification

The short length of newspaper and magazine articles can easily lead writers to oversimplify complex issues. For example, many pieces on mutual funds focus on a fund's returns and investment philosophies, devoting little, if any, space to the risks or tax consequences of investing in recommended funds. Other pieces oversimplify something that's more complex and end up offering flawed advice.

Consider a short piece entitled "Index Funds: Size Matters" in the October 12, 1998, issue of *Time* magazine. Using data from Morningstar, the article argues, "To invest in large companies, buy a low-fee index fund. But to invest in smaller stocks, it's worth paying more for an active fund manager."

According to the *Time* article, for the five-year period ending August, 31, 1998, 0 percent of actively managed mutual funds investing in large company stocks were able to beat the corresponding market index — the Standard & Poor's 500 (S&P 500). By comparison, the article says, a whopping 98 percent of actively managed mutual funds investing in a mix of small company stocks were able to beat its corresponding market index — the Russell 2000. This data does seemingly lead to the conclusion offered in the article: Use index funds for investing in large company stocks but shun index funds and use actively managed funds when investing in small cap stocks. The data is compelling.

There's a big problem, however, with the article's analysis of Morningstar's data: It is wrong, and wrong in a big way. Like many such articles in media publications, the genesis for this piece was an already-published piece, in this case in Morningstar's *FundInvestor* publication. Like too many reporters who cover investing these days, the reporter behind this piece was either too busy or (more likely) too financially ignorant to understand Morningstar's article.

What Morningstar's piece actually demonstrated was how frequently over the past five years (over the various 12-month periods) the average return for a fund in a given fund category beat the corresponding index performance for the category. However, this data is quite different from what portion of the individual funds in a given category outperformed the corresponding index over the five-year time period.

Readers who perused this *Time* piece were left with the erroneous conclusion that actively managed stock funds investing in large cap stocks never beat the S&P 500 but that small cap stock funds almost always beat their corresponding index — the Russell 2000. I asked Morningstar to compile its data in the way in which *Time* presented it. For each fund category, Morningstar told what portion of the funds were able to beat the comparable market index over the same five-year period.

Among large company stock funds, just over 17 percent (a far cry from 0 percent) of them beat the S&P 500 over the five-year time span in question. Among small company stock funds, about 50 percent (again, a big difference from the 98 percent cited by *Time*) beat the Russell 2000.

You should exercise great caution even in using this correct data to assert that it's better to buy index funds when investing in large company stocks. During the five-year period study, larger cap stocks did far better than small cap stocks — the S&P 500 returned an annualized 18.2 percent, more than double the annual returns of the Russell 2000 of 8.1 percent. Many mutual funds focusing on small company stocks tend, because of the large assets of the fund, to hold a portion in larger cap stocks. Thus, many small cap funds were able to best the Russell 2000 index, thanks to higher returns provided by large cap holdings.

You also shouldn't simply use one five-year period of data to determine the value (or lack thereof) of particular index funds. The results of various studies I've examined demonstrate that the majority of actively managed funds underperform the market indexes. Although a somewhat greater proportion of larger cap funds tends to fall short of their mark, small company stock index funds have value too.

Hype and horror

Whenever the stock market suffers a sharp decline, many in the media bring out the gloom and doom. Front page headlines, such as "The Beginning of the End" torment investors about holding onto their stocks.

Scores of articles horrify parents with the expected cost of a college education. The typical advice: Start saving and investing early so that you don't have to tell Junior that you can't afford to send him to college.

Completely overlooked and ignored are the tax and financial aid consequences of the recommended investment strategies. For example, if parents don't take advantage of tax-deductible retirement accounts and save instead outside them, they not only pay more in taxes, but they also generally qualify for less financial aid. Sound investing decisions require a holistic approach that acknowledges that people have limited money and must make these sorts of tradeoffs.

Poor advice

Consider the gaffe made by a June 1987 *Money* magazine piece entitled "Where to get safe, high yields." The title itself should have been a red flag: It's impossible to find a *safe,* high yield. To get high yields, you must be willing to accept more risk. In the *Money* article, three of the recommended investments were limited partnerships (LPs) sold through commission-based brokers. These products' high commissions and ongoing fees doomed even the luckiest of investors to mediocre or dismal investment returns.

The *Money* article even asserted that investors could earn annual returns as high as 18 percent on some LPs. Students of the financial markets know that the best ownership investments, such as stocks and real estate, return no more than 10 to 12 percent per year over the long haul. To expect more is to hold unrealistic expectations.

Four years after the magazine published that article, Marshall Loeb, former managing editor of *Money,* wrote *Marshall Loeb's Money Guide.* In his book, Marshall said, "For most investors who don't have the skill to do the necessary research, limited partnerships are just too risky." Although an improvement over the poor advice *Money* published four years earlier, Loeb's advice still missed the mark. The point isn't risk. In fact, limited partnerships, like other bundled investments such as mutual funds, are only as risky as the component investments they hold. The major issue is cost. Even financially unsophisticated types would take a pass if they knew that broker-sold limited partnerships took 15 percent of their up-front investment for commissions and other start-up expenses, as well as 3 percent per year in operating fees. Another issue is lack of liquidity. LP investors typically don't have access to their money for seven to ten years.

Quoting experts who are not

Historically, one way that journalists have attempted to overcome technical gaps in their knowledge is to interview and quote financial experts. Although this may add to the accuracy and quality of a story, journalists who aren't experts themselves sometimes have trouble discerning among the self-anointed experts.

I continue to be amazed at how many newspaper and magazine financial writers quote investment newsletter writers' advice. As I discuss later in this chapter, the predictive advice of newsletter writers is often wrong and causes investors to earn lower returns due to frequent trading than if they simply bought and held.

Focus on noise and minutiae

In addition to not doing their homework on their sources, daily financial press reports tend to cause people to be shortsighted. Today it's common for daily newspaper charts to show the stock market's movements at five-minute intervals throughout the previous day. This focus on the noise of the day causes nervous investors to make panicked, emotionally based decisions, such as selling *after* major stock market falls.

Of course, the daily print media aren't the only ones chronicling the minutiae. As I discuss elsewhere in this chapter and this part, other media, including television, radio, and the Internet, cause many investors to lose sight of the long term and the big picture.

Making the most of newspapers and magazines

So what should you do if you want to learn more about investing but don't want to be overloaded with information? Educate yourself and be selective. If you're considering subscribing to financial publications, go to the library first and review some old issues. Was the information and advice useful and error-free? The more you learn, the easier it is to separate the wheat from the chaff. Shy away from publications that purport to be able to predict the future — few people can, and those who can are usually busy managing money.

Read bylines and biographies and get to know writers' strengths and weaknesses. Ditto for the entire publication. Any writer or publisher can make mistakes. Some make many more than others — follow their advice at your own peril. Start by evaluating advice in the areas that you know the most about. For example, if you're interested in investing in Microsoft or Intel and are reasonably familiar with the computer industry, find out what the publications say about technology investments.

And remember that you're not going to outfox the financial markets because they are reasonably efficient (see Chapter 4). Spend your time seeking out information and advice that help you flesh out your goals and develop a plan with specific recommendations.

Investment Newsletters

Particularly in the newsletter business, prognosticators fill your mailbox with promotional material making outrageous claims about their returns. Private money managers, not subject to the same scrutiny and auditing requirements as mutual funds, can do the same.

Be especially wary of any newsletters making claims of high returns. Stephen Leeb's *Personal Finance* newsletter, for example, claims that he has developed a brilliant proprietary model, which he calls the "Master Key Indicator." His model supposedly has predicted the last 28 upturns in the market in a row without a single miss. The odds of doing this, according to Leeb, are more than 268 million to 1! The ad goes on to claim that Leeb's "Master Key" market timing system could have turned a $10,000 investment over 12 years into $39.1 million, a return of 390,000%!

Turns out that this outrageous claim was based on *backtesting*, looking back over historic returns and creating "what if" scenarios. In other words, Leeb didn't turn anyone's $10,000 into $39 million. Much too late after that ad appeared, the SEC finally charged Leeb with false advertising. Leeb settled out of court for a mere $60,000 fine (far less than he cost investors).

According to the *Hulbert Financial Digest*, which looks at risk as well as return, no newsletters have outperformed the market averages over the past 15 years. The worst investment newsletters have underperformed the market averages by dozens of percentage points; some would even have caused you to lose money during a decade when the financial markets performed extraordinarily well.

Newsletter purveyor Joe Granville, for example, has long been known for making outrageous and extreme stock market predictions and is often quoted in financial publications. He claims to have the #1 rated newsletter — omitting that it was for one year — 1989. Over the past decade — one of the best decades ever for the stock market (with U.S. stocks more than quadrupling in value) — followers of Granville's advice *lost* 99 percent of their investment!

Be highly suspicious of past investment performance claims made by investment newsletters. Don't believe a track record unless it has been audited by a major accounting firm with experience doing such audits. In order for you to make sound investing choices, you don't need predictions and soothsayers. If you choose to follow these prognosticators, and you're lucky, little harm will be done. But more often than not, you can lose lots of money following their predictions. Stay far away from publications that purport to be able to tell what's going to happen next. No one has a crystal ball.

Radio and Television Programs

As you move from the world of magazines and newspapers to radio and television, the entertainment component usually increases. In this section, I highlight some common problems with radio and television programs and offer some recommendations for the better programs.

Problems with radio and television programs

I've been a guest on many a radio and television program. Just as in the *Wizard of Oz,* seeing how things work behind the scenes tends to deglamorize these mediums. Here are the main problems I've discovered from my years observing radio and television.

You often get what you pay for

Some of the worst financial advice is brought to you, not surprisingly, for "free." Nationally, thousands of radio stations have financial and money talk shows. Money and investing shows are proliferating on television cable channels. Because listeners don't pay for these shows, advertising often drives who and what gets on the air.

Some of these shows are "hosted" by a person who is nothing more than a financial salesperson. That person's first, and sometimes only, motivation for wanting to do the show is to pick up clients. Many local radio investing programs are hosted by a local stockbroker (who usually calls himself a financial consultant or planner). A broker who reels in just one big fish a month — a person with, say, $300,000 to invest — can easily generate commissions totaling $15,000 by selling investments with a 5 percent commission.

But radio suffers from more than brokers trolling for new clients as evidenced by the case of Sonny Bloch, a New York radio personality who was indicted for fraud in 1995. The Securities and Exchange Commission found that Bloch was receiving kickbacks from investment brokers for endorsing some pretty crummy investment products on his nationally syndicated radio show. The SEC also filed a complaint against Bloch for defrauding investors of millions of dollars to supposedly purchase some radio stations. Instead, according to the SEC, Bloch and his wife used hundreds of thousands of dollars to purchase a condominium. Partners in a precious metals firm (DeAngelis Brothers Collectibles) that Bloch regularly endorsed on the air were arrested for theft and ended up in bankruptcy. Again, Bloch was accused of receiving kickbacks.

I know from personal experience what too many radio stations look for in the way of hosts for financial programs. The host's integrity, knowledge, and lack of conflict of interest don't matter. Willingness to work for next to nothing helps: One radio station program director told me that she liked the broker who was hosting a financial talk show because the broker was willing to work for so little compensation from the radio station. Never mind the fact that the broker rarely gave useful advice and was obviously trolling for new clients. The program director told me, "We're in the entertainment business."

Information and hype overload

The opening bell will sound in 5 minutes, 32 seconds on the floor of the New York Stock Exchange. A digital clock counts down the seconds on-screen as CNBC reporter Maria Bartiromo crams sound bite after sound bite into her monologue.

The previous day, Federal Reserve Board Chairman Alan Greenspan made an unexpected 0.25 percent cut in the Fed Discount Rate, and stocks jumped sharply. Now, on the morning after, CNBC tries to pump this short-term excitement for all its worth. Bartiromo talks so frenetically that she has to continually brush her hair back after every time she whips her head around. Like a runner near the end of a sprint, she's practically out of breath. Although Bartiromo is technically reporting, her real job is to keep CNBC viewers glued to their TV screens for the opening of the world's biggest stock market.

At 9:30 a.m. EST the market opens and transactions start streaming across the bottom of the television screen. Changes in the major market indexes — the Dow Jones Industrial Average, the S&P 500, and the NASDAQ index — also flash on the screen. In fact, these indexes are updated almost every five *seconds* on the screen. Far more exciting than a political race or sporting event, this is an event that never ends and has constant change and excitement. Even after the markets close, reporting of still-open overseas markets continues. The performance of futures of U.S. stock market indexes then appears on CNBC.

Does all this reporting and data make us better investors? Of course not. But the conventionally accepted notion is that this information overload levels the playing field for the individual investor. I know too many investors who make emotionally based decisions prodded by all this noise, prognostication, opinion, and hearsay.

How programs select guests

Some journalists, often in an effort to overcome their own lack of knowledge, like to interview "experts." However, journalists who are themselves not experts sometimes have trouble discerning among the self-anointed experts. A classic example of this problem is the media exposure that author Charles Givens used to receive. Givens became a darling of the media and the public following unprecedented, consecutive three-day appearances on NBC's *Today* show.

"When Charles Givens talks, everyone listens," said Jane Pauley, then-cohost of the *Today* show. Bryant Gumbel, the other cohost, said of Givens, "Last time he was here, the studio came to a complete stop. . . . Everyone started taking notes, and I was asking for advice." Givens regularly held court on the talk show circuit with the likes of Larry King, Oprah Winfrey, and Phil Donahue.

The Givens case highlights some of the media's inability to distinguish between good and bad experts. It's relatively easy for the financially sophisticated to see the dangerous, oversimplified, and biased advice that Givens offers in his books. In his first best-seller, *Wealth Without Risk,* Givens recommended investing in limited partnerships and provided a phone number and address of a firm, Delta Capital Corporation in Florida, through which to buy the partnerships. Those who bought these products ended up paying hefty sales commissions and owning investments worth half or less of their original value. Besides the problematic partnerships he recommended, court proceedings against Givens in a number of states have uncovered that he owned a major share of Delta Capital.

Other investing advice from Givens that gives cause to pause: In his chapters on investing, he said that the average yearly return you'll earn investing in mutual funds will be 25 percent or 30 percent on discounted mortgages. The reality: An investor would be fortunate to earn half of these inflated returns.

So how did Givens get on all these national programs? A shrewd publicist combined with show producers who either didn't read his books and/or were themselves financially illiterate. Talk shows and many reporters often don't take the time to check out people like Givens. I know this for a fact because I've been on dozens of radio and television programs and understand how they work. Most of the time, the books are never read. Producers, who themselves are financially illiterate, often decide to put someone on the air on the basis of a press kit or a call from a publicist.

The best radio and television investing programs

Okay, so I've warned you about a number of problems with relying on radio and television programs investing advice. There are some good programs and hosts among the bad apples. The following are my picks for the best of the lot:

- ✔ **"Right on the Money."** This relatively new PBS television series is hosted by Chris Farrell, whom I've long found to be an honest, down-to-earth, intelligent financial journalist. Farrell stays away from hype and sensationalism and helps you focus on the basics that work.

- ✔ **"Money Talk."** Bob Brinker's ABC radio program airs weekend afternoons in most parts of the country. Brinker is an advocate of investing in mutual funds. The one area where Brinker and I disagree is that he does advocate market timing — he puts out a newsletter called *MarketTimer,* whose investment picks haven't performed as well as the market averages over the long term. That said, Brinker does help listeners stay focused on the big picture and headed in generally the right direction.

- ✔ **"Sound Money."** This weekly PBS radio program airs live in most areas on Saturday morning and is tape-delayed in other areas. Host Bob Potter actually has worked many years with Chris Farrell and shares his redeeming qualities.

- ✔ **Other.** There are many other programs out there. Worthy of honorable mention are the *Wall Street Journal's* syndicated television show and NPR's "Marketplace."

Chapter 19

Books, Glorious Books

. . . .

. . . .

*O*ver the years, I've read hundreds of investing and financial books. I hope you haven't subjected yourself to this task!

While most books have something to offer, too many investing books are burdened with wrongheaded advice and misinformation. As a non-expert, you may have a hard time sifting through the dung heap for the tidbits of treasure. The bad stuff can pollute your otherwise intelligent thinking and cause you to make investing mistakes that millions before you have made.

I hope that I'm not the first person to tell you not to believe everything you read. Publishing is no different than any other business — companies are in it to make money. As with other industries, the shortsighted desire to reap quick profits causes some companies to publish content that seems attractive in the short-term but is toxic to readers long term.

In this chapter, I help you sift through the confusion to find books worth reading.

Beware of Infomercials Disguised as Books

The worst books tend to confuse more than they convey. Why would an author want to do that? Well, some authors have an incentive to make things complicated and mysterious. Their agenda may be to sell you a high-priced newsletter or convince you to turn your money over to them to manage.

One book author said to me, "Royalties, schmoyalties . . . I write books to hook people into my monthly newsletter. I can make $185 per year off of a $195 newsletter sale. You can't do that with a book." You sure can't, but this author's books were short on information and advice and said that you needed to keep up with the latest developments to make the right investments. When you subscribe to his newsletter, you're told that the financial markets are so complicated and rapidly changing that the newsletter is really no substitute for using his money-management service!

The worst books steer you toward purchasing a crummy investment product that the author has a vested interest in selling you. Unfortunately, most publishers don't do their homework to check out prospective authors. Most publishers don't care what the author is up to, or if the author is indeed an expert on the topic, as long as he or she is willing and able to write a salable book. Authors who run around the country conducting seminars are a plus to the publisher.

In his books and seminar promotional materials, Wade Cook claims to be able to teach people how to earn monthly returns of 20 percent or more (that's right — *monthly*, not yearly) using his stock market investing strategies.

Cook's self-published best-selling books are short on specifics and are largely infomercials for his high-priced seminars. Cook's get-rich-quick investment seminars — which cost a whopping $4,695 — have been so successful at attracting attendees that Cook's company, Profit Financial Corporation, went public and generated more than $118 million in 1998 revenues!

Cook isn't shy about promising people they can get rich quick without much effort. Here's a passage from his book, *Stock Market Miracles*:

> "I want millions of dollars and I don't want to have to work a 9 to 5 job to get them. Boy, that's a conundrum. It's almost impossible to work a typical American job, with average income and accumulate millions. Yes, in 40 to 50 years maybe, but who wants to wait that long? That's the rub — accomplishing the task of having millions without having to work for millions.
>
> "You see my method is simple. I want to use a small amount of money — risk capital if you will, to generate cash flow which will exponentially generate more income."

Cook promises his followers several hundred percent annualized returns by teaching them how to successfully gamble (not invest) in the stock market. Cook's "techniques" include trading in and out of stocks and options on stocks after short holding periods of weeks, days, or even hours.

His trading strategies are loosely based upon technical analysis — that is, examining a stock's price movements and volume history through charting. (See Chapter 7 for more details on the foolishness of technical analysis.) More best-selling books have appeared in recent years touting how people can get rich day trading stocks, which is quite similar to Cook's recommended approach.

With the booming stock market in recent years, some people have been earning higher-than-average (10 percent) annualized returns. But Cook's investment seminar, which is offered in cities throughout the country, is marketed to folks like this: "If you aren't getting 20 percent per month, or 300 percent annualized returns on your investments you need to be there."

Steven Thomas, a truck driver, went to a seminar with his wife so that both of them could follow and implement Cook's strategies. In addition to spending $4,695 on the seminar, they also spent another $2,000 on audio and video-tapes. Six months later he spent $1,500 on a paging system from Cook's company. The results: Thomas lost $36,000, which he borrowed against his home's equity. "I saw this as an opportunity to quit my job and just invest in the stock market," says Thomas. "This has had a terrible impact on my family and I'm super depressed."

Of course, if Cook were indeed earning the 300 percent annual returns his seminars claim to be able to teach the masses how to achieve, he would, in about a decade, become the world's wealthiest individual if he invested just one million of the dollars he supposedly earned in real estate. Look out, Bill Gates and Warren Buffett! Any investor starting with just $10,000 would vault to the top of the list of the world's wealthiest people in about 15 years if Cook's teachings really worked!

So how did Cook get his start in the investing world? Here's what his Web site says:

> "He was a taxi cab driver in the '70s. Borrowing $500 from his father, Wade Cook started buying real estate. His innovative ideas and gutsy follow-through enabled him to turn that $500 into several million. But that's nothing compared with what he's doing on Wall Street. Starting with $1,300, using his "Rolling Rock" and "Range Rider" methods, he's showing students how to create millions.

> "Why is Wade so smart? He says he's 'street smart.' What he discovered driving a cab changed his life forever. While his fellow cabbies were out looking for the big runs, Wade was taking every little run he could find — $4 here, $5 here. You see it costs $2 just to get into a cab (something called a meter drop) even if you only go two blocks. At the end of a month, Wade made three times what every other taxi cab driver made. Now, Wade applies his 'meter drop' technique to his stock market investment business — making a ton of money on a lot of little deals."

What's the real story behind Cook's wealth? Although Cook's investment return expectations are completely unrealistic, he got away with claiming hyped and undocumented returns for many years because he doesn't manage money for others. Seminar promoters and newsletter writers face no SEC scrutiny of their inflated performance claims or what they do in their seminars as long as no securities laws are violated. The SEC refers to such organizations as "non-regulated entities."

Of course, Cook isn't the first person to profit in this fashion. Numerous other seminar promoters and authors (some are discussed later in this chapter) have cleaned up as well, including the Beardstown investment club, which could not document their supposedly market beating returns of 23+ percent per year (see the next section for details).

In addition to puffed-up expected stock market returns, there's more to Cook's past than simply driving a taxi. According to *Smart Money* magazine, Cook's dubious business practices had him in trouble throughout the '80s. At the end of his real estate seminars, which touted that average people could become millionaires buying property with little money down, Cook began peddling stock in his own business ventures.

By 1990, state securities regulators in six states — Missouri, Utah, Minnesota, Illinois, Oregon, and Arizona — issued him cease-and-desist orders for selling securities without a license, selling unregistered securities, and omission of material facts — like the fact that he had declared bankruptcy in 1987.

In fact, Arizona charged that Cook had duped $390,841 out of 150 investors by selling unregistered securities, funneling $48,000 of that money into a Scottsdale home purchase and federal income tax payments. The state ordered him to pay back the money and slapped him with a $150,000 penalty.

Cook answered by filing bankruptcy (again). Arizona shot back by indicting Cook on 18 counts of securities fraud. The case has been battled all the way to the Supreme Court. Most of the counts were dismissed on a technicality (double jeopardy); the rest were settled when Cook paid $70,500 in restitution.

Cook then moved back up to his home state of Washington, where he didn't lay low for long. His new company, Profit Financial Corporation, has become wildly successful selling his Wall Street Workshop seminars and publishing his two stock-picking books. The attorneys general of California and Texas, who are seeking millions of dollars in consumer refunds, are now suing the company. Both allege the company lied about its investment track record (now that's a big surprise — this company claimed you would make 300 percent per year in stocks!). Cook is under investigation in numerous other states, and his company is millions in arrears in IRS tax payments.

Although a public company, SEC documents show that Profit Financial Corporation is not exactly shareholder friendly. Cook has set up a rather clever business structure whereby the public company (of which he is the

Can you be like Warren Buffett?

In recent years, Warren Buffett has received lots of attention for his investing prowess. Numerous books have been published about him (none by Buffett himself), most of which were written and promoted from the philosophy embodied in the marketing slogan, "He did it his way; now you can, too," for the book, *The Warren Buffett Way.*

You can read every book ever written about Buffett, and the odds are about 10 million to 1 that you're going to be able to invest like he does. It's not that you're not an intelligent, willing-to-learn kind of person. But consider that you can't invest like Buffett for the same reason that you can't learn to be a professional basketball player by reading books about basketball greats Larry Bird and Michael Jordan, even if they themselves wrote the books.

One financial market commentator said of Buffett and the financial markets, "If making money in the market is so easy, why has only Warren Buffett made $14 billion picking stocks?"

However, Buffett did not make $14 billion picking individual stocks. It's true that Berkshire Hathaway, the firm that Buffett purchased in 1965 and still runs today, makes substantial investments in the stocks of individual companies. But Buffett built much of his great wealth through his buying and managing a variety of businesses, particularly insurance companies.

In addition to 13 insurance companies, Berkshire Hathaway owns divisions such as See's (candy manufacturer), the *Buffalo News* (newspaper), Nebraska Furniture Mart (home furnishings retailer), Borsheim's (jewelry retailer), *World Book* (encyclopedia publisher), Kirby's (home cleaning products manufacturer), Fechheimer Brothers (uniform manufacturer), and H.H. Brown and Dexter (shoe manufacturers).

The property and casualty insurance businesses that Berkshire Hathaway bought, most of which are located in Nebraska, afforded Buffett lots of low-cost money, which his firm could invest in a tax-favored way. Specifically, insurance companies collect premiums from policyholders and invest the money, called *float,* until insurance claims need to be paid. Unlike almost all other insurers, Berkshire Hathaway, which is in Nebraska, a state with loose insurance company regulations, can invest much of its float in riskier investments like stocks.

Although most other insurers invest no more than 20 percent in stocks, with the remainder in conservative, boring, low-return bonds, Buffett has taken full advantage of Nebraska's loose regulations, investing at times more than 95 percent of the float in stocks. Buffett likes to buy name-brand company stock and is attracted to almost anything that hooks consumers. Witness his investment in tobacco companies, of which he said, "I'll tell you why I like the economics of the cigarette business. It costs a penny to make. Sell it for a dollar. It's habit-forming. And there's fantastic brand loyalty."

The float is also invested in a tax-favored way as these reserves compound tax-free and the final capital gains are taxed at a reduced rate thanks to the protection afforded insurance companies. Buffett's insurance operations have also shrewdly kept their float reserved from claims at higher-than-needed levels to take full advantage of these tax benefits.

As Berkshire Hathaway grew over the years, acquired more businesses, and squirreled away more money to invest, Buffett's wealth also ballooned, thanks to his 41 percent ownership stake in the outstanding stock of the company. So to say that Buffett built his wealth through stock picking and that you can replicate what he did simply by reading books is ludicrous!

majority owner) must pay him for the right to print his words and teach his methods; that way Cook funnels much of the revenue stream directly into his pockets before it ever gets to the shareholders. According to SEC filings, Cook's total corporate compensation last year exceeded $8 million!

Ignore Unaudited Performance Claims

Book authors avoid careful scrutiny of claims of especially high returns. Some book publishers are happy to look the other way or even to solicit and encourage great boasts that they use in the packaging to sell books. Consider these two recent books: *The Beardstown Ladies' Common-Sense Investment Guide: How We Beat the Market — and How You Can, Too* and *The Whiz Kid of Wall Street's Investment Guide* by Matt Seto.

The Beardstown investment club claimed a whopping 23.4 percent annual return since the club's inception in 1983. In the book, the authors advocate forming an investment club, pooling your money, and using a simple stock selection method to beat the pants off the market and the suspendered managers of mutual funds. The bulk of this book walks the reader through how this investment club evaluated and selected individual stocks.

Seto's book boasts, "Matt Seto manages a portfolio that consistently outperforms 99 percent of all mutual fund managers . . . and returns an annual average of 34 percent." In his book, this 17-year-old investing genius says to forget bonds, real estate, and mutual funds and grow rich by investing entirely in individual stocks.

Each of these books makes prominently displayed and marketed performance claims. The Beardstown club's returns and Seto's returns, versus the market averages, place them shoulder to shoulder with the legendary Peter Lynch, of the now famous Fidelity Magellan fund, and Warren Buffett, an investor who Peter Lynch described as "the Greatest Investor of them all." Problem is, neither book contains information as to how these investment gurus calculate their returns, nor are the authors able to substantiate them when asked to.

When I first wrote about the Beardstown book for the *San Francisco Examiner* in 1995, I offered to work with an accounting firm to calculate the club's returns if the club supplied the necessary information. I asked the same of Seto when I read his book in late 1995. Neither of these authors could supply the documentation to prove their claims, and they backpedaled when pressed.

Initially, the Beardstown club said it would send the information, but months passed, and it never arrived. The club's media spokesperson then told me that the club has ". . . chosen not to make our return an issue. . . . we're not out to be bragging." This statement was surprising, given the claims prominently plastered all over its book.

WARNING!

Other dangers in narrowly focused advice guides written by novices

Although I disagree with the Beardstown guide's premise — that an investment club can pick individual stocks and beat the market and the best professional money managers — the book has even bigger problems that are common to many narrowly focused investment books pitching one investment. The book does not address the importance of choosing investments that fit an investor's overall financial strategies and goals, which, as you can read throughout this book, is something that is essential to smart investing. Making sound investing decisions, of course, involves more than picking "good" investments. The Beardstown book completely ignores the rest of your financial situation, such as your tax bracket and your ability to contribute money to retirement accounts. Pooling money through investment clubs doesn't work well because different club members have different investing and tax needs.

"Our individual needs were not a factor in the selection of the stocks. We didn't consider taxes," says the club's spokesperson. A number of the stocks that the club invested in paid healthy dividends. Although appropriate for retired members of the club, such stocks unnecessarily add to the tax burden of younger club members, who are still in their working years.

Also surprisingly absent in the book was advice to take advantage of funding tax-deductible retirement accounts. The club spokesperson, for example, says, "I don't put the maximum possible in my 401(k). I put up to the amount that my employer matches." She believes that she can earn higher returns investing in individual stocks outside of a tax-sheltered account than she can investing in the funds provided by her employer in its 401(k) plan. Even if she could earn higher returns picking her own stocks, she might rethink whether she'll end up with higher returns. The lost tax benefits from not using her 401(k) plan are huge (see Chapter 3).

A 1998 piece in *Chicago* magazine proved that although the Beardstown investment club claimed 23 percent per year returns versus 14 percent for the market, it turns out they tremendously underperformed the market and only earned 9 percent per year. Now the club is being sued by its book buyers in a class action lawsuit. Do you think the Beardstown Ladies would have gotten their book deal (and landed on best-seller lists) if the facts had been known?

Seto, likewise, could not prove his claim of an astounding 34 percent return. Meanwhile, the printing presses crank away.

Investing Books Worth Reading

Exceptional investing books — ones that are readable, educational, and insightful — are rare. Some of the better investment books are technical in nature and are written by career investment folks, so don't be surprised if they require more than one read. Make the investment of time; it'll pay big dividends (and capital gains!). Following are my picks for books that are worth the trouble of tracking down and reading.

A Random Walk Down Wall Street

Now in its sixth edition, *A Random Walk Down Wall Street* (Norton), by Burton Malkiel, is a classic that was first published in 1973. Malkiel is an entertaining and intelligent writer. Drawing from examples from this century and others, Malkiel teaches how *speculative bubbles* (frenzied buying) and fear and greed, as well as economic and corporate fundamentals, can move the financial markets.

One of the fundamental premises of his book is that the financial markets can't be predicted, especially in the short term. Common sense confirms this premise: If someone could figure out a system to predict the markets and make a fortune, then that person wouldn't waste time writing a book, publishing a newsletter, and so on. Malkiel, in fact, is one of the pioneers and proponents of *index mutual funds,* which simply invest in a relatively fixed basket of securities in order to track the overall market performance rather than to attempt to beat it. (See Chapter 9 to find out about index funds and how to use them.)

Needless to say, many Wall Street types aren't enamored of this book. As Malkiel says, the very term *random walk* is an "obscenity." But Malkiel presents a mountain of compelling arguments and data to support his case that most Wall Street firms and their investment research aren't worthy of an investor's hard-earned money. He also convincingly rebukes the whole field of technical analysis, which purports to be able to predict security prices based on charting and following past price movements. (See Chapter 7 for more about technical analysis.)

Malkiel explains how to look at some common-sense indicators, such as whether the stock and bond markets are fairly valued and your own personal goals and desire to take risk, to develop a thoughtful and successful investment plan. Rather than trying to predict the future, Malkiel explains how the level of risk an investor accepts with investments will ultimately determine future returns.

Stocks for the Long Run

Wharton School, University of Pennsylvania, Professor of Finance Jeremy J. Siegel loves investing data, especially examining it over long time periods. In *Stocks for the Long Run: The Definitive Guide to Financial Market Returns and Long-Term Investment Strategies* (McGraw Hill), Siegel presents an analysis of U.S. stock and bond returns since 1802!

The book is packed with charts and graphs, some of which you won't readily comprehend unless you're the analytic, graphical sort. Even so, Siegel provides comprehensive discussion of the worldwide financial markets. The book focuses on stock market investing, although bonds are discussed if for no other reason than to compare their returns and risk to that of stocks.

Built to Last

Some people may think that this book is just for the small number of people who want to build a large company. However, *Built to Last: Successful Habits of Visionary Companies*, written by management consultant James Collins and Stanford Business School Professor Jerry Porras, is an excellent book for all entrepreneurs and people who work in leadership positions in companies, as well as people interested in investing in individual stocks. Rarely does a great book make it to the business best-seller lists, but *Built to Last* did.

The book presents the findings from an extensive six years' worth of research into what's behind the success of companies such as 3M, Boeing, Ford, Hewlett-Packard, Motorola, Sony, and Wal-Mart, all of which have achieved great success in their respective industries over many years. The average company in Collins and Porras's study was founded in 1897. In all, the authors tracked 18 extraordinary companies (referred to as the gold medal winners in their respective industries) and compared the traits of these companies with similarly long-lived but less successful peer companies (in the same industries).

Collins and Porras's findings not only yield insight into how to build or identify a great business in which to invest, but also destroy some commonly held myths. For example, some people feel that a great idea is behind every great company. This concept is wrong, and in fact, according to the authors' research, companies founded on the basis of a great idea can lead to a focus on the idea rather than on laying the groundwork for building a great company. Sony's founder, for example, wrote a nine-page philosophical prospectus setting the stage for this great company, yet had few product ideas in his firm's early days. Early products, such as a rice cooker, failed miserably.

Great, visionary companies also are rigid and unyielding when it comes to respecting their core ideologies and principles. On the other hand, such companies tinker and experiment to stimulate positive change and innovation. And despite their often-stunning financial success, great companies usually have a higher or equal aspiration to maximizing profits: fulfilling a purpose and being driven by values. This book is packed with insights, information, and examples, so don't expect to absorb all its contents in one reading.

Mutual Funds For Dummies

Okay, I'm a tad biased about *Mutual Funds For Dummies* (IDG Books Worldwide, Inc.), which I wrote! However, it's the perfect complement to this book because it details how to build and manage a stock and bond portfolio using the best mutual funds. I discuss dozens of the best funds available today and provide sample portfolios for investors in differing situations.

Chapter 20

Internet and Software Resources

. . . .

In This Chapter

▶ Choosing investing software

▶ Recognizing Internet pitfalls and opportunities

▶ Finding the best investing Web sites

. . . .

Computers and technology are supposed to make our lives more efficient and entertaining. In the investment world, hundreds of software packages and thousands of Web sites and online service providers claim to be able to make your investments more profitable and easier to manage. As with most other advertising claims, the reality of using your computer for investing and other tasks falls short of the promises and the hype.

In this chapter, I show you ways your computer may be able to help you with your investing challenges and chores. Throughout this discussion, however, please remember several important caveats:

✔ Many highly successful investors don't use their computers (or use them quite little) to manage their investments.

✔ You may subject yourself to information overload and spend a fair amount of money without seeing many benefits.

✔ Don't believe everything that you read, especially in the online world, where filters and editors are often absent. (Of course, as I discuss elsewhere in this part of the book, filters and editors don't guarantee that you'll find quality investment advice and information when you read financial publications.)

Exploring Investment Software Options

Good investment software must be user-friendly and guide you to good information and sound decisions. Software that helps you make personal investment decisions also needs to provide accurate information and, if applicable, well-founded advice.

Which software is best for you depends on what you're trying to accomplish, as well as your level of investment knowledge and computer savvy. Software can help you with a variety of investment tasks, from tracking your investments to researching, planning, and placing trades through your computer (a topic that I discuss in Chapter 10). The following sections help you find the best software for your needs.

Investment tracking software

Most investors don't know how they're doing — that is, what returns their investments are producing. People usually know their CD and bond yields, but ask most people investing in individual stocks and bonds what the total return was on their entire portfolio, and at best, you'll get a guess. It's the rare person who can quote you total returns or tell you if her returns are on track to reach her future financial goals. If someone does know his investments' returns, he probably doesn't know if that return is good, bad, or otherwise. Feel good having made 22 percent on your portfolio of stocks last year? Maybe you wouldn't if an index of comparable stocks was up 35 percent over the same period.

Beyond knowing what your returns are, wouldn't it be nice to know the total value of all your investments and where all your money is currently residing? The fact that investors lose billions of dollars annually to *escheatment* — a situation in which financial institutions turn money over to the state because the owner loses track of his investment (often because the investor moved or passed away) — is testimony to the disarray of some investors' tracking systems.

Many software makers produce programs that claim to solve these and other investment-tracking quandaries. However, investment tracking software is not a painless panacea for investors who want to track their investments and returns.

Many people buy these programs thinking that the programs will, after a small investment of time, simplify their investment lives. My review of many investment tracking packages suggests that you should be prepared to make a substantial time commitment to learn how to use these packages and should know that other, less high-tech, alternatives may be more efficient and enlightening. Also know that a good portion of program users tire of entering all the required data and then feel guilty for "falling behind."

One of the best benefits of these packages is that using them can help you get organized. If you enter your investments into the program, the software can help you make sure that you don't lose track of your holdings. (Keeping a current copy of each of your investment statements in a binder or file folder can accomplish the same purpose.) Of course, if your home burns to the ground and you don't have a back-up copy of your files or software off-site, you have to start your documentation from scratch.

In addition to organizing all your investment information in one place, investment software allows you to track your original purchase price, current market values, and rates of return on your investments. If you have accounts at numerous investments firms, using software can reduce some of the complications involved in tracking your investing kingdom. (You can accomplish the same things by consolidating your investments at one investment company. See my discussion of discount brokers in Chapter 10.)

Software that can help you with investment tracking fall into one of two main groups: personal finance software that also includes investment-tracking capabilities, and software that focuses exclusively on investment tracking.

The broader personal finance packages such as Quicken, Managing Your Money, Kiplinger's Simply Money, and Microsoft Money are more user-friendly and are probably more familiar if you already use these packages' other features (such as bill paying).

If you want to see what your investment returns have been over a longer period of time, beware that entering historic data from your account statements (if you can find them) is a time-consuming process, regardless of which package you use. In order to calculate your returns, you generally need to enter each new investment that you made as well as all of your re-investments of dividends, interest, and capital gains distributions (such as those made on mutual funds). Ugh!

Investment tracking software can be more useful for stock traders. In my experience, stock traders, the people who would most benefit from using these programs, often don't track their overall returns. If they did, they could calculate the benefit (or lack thereof) of all their trading. (I've never worked with a stock picker who completed this exercise with me and had return numbers that beat the market indexes over the long term.)

If you are a buy-and-hold mutual fund investor, tracking software gives you limited benefits because of the time that entering your data requires. Mutual funds and many other published resources tell you what a fund's total return was for the past year, so you don't need to enter every dividend and capital gain distribution.

As for calculating the return of your overall portfolio, there are fairly simple ways to estimate your return using an old-fashioned paper and pencil. Simply weight the return of each investment by the portion of your portfolio that's invested in it. For example, with a simple portfolio equally divided between two investments that returned 10 percent and 20 percent respectively, your overall portfolio return would be 15 percent (10 x .50 + 20 x .50 = 15).

People who make investments at various times throughout the year and want to know what their actual returns were during the year can get answers from software. Unless you're a frequent trader and are trying to measure the success of your trading, knowing the exact returns based on the precise dates that you fed money into investments has limited value. This fact is especially true if you're a regular, dollar-cost-averaging investor (see Chapter 3). If you're a frequent trader, using a financial calculator works as well as software in calculating your returns based on the timing of your investments.

Investment research software

Investment research software packages usually separate investment beginners (and others who don't want to spend a lot of their time managing their money) from those who enjoy wallowing in data and conducting primary research. If you already have a plan in mind and just want to get on with investing, then go to it! But even if you don't want to conduct more-specific research, some of the packages that I discuss in this section can also help you conduct online investment transactions and track an investment's performance.

Investment software packages do not lack information and research data. In fact, you may have the problem of sifting through too much data and differentiating the best from the mediocre and the downright awful. And, unless cost is no object, you need to make sure that you don't spend too much of your loot simply accessing the information.

Before you plunge into the data jungle and try to become the next Peter Lynch or Warren Buffett and pick individual stocks, be honest about your reasons for wanting to research. Some investors fool themselves into believing that their research will help them beat the markets. Few investors, even so-called professionals, ever do. Witness the fact that over long time periods (ten-plus years), mutual funds that invest in a fixed market index, such as the Standard & Poor's 500, outperform three-quarters of their actively managed peers thanks to the former's lower operating expenses (see Chapter 9).

Researching individual securities

If you like to invest in individual securities, the Value Line Investment Survey for Windows helps you research individual stocks using the data that the Value Line Investment Survey provides (as I discuss in Chapter 7). This software package lets you sift through Value Line's data efficiently. You can also use it to track your stock portfolio.

A two-month introductory offer for Value Line's large company stock directory costs $55 ($95 for the bigger directory, which also tracks small-and medium-company stocks), and an annual subscription costs $595 for monthly updates of the large-company stock directory ($995 for the more comprehensive version). The software is available from Value Line at 800-654-0508.

Understanding how software calculates returns

Most software programs calculate returns in one of two ways. First, the programs can calculate your effective or "internal" rate of return (IRR) by comparing your original amounts invested to the current market value. Of those programs that I've tested that calculate IRR — and a surprising number don't — the results were accurate. After you calculate your returns, knowing how they compare with relevant market averages would be nice. Unfortunately, not all programs allow you to compare your performance to various market indexes.

The tax or cost basis method is the second way software may calculate your returns. All the packages that I've reviewed calculate your cost basis for accounting purposes. Your cost basis is your original investment plus reinvested dividends and capital gains, for which you have already paid taxes in a non-retirement account. To get an accurate cost basis, you need to key in all your investments, including reinvested distributions. Time-starved investors can take solace in the fact that most investment companies, particularly larger mutual fund providers, provide cost basis information for you upon request or when you sell an investment.

Some packages only provide this cost basis information and don't report actual returns. Cost basis reports make your returns look less generous because reinvested distributions increase your original investment and seemingly reduce your returns. I know from direct experience that investors often look at cost basis reports and assume that the reports tell them what their investment returns are. This happens partly because of the cost basis reports' misleading names such as "investment performance" or "investment analysis."

The difference between the rate of return using the cost basis and internal rate of return methods is generally insubstantial. For the data that I used in my research, the cost basis method software calculated a 2.7 percent annual return, and the internal rate of return method software calculated a 13 percent annual return. The actual portfolio's total return was 13 percent, but an investor using a software package that only calculates cost basis is led to believe that her profit was just 2.7 percent (which is correct for tax purposes only for a non-retirement account).

Is all this calculation method mumbo jumbo too technical for your taste? Because they already have the data on your accounts, investment firms can and hopefully someday will be able to send you your account's performance numbers.

Researching mutual funds

For mutual funds, Morningstar and Value Line both publish a number of software packages, the best of which are similar in price to the Value Line Investment Survey. These packages are geared toward more sophisticated investors who understand mutual funds and how to select them. For more details, pick up a copy of my book, *Mutual Funds For Dummies* from IDG Books Worldwide, Inc.

Choosing Internet Investing Resources

As people interested in managing their money go online, thousands of sites are springing up to meet the demand. Although the low barriers to entry in the online world make it easy for scamsters and incompetents to flog their wares and flawed advice, this new medium can offer some helpful resources if you know where to look and how to discern the good from the not-so-good.

The Securities & Exchange Commission shutters numerous online scams, such as the one run by two individuals (Gene Block and Renate Haag), which bilked investors out of more than $3.5 million by promising to double investors' money in four months in a fictitious security they called prime bank.

Although you may be smart enough to avoid offers that promise pie in the sky, you're far more likely to fall for unsound financial advice. For example, at the stock-picking Motley Fool's site, an online scribe posted a column entitled, "Paying your mortgage off early? Might as well put the money under your mattress." In the poorly reasoned piece, this person argues: "If you move before the mortgage is paid, the money you gave your bank actually saved you nothing. All your money did is reduce your principal amount by the exact extra amount you paid. Sounds like a mattress savings account to me."

Paying your mortgage balance off faster *can* be a good investment, regardless of whether you move. See Chapter 3 for a discussion of the merits and drawbacks of paying your mortgage off faster.

You can find plenty of self-serving advertorial content and bad advice online, so you should be wary and cautious. The next section offers tips for evaluating Internet resources.

Evaluating online resources

Fraud and bad financial advice existed long before the Internet ever came around. The SEC describes online scams as "new medium, same message." The tips in the following sections can help you find the nuggets of helpful online advice and avoid the landmines.

Check out agendas

Get an idea of who's behind a site before you trust its information. When navigating the Net for investment purposes, remember that financial service companies that want to sell you something erect the vast majority of sites. Thus, the "free" entrance fee to these sites is driven by companies wanting you to buy what they're selling.

Some sites go to extraordinary lengths — including providing lots of information and advice and attempting to conceal the identity of the company that runs the site — to disguise their agendas. Therefore, don't turn to the Web for advice or opinions, which usually aren't objective. Approach online financial calculators with skepticism. Most are incredibly simplistic and biased.

Most sites have icons that you can click on to see some background on the site's sponsor and to find out whether the site solicits potential advertisers. With a simple click, you can quickly see that a site purporting to be a reference service of the best mortgage lenders may be nothing more than an online yellow pages to which gaining entry is as simple as paying an advertising fee. Look for sites that exercise quality control in what they post and use sensible screening criteria for outside information or companies they list.

Just because every Tom, Dick, and Jane can easily and at relatively low cost set up an Internet site doesn't mean that their Web sites and advice are worthy of your time. Stake a lot on the reputation of the name. Not surprisingly, the financial companies with reputations for integrity offline are the ones that offer some of the best integrity online. For example, as you see later in this section, the leading and most investor-friendly investment companies often have the best education-oriented Web sites.

Solicit grassroots customer feedback

The Internet can be a useful place to do consumer research. The more enlightening message board conversations that I've encountered start with someone asking what others thought about particular financial service firms, such as brokerage firms. If you're investigating a certain financial service, the Internet can be an efficient way to get feedback from other people with experience dealing with that firm.

In order to find a dozen people offline who have done business with a given firm, you'd probably have to speak with hundreds of people. Online, finding customers is a snap. Those who feel wronged by a particular firm are more than willing to share their gripes. As in the offline world, though, don't believe everything you hear, and watch out for employees of a given firm who post flattering comments about their firms and diss the competition.

Verify advice and information offline

You can enhance the value of the online information you gather by verifying it elsewhere. You can do some fact-checking both online and offline. For example, if you're contemplating the purchase of some stock based on financial data that you read on an investing site, check out those numbers at the library or at one of the Web sites I recommend later in this chapter before buying.

Lots of Internet investment advice (and most of the scams) focus on smaller companies and investment start-ups; unfortunately, these are often the most difficult businesses to locate information about. The SEC requires companies that are raising less than $1 million to file a "Form D," which you can obtain by calling the SEC at 202-942-8090. Also check with your state securities regulator; the numbers for all 50 regulators are on the SEC's Web site at www.sec.gov.

And, if something does sound too good to be true, check out and possibly report your concerns to Internet fraud-fighting organization sites. In addition to the SEC's Web site, check out the National Association of Securities Dealers' Regulation Web site (www.nasdr.com) and the National Consumers League's National Fraud Information Center (www.fraud.org, 1-800-876-7060).

The best investment Web sites

Although you can live without the Internet and not suffer any ill financial or educational consequences, the quality of what's on the Net is slowly increasing, and a handful of sites are setting a high standard. You can find the best sites through the Internet rather than through online service providers such as Prodigy and America Online. If you're tiring of those services' busy signals and their increasing focus on entertaining rather than informational content, consider switching to a lower cost Internet service provider.

In addition to the consumer advocacy sites that I recommend earlier in this chapter, here are my top picks for investing sites worthy of your online time.

Hoover.com

Hoover's Web site (www.hoover.com) provides lots of useful tools, especially if researching individual stocks interests you. At this site you can find reports on individual companies, industry news, links to SEC filings, stock screening tools, and analyst reports.

You can only access the most basic information for free. For stock reports, you must pay a $99.95 annual membership fee to access the more detailed company reports that include comprehensive product line information and competitor analysis.

Investorguide.com

For a thorough and well-organized listing of lots of investment Web sites, peruse Investor Guide (www.investorguide.com). Created by Gary Karz, CFA, the site is a reference of the best and most popular Internet investment sites that I've seen. And, for now at least, the price to use it is right — accessing the site is free, and you won't bump into any advertising.

In addition to providing links to many Internet investing sites, Karz has also drafted a good deal of his own content on various investing topics. Karz is intelligent and knowledgeable and has great investigative skills and instincts. For example, he broke the story about how The Motley Fool's Internet investment site, which has hyped the performance of some of their stock picks

Look who's talking

If you're at a cocktail party and you receive advice from someone you've just met, you hopefully check him out to determine how much credence you should give to his words. And no matter how wise he seems, you shouldn't judge him on the basis of just one conversation.

In the online world, you need to do the same, but you may have greater difficulty determining who's doing the talking and why he or she is talking. On some Internet sites, visitors may post comments and opinions on *message boards* (the online equivalent of a big bulletin board).

As the National Association of Securities Dealers (NASD) says on its Web site, "In most instances, there is simply no way to uncover someone's true identity. Are you getting information from a broker, short seller, corporate insider, amateur investor, or stock touter?" You have to use a little induction and a lot of intuition. Start by eliminating any advice from posters who are totally anonymous. Pseudonyms are common online, and some salespeople will to try to hide their true identities. Aliases are especially easy on America Online, where users can have up to five self-chosen screen names.

Among the more popular message boards on the Net are those where people debate and discuss the prospects for individual stocks. The postings in stock folders often play fast and

loose with the facts. "Investors need to understand that while they might be reading honest conversations, they could just as easily be looking at the work of a corporate insider, stock promoter, or short seller using an alias to deceive the unsuspecting or to manipulate the market," says the NASD Regulation unit.

The commercial online services have more oversight and eliminate clear sales pitches. However, don't expect complete oversight because fact checkers or technical reviewers don't exist. You can find the Wild West of message boards on the Internet Usenet NewsGroups — places such as `misc.invest`, `alt.invest.penny-stocks`, and `misc.invest.futures`. These newsgroups are unregulated and unmonitored forums to which any Net surfer in the world has access. These sites are bombarded with solicitations for "get rich quick" and "too good to be true" investments schemes such as "Turn $30 into $2,150 . . . Over, again & again!" Pyramid schemes abound, as do IPOs for "Internet" companies. Despite their lack of practical usefulness, the Usenet sites are worth a look by investors because they are such a caricature of the dangers of online advice. Investors get an immediate crash course on what to watch out for and can apply the lessons that they learn to more subtle postings on "monitored" forums.

(see the "The Motley Fools: Online investing geniuses?" sidebar in this chapter), had hidden some of their earlier model stock portfolios that performed poorly. Karz's research on this topic was so thorough and compelling that investment newsletter evaluator Mark Hulbert picked up on it and wrote an entire column about the Motley Fools, citing Karz's original research.

Entrepreneurs like Karz who are more interested in providing good information rather than making a quick buck are a rare breed on the Internet. There aren't that many good investing sites — most of what's out there is from companies with something to sell. The trick for people like Karz is to figure out how to make money providing quality content online. In the meantime, surf and choose your sites carefully.

Sec.gov

All publicly held companies and mutual funds must file annual and quarterly reports and other documents electronically with the U.S. Securities and Exchange Commission (SEC). In the past, the simplest way to access this information was to pay a private service. Now this information is easily accessible for free (paid for by tax dollars) on the SEC Web site (www.sec.gov).

If you're researching individual companies, you can find all the corporate reports — annual reports, 10-Ks, and the like — that I discuss in Chapter 7 on this Web site. Alternatively, you may call the individual companies that interest you and have them mail you the desired material.

The SEC site isn't pretty, and searching the Electronic Data Gathering, Analysis, and Retrieval system (EDGAR) database can be overwhelming, especially for the novice investor. But if you're tenacious you may find something that is hard to come by on the Web these days: cold, hard facts and no spin.

Stockpoint.com

Named by *Barron's* as one of the top ten investment Web sites, Stockpoint (www.stockpoint.com) is home to my daily question-and-answer column. Additionally, you can find all sorts of business and other news, charting capabilities, worldwide stock market indexes, and stock and fund screening tools.

The site is quite basic and won't win any awards for slickness — I guess that's one of the reasons Stockpoint asked me to write for them! Skip the newsletter section of this site — the sample freebies come from a rather motley group of newsletters.

Vanguard.com

Few sites run by investment companies are worth visiting unless you're an account holder at the firm and you want to review your accounts or conduct transactions online. The reason: Much of the content is self-serving, biased, and advertorial in nature. That said, the nation's second-largest mutual fund company, the Vanguard Group, operates a site (www.vanguard.com) that is the exception.

Of course, you can find details on Vanguard's fine family of funds here, but you also find some of the best educational materials that I've seen online. I'm not surprised that Vanguard did an excellent job with its Web site. One of the reasons that I've long liked the company is that it advocates what's in an investors' best interests (see Chapter 9).

And, if you're one of the millions of Vanguard shareholders, you can access your accounts and perform most transactions online. In recent years, Vanguard has also expanded its discount brokerage division, also accessible online, to allow for investing in many other fund companies' funds (as well as Vanguard's) through a single account.

Yardeni.com

Economist Dr. Ed Yardeni, who is currently with Deutsche Bank, has a site (www.yardeni.com) that's a good compendium of economic and financial market data and news. You can also find a great deal of information here on the Federal Reserve and Fed policy as well as economic history.

My favorite feature of this site is the excellent long-term charts that it provides for various financial market indicators and economic data. In a world where the media focuses on what happened in the last half-hour, Yardeni's multi-decade charts are a breath of fresh air that can help you keep a much needed longer-term investing perspective.

There are many other sites out there. Remember that I've recommended the best here. Quality is far more important than quantity when you do some of your investing homework online.

The Motley Fools: Online investing geniuses?

David and Tom Gardner launched their own printed monthly investment newsletter but were "depressed" when only a few dozen people subscribed in 1993. So the next year, the Virginia-based Gardners moved their wares onto America Online to enhance their visibility. Thus was born The Motley Fool (also on the Internet at www.fool.com).

The Gardners claim that novices can "...nearly double the S&P 500 posting returns in excess of 20 percent per year...you might be able to fish out greater than 30 percent per year on your own without assuming considerably greater risk." They also say, "It's not an exaggeration to say that fifth graders can wallop the market after one month of analysis. You can too."

Although they claim to have walloped the market averages with their stock picks, according to research by Investorhome.com, which I

discuss later in this section, only one of their seven portfolios has actually performed better than the market averages — two of their portfolios were shuttered after poor performance (one of which plunged 50 percent during its short six-month existence).

The Fool story is rich in lessons for all consumers of investment newsletters online (and off):

✔ **Beware of promises of easy riches.** To deter investors from mutual funds, the Fools say of their stock picking, "We hope to have put you in position to nearly double the S&P 500...it'll demand little research per year, and present you little, if any, long-term risk." If investing were that easy, we'd all be rich! And as any professional money manager knows firsthand, successfully managing a portfolio of individual stocks takes time, not just a few hours per year.

(continued)

(continued)

✔ **Beware of bloated performance claims.**
The Fools love to compare their integrity
and accountability to the notoriously shady
marketing practices of other financial
newsletters. As the Gardners repeatedly
point out, The Fool portfolio uses real money,
and calculated returns account for trading
commissions. However, their real-money
portfolio is a non-retirement account, and
the Fools fail to calculate and report their
returns taking into account their greatest
investment cost of all: taxes. In fact,
because of trading, the Fools' one portfolio
that looks like it has beaten the market
averages has only performed on par with
what an investor could have earned, with no
ongoing research time required, in a low
cost index fund. Ironically, the Gardners say,
"If you can't beat the index after all costs
are deducted, you've blundered."

By early 1996, the Fools were basking in the
media spotlight. However, the deluges of
newcomers to their online site soon learned
about the perils of hitching your investment
cart to a shooting star. Since that time,
a stock that they aggressively promoted —
Iomega — has plunged from $27½ to $4. A buy
recommendation for ATC Communications
at $23 in late 1996 proved disastrous when the
stock crashed to less than $4 just one year
later, before the Fools threw in the towel.

✔ **Beware of actions that contradict the
newsletter's stated philosophy.** "We invest
for the long-term" is the Fool mantra,
invoked in their portfolio report on a regular
basis (almost daily when the portfolio performs poorly). They add that "Part of the
enduring beauty of long-term equities
investing is the advantage of buying and
holding — never touching — stocks like
General Electric, which rack up 20 percent
annualized gains over a decade or more.
We're talking compounded returns
untainted by capital gains taxes."

The portfolio's trading history, however, tells
another story. The Fools have closed out on
average about seven investment holdings
annually (in a portfolio with typically just ten
stocks) and have held just one stock — in
fact just a portion of the original position —
since their portfolio started under five years
ago! Moreover, the Fools engage in risky
short selling (and have lost money overall
doing it) where you sell borrowed stock in
the hope that you can buy it back later at a
lower price. If this is long-term investing,
then perhaps the Fools' definition of a long-
term trader is anyone who doesn't day
trade!

✔ **Successful investing doesn't require following the market closely.** Buying and
holding index or other quality mutual funds
for many years doesn't take much review
time — perhaps as little as an hour once per
year to read the fund's annual report.
Although the Fools rightfully criticize the
financial media's short-term reporting —
"So many are lost in the day-by-day noise
of stock moves" — the Fools themselves
report on the biggest stock price changes
of the day not once, but twice a day. This
daily tracking of stock prices causes
investors to lose site of the long-term and
the big picture (although it draws more visitors to the site, which satisfies advertisers
and enriches the Gardners).

The bottom line? Be skeptical of financial
newsletters, online or off. Like politicians,
they're out to make themselves look as good as
possible, taking credit for when things go well
and blaming external forces when they don't.
According to *Hulbert's Financial Digest,* not a
single investment newsletter has beaten the
market averages over the past 15 years. During
the period that Hulbert has tracked the Fools'
stock picks, they have not performed among the
best newsletters. See Chapter 18 for more about
investment newsletters.

Part VI
The Part of Tens

The 5th Wave   By Rich Tennant

"I don't see it as a chart of a poorly performing stock as much as a sign to invest in lava lamps and portable televisions."

In this part . . .

The Part of Tens contains shorter chapters, each including about ten items on important investing topics that don't quite fit elsewhere in the book. The topics in this part cover the psychological issues to overcome to be a successful investor and what you need to know when you're considering selling an investment.

Chapter 21

Ten Psychological Investing Obstacles to Conquer

· ·

In This Chapter

▶ Putting faith in experts

▶ Letting your emotions guide your investment decisions

▶ Giving up when the market takes a plunge

▶ Ignoring your financial big picture

· ·

*J*ust as with raising children or in one's career, "success" with personal investing is in the eye of the beholder. In my work as a financial counselor and lecturer, I've come to define a successful investor as someone who, with a minimal commitment of time, develops an investment plan to accomplish financial and personal goals and earns returns commensurate with the risk he is willing to accept.

In this chapter, I point out ten common psychological obstacles you may face and share tips and advice for overcoming them on the road to investing success.

Trusting Authority

Some investors assume that an advisor is competent and ethical if she has a lofty title (financial consultant, vice-president, and so on), dresses well, and works in a snazzy office. The lure of such accessories are often indicators of salespeople — not objective advisors — who recommend investments that will earn them big commissions — commissions that come out of your investment dollars.

Additionally, if you over-trust an advisor, you may not research and monitor your investments as carefully as you should. Figuring that Mr. Vice President is an expert, some investors blindly follow along without ever questioning his advice or watching what's going on with their investments.

You can't possibly evaluate the competence and agenda of someone you hire until you yourself understand the lay of the land. Read good publications on the topic to learn the jargon and how to evaluate investments. Seek independent second opinions before you act on someone's recommendations. If you're in the market for a broker, be sure to read Chapter 10.

Getting Swept Up by Euphoria

Feeling strength and safety in numbers, some investors are lured into buying hot stocks and sectors (for example, industries) after major price increases (see Chapter 5). Psychologically, it's reassuring to buy into something that's going up and gaining accolades. The obvious danger with this practice is buying into investments selling at inflated prices that too soon deflate.

For example, Robert Shiller, professor of economics at Yale University, conducted a survey of Japanese investors and found that few (14 percent) expected a major correction at that market's peak in 1989 when Japanese stocks were selling at outrageous price-earning multiples (see Chapter 5). By the mid-1990s, when tremendous damage had been done and the Japanese market was off more than 60 percent from its peak and selling at less risky levels, far more investors (32 percent) expected a crash.

Develop an overall allocation among various investments (especially diversified mutual funds) and don't make knee-jerk decisions to change your allocation based upon what the latest hot sectors are. If anything, de-emphasize or avoid stocks and sectors that are at the top of the performance charts. Think back to the last time you went bargain shopping for a consumer item — you looked for value, not high prices. After taking such a bad beating in 1997 and 1998, stocks in emerging markets, for example, offered excellent value with far less downside risk.

Being Overconfident

As I discuss in Part V, newsletters, books, and even some financial periodicals lead investors to believe that you can be the next Peter Lynch or Warren Buffett if you follow a simple stock picking system. The advent of the Internet and online trading capabilities have spawned a whole new generation of short-term (sometimes even same-day) traders.

Dr. Paul Linton is a marriage and family counselor. Despite his expertise in psychology, when the stock market crashed in 1987, Linton had to come to terms with his own relationship to money and the psychological obstacles that he faced as an investor.

"I got overconfident with my stock picking when some of my technology stocks soared and from my work in benefits in a previous company where I was responsible for choosing investment funds, one of which returned 90 percent one year," says Linton. When the market crashed, Linton was "psychologically devastated" because he lost about two-thirds of the money that he had saved over the previous 10 years.

Linton's challenge was that his early investment successes during a strong stock market led him to believe that he had a magic investing touch. This led him to excessive trading and risk taking, and eventually, losses when the market reversed its course. "I realized that if I was going to be a stock trader, I had to work at it full-time and be prepared anxiety wise to handle it," says Linton.

If you have the speculative bug, earmark a small portion of your portfolio (no more than 20 percent) for more aggressive investments. Linton traded in most of his high-risk, frequently traded individual stock portfolio for diversified mutual funds that he buys and holds. If over-trading is a problem, go to Gambler's Anonymous (see Chapter 6 for more information).

Throwing in the Towel When Things Look Bleak

For inexperienced or nervous investors, it's tempting to bail out when it appears that an investment is not always going to be profitable and enjoyable. Some investors dump falling investments precisely at the times when they should be doing the reverse — buying more. Whenever the U.S. stock market drops more than a few percentage points in a short period, it attracts a lot of attention, which then leads to concern, anxiety, and, in some cases, panic.

I remember when a major earthquake struck the San Francisco Bay Area, my home, in 1989. I had just left an office building in San Francisco's financial district when the ground started to shake, rattle, and roll. My first panicked thought as I looked at all the glass-windowed skyscrapers towering over me was that someone would find me buried under piles of shattered glass. Although unpleasant, the thought wasn't original. I had heard others explain this scenario. Although the quake was scary, the only thing that I lost that day was a bit of my courage — and a little more of my hair, I'm sure!

Immediately following the earthquake, some of my East Coast friends and family thought that the entire Bay Area was in ruins, based on early TV coverage. Television news programs typically played a few minutes' worth of tape showing a collapsed freeway near the city of Oakland, several partially collapsed and fiery buildings in the Marina district of San Francisco, and a fallen portion of the upper deck of the Bay Bridge. The media played these segments over and over again.

Now I don't want to diminish the tragedy, loss of life, and damage that the earthquake caused. However, watching these news programs throughout the week following the quake, you'd never have known that more than 99 percent of the Bay Area was just fine, except for people with shaken nerves and a few broken vases. Far fewer people died as a result of this earthquake than die every day from driving on U.S. roadways or from guns.

When the financial markets suffer earthshaking events, some investors worry that their investments are in a shambles. As I discuss in Part V, the media is often to blame because it hypes short-term events and blows those events out of proportion to captivate viewers and listeners. History has shown that financial markets recover; recovery is just a question of time. If you invest for the long-term, then the last six weeks — or even the last couple of years — is a short period. Plus, a mountain of evidence and studies demonstrate that no one can predict the future, so you gain little from trying to base your investment plans on predictions. In fact, you can lose more money by trying to time the markets.

A big danger that larger-than-normal market declines hold is that they may encourage decision-making that's based on emotion rather than logic. Just ask anyone who sold *after* the stock market collapsed in 1987 — the U.S. stock market dropped 35 percent in a matter of weeks in the fall of that year. Since then, the U.S. market has risen more than five-fold!

I remember following the daily gyrations of the stock market more than two decades ago when, as a high school student, I performed a science fair project that attempted to discover what caused the market to fluctuate. My interest developed because my father, who lost his job during the recession that began in 1973, found himself in the new position of investment manager of his own money. His former employer gave him a chunk of money that, at the time, represented virtually all of his long-term money for retirement.

Dad started trading individual securities through a broker and soon found himself in a rapidly dropping market. I'll never forget the day we drove to see the broker in person because the market, as measured by the Dow Jones Industrial Average, was down more than 20 points (which at that time was a lot because the Dow was around 700). To make a long story short, Dad sold most of his stock holdings, with his broker's encouragement and blessing, pretty much near what turned out to be, in retrospect, one of the better buying opportunities of this century.

My dad, a self-educated mechanical engineer, is a smart man — I'm not just saying that because of his familial linkage to me. However, he sold his stock for the wrong reasons. He didn't need the money at the time for some other purpose; he simply sold out of fear of losing more money.

Investors who are unable to withstand the volatility of riskier growth-oriented investments such as stocks may be better off not investing in such vehicles to begin with. Examining your returns over longer periods helps you keep the proper perspective. If a short-term downdraft in your investments depresses you, avoid tracking your investment values closely. Also, consider investing in highly diversified, less volatile funds of funds that hold stocks worldwide as well as bonds (see Chapter 9).

Investing Too Much to Quit

Although some investors realize that they can't withstand losses and sell at the first signs of trouble, other investors find selling a losing investment so painful and unpleasant that they continue to hold a poorly performing investment, despite the investment's poor future prospects. The late Amos Tversky, a Stanford psychology professor, and Daniel Kahneman of Princeton documented how people find accepting a given loss twice as painful as the pleasure of accepting a gain of equal magnitude.

Analyze your lagging investments to identify why they perform poorly. If a given investment is down because similar ones are also in decline, hold on to it. However, if something is inherently wrong with the investment — such as high fees or poor management — make taking the loss more palatable by remembering two things:

- ✔ If your investment is a non-retirement account investment, remember that losses help reduce your income taxes.

- ✔ Consider the "opportunity cost" of continuing to keep your money in a lousy investment — that is, what returns can you get in the future if you switch to a "better" investment?

Over-Monitoring Your Investments

The investment world seems so risky and fraught with pitfalls that some people believe that closely watching an investment can help alert them to impending danger. "The constant tracking is not unlike the attempt to relieve anxiety by fingering worry beads. Yet, paradoxically, it can increase emotional distress because it requires a constant state of vigilance," says psychologist Dr. Paul Minsky.

In my work as a financial counselor, I see time and time again that investors who are the most anxious about their investments and most likely to make impulsive trading decisions are the ones who watch their holdings too closely, especially those who monitor prices daily. The proliferation of Internet sites and stock market cable television programs offering up-to-the-minute quotations give these investors more temptation to over-monitor investments.

Restrict your "diet" of financial information and advice. Quality is far more important than quantity. If you invest in diversified mutual funds, you really don't need to examine your fund's performance more than once per year. An ideal time to review your funds is when you receive their annual reports. Although many investors track their funds daily or weekly, far fewer read their annual reports. Reading your annual reports can help you keep a long-term perspective and gain some understanding as to why your funds perform as they do and how they compare to major market averages.

Being Unclear about Your Goals

All of this talk about psychological issues may create the impression that investing is more complicated than simply setting your financial goals (see Chapter 3) and choosing solid investments to help you achieve them. Unfortunately that's true, however, awareness and understanding of the less tangible issues can maximize your chances for investing success.

In addition to considering your goals in a traditional sense (when do you want to retire, how much of your kids' college costs do you want to pay) before you invest, you should also consider what you want and don't want to get from the investment process. Do you treat investing as a hobby or simply as another one of life's tasks, such as maintaining your home? Do you enjoy the intellectual challenge of picking your own stocks? Don't just ponder these questions on your own; discuss them with family members, too — after all, you're all going to have to live with your decisions and investment results.

Ignoring Your Real Financial Problems

I know plenty of high-income earners, including more than a few who earn six figures annually, who have little to invest. Some of these people have high interest debt outstanding on credit cards and auto loans yet spend endless hours researching and tracking investments.

I also know many people who built significant personal wealth, despite having modest-paying jobs. The difference: the ability to live within your means.

If you don't earn a high income, it's tempting to think you can't save. Even if you are a high-income earner, you may think that you can hit an investment home run to accomplish your goals, or that you can save more if you can bump up your income. This way of thinking justifies spending most of what you earn and saving little now. Investing is far more exciting than examining your spending and making cutbacks. If you need help coming up with more money to invest, see my first book, *Personal Finance For Dummies*.

Overemphasizing Certain Risks

Saving money is only half the battle. The other half is making your money grow. Over long time periods, earning just a few percent more makes a big difference in the size of your nest egg. Earning inflation-beating returns is easy to do if you're willing to invest in stocks, real estate, and small businesses. Figure 21-1 shows you how much more money you'll have in 25 years if you can earn investment returns that are greater than the rate of inflation (which is currently running at 3 percent).

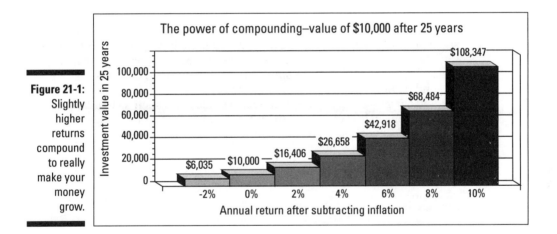

Figure 21-1: Slightly higher returns compound to really make your money grow.

As I discuss in Chapter 2, ownership investments (stocks, real estate, and small business) have historically generated returns greater than the inflation rate by 6 percent or more, while lending investments (savings accounts and bonds) tend to generate returns of only 1 to 2 percent above inflation. However, some investors keep too much of their money in lending investments out of fear of holding an investment that can fall greatly in value. Although ownership investments can plunge in value, you need to keep in mind that inflation and taxes eat away at your lending investment balances.

Believing in Gurus

Stock market declines, like earthquakes, bring all sorts of prognosticators, soothsayers, and self-anointed gurus out of the woodwork, particularly among those in the investment community that have something to sell, such as newsletter writers. The words may vary, but the underlying message does not: "If you had been following my sage advice, you'd be much better off now."

People spend far too much of their precious time and money in pursuit of a guru who can tell them when and what to buy and sell. Peter Lynch, the former manager of the Fidelity Magellan Fund, amassed one of the best long-term stock market investing track records. His stock-picking ability allowed him to beat the market averages by just a few percent per year. However, even he says that you can't time the markets, and he acknowledges knowing many pundits who have correctly predicted the future course of the stock market "once in a row"!

We live in a society that likes to build up gurus. I'm not going to argue that some people aren't more expert than others in their respective professions. Clearly, in the world of investing, the most successful investors earn much better returns than the worst ones. But what may surprise you is that you can end up much closer to the top of the investing performance heap than the bottom if you follow some relatively simple rules such as regularly saving and investing in low cost, growth investments. In fact, you can beat many of the full-time investment professionals.

Chapter 22

Ten Issues to Consider When Selling an Investment

*T*he best investments can and should be held for years and decades. Each year, people sell trillions of dollars' worth of investments. My experience working with and teaching people about investments suggests that too many people sell for the wrong reasons and hold onto investments that they should sell. In this chapter, I highlight some issues to consider when you contemplate selling your investments.

What Are Your Personal Preferences and Goals?

If you've inherited investments or your life has changed, your current portfolio may no longer make sense for you. The time that it takes you to manage your portfolio, for example, is a vital matter if you're starved for time or weary of managing time-consuming investments.

Leo, for example, loved to research, track, and trade individual stocks — until his daughter was born. Then Leo realized how many hours his hobby was taking away from his family, and that realization put his priorities into perspective. Leo now invests in time-friendly mutual funds and doesn't follow them like a hawk.

One of my clients, Mary, loves investing in real estate because she enjoys the challenge of researching, selecting, and managing her properties. She works in a job where she has to put up with lots of controlling, stressed-out bosses. For Mary, real estate isn't just a profitable investment, it's also a way of expressing herself and growing personally.

What Does Your Overall Portfolio Look Like?

A good reason to sell an investment is to allow you to better diversify your portfolio. Suppose that before reading this book, you purchased a restaurant stock every time you read about one. Now your portfolio resembles several bad strip malls, and restaurant stocks comprise 80 percent of your holdings. Or maybe, through your job, you've accumulated such a hefty chunk of stock in your employer that this stock now overwhelms the rest of your investments.

It's time for you to diversify. Sell off some of the holdings that you have too much of and invest the proceeds in other good investments, such as those that I recommend in this book. If you think that your employer's stock is going to be a superior investment, holding a big chunk is your gamble. At a minimum, review Chapter 7 to see how to evaluate a particular stock. But remember to consider the consequences if you're wrong about your employer's stock.

Conservative investors often keep too much of their money in bank accounts, Treasury bills, and the like. Read Chapter 3 to come up with an overall investment strategy that fits with the rest of your personal financial situation.

Which of Your Investments Are Good or Bad?

Often, people are tempted to sell an investment for the wrong reasons. One natural human tendency is to want to sell investments that have declined in value. Some people fear a further fall, and they don't want to be affiliated with a loser, especially when money is involved. I think this reaction resembles the phenomenon of piling into the lifeboats when a ship springs a leak.

Take a step back, a deep breath and examine the merits of the investment you're considering selling. If an investment is otherwise still sound, why bail out when prices are down and a sale is going on? What are you going to do with the money? If anything, you should be contemplating buying more of such an investment. Don't make a decision to sell based on your current emotional response, especially to recent news events. If bad news has recently hit, it's already old news. Don't base your investment holdings on such transitory events.

Use the criteria in this book for finding good investments to evaluate the worthiness of your current holdings. If an investment is fundamentally sound, don't sell it.

A better reason to sell an investment is that it comes with high fees relative to comparable investments. For example, if you own a bond mutual fund that is socking it to you with fees of 1 percent per year, check out Chapter 9 to discover high-performing, lower-cost funds.

What Are the Tax Consequences?

When you sell investments that you hold outside a tax-sheltered retirement account such as an IRA or a 401(k), taxes should be one factor in your decision. (See Chapter 3 to find out about tax rates that apply to the sale of an investment as well as to the distributions that investments make.) If the investments are inside retirement accounts, taxes aren't an issue because the accounts are sheltered from taxation, unless you're withdrawing funds from the accounts.

Just because you pay tax on a profit from selling a non-retirement account investment doesn't mean that you should avoid selling. With real estate, you can often avoid paying taxes on the profit that you make (see Chapters 11 and 12).

With stocks and mutual funds, things get more complex because you can specify which shares you want to sell. This option makes selling decisions more complicated, but you may want to consider specifying what shares you're selling because you may be able to save taxes. (Read the next section for more information.) If you sell all your shares of a particular security that you own, you need not concern yourself with specifying which shares you're selling.

Which Shares Cost You More?

When you sell a portion of the shares of a security (for example, stock, bond, or mutual fund) that you own, specifying which shares you are selling may benefit you tax-wise. Here's an example to show you why you may want to specify selling certain shares — especially those shares that cost you more to buy — so that you can save on your taxes.

Suppose that you own a total of 300 shares of a stock, Technology.com, and you need to sell 100 shares to pay for a root canal. Suppose further that you bought 100 of these shares a long, long time ago at $10 per share, 100 shares two years ago at $16 per share, and the last 100 shares one year ago at $14 per share. Today the stock is at $20 per share. While you didn't get rich, you're grateful that you haven't lost your shirt the way some of your stock picking pals have.

The good tax folks at the IRS allow you to choose which shares you want to sell. Electing to sell the 100 shares that you purchased at the highest price — in other words, those that you bought for $16 per share two years ago — saves you in taxes. (To comply with the tax laws, you must identify the shares that you want the broker to sell by the original date of purchase and/or the cost when you sell the shares. The brokerage firm through which you sell the stock should include this information on the confirmation slip that you receive for the sale.)

The other method of accounting for which shares are sold is the method that the IRS forces you to use if you don't specify before the sale which shares you want to sell — the *first-in-first-out* (FIFO) method. FIFO means that the first shares that you sell are simply the first shares that you bought. Not surprisingly, because most stocks appreciate over time, the FIFO method leads to you paying more tax sooner. In the case of Technology.com, the FIFO accounting method leads to the conclusion that the 100 shares you sell are the 100 that you bought long, long ago at $10 per share. Thus, you owe a larger amount of taxes than if you sold the higher-cost shares under the specification method.

Although you save taxes today if you specify selling the shares that you bought more recently at a higher price, remember that when you finally sell the other shares, you'll then owe taxes on the larger profit. The longer you expect to hold these other shares, the greater the value is that you'll likely derive from postponing realizing the larger gains and paying more in taxes. If you expect your tax rate to decline in the future, you have another good reason to hold off selling the shares in which you have greater profit.

In case you care — and if you don't, I completely understand — when you sell shares in a mutual fund, the IRS has yet another accounting method, known as the *average cost method,* for figuring your taxable profit or loss when you sell a portion of your holdings in a mutual fund. This method comes in handy if you bought shares in chunks over time or reinvested the fund payouts into purchasing more shares of the fund. As the name suggests, the average cost method allows you to take an average cost for all the shares that you bought over time.

Selling Investments with Hefty Profits

Of course, no one likes to pay taxes, but if an investment you own has appreciated in value, someday you will have to pay tax when you sell it, unless you plan on passing the investment to your heirs upon your death. The IRS wipes out the capital gains tax on appreciated assets at your death.

Capital gains tax applies when you sell an investment at a higher price than you paid for it. As I explain in Chapter 3, your capital gains tax rate is different than the tax rate that you pay on ordinary income (such as from employment earnings or interest on bank savings accounts).

Odds are, the longer you've held securities such as stocks, the greater the capital gain you'll have, because stocks tend to appreciate over time. If all your assets have appreciated greatly, you may resist selling to avoid taxes. However, if you need money for a major purchase, sell what you need and pay the tax. Even if you have to pay state as well as federal taxes totaling some 35 percent of the profit, you'll have lots left (for "longer-term" profits from investments held more than one year, your taxes would probably be less than 30 percent). Before you sell, however, do some rough figuring to make sure that you'll have enough money left to accomplish what you want. If you want to sell one investment and reinvest in another, you'll owe tax on the profit unless you're selling and re-buying real estate (see Chapters 11 and 12).

If you hold a number of assets, in order to diversify and meet your other financial goals, give preference to selling your largest holdings with the smallest capital gains. If you have some securities that have profits and some with losses, you can sell some of each in order to offset the profits with the losses.

Selling Securities with Losses

Perhaps you own some turkeys in your portfolio. If you need to raise cash for some particular reason, you may consider selling some securities at a loss. You can use losses to offset gains as long as you hold both offsetting securities for more than one year (long term) or you hold both for less than one year (short term). The IRS makes this delineation because the IRS taxes long-term gains and losses on a different rate schedule than short-term gains and losses (see Chapter 3).

If you need to sell securities at a loss, be advised that you cannot claim more than $3,000 in net losses in any one year. If you sell securities with net losses totaling more than $3,000 in a year, you must carry the losses over to future tax years. This situation not only creates more tax paperwork, but it also delays realizing the value of deducting a tax loss. So try not to have _net losses_ (losses + gains) that exceed $3,000 in a year.

Some tax advisors advocate doing year-end tax-loss selling with stocks, bonds, and mutual funds. The logic goes that if you hold a security at a loss, you should sell it, take the tax write-off, and then buy it (or something similar) back.

When selling investments for tax-loss purposes, be careful of the so-called *wash sale* rules. The IRS doesn't allow the deduction of a loss for a security sale if you buy that same security back within 30 days. As long as you wait 31 or more days, no problem. If you're selling a mutual fund, you can purchase a fund similar to the one you're selling to easily sidestep this rule.

If you own a security that has ceased trading and appears worthless (or you've made a loan that hasn't been repaid), you can likely deduct this loss. Peruse *Taxes For Dummies* (IDG Books Worldwide, Inc.) for more information on what situations are deductible and how to claim these losses on your annual tax return.

Selling an Investment When You Don't Have a Clue About Its Cost

You may not know what some investments originally cost you or the person who bought them and later gave them to you. If you can't find that original statement, start by calling the firm where the investment was bought. Whether it's a brokerage firm or mutual fund company, the company should be able to send you copies of old account statements, although you may have to pay a small fee for this service.

Also, increasing numbers of investment firms, especially mutual fund companies, tell you when you sell what the investment cost you. The cost generally calculated is the average cost for the shares that you purchased. See *Taxes For Dummies* for more ideas of what to do when original records aren't available for other assets, such as real estate.

All Brokers Are Not Created Equal

If you're selling securities such as stocks and bonds, you need to know that some brokers charge more — in some cases tons more — to sell. Even if the securities that you want to sell currently reside at a high-cost brokerage firm, you can transfer them to a discount brokerage firm. See Chapter 10 to read about the virtues of using a discount brokerage firm.

Who Can You Trust?

You aren't stupid. Before you picked up this book, you may have considered yourself an investing dummy. I didn't, and I still don't, but hopefully you feel less like a dummy after reading this book. If you delegate your investment decision-making to an advisor, you're likely to be disappointed.

Few financial advisors offer objective and knowledgeable advice. Unfortunately, if you're grappling with a selling decision, finding a competent and impartial financial advisor to help with the decision is about as difficult as finding a politician who doesn't accept special interest money. Most financial consultants work on commission, which can cloud their judgment. And among the minority of fee-based advisors, almost all manage money, which creates other conflicts of interest. The more money you give them to invest and manage, the more money these advisors make. If you need advice about whether to sell some investments, turn to a tax or financial advisor who works on an hourly basis.

Index

• *E* •

Notes

Notes

Notes

Notes

Notes

Notes

Notes

Notes

Notes

Notes

Ready for more financial insights and advice?

Check out these great ...For Dummies™ books from best-selling author and personal finance expert Eric Tyson!

Personal Finance For Dummies™
ISBN 0-7645-5013-6
$19.99 US $27.99 CAN
With 1 million copies in print, this is the #1 bestselling Dummies finance title ever! Eric Tyson shows you the best ways to establish and accomplish your financial goals, reduce your spending and taxes and make wise personal finance decisions.

"Eric Tyson...is helping people at all income levels to take control of their financial futures."
—James C. Collins, Co-author of the bestseller *Built to Last*, on
Personal Finance For Dummies

Mutual Funds For Dummies™, 2nd edition
ISBN 0-7645-5112-4
$19.99 US $27.99 CAN
Anyone planning for a secure retirement or establishing other important goals should invest in this indispensable guide! Let Eric Tyson help you design a mutual fund investment plan suited to your income and lifestyle.

"You don't have to be a novice to like *Mutual Funds For Dummies* ... Eric Tyson clearly has a mastery of his subject."
—*Kiplinger's Personal Finance* magazine

Home Buying For Dummies™
ISBN 1-56884-385-2
$16.99 US $24.99 CAN
With sound financial advice from Eric Tyson and frontline real estate insights from real estate veteran Ray Brown, you'll have the tools and resources at your fingertips to take the trauma out of buying a home. For your other real estate needs, check out House Selling For Dummies and Mortgages For Dummies from Tyson and Brown.

House Selling For Dummies™
ISBN 0-7645-5038-1
$16.99 US $24.99 CAN

Mortgages For Dummies™
ISBN 0-7645-5147-7
$16.99 US CAN $24.99

"Takes you step-by-step through the process ... humorous insights that keep the pages turning. This is a reference you'll turn to time after time."
—Judy Stark, *St. Petersburg Times*

And When Tax Season Comes Around, Don't Forget To Pick Up a Copy of Taxes For Dummies™ To Help You Prepare Your Tax Return and Reduce Your Future Taxes!

Look for these national bestsellers wherever ...For Dummies books are sold!

IDG BOOKS WORLDWIDE BOOK REGISTRATION

We want to hear from you!

Register This Book and Win!

Visit **http://my2cents.dummies.com** to register this book and tell us how you liked it!

- ✔ Get entered in our monthly prize giveaway.
- ✔ Give us feedback about this book — tell us what you like best, what you like least, or maybe what you'd like to ask the author and us to change!
- ✔ Let us know any other *...For Dummies*® topics that interest you.

Your feedback helps us determine what books to publish, tells us what coverage to add as we revise our books, and lets us know whether we're meeting your needs as a *...For Dummies* reader. You're our most valuable resource, and what you have to say is important to us!

Not on the Web yet? It's easy to get started with *Dummies 101*®*: The Internet For Windows*® *98* or *The Internet For Dummies*®, 6th Edition, at local retailers everywhere.

Or let us know what you think by sending us a letter at the following address:

...For Dummies Book Registration
Dummies Press
7260 Shadeland Station, Suite 100
Indianapolis, IN 46256-3945
Fax 317-596-5498

...FOR DUMMIES™

BESTSELLING BOOK SERIES FROM IDG